Bob Dylan & William Shakespeare

The True Performing Of It

Andrew Muir

By the same author

Razor's Edge: "Bob Dylan and the Never-Ending Tour"
(Helter Skelter Publishing, 2001)
Troubadour: "Early and Late Songs of Bob Dylan"
(Woodstock Publications, 2003)
One More Night "Bob Dylan and the Never-Ending Tour"
(CreateSpace, 2013)
Shakespeare in Cambridge: A Celebration of the Shakespeare Festival
(Amberley Publishing, 2015)

———————————

A catalogue record for this book is available from the British Library

This edition © Red Planet Books 2019
Text © Andrew Muir 2019

ISBN: 978 1 9127 3395 8

Printed in the UK

Cover design: Harry Gregory

Publisher: Mark Neeter

www.redplanetmusicbooks.com
Email: info@redplanetzone.com

CONTENTS

Dedication

To Joe McShane and David Bristow,
for outstanding companionship at
numerous performances of both
Shakespeare and Dylan over the last
three decades. Thanks, gents, for having
heard the chimes at midnight with me.

Note

Unless otherwise stated, all Shakespeare quotations come from the
New Cambridge editions; all Dylan quotes from his official lyrics,
and all Bible quotes from the King James Version. All direct quotes
from Shakespeare and Dylan are typeset in italics. A line space has
been inserted above longer quotes for ease of reading.

Chapter One

INTRODUCTION

B ob Dylan has been regularly compared to Shakespeare for many
years. In the Sixties, *The New York Times* called him 'the Shakespeare
of his generation'. As the decades have passed, many more have done
so. Some have noted his works' scope and depth as being comparable
to Shakespeare's, while others have acclaimed certain of his writing
techniques as 'Shakespearean' in both style and quality. [1]

The comparison has become so commonplace that it can even be
expanded and reversed. "Leonard Cohen is John Donne to Bob Dylan's
Shakespeare" declared a headline in *The Guardian*. Donne is considered
later, making this quote from the biography *The Ballad of Bob Dylan* all the
more intriguing: "For two years Zimmerman sat in the front row of Rolfzen's
class, third seat from the door, transfixed by the teacher's lively Donne and
Shakespeare." [2] Rolfzen's influence may be pivotal. He concentrated on the
effects of individual words and his engaging and insightful approach to
poetry was considered inspirational. Dylan's close friend at the time, John
Bucklen, said: "I remember him getting me to appreciate Shakespeare. He

was a good teacher of literature because you could sense that he really enjoyed and knew and loved literature."[3]

Reversals include the following two, firstly a knowing and impish statement by Professor Christopher Ricks and then an instintive comment by an actor from the Shakespeare Globe company. Professor Ricks, in acclaiming Dylan as "the greatest living user of the English language," justifies his claim in part by referring to "that Dylanesque writer, William Shakespeare." Phil Daniels, an actor at the Globe Theatre, describing what he likes about Jacobean and Shakespearean theatre, said:

"Well, they are just such good plays usually. I mean, they're so well written. I went to see *The Duchess of Malfi* the other night, and it's so clever, so brilliantly written word wise. ... And it's like Shakespeare as well, such wonderful stories and so brilliantly written, and so astute and lyrical. They're kind of like the Bob Dylan of their ages really, these guys. They really could write. And people don't write like that anymore. I mean there are some brilliant writers about but just that style is so fantastic".[4]

Bob Dylan does not see the fact that "people don't write like that anymore" as a terrible loss, however, because we can still experience the originals in performance:

"...of course nobody writes like Shakespeare either, but you know, it doesn't matter those things can still be performed. They don't have to be written – just like folksongs".[5]

It appears incumbent upon me, for the sake of clarity, to underline that I am not claiming that Dylan is the artistic equal of Shakespeare. It hardly belittles Mr. Dylan to state so, as neither is anyone else. As Dylan has remarked: *"Have you ever seen a Shakespeare play? I mean, it's like the English language at its peak".*[6] Instead, I am drawing what I believe are revealing and fruitful comparisons between these two artists.

That comment by Dylan on Shakespeare is one of many he has made throughout the years, as can be seen in the appendix at the end of the book. In 1978, when he was asked about his 'strong feelings for giving people a really strong, intense, emotional show', Dylan responded:

"That's because the songs are intense. There's a wide range of emotions there. To me it's like a Shakespeare play, even after all these years you can still go and see a

group doing Shakespeare. It might not be the way it was when it was happening but it's a pretty fair account of it, and this is the same way, the songs all run together in a way that if you was going to sit down and break 'em all down you'd have some kind of story there. You really would. It's that... it's more... it's a play. And I'm singing all the songs. Maybe all the elements are out there. A lot of these songs I could see better, with more, I could see them definitely being more romantic and using different elements of theatre but I can't do everything, you know."[7]

It is common with many creative people to allude to Shakespeare, and this has become so regular with Dylan in interviews as to have become something of a constant. Again we find Shakespeare appearing as a touchstone, as a reference, and perhaps even as an implied comparative quality.

Sometimes there can be an air of over-reaching about this use of Shakespeare's cultural authority; not just from Dylan, but from anyone trying to justify something they have created. Dylan is our interest here, however, and Dylan had, thankfully, never felt any need to 'justify' his musical output as he produced his masterpieces of the Sixties and seventies. However, when he moved into the realm of cinema, 1978's *Renaldo and Clara*'s reception – a mixture of hatred, misapprehension and boorishness – plus, more destructively, the film's inherent weaknesses, led him to 'explain' his art in a series of interviews. As one example, the staged 1978 discussion with the poet Allen Ginsberg was a promotional piece for, and justification of, *Renaldo and Clara*. After the two men list some of the major images in the film, Ginsberg says: "Pound's Cantos are constructed in this way – image to image." Dylan replies: *Every great work of art is when you think about it, Shakespeare. The point to get is that the film is connected by an untouchable connective link."*

However, many of Dylan's more recent mentions of Shakespeare have been particularly astute. Most of them spark analogies to Dylan's work either implicitly or explicitly. An example of this was in his 2015 MusiCares speech, where Dylan picked up on a connection to the roots of Shakespeare's drama:

"I'm glad for my songs to be honored like this. But you know, they didn't get here by themselves. It's been a long road and it's taken a lot of doing. These songs of mine, they're like mystery stories, the kind that Shakespeare saw when he was growing

up. I think you could trace what I do back that far. They were on the fringes then, and I think they're on the fringes now."[8]

The reference is exact and telling. It seems highly probable that the young Shakespeare was taken to nearby Coventry to witness that city's famed cycle of mystery plays. These enactments of major episodes were a mixture of awe-inspiring spiritual drama intertwined with clowning and crude jokes. This mixture appears, too, in Minstrelsy and its ethos, style and sprinkling of mixed-up Shakespeare plots and characters was recreated on Dylan's *"Love And Theft"*. That album, like those mystery plays, mixes the sublime and the corny, and the religious with earthy comedy, as does *The Basement Tapes* collection.

As Dylan noted in a 2011 interview: *"One song is always using a line from another song to brace it. But then goes off on another tangent. Minstrels did it all the time. Weird takes on Shakespeare plays, stuff like that. It's just done automatically."*[9]

***

Some important shared areas are not in separate chapters but instead run throughout. Our artists have a common folk hinterland of ballads, fairy tales and nursery rhymes. Probably Dylan's most celebrated song, 'Like A Rolling Stone', opens with the words *"Once upon a time..."* in one of his many allusions to the rich world of fairy tales. Cinderella appears in a song on the same album. The Cinderella myth lies underneath, but close to the surface, of the opening to arguably Shakespeare's most profound play, *Lear*. This play also features the children's game and nursery allusion 'Handy Dandy', as does Dylan's song of that name from an album built on the magic of nursery rhymes. Even more than fairy tales and nursery rhymes, the ballad and folk song world suffuses the work of both. Specific examples of these will be examined in the chapter, *The Tempest* and *Tempest*, as well as in those on sources and wordplay.

***

Given the range and sweep of both writers, there are bound to be many similarities, and it is not difficult to build correspondences between any two artists. Needless to say, there are also numerous differences and a book on those would be a very large volume indeed. At a fundamental level, in addition to the differences in the societies of sixteenth-century England and twentieth-century America, we can add the disproportionate length of their careers. As Dylan heads into his sixth decade, we have to remember that Shakespeare's work was concentrated mainly in the last decade of the sixteenth century and the first of the seventeenth. We have an overwhelming amount of information on Dylan and a frustrating paucity on Shakespeare.

This book is not concerned with these dissimilarities but instead concentrates on connections and parallels at the core of their working practices. As such it deals with the primacy of the performance of words which are simultaneously of the highest literary value.

In the prologue to *Henry V*, Shakespeare implores his audience to use their imagination to transform the words they hear into pictures in their minds, *"Think when we talk of horses, that you see them"*. Somewhat similarly, this book depends on readers recalling or experiencing performances of Shakespeare and by Dylan. Productions of Shakespeare and performances by Dylan are so readily available as to be overwhelming in number in both cases. It is to these and to your private memories of the ones you have experienced that this study addresses itself.

A major theme of the book is the convergence of popular art with academic studies and so, in tandem with this, its approach attempts to marry the rigorous research of the latter with a widely accessible tone.

***

Following on from this introduction, chapter two looks at the universality of Bards in general, and the two under discussion in particular. We note the wide range of genres they cover, due, in no small measure, to them being providers of popular entertainment. This leads us to chapter three, where the implications of song and play scripts being treated as literature are considered. Live performances are never the same, and one of the many consequences of this is that there are no definitive textual versions; instead, multiple texts contribute to our rather nebulous concept of each specific "song' or 'play'. The same chapter investigates what happens when what had initially been popular art comes to be regarded as high art.

Chapter four is concerned with the virulent opposition that acting and rock music faced from both civic authorities and self-appointed cultural guardians in the sixteenth and twentieth centuries, respectively. These condemnations may have been separated by four hundred years, but their content and tone turn out to be startlingly similar. Religious leaders may have been prominent in these opposing forces, but religion plays a significant role in the lives and art of our bards. Consequently, chapter five focuses firstly on the continuing controversies over whether Shakespeare was a Protestant or a Catholic and whether Dylan is Christian or Jewish. After examining the evidence and the arguments proposed in these regards, there is an exploration of how Biblical symbolism and themes form an ever-present backdrop to their writing.

The following two chapters take us from parallels to direct connections. We first examine the many references to Shakespeare's plays and characters throughout Dylan's songs, prose and film scripts before the next chapter concentrates on Shakespearean productions which have featured Dylan songs.

Chapter eight enjoys the shared delight in wordplay, featuring Shakespeare and Dylan's favoured conceits and love of puns. Additionally, there is an investigation into how both artists are also very driven to explore, develop and investigate the very language that they use and what it means to use language in the first place.

The following chapter provides an examination of copying, in all its myriad forms, in the works of both writers from the transmutation of source material into magic, through the concepts of *imitatio*, the nature of originality, the folk process and on to what appears to be unabashed plagiarism.

The final chapter, before the conclusion, provides a practical demonstration of all the theories in the book by considering, together, Shakespeare's play *The Tempest* and Dylan's album *Tempest*.

INTRODUCTION

NOTES

1 Journalists make the link with regularity. In the Sixties, Richard Goldstein of *The New York Times* wrote that Dylan is "Shakespeare and Judy Garland to my generation. We trust what he tells us." According to Paul Zollo "...to sit at a table with him and face those iconic features is no less impressive than suddenly finding yourself sitting face to face with William Shakespeare." Adrian Deevoy started an interview piece by declaring: "There can be no greater validation for a songwriter than knowing that Bob Dylan likes your work. It's a little like Shakespeare approving of your latest sonnet."

It is not just the journalists; headline writers also get in on the act, as they, too, often refer to the two artists as being alike. "Shakespeare in crocodile slippers" was the heading of an interview in *Der Spiegel*, while in the UK, *The Guardian* put it plainly in the headline: "Dylan's a modern Shakespeare."

Musicians, as you would expect, contribute more than any other group even exceeding journalists and critics. Antony Scaduto, in his 1972 biography, quotes folk-singer Phil Ochs as saying: "From the moment I met him I thought he was...a genius, Shakespearean". Charlie Daniels: "I kind of compare Dylan in his time and his vernacular to Shakespeare's very unique way with words." Alex Levy: "I think that we all should be grateful that we are living in a world with Bob Dylan. It's maybe how people felt when they saw a Shakespeare play, when he was alive, that's how major he is. It's pretty obvious that this guy has done something with language that has transcended the status quo, that's for sure." Kelly Jones of the Stereophonics on hearing Dylan had said he was a fan of the band: "...to have something like that come from a guy who's kind of the Shakespeare of music? It's very... it's a jab in the arm for sure."

Rock critic Paul Williams had similar feelings to Alex Levy: "If Shakespeare was in your midst, putting on shows at The Globe Theatre, wouldn't you feel the need to be there, to write down what happened in them?" The back page of the book *The Philosophy of Bob Dylan* is emblazoned with the words, all in capitals: "The poet who has given us more phrases than any poet since Shakespeare".

There's a wider gamut of people who do the same. Professor Christopher Ricks is often quoted with perkily provocative remarks linking the two: "I'm not so besotted with Dylan's genius not to know that not all of his work is perfect. He's only as good as Shakespeare, who had a lot wrong, too!" Ricks has also pointed out one of the connections core to this volume: "Dylan is a great amuser, a great entertainer, who belongs with the artists who've looked for the widest popular constituency, like Dickens and Shakespeare." An Internet Radio programme recently entitled an interview: "Is Bob Dylan the Shakespeare of Song?" without feeling the need to mention Shakespeare even once. "Bob Dylan may be the Shakespeare of our time", speculated Dylan's high school English teacher Boniface J Rolfzen. Man of many parts, Penn Jillette put it this way: "If we have anybody who's Shakespeare in our time, it's Dylan, and he just speaks to me more and more...." Pamela Des Barres, writer and groupie, places Dylan at the pinnacle of all the men she wanted because: "he is our bard, our modern day Shakespeare".

There is a reliance on the convenience of Shakespeare as a touchstone involved in all of this, as his name provides a form of shorthand. The use of the name of the greatest writer, by general accord, is applied to whomsoever one is claiming as the greatest writer in a specific sphere. Hence, Hank Williams was known as the "Shakespeare of Country music", and Bob Dylan himself referred to Chuck Berry as "the Shakespeare of rock and roll".

I would suggest that it is also much more and that consciously or subconsciously, many of the people quoted are responding to one or more of the areas covered in this book, such as the popular basis of their appeal or their ability to capture the zeitgeist in memorable phrases and to use the language in unforgettable ways.

These quotes, in order, come from the following sources:

Paul Zollo *Bob Dylan: The Song Talk* Interview 1991

http://www.dailymail.co.uk/home/event/article-4970810/Imelda-getting-shout-Bob-Dylan.html#ixzz4vnCDb7yT,

Der Spiegel, October. 16, 1997

http://www.theguardian.com/culture/2001/sep/11/artsfeatures.bobdylan,

Charlie Daniels, *Close Up* (Country Music Association magazine), 1993

https://eu.tennessean.com/story/entertainment/music/2017/05/19/dylan-fest-nashvilles-coolest-all-star-concert/328900001/

http://amp.timeinc.net/nme/news/music/stereophonics-respond-bob-dylan-fan-music-2148819?source=dam,

http://www.rollingstone.com/music/news/tangled-up-in-dylan-20010412

BJ Rolfzen quoted in Lee Marshall's *Bob Dylan: The Never Ending Star* Polity Press September 28, 2007

Penn Jillette, Reason TV interview (2 August 2016), http://erinlynnviolettelifeinla.blogspot.com/2012/,

Bob Dylan and Philosophy (Open Court, 2006)

https://cohencentric.com/2016/10/17/bob-dylan-congratulates-pen-lyrics-award-winners-chuck-berry-shakespeare-rock-roll-leonard-cohen-kafka-blues/

https://www.theguardian.com/music/2016/nov/19/leonard-cohen-music-recalls-john-donne-poetry,

http://www.cbc.ca/radio/writersandcompany/christopher-ricks-on-why-bob-dylan-is-the-greatest-living-user-of-the-english-language-1.3803292

2 Quoted in *The Ballad of Bob Dylan: A Portrait* Souvenir Press Ltd., March 2012 Daniel Mark Epstein. I have endeavoured, without success, to gain more information on this comment and to trace the original source

3 Howard Sounes, *Down The Highway*, Grove Press May 2011

4 http://www.shakespearesglobe.com/discovery-space/adopt-an-actor/archive/citizen-played-by-phil-daniels/pre-rehearsal accessed July 24, 2018

5 Quoted in the *Miami Times*, and by Kathryn Baker in an interview entitled "Love Me or Leave Me" September 1988

6 *Ibid.*

7 Marc Rowland interview 23rd September 1978, (Collected in John Baldwin's privately published *Fiddler Now Upspoke Volume 3*)

8 Musicares Acceptance Speech February 6, 2015. Transcript here: https://www.rollingstone.com/music/music-news/read-bob-dylans-complete-riveting-musicares-speech-240728/

9 http://www.bobdylan.com/us/bobdylan101/john-elderfield-interview-bob-dylan-spring-2011

Although still listed in the site's contents and listed on 'search', it was unavailable as of July 24, 2018

Chapter Two

BARDS

**The muse has taught them songs
and loves the race of bards**

Dictionaries tend to give two primary meanings for the word 'bard'. Merriam-Webster defines it firstly as that of a tribal poet-singer skilled in composing and reciting verses on heroes and their deeds and, secondly, as a name for any lyric poet. If we write the word with a capital 'B', then the aptness for both Shakespeare and Dylan becomes immediately apparent.

This is because 'Bard' has primarily come to mean the voice of a people: be it a nation, class, religious or other grouping. Shakespeare may differ from the original definition of the word 'bard', in most aspects of the term, but it is used to elevate him above other poets, even those of genius. He is, as it were, the Bard of Bards.

Dylan is close to the first definition of bard, although he is not strictly an 'epic poet'. He is the perfect embodiment of the second, being a lyric poet and the most immediately identifiable minstrel of his times. We find him as a bard with an upper case 'B' as "the Bard of his generation". For many, at least in the Western world, he is the Bard of our times, and the leading poetic voice of the last six decades.

One thing that Bards of this kind, over and above the value of the poetic output, also share, is the ability to influence the language, and therefore the minds, of their and future generations. A third bard, one Dylan has called his "inspiration", who exemplified this strikingly, is Robert Burns, the Bard of Scotland, and, in his day, much further afield. It is often forgotten, nowadays, but in his time, Burns' influence on everyday speech spread far further than Scotland. He exerted a powerful influence southwards to at least the English Midlands. His rhythm, phrases and language were quoted or embedded in everyday exchanges even by those who had never read him or heard his poetry recited, or songs sung. Due to a concerted and orchestrated cultural blitzkrieg on Scottish dialects, followed by ever-increasing globalisation, the only remnant of this left today, and it too is fast disappearing, is in Ulster.

In both his verse and prose, Seamus Heaney, from that part of the world, is very acute in acknowledging this influence. In the poem "A Birl for Burns", which begins:

From the start, Burns' birl and rhythm,
That tongue the Ulster Scots brought wi' them
And stick to still in County Antrim
Was in my ear.
From east of Bann it westered in
On the Derry air.

Heaney notes that the tongue is "going, gone" and although he knows it will live on in Burns' work, that will need to be heavily glossed, and Heaney rues the passing of it, after centuries of common usage, in his homeland:

Old men and women getting crabbed
Would hark like dogs who'd seen a rabbit,
Then straighten, stare and have a stab at
    Standard habbie:
Custom never staled their habit
    O' quotin' Rabbie.[1]

In those lovely last lines, Heaney deftly brings the attribute of 'infinite variety' to the Rabbie they are quoting by the reference to the unforgettable description of Cleopatra in Shakespeare's *Antony and Cleopatra*: '*Age cannot wither her, nor custom stale her infinite variety.*'

Heaney again highlights a connection with Shakespeare when he approaches the same theme in his prose writing. Here with the added benefit for this book in highlighting the connection with folk ballads and Shakespeare's English:

> "... *what Nadezhda Mandelsiain called the nugget of harmony' and the guarantee of Burns' genius as a poet of the Scots and English tongues, for 'och', like 'wee', also belongs north of that Berwick/Bundoran line where the language of Shakespeare and the Bible meets the language of Dunbar and the ballads and where new poetic combinations and new departures are still going on*".[2]

Heaney repeatedly notes the importance and effect of a poet's language on everyday speech, its rhythms, cadence and accents and the cumulative history it brings with it. Burn's language was important to him in the same way that Dylan's is to those of his time, because:

"It gets into the boundless language of poetry by reason of its totally unchallengeable rightness as utterance, its simultaneous at-oneness with the genius of English and Scottish speech; and it got under my official classroom guard and into the kitchen life, as it were, of my affections by reason of its truth to the life of the language that I spoke while growing up in mid-Ulster, a language where trace elements of Elizabethan English and Lowland Scots are still to be heard and to be reckoned with as a matter of pronunciation and even, indeed, of politics."[3]

Heaney highlights crucial factors of being a Bard in these quotes. The Bard is seen to look back, to have the wisdom of the ages behind him, while simultaneously being absolutely at one with now. We can complete the temporal arc by adding the future, as the authentic bard is also seen to be a Poet-Seer with more than a touch of the prophet in him. He is, as Ben Jonson memorably wrote of Shakespeare: 'not of an age, but for all time'. At the same time, however, in his writing, he encapsulates his age like no other can.

F.R. Leavis captured this particular bardic quality well, when he wrote of T.S. Eliot's *The Love Song of J. Alfred Prufrock*: "We have here, in short, poetry that freely expresses a modern sensibility, the ways of feeling, the modes of expression, of one fully alive in his own age."[4]

John Clellon Holmes, when interviewed in the mid-Sixties, saw this same attribute in the young Bob Dylan: "He has the authentic mark of the bard on him, and I think it's safe to say that no one, years hence, will be able to understand just what it was like to live in this time without attending to what this astonishingly gifted young man has already achieved."[5]

This element of "unchallengeable rightness as utterance" is evident in the way so many of Dylan's words have become common usage already. Phrases like: '*the times they are a-changin*', '*blowin' in the wind*', '*to live outside the law, you must be honest*', '*you'll find out when you reach the top, you're on the bottom*', and so forth.

Shakespeare, being Shakespeare, and with over four hundred years of quotation already in his favour, is everywhere in our language, not only for things he originated but, like Burns and Dylan after him, for the proverbs, sayings and clichés which, in the hands of Bards, are re-minted. Thus re-energised by new context and the patronage of a later bard, they are re-popularised.

This is so much the case that many sayings which are credited to Bards actually date back to previous writers both known and anonymous. A major source of these is *The Tyndale Bible*, in particular via its pervasive influence on the 1560 *Geneva Bible* for Shakespeare and the *King James Version* for Dylan. William Tyndale's extraordinarily adept and memorable phraseology, and pithy quotes are often misattributed to Shakespeare. Which is not to deny, of course, that Shakespeare gave the English language a multitude of the very same, coined from his own fertile verbal imagination. Notwithstanding this, Tyndale is quite possibly the single most significant writer to have so profoundly affected both of our two bards. Throughout this book, when I quote Dylan referencing the *King James Bible* and Shakespeare the *Geneva*, it is worth remembering that the bulk of both texts come directly from Tyndale.

Other commonplaces go back even further. The proverb we use nowadays, 'all that glitters is not gold' is usually traced to Shakespeare's *Merchant of Venice* Act II Scene iv:

All that glisters is not gold;
Often have you heard that told.

The term "glisters" became glitters in time; it is, in effect, the same word.

People had indeed 'often heard that told', prior to Shakespeare, Chaucer had it as: *"Hit is not al gold, that glareth"*. So, it was known in English poetry before Shakespeare even got to it. It is such an obvious truth that it is no surprise to discover that earlier civilisations used the same phrase. The Roman poets Shakespeare appears to have immersed himself in, and from whom Dylan, who also studied them at school, liberally quotes, include, amongst their lines, *nōn omne quod nĭtet aurum est* ('Not all that glitters is gold'). It was a Latin proverb and well-known enough as to appear in *Corpus Juris Civilis* (the Book of Civil Law) some two and a half thousand years ago.

Dylan puts a version of this ancient saying into the mouth of a grandparent dispensing a list of clichéd advice. Dylan thus acknowledges, as Shakespeare did, that here was an old truth, while simultaneously giving an intriguing twist to the concept:

Grandma said, "Boy, go and follow your heart
And you'll be fine at the end of the line
All that's gold isn't meant to shine
Don't you and your one true love ever part"

As with other things we have heard and read and thought many times in our life, many of us never come across a version of this phrase without either hearing it in Dylan's voice or thinking of its use in Shakespeare's play and the extra resonance those bring to it. Such is the power of Bards.

There is a side-effect to this that Dylan finds unpleasant, namely that lines from songs are often taken as though they are his personal statements. Dylan refutes this: "*...I'm not the songs. It's like somebody expecting Shakespeare to be Hamlet, or Goethe to be Faust.*"[6]. In the same way that we are repeatedly told that Shakespeare said *"To thine own self be true"*, people will hear in the future that "Dylan said: *'All that's gold isn't meant to shine"*. In reality, as Dylan is so keen to underline, it is not themselves, but characters they have created who are speaking, and in Shakespeare's case here it is Polonius in *Hamlet*, a character who is being openly mocked for his sententious, fussy nature.

Many phrases that do not originate with Bards can become so firmly associated with them that we think they do. This is not entirely unjust as, in many cases, the phrases would undoubtedly have dropped out of common use were it not for the Bard preserving and reinvigorating them. In doing this, they provide an intriguing and poetic strand to our regular communication in which complex concepts and emotions can be conveyed by a few words that carry within them a resonant cultural history and force.

A simple three-word phrase like 'not dark yet' will take on added significance because of Dylan's use of it in his song of that name. The same could be said for the whole line, but the remaining words will in time, and already have for many of us, become 'encoded' as an automatic extension of the first three, and they no longer need to be uttered. It serves as intuitive, folk shorthand.

To take an example from the past, so that the effect over time can be observed, the poet John Donne, a bard himself and a potential Bard had he not been a contemporary of Shakespeare, wrote lines so memorable as to have become proverbial. Thus, the phrase 'No man is an island' no longer 'needs' its succeeding words:

> entire of itself; every man
> is a piece of the continent, a part of the main;[7]

Instead, we accept them all as part of the short phrase itself. That same short verse, which is, incidentally, alluded to on the Dylan albums *Time Out of Mind* and *"Love and Theft"*, ends with another instance of the same phenomenon. The last four words are rarely quoted, because they are, literally, 'taken as read':

> *never send to know for whom*
> *the bell tolls; it tolls for thee.*

The same thing, I suggest, is already happening with Dylan's *"but it's getting there.*" In both cases, given our mortality, we all know how it ends.

Another thing about bards, associated with their raising of everyday speech to high art, is that they are generally claimed to have sprung naturally from the soil, or from the common mass of humanity. They are, in other words, not only our spokespeople but also one of us.

Although feted as literary geniuses, they are all acclaimed as having sprung naturally from the communal, oral art of 'the people'. So strong is the wish for this to be the case that a risible series of claims attach themselves to Bard mythology. Poetic seers who are sons of the soil has always been an attractive image. Thus, we get Milton referring to Shakespeare as a rustic genius: "warbling his native woodnotes wild", Burns being known as 'the heaven-taught ploughman'. Dylan himself peddled the myth of the kid who ran away and grew up in a carnival in the middle of twentieth century America and picked up everything he knew in a similar, near mystical, manner.

In reality, all things point to Shakespeare having been given a very firm grounding in the classics and rhetoric; Burns, despite the grinding poverty of his life, lived in Scotland at a time when education was revered and he was well read in the classics, as well as in both Scottish and English poetry and, naturally, in Shakespeare. Dylan attended a well-funded, palatial school in the richest country in the world.

Bards encompass all of life in their work and give a voice to everyone in society. As Walt Whitman put it: "I contain multitudes". In the works of Shakespeare, Burns and Dylan you will find the sordid and the sublime, and the earthy and the divine. Burns being a farmer knew that nature was no idyll but hard work and full of dirt, death and a plethora of physical unpleasantries. Shakespeare wryly notes the reality of country life and punctures the pastoral idyll in *As You Like It* when Corin refuses to shake hands, pointing out that: *'Why, we are still handling our ewes, and their fells, you know, are greasy'* and adding that *'they are often tarred over with the surgery of our sheep'*.

All three poets revelled in their use of bawdy. Burns' barnyard verse is legendary, and he was comfortable writing it side by side with elevated verse. Shakespeare and Dylan's extensive forays into vulgarity are discussed in chapter eight. Such mixing of high and low elements was to disappear after Burns. William Wordsworth and the following Romantic Movement saw the countryside as part of sublime nature, while the Victorians shied away from any mention of bodily functions. It returned though, in time, and is gloriously present in Dylan's rich corpus. It is something he is aware of, as you can tell from the quote in the introduction where he equates his songs with the very Mystery Plays that the young William Shakespeare is likely to have seen. These formed one of the foundation stones of Elizabethan theatre where scenes of key biblical events were interspersed with rude humour of the lowest variety.

A gift for polyphonic universality is another characteristic of Bards. They speak out in the voices of people from all walks of life and they say things in such a way that we think they are voicing our own thoughts. As David Bowie put it in his 'Song for Bob Dylan': "And you sat behind a million pair of eyes/And told them how they saw."

Voicing the innermost thoughts of another person and somehow encapsulating their inner essence is one of Shakespeare's keenest triumphs. He did not just do this for the main characters in his plays but for all of them. The examples are legion throughout his work. To take just one example: the very short Act II Scene iii in *Henry V*, when Falstaff's death is reported, is a sideshow to the main action. Yet it provides an insight into the humanity with which Shakespeare imbues his characters. Bardolph, Nym and Pistol all feel very real and the Hostess is magnificently realised, as is the meticulously observed ending of the absent Falstaff through Quickly's garbled words. Hundreds of characters have such authentic life breathed into them by the master dramatist. On a smaller scale, not being dramatists, Burns and Dylan also display this ability. Being Bards, they too can adopt the voice and persona of others in an utterly convincing manner.[8] Consider Burns as a young man known for his promiscuous lifestyle, putting into words and song, adapted from a luridly bawdy folk source, the touching view of a wife looking back on a long, faithful marriage and towards a joint ending of life in "Jon Anderson, My Jo"; or the young man, Bob Dylan, putting into words and song, again based on a folk source, the pitiful lament of the abandoned wife and soon to be abandoned mother of 'North Country Blues".

Shakespeare's universality has proved to be perdurable. Midway through the four centuries since Shakespeare was writing his masterpieces, Coleridge lectured:

"If Shakespeare be the wonder of the ignorant, he is, and ought to be, much more the wonder of the learned: not only from profundity of thought, but from his astonishing and intuitive knowledge of what man must be at all times and under all circumstances, he is rather to be looked upon as a prophet than as a poet. Yet, with all these unbounded powers, with all this might and majesty of genius, he makes us feel as if he were unconscious of himself and of his high destiny, disguising the half god in the simplicity of a child."[9]

Even as our contemporary, Dylan's career longevity has allowed him to already have influenced generations. It is an all-pervasive influence, as Neil McCormick noted when praising the decision of the Nobel Committee to award Dylan the Prize for Literature:

The Nobel committee say they are honouring Dylan "for having created new poetic expressions within the great American song tradition" but he did way more than that. Dylan utterly exploded the form, enabling the simple song to become a vehicle for every shade and nuance of human thought and expression, unleashing incredible forces of creativity on this ancient, sturdy folk medium – and did it with a flowing, electrifying wordsmithery and innate, almost mystical wisdom that has created a body of mindblowing work that will resonate for centuries to come.

As a supernaturally gifted youngster, he brought into folk music a poetic license that married the romantic flourish of Shelley and Yeats, the cryptic intelligence of Ezra Pound and T.S. Eliot, the beatnik exuberance of Ginsberg and Kerouac and the Old Testament weight of the St James Bible crossed with the hardboiled, deadpan American wit of pulp fiction. Then he took that all into rock and roll, the most brash and exciting electric sound of the post-War generation, and no part of popular culture was left untouched by his influence."

It aids in their universality that both writers cover such a wide range of genres. Due to *The First Folio* of 1623, we are conditioned to pigeon-hole Shakespeare's plays into "Comedies, Histories, and Tragedies". However, we know the categories range much further. Within comedy alone, there is light comedy, dark comedy, very black comedy, satire, city comedies, pastoral and farce. There are the wondrous later Romances; there's the gore-fest horror of *Titus Andronicus*, revenge thrillers and more. Dylan, in the Sixties alone, went from folk-blues, folk, protest, to singer-songwriter, to rock, and on to country and that was just the first decade of an artist still producing surprises in the sixth one of his career. Dylan has written every manner of song, in almost every musical genre imaginable; visionary, political, religious, satirical, epic, tender, philosophical, riotous fun, relaxing, vitriolic, peaceful and contemplative.

Their universality is also a driver behind the timelessness of the works of bards. Individual verses, lines, and scenes inevitably speak to the current moment with uncanny pertinence even after much time has passed since they were first penned. Listeners feel that their own inner apprehensions are being given verbal utterance in a way that appears almost magical. Songwriter, poet and novelist, Richard Farina, captured this phenomenon well when he told Dylan biographer, Robert Shelton:

"But I don't believe that I understand what is going through his mind. The particular magic that Dylan has over, say, twenty million people, is the paradox and the inaccessibility of him. In his music, people are struck by something and yet they don't really seem to know what it is. That's always been the case with the most acute and exalted poetry. There are lines of Shakespeare like this, in which you don't have to know who plays what to be struck by the magic of words. Then the insight of the listener is followed by intense perplexity. We hear something that we finally realize is saying something we think ourselves..."[10]

***

One example of their universality, their ability to speak for us, in our own voices, their prophetic natures, and their encompassing of all human life can suffice to conclude this chapter. Professor Marjorie Garber pointed out the close affinity that exists between Shakespeare's *Romeo and Juliet* and Dylan's 'The Times They Are A-Changin'.[11] The play, she states, is: "concerned with youth, sexuality, media, and generational conflict ... the love story of two young people and the failure of parents to understand their idealistic and rebellious children. Romeo's outburst to Friar Laurence *"Thou canst not speak of that thou dost not feel"* was, effectively, the cry of a generation."

That generation being the one who acclaimed Dylan as their bard. Garber notes that 'The Times They Are A-Changin' 'became the anthem for a generation. Its lyrics speak, almost uncannily, to the Romeo and Juliet situation ... This logic of inversion (the slow will be fast, the present will be past, the sons and daughters will be in command) is, as we have already seen, the logic of *Romeo and Juliet*."

Around the world people still quote lines from both play and song whether they have seen the Shakespeare play or heard Dylan sing his song. Such is the enduring power and popularity of Bards. They both arose at times of considerable social upheaval which leaves people disorientated and in need of such voices. Bruce Springsteen remembers exactly how it felt hearing Bob Dylan in a time of flux and uncertainty and captures the effect and force that the voice of a Bard carries:

"He inspired me and gave me hope. He asked the questions everyone else was too frightened to ask, especially to a 15 year old: "How does it feel to be on your own?" A seismic gap had opened up between generations and you suddenly felt orphaned, abandoned amid the flow of history, your compass spinning, internally homeless. Bob pointed true north and served as a beacon to assist you in making your way through the new wilderness America had become. He planted a flag, wrote the songs, sang the words that were essential to the times, to the emotional and spiritual survival of so many young Americans at that moment."[12]

NOTES

1 Seamus Heaney from *Addressing the Bard: twelve contemporary poets respond to Robert Burns,* edited by Douglas Gifford, Scottish Poetry Library, 2009

2 Seamus Heaney *Finders Keepers: Selected Prose 1971 – 2001* Faber & Faber

3 Seamus Heaney *Burns' Art Speech* Faber & Faber; 2002

4 F.R.Leavis *New Bearings in English Poetry* first published in 1932. The aptness of this quote has previously been pointed out by Michael Gray

5 Yurchenco, Henrietta 'Folk-Rot: in Defence", *Sound and Fury* April 1966. Reprinted in *The Bob Dylan Companion,* Schimer, New York, *1987*

6 "Dylan Revisited" by David Gates *Newsweek* May 10, 1997

7 John Donne. *Devotions Upon Emergent Occasions* Meditation 17, 1624

8 In John Donne's "Break of Day" he also writes from a female viewpoint

9 Samuel Taylor Coleridge, *Lecture ix*

10 Richard Farina quoted in *Bob Dylan: No Direction Home, the Life and Music of Bob Dylan* by Robert Shelton, Beech Tree Books, 1986

11 Shakespeare and Modern Culture By Marjorie Garber Knopf Doubleday Publishing Group, December 9, 2008

12 Bruce Springsteen *Born To Run*, Simon and Schuster, 2016

Chapter Three

PERFORMANCE

Cry out against the non-performance

A key similarity between these two Bards is that they are both primarily known as writers of poetic verse that is not poetry *per se*, but rather scripts to be performed and lyrics of songs to be sung. A dogged avoidance of this simple truth has been the cause of much obfuscation through the years. Clearly put, Shakespeare wrote prose and verse that was designed to be performed in front of audiences by a cast of actors, not studied alone in a quiet library. Dylan has time and again stated that he wrote songs to have something to sing to audiences and that he views his albums as holding mere blueprints[1] of the songs that take full life when he performs them, nearly always accompanied by other musicians. In Martin Scorsese's 2006 film *No Direction Home*, Dylan tells us that: *"I wrote the songs to perform the songs. I needed to sing in that language, which was a language I hadn't heard before."* Furthermore, he points out that: *"The ideal performances of the songs would then come on stages throughout the world. Very few could be found on any of my records. Reaching the audience is what it's all about."* [2]

Aiming your work at an audience rather than a private reader obviously has profound implications, especially when satisfying those audiences is how you intend to make your living. Both artists strived to have 'hit shows', and to both entertain and be successful while doing so:

> *"... Shakespeare was a working dramatist in a very competitive world; he was writing highly topical plays to catch a particular market, and if he did not pull in an audience, the theatrical company in which he had a substantial financial share did not eat that week. What he and his fellows were selling was not a printed book but a heard and seen experience. As a result, he was far more concerned with the design of a very complex system of communication, as a tool to make the audience respond as he wished, than with a merely verbal text."* [3]

Dylan views a live audience as being of paramount importance. Mikal Gilmore put the following question to him in 2012: "Miles Davis had this idea that music was best heard in the moments in which it was performed – that that's where music is truly alive. Is your view similar?" Dylan's response chimed with similar comments he had made previously: *"Yeah, it's exactly the same as Miles' is. We used to talk about that. Songs don't come alive in a recording studio. You try your best, but there's always something missing. What's missing is a live audience. Sinatra used to make records like that - used to bring people into the studio as an audience. It helped him get into the songs better.*[4]

These two artists, however, are putting on performances while also pursuing their creative dreams and following their artistic principles. As a consequence, what audiences may want to hear is not necessarily what the artist wishes to write and so commercial and artistic tensions can arise. One of Shakespeare's biggest successes in his day was the relatively little known *Titus Andronicus* while *King Lear* seems not to have been particularly popular. Dylan's *Self Portrait* sold double the number of the much superior *Blonde on Blonde* upon release. The latter is far more influential and has subsequently garnered impressive sales; in 1966, though, it was too far ahead of its time to ensure sales commensurate with its fame and the acclaim accorded to it. *King Lear* was so in advance of its time that it would be hundreds of years before it was adequately appreciated or, it appears, successful in drawing audiences in its Shakespearean form. When it was staged, during the Restoration and thereafter, it was always drastically re-written.

The popular 'gore-fest', *Titus Andronicus*, was one of the plays that the adolescent Thomas Middleton saw when his trips to the theatre inspired him to become a playwright. He presumably looked up to Shakespeare as a leading light in the old guard in the same way younger pop and rock people look up to Dylan. Middleton was also, later in life, a direct competitor as well as a collaborator. Various music figures have followed a similar path in relation to Dylan.

In Shakespeare's London, most plays were only performed a handful of times before being discarded and replaced with 'the latest thing'. This provides a stark contrast to the Royal Shakespeare Company's schedule in current times. Shakespeare's theatre, just like the rock music of Dylan's decades, was inherently influenced by changes in fashion and style. Relentless demands for novelty and hits drove both industries and this had an impact on our two artists in fundamental ways. Just as Dylan went after the latest, but deeply unpleasant, studio sound in the mid-Eighties and jumped, or rather sank, into the pop video market, so Shakespeare had to move into whatever area the current fashion dictated. If plays featuring prostitutes and witches were in demand, then that is what was written. Popular entertainers need to remain fashionable.

Nonetheless, as ever our pair of artists were impressively resourceful even while working under such constraints. Shakespeare was the only major playwright of his day to avoid writing for the boys' companies whose fashionable reign over London theatres drove him and his company out on tour as adult actors became unwanted in the capital. While Dylan, to his eternal credit, has largely fought against such market imperatives; perhaps even going so far as to make a career out of defying career paths and audience expectations by going where his instinct led him. In the Sixties this resulted, more often than not, in everyone following Dylan rather than the opposite. He was, nonetheless, a hungry, itinerant would-be folk singer at that decade's opening, before rising to the stardom he had started out craving. His slip in the mid-eighties into following the off-putting production techniques of that period came at a time when, as he has acknowledged, he had lost direction and faith in his own work. It reminded him of why he hated studios:

> *"The recording process is very difficult for me. I lose my inspiration in the studio real easy, and it's very difficult for me to think that I'm going to eclipse anything I've ever done before. I get bored easily, and my mission... becomes very dim after a few failed takes."*[5]

The restrictions involved in making records, rather than playing live, were exacerbated by the ever increasing use of technology in the studios. Dylan's aversion to this, and the sound it produced on his albums, propelled a late career resurgence by encouraging him to thereafter battle against its detrimental effects:

"My music, my songs, they have very little to do with technology ... We all know what the thing should sound like. We're just getting further and further away from it," Dylan says. "I wanted something that goes through the technology and comes out the other end before the technology knows what it's doing."[6]

Dylan had always preferred live performing to studio work; *"My songs always sound a lot better in person than they do on the record"*, he told *Rolling Stone*'s Jann Wenner, in 1969.[7]

While neither Shakespeare nor Dylan created the biggest commercial successes of their times, they nonetheless were and are among the top names with solid, occasionally spectacular, successes over decades in their respective cut-throat industries. Shakespeare and Dylan's pre-eminence as writers of plays and songs allowed them to move from genre to genre almost gleefully, one sometimes feels, artistically topping the efforts of everyone else in all fields. You think of Shakespeare conquering romantic comedy, history, tragedy, city comedies and Dylan moving from folk to the pop charts to rock to country to gospel and excelling in each.

The primacy of performance dominates their thoughts. To return to Dylan's Nobel Lecture, we find him musing on the practicalities of 'putting on a show':

"I began to think about William Shakespeare, the great literary figure. I would reckon he thought of himself as a dramatist. The thought that he was writing literature couldn't have entered his head. His words were written for the stage. Meant to be spoken not read. When he was writing Hamlet, I'm sure he was thinking about a lot of different things: "Who're the right actors for these roles?" "How should this be staged?" "Do I really want to set this in Denmark[8]?" His creative vision and ambitions were no doubt at the forefront of his mind, but there were also more mundane matters to consider and deal with. "Is the financing in place?" "Are there enough good seats for my patrons?" "Where am I going to

get a human skull?" I would bet that the farthest thing from Shakespeare's mind was the
question "Is this literature? But, like Shakespeare, I too am often occupied with the pursuit
of my creative endeavors and dealing with all aspects of life's mundane matters. "Who
are the best musicians for these songs?" "Am I recording in the right studio?" "Is this song
in the right key?" Some things never change, even in 400 years. Not once have I ever had
the time to ask myself, "Are my songs literature?"[9]

This might also be the explanation, or at least part of it, as to why neither
seems to have been concerned, at least for a substantial period from the
beginning of their careers onwards, about their plays or songs being accurately
recorded in print. Dylan was the first major rock figure to have a book of
lyrics but it was a woefully slipshod production, and his LP sleeves had been
issued without the accompaniment of lyrics printed on them.[10] This was in
conspicuous contrast to many of his contemporaries, and made all the more
glaring by his pre-eminent position as a lyricist. The printing of Shakespeare's
plays in quarto format had nothing do with him and were instead profit
making enterprises for others, and this alone could explain Shakespeare
ignoring their many infelicities. With one possible exception, no 'authorial'
versions were put out in correction and it was left to friends to bring out the
Folio version seven years after Shakespeare's death.

While their feelings towards printed versions of their words is, at best,
ambivalent, the effect they have on an audience is always uppermost in
their minds. Dylan, as we have just seen, has gone so far as to say that the
only reason he began writing songs at all was because he needed material
to perform. It is a point that he has returned to: *"I wanted just a song to sing,*
and there came a certain point where I couldn't sing anything. So I had to write what I
wanted to sing 'cos nobody else was writing what I wanted to sing.[11]

Dylan, bemoaning the proliferation of the ubiquitous, held-aloft mobile
phones at his shows in the opening decade of this century, stated to *Rolling*
Stone's Douglas Brinkley in 2009 that:

"You have to go deal with the people who are actually there from night to night.
But most of those people aren't there to record or to take pictures. They're there for
enjoyment reasons. They are a lot of people who are having a night out. If you're
doing something else while we're playing... [shakes head]. I say it's like going to a

Shakespeare play and taking pictures. You're not going to feel the effect."

***

A fundamental difference in witnessing a performance of a Shakespeare play, rather than reading it, is that physical movement transforms text. The dramas were all written with this as their guiding principle. Certain passages make no sense without accompanying action, while gestures and even a silent presence can alter meaning. In addition, gestures and movement are partly subconscious enactments of the thoughts and feelings being portrayed. Over and above this, there was a significant contribution in the plays of purely physical entertainment; elaborate displays of sword-fighting, battle scenes, multiple murders, executions, wrestling matches, juggling, mummery, mimicking and bodily bawdiness. A considerable proportion of what we comprehend comes via movement, and the strength and subtleties of emotions that are communicated through the rhythms of speech rather than its content, in both prose and poetry.

This is one of the reasons why Shakespeare performances attract large numbers of non-native English speakers. As with the native speaking audience members, these are people drawn from all walks of life and their level of understanding English ranges from beginner to bilingual. Everyone can still enjoy the plays and it is worth remembering that much of what we know of Elizabethan play-going comes from the enthusiastic reports of performances by foreign travellers, some with little or no English at all.

Dylan would voluntarily swap positions with them:

"I like to see Shakespeare plays, so I'll go — I mean, even if it's in a different language. I don't care, I just like Shakespeare, you know. I've seen Othello and Hamlet and Merchant of Venice over the years, and some versions are better than others. Way better. It's like hearing a bad version of a song. But then somewhere else, somebody has a great version."[12]

Again, fluidity is stressed. Performances vary, and experiences change, not least because putting on performances also necessitates teamwork. All dramatic productions are collaborative in nature. This can begin at the writing stage and always occurs in the performances themselves.

For writing, it is indisputable that Shakespeare would have collaborated at some junctures. What is often disputed is the extent of this collaboration and when and where it took place. Collaboration was the norm in the theatres of his day; but Shakespeare would appear to have been less involved in this than most, perhaps due to his long association as shareholder, actor and playwright for the one company. Due to Shakespeare's reputation, it is nearly always thought, the early *Henry VI* trilogy aside, that he was the central player in his collaborations and the younger writers were benefiting from his experience, but it may well be that the dynamic was very much that of an old "star" linking his name with the 'latest hot names'. When Shakespeare co-wrote with Fletcher at the end of his career, it is quite likely the latter's name was the one selling the tickets.

Similarly, when Shakespeare linked up with Middleton, we think of Shakespeare as the dominant partner. Yet, at the time, despite writing what we now regard as many of the greatest of his works, Shakespeare was seen as 'yesterday's man'. Audiences wanted new genres, new themes, and young blood. We think of The Globe as 'Shakespeare's Globe', but Middleton had a bigger success there than Shakespeare ever did. Consequently, when Shakespeare teamed up with Middleton, it may have been for much the same reason as Dylan teamed up with The Grateful Dead and Tom Petty, that is, to sell tickets. Similarly, when Shakespeare co-wrote with Middleton, this may have been similar to Dylan co-writing 'Love Rescue Me' with U2 on their *Rattle and Hum* album, or Dylan co-authoring the song "Steel Bars" with Michael Bolton. There are other examples both surprising (Gene Simmons) and predictable (George Harrison) sprinkled throughout Dylan's career.

As for performing, Dylan, like Shakespeare, can only put on shows via interacting with others. Even when performing 'solo', Dylan relies on, or interacts with, stage hands, lighting and sound engineers and, crucially, the audience. When with a band, the resultant musical interplay is clearly of central import.

Shakespeare was an actor in his own plays and presumably also performed the role of on-the-spot editor and at least some of the roles we would now associate with directors and producers. Dylan came to the fore as a solo performer but for the majority of his live work he has been backed by various groups of musicians. Dylan dominates any band he shares a stage with but, nonetheless, both writers present their work, in the majority of cases, to an audience via an ensemble of creative artists striving to project their visions. Just as Bob Dylan views his songs as mere 'blueprints' for performance, so Shakespeare's scripts stand in the same relation to performances of them. Furthermore, others are involved in any live production; prompters, stage assistants, designers, lighting personnel, sound engineers and so forth.

Numerous people have varying degrees of input in transforming that text into performance. Shakespeare gives a comic rendition of this process in *A Midsummer Night's Dream* and, risible though the 'rude mechanicals' in that play are, he was clearly having fun with a process he, his players and his audience could all relate to, on knowing and familiar terms. What makes a live performance is not the blueprint *per se* but the interpretation of it by the physical bodies of the actors, plus the setting, the props, the costumes, the music and a host of other ingredients.

It would be fascinating to know how much control Shakespeare exerted over the actors in his company while they performed his, and others', plays. Unfortunately, though, we will never know what Shakespeare told his actors, or what his actors impressed upon him should be done, in the staging. Some clues survive in the scripts but nearly all such information will have been passed on verbally, *in situ*, and is lost to the ages. We wonder if the company were headstrong, audience led improvisers or were more under Shakespeare's control than that. Alternatively, if they were a mixture of these tendencies, then which tendencies predominated would be the question. Much has been read into the original clown Will Kempe leaving the company and his improvised tom-foolery being replaced by the sophisticated and witty Robert Armin. Critical orthodoxy holds that Shakespeare had tired of Kempe taking certain stage with improvised tomfoolery and extensive ad-libbing. Certainly the comic turn was the big attraction for many. It was the clown's name that appeared on cover of the first, pirated, printings of Shakespeare's plays, not the playwright's. Their on-stage dynamic when Shakespeare acted alongside him must have been compelling viewing.

On-stage dynamics with Dylan and his bands always are, too. Dylan unquestionably leads his bands. The guitarist Duke Robillard, who had worked successfully with Dylan in the studio, joined his touring band in 2013. Problems arose almost immediately and Robillard soon found himself out of the band and posting a bitter 'Dylan albums for sale' notice on social media. Robillard was used to being his own man, and running the show. Perhaps he was taken aback at how Dylan, although a lover of improvisation, keeps overall control of everything on his stage.

Over and above all these other involved personnel are the audiences, the *sine qua non* for all performing art, with the dynamic exchanges between artist and audience being the most vital of elements. This is what Dylan finds such a loss when recording in the studio. Shakespeare and Dylan began their performing careers in communal environments where there was little or no distance between audience and performer, and where folk material was re-presented to audiences already familiar with its content. The original authorship was not a matter of concern, as the material performed was by, and for, everyone in those communities.

Starting out in these environments also meant that Shakespeare and Dylan learnt to write with audiences in mind and had their onstage experiences to guide them. Dylan thought back to this in his Nobel Award banquet speech: *"As a performer I've played for 50,000 people and I've played for 50 people and I can tell you that it is harder to play for 50 people. 50,000 people have a singular persona, not so with 50. Each person has an individual, separate identity, a world unto themselves. They can perceive things more clearly. Your honesty and how it relates to the depth of your talent is tried."*[13] Moving away from this initial environment was a cause of much resentment as can be seen in the closing pages of the following chapter.

Inevitably, the differences between reading a book and watching a live drama or musical show begin in their fundamentally opposed physical and mental conditions. A reader is in control over the speed at which they absorb the words and s/he sets the overall timescale. It is they who dictate when the story starts and stops and whether or not there are pauses and the length of any breaks they choose to take. Crucially, too, certain passages can be lingered over and perhaps re-read several times before the reader progresses. At any point of the unfolding of the plot, a reader can return to earlier scenes to remind themselves of what has occurred, or to trace connections of character, plot or imagery. In an even more radical contrast, a reader can skip ahead, including reading the ending first if they so desire. In total contrast, a play or a live Dylan show follows events in a timeframe outside of the audience members' control.

Performance is the be-all for both Bards, so the text itself is merely a starting point, and a launch pad towards whatever it is that they are striving to fully express on stage. Furthermore, the very nature of live performance means that the realisation of this expression can never be a fixed one. There is always another version, another take, and another set of circumstances. Live performances of the same work can never be identical experiences. This is the case in any setting, but is particularly so in touring companies, theatrical or musical with changing theatres and cast availability. This is especially true of recreated Elizabethan' stages or outdoor locations. These afford a degree of approximation as to how Shakespeare would have envisaged his plays being performed.

Outdoor performance with its variable weather, lighting, and unpredictable audience interaction is very much a 'happening experience'. For the actors who revel in it, this is 'the real stuff' of performance, just as touring is for Dylan. Contrastingly, a filmed performance is frozen forever, like a studio cut. Both are reminiscent of a butterfly pinned behind a glass cover; that is, a pale reminder of the ever-changing glory of the living creation. Yet, we often consider that those 2-D or audio-only recordings fully represent the work. For Dylan, it is still probably the norm that one particular album version is considered by his wider audience as the 'real' version rather than the blueprint he sees it as, though the continued official releases of *The Bootleg Series* challenge this to a degree.

So embedded in performance are nearly all our writers' works that many people feel that Shakespeare's Sonnets are 'little dramas'. John Barton's *Playing Shakespeare*[14] video demonstrates why people feel this way about the sonnets very effectively. Dylan, unsurprisingly, apprehends poems as songs, and so experiences Shakespeare's sonnets not as mini-dramas but in the light of his own performance mode:

"At certain times I read a lot of poetry. My favorite poets are Shelley and Keats. Rimbaud is so identifiable,Lord Byron, I don't know. Lately if I read poems, it's like I can always hear the guitar. Even with Shakespeare's sonnets I can hear a melody because its all broken up into timed phrases so I hear it. I always keep thinking, what kind of song would this be?"[15]

Multiplicity of text(s)

One of the many consequences of the malleability of script or lyric in performance is that there are no definitive textual versions and, instead, multiple texts contribute to our somewhat nebulous concept of each specific 'song' or 'play'. It is evident from the various versions that have survived that Shakespeare edited his scripts after the plays were staged, perhaps in the light of changing circumstances or as his own ideas progressed. The changes to *King Lear*, in particular the ending, give us two very different experiences as an audience.

Hamlet is an even more explicit example of this trait. We have two quarto editions plus the folio version.[16] As a result, any production that you have seen or read is an editor's conflation of sections he has chosen for a particular staging or edition. Scenes are not consistently in the same order. Shakespeare, or someone in his company, played around with it too; topical references appear that post-date the time of its first incarnation, and performances varied dramatically in length. They still do and can range from just over two hours to barely under four with scenes regularly played in different sequences. Yet, we refer to all of these as the one thing, as Shakespeare's *Hamlet*.

Dylan often plays songs from his albums in concert with many verses missing or rewritten, or with new ones added. Yet, a 'Desolation Row' played with eleven verses or five, to a rock or folk sound, and with a backing band or solo, is similarly always called Dylan's 'Desolation Row', again, as though a definitive entity objectively exists somewhere. These mythical, Platonic ideal entities are probably thought by many to be Dylan's original studio cuts and the First Folio versions of Shakespeare's plays. There is no evidence to think that these are the author's ideal versions though, in fact all evidence points to the author disclaiming that very thing, in Dylan's case, or not being alive to authenticate it, in Shakespeare's. Even when in the studio, Dylan is famous for conjuring up radically divergent versions from take to take. There are two officially released versions of the song 'Ain't Talkin'. One features around a dozen lines from Ovid, the other features none. We talk about the song in the singular, nonetheless.

When talking of literature we are accustomed to referring to fixed texts. This is an inapplicable approach to performance text. As director Nicholas Hytner forcefully reminded an audience when giving a lecture on Shakespeare: "... as plays, these great works don't have one meaning, they are scripts. Half of the meaning is in how they are performed... Shakespeare was an actor. He knew what he was doing, he was writing for other actors. And as I've so often pointed out, he didn't think that he was writing literature. He took no care the publication of these things at all, none at all."[17]

As if the texts were not already conceptually volatile enough, further instability arises when we look deeper into the situation. Instead of a single experience we have a mesmerising multitude of divergently experienced realities. Even if there was, somehow, a definitive text it would still not represent *Hamlet*. The *Hamlet* we know is the *Hamlet* we remember from having read at school, or the *Hamlet* we read when we were twenty-six, fifty-six or any other age. It is also the *Hamlet* we saw performed by students, the *Hamlet* we saw at the RSC, the National, the Globe, on TV, perhaps David Tennant is Hamlet in our minds or perhaps John Gielgud is, or one of the many others who have taken on the role. Demonstrating this shifting nature of performance, the role was recently played by Michelle Terry in a 'gender and disability blind production', at the re-constructed Globe Theatre.

When we next see *Hamlet* we carry bits of some, or all, of these with us and yet we will say it is a 'good', a 'bad' or even an 'authentic' *Hamlet* as though there was an agreed upon blueprint or standard to which each performance should aspire. In a way, this is true for us on an individual level. Yet, we could never definitively identify it as it is never fixed, but instead exists forever in motion. The more we learn about the play, the more productions we see and the more our life experience grows to allow us to appreciate aspects which we may have hitherto overlooked, then the more our response to the play changes. As a result, what we once held as a template in our minds has become a different template and will continue to change as time passes.

Again, much the same is true with Dylan's songs. 'Tangled up in Blue', for example, is not one song, as again there is no definitive text. We have 1974 studio versions and we have all the live versions, most dramatically the 1984 'rewrite', officially released on the album *Real Live*. Dylan re-wrote it for stage performances in 2018 and those alterations appeared in a set of lyrics that included completely re-written verses at a major exhibition in London in October and November that year.[18]

In most people's minds, the *Blood On The Tracks* album version, or the first version they ever hear, takes precedence as their personal 'template' version. Again, though, the template will always change, for the same reasons as above. A *Bootleg Series* volume of *Blood on the Tracks* alternate takes was released in November, 2018 that included many more versions of the song from the original sessions. As such, our idea of the 'original template' has changed, or rather it has for those of us who have these newly released version(s) and pay close attention to such things. The person we stand next to at the next concert Dylan sings it at may not have heard this new variant, and so they will have another template in mind with which to compare the latest live rendition.

Dylan still rewrites lines from *Blood On The Tracks*' songs in live performance, as he has done over the decades. Audiences and reviewers nearly always discuss these changes as though he were consciously re-working the 1975 album version. For the author himself, however, the perspective is different. The original album version is, to him, just one more version of a continually evolving song and experience. For Dylan, the song began with a few lines jotted down in a notebook and then existed in a variety of forms prior to the first released version. Different versions were played to friends and some were recorded. Later, it was run through at the studio and one version was selected for release. This was then re-done at an additional session in Minneapolis and that later version appeared on the released album. Soon he was touring and the song emerged in a new musical setting and changed again. This was to happen repeatedly on later tours, and continues up until the present day.

It is not just the words but also the music that changes. 'Tangled Up In Blue' has appeared in a wide range of musical formats. This is true of nearly all the songs that Dylan has performed and if your first exposure to, say, his signature tune, "Like A Rolling Stone" was on the live album *Before the Flood* or from a concert you attended on a later tour then you may have a different template from someone who has heard only the single or *Highway 61 Revisited* album version.

Even with the same musical style and backing musicians, or when solo, Dylan's immeasurably informing intonation brings variable meanings to each line, verse, chorus and song he sings. All emotions are expressed, in their innately fluctuating forms, with nuances, subtleties and import of expression changing from one performance to the next. A line or phrase that was bitter can become wistful, or he can make something that was playful become serious. Dylan's delivery is in constant flux. If he plays the same song even ten minutes later it can, and usually does, convey a different experience to the listener, and the performer, too, come to that. Consequently, no two performances are ever identical even if there are no set-list or personnel changes. This salient fact, so often overlooked, is at the core of Dylan's art:

"There's always new things to discover when you're playing live. No two shows are the same. It might be the same song, but you find different things to do within that song which you didn't think about the night before. It depends on how your brain is hooked up to your hand and how your mind is hooked up to your mouth."[19]

Shakespeare might have influenced his company into different interpretations, night to night, but that is something we will never know for certain. We do know, though, that the same company had to play the same play for different lengths of time in different locations, both open to the elements and indoors and to audiences varied in size, taste and social composition. Adaptability was, undoubtedly, the name of the game.

This is without even getting into the realm of covers, but it is worth noting in passing that millions of people will have heard Clapton or Guns n' Roses performing 'Knocking on Heaven's Door' before they heard Bob Dylan sing it. Most people think of Hendrix when they think of 'All Along the Watchtower' and so forth. Similarly, Shakespeare's plays have been produced in many re-written versions and adaptations.

Our two successful artists inspired spin-offs, parodies, follow-ups and, especially, covers of their work. These covers have ranged from the genuinely, if less reachingly, inspired down to the most atrocious of misrepresentations. In Dylan's case, the actor William Shatner, who was also responsible for a Shakespeare 'cover version' by directing *Henry V*, released a recitation of 'Mr Tambourine Man' that is as far from artist's original vision as could possibly be conceived. Shakespeare's originally verbally rich, scenically deficient productions were transformed in Victorian times into mega-visual spectaculars. Before the Victorians, the Restoration had covered Shakespeare in their own inimitable and rule-bound manner. In 1815, William Hazlitt described a performance of *The Tempest* as "anomalous, unmeaning, vulgar and ridiculous". He noted that: "To call it a representation is, indeed, an abuse of language: it is travestie, caricature, anything you please but a representation."

Nonetheless, misrepresentations can be commercially successful by stressing the elements likely to appeal widely. The Byrds' version of 'Mr Tambourine Man' and the Restoration take on *King Lear* would be two examples of altering the original 'text', while covering, which were successful with audiences. The restoration of the traditional happier ending for Lear and Cordelia brought Shakespeare's play, albeit artistically neutered, to its first popular appeal. The Byrds' happy, frothy summer single, truncated the original and trivialised its beautiful and profound artistic achievement. Nonetheless, it was an outstanding pop single that achieved widespread sales and acclaim.

We should note that covers are a two-way street. Shakespeare and his company, in turn, covered the plays of others, as Dylan has covered so many songs written and performed by others from the beginning of his career right up to the current day. His last three album releases have consisted of the American Songbook, mainly those associated with Frank Sinatra, and the last of these was a three disc set.

Songs have been ever-mutable in Dylan's "Never Ending Tour", tour, too which was, until the last few years, known for its changing set lists and changing styles. For many years it was an expression of his abiding artistic impulse as he presented blues, rock, country or reggae versions of the same songs on the same tour, sometimes even night to night, in constantly changing set-lists. It was something he had done over previous periods of his career, too. The extremely varied forms of 'One Too Many Mornings' in 1963, 1966 and 1975, for just one of numerous examples, exemplifies the urgency and artistry of the re-staging of the same song as something vibrantly new.

You can expand the thought of play and song variations and changeability to a near never-ending degree but hopefully what I have written above establishes that there is an extreme instability at the core of the 'text' of either a Shakespeare play or a Dylan song.

Poetic Brilliance

The above is, however, only part of our story. There is a reason that Dylan's songs are famous for their lyrics, and Shakespeare's scripts are regarded as the pinnacle of poetry. In both their fields they are unparalleled for insight, for capturing the complexity and the simplicity of life, for expanding consciousness and understanding among their lucky audiences through their literary genius. Their words, as we noted in the chapter on 'being bards' and as we shall see in the chapter on wordplay, are endless delights, which offer revelatory insight into the human condition.

Shakespeare, as performed on a bare stage, throws the weight back on the words, and the same holds true when I listen intently to Dylan performing live. The 'blueprints' are not only launch pads but also key to the whole experience, as they are the seeds which flower on stage. Even the director Peter Brook, a leading advocate of the primacy of performance over text, notes that:

"Verse speakers and opera singers could learn a great deal if they listen to all forms of popular music from Billie Holiday to Edith Piaf, where the passion, the feeling, the intonation, the tempo all arise from the word. In Broadway jargon, this is called 'reading' a song. I once asked Richard Rodgers, composer of Oklahoma! and countless other musicals, whether he had a stash of melodies in a top drawer, waiting to be used. 'Of course not!' he said. 'I need the words.' Like every composer of songs, it is the words that are proposed by a lyric that awaken the tune".[xiv]

We left his Nobel banquet speech with Dylan turning from his musings on Shakespeare's performance producing pragmatism to his own art and the literary award which he was receiving. He had said: *"Not once have I ever had the time to ask myself, "Are my songs literature?".* He then ended, however, with the following words: *So, I do thank the Swedish Academy, both for taking the time to consider that very question, and, ultimately, for providing such a wonderful answer."*

The wonder of our two bards lies not just in their performing art, but in their unforgettable words. Words which move and thrill us, which open up our minds and senses and which seem uncannily applicable to incident after incident in our own lives.

Dylan draws a parallel between hearing the brilliance of language in Shakespeare plays and listening to traditional folk songs:

"Have you ever seen a Shakespeare play? I mean, it's like the English language at its peak where one line will come out like a stick of dynamite, and you'll be so what-was-that! But then the other stuff is rolling on so fast you can't even think, and then you have to struggle to catch up to where you are in the present. And folk songs are pretty much like the same way. "Of course, nobody writes like Shakespeare either," he said. "But, you know, it don't matter. Those things can still be performed. They don't have to be written, just like folk songs."[20]

The language and the performance are entwined, and it is not just academia that has struggled with this two-way pull of performance and print. Some scholars, it is worth noting, believe that Shakespeare was, in later life, in favour of having his plays immortalised in a Folio version, as they eventually were after his death, perhaps inspired by his long time friend and rival, Ben Jonson, having already overseen one for his collected works. Dylan himself has made many conflicting claims regarding the relative worth of his words or music, such as:

"I'm using the old melodies because they're there. I like the melodies. Besides, if they can hear the old melodies in my new songs, they'll accept the songs more. It ain't the melodies that're important, man, it's the words. I don't give a damn 'bout melodies."[21]

Yet Dylan makes a pertinent complaint at the concentration on his words, the literary-only part of his art in *Chronicles*:

...if my songs were just about the words, then what was Duane Eddy, the great rock-and-roll guitarist, doing recording an album full of instrumental melodies of my songs? Musicians have always known that my songs were about more than just words, but most

people are not musicians ... I was sick of the way that my lyrics had been extrapolated.

These are just two of the many contradictory things Dylan has said on the subject. In the summer of 1978 he remarked, "I consider myself a poet first and a musician second" whereas in autumn of the same year he declared: "I'm a musician first and a poet second."[22] Dylan is very aware he does this, "I am inconsistent, even to myself" he remarked in one interview, and in another interview said his views were like a passing cloud and if he was asked the same question some minutes later then the answer, like the cloud, would have changed. Nonetheless, this does not preclude Dylan from coming up with insightful comments on the matter:

"I only look at them musically...as things to sing. It's the music that the words are sung to that's important. I write the songs because I need something to sing. It's the difference between the words on paper and the song. The song disappears into the air, the paper stays. They have little in common. A great poet, like Wallace Stevens, doesn't necessarily make a great singer. But a great singer always – like Billie Holiday makes a great poet."[23]

It is from the combination of words, music and voice that his magic arises. All the way up to presenting his Nobel Speech backed by a tinkling, jazz tinged lounge piano piece, Dylan has always understood this, whatever his particular emphasis at various points in his career or how he was feeling at the time of one interview or another. Discussing the early influences of poetry during an interview, Dylan remarked that:

"...There used to be a folk music scene and jazz clubs just about every place. The two scenes were very much connected, where the poets would read to a small combo, so I was close up to that for a while. My songs were influenced not so much by poetry on the page but by poetry being recited by the poets who recited poems with jazz bands.[24]

Shakespeare and Dylan's performance arts are made up from numerous elements. We cannot witness Shakespeare's own acting but we do have the blessing of Dylan's extraordinary vocal gifts and that voice, like the words and the music, is an essential ingredient. As is his harmonica playing, as the recent releases of 1966 and 1979 box sets have once again demonstrated. The harmonica is absolutely crucial to the effect of, as stand-out examples, 'Mr Tambourine Man' in 1966 and 'What Can I Do For You' in 1979. It is yet another critical element that is entirely absent from the printed page. As Dylan put it in a 1979 interview about his shows of the time: *"You can't separate the words from the music. I know people try to do that. But they can't do that. It's like separating the foot from the knee."*[25]

Dylan was succeeded in winning the Nobel Prize for literature by one of the leading novelists of our time, Kazuo Ishiguro. After his award an interviewer tried to pull Ishiguro into the controversy that had surrounded the award to his predecessor. Ishiguro was having none of this and stressed how much better it made winning the award to have known he was succeeding one of his main inspirations, Bob Dylan. Ishiguro stated that without Dylan's songs he would never have become a writer in the first place. The novelist went on to stress the importance of singers' voices in helping him create literature of the highest quality, in his 2017 Nobel Lecture:

> *Over the years, specific aspects of my writing have been influenced by, among others, Bob Dylan, Nina Simone, Emmylou Harris, Ray Charles, Bruce Springsteen, Gillian Welch and my friend and collaborator Stacey Kent. Catching something in their voices, I've said to myself: 'Ah yes, that's it. That's what I need to capture in that scene. Something very close to that.' Often it's an emotion I can't quite put into words, but there it is, in the singer's voice, and now I've been given something to aim for.*[26]

Dylan's voice attracted many fans even before they became devoted to his words. In that magical apprehension which leading art inspires in you, you somehow know before you make out what the voice is saying that it is of profound beauty and import, and that it will change the way you see the world. As John Lennon said of Dylan:

"I loved him because he wrote some beautiful stuff. I used to love his so-called protest things. But I like the sound of him. I didn't have to listen to his words. He used to come with his acetate and say, "Listen to this, John. Did you hear the words?" And I said, "That doesn't matter, just the sound is what counts. The overall thing." You didn't have to hear what Bob Dylan's saying, you just have to hear the way he says it, like the medium is the message."[27]

Dylan is also aware of how vital his vocals are, as well as his musical skills on guitar, piano and harmonica. In an interview with *Song Talk*, (while discussing Shakespeare and the longevity of his plays,), he was asked: "Aren't there songs of your own that you know will always be around?" Dylan's reply was very revealing:

Who's gonna sing them? My songs really aren't meant to be covered. No, not really. Can you think of... Well, they do get covered, but it's covered . They're not intentionally written to be covered, but okay, they do.[28]

Dylan, as ever, is thinking of future artistic survival as residing in new performances, rather than listening to previous ones. He is customarily very courteous towards covers of his work and this comment came across almost as though a mask had slipped for a moment. As his art relies on his continually evolving performance based re-interpretations and new creations, the analogy the interviewer was pursuing of how future performances of Dylan's work might compare with those of Shakespeare's plays opened up the problem of Dylan's own presence being irreplaceable.

Dylan's concentration on live performances is a constant. Dylan told Edna Gundersen, in 1989, that:

"The song is going to live or die {on stage}. On record, it's deceiving. You hear it in privacy, so it creates its own world when it plays itself for you. But when you see that person doing it live, you can tell if it's real or somebody up there wasting your time or faking it. Faking it is real popular."[29]

Performance Art and Literary Studies

The pre-eminence of performance has not been a barrier to popular art being transformed into high art and subsequently performance art texts becoming part of the domain of academic literary studies. It is time to look at what has happened to Shakespeare in academia, and what had already begun to happen to Dylan, and has accelerated exponentially since he was presented with the Nobel Literature Award in 2016. The lustre of the writing is dazzling but its combination with the necessity of performance has led to difficult times in the structuring of academic appreciation of the two Bards.

We have established that Shakespeare was first and foremost a jobbing dramatist. He was a writer, actor, collaborator and editor of texts whose purpose was to be acted on stage and to prove popular enough to keep audiences coming back to pay for more. His business was that of pleasing audiences to increase the company's cash flow. Genius and commerce are not always separate despite our romantic myths of starving artists in tiny garrets. Dylan remarked to biographer Robert Shelton, in 1978: "the myth of the starving artist is just that – a myth".[30] Genius can also be at the beck and call of the need for cold, hard cash. One thinks of Dostoyevsky producing the most extraordinary series of novels in order to settle debts, and of Charles Dickens' mass-marketed outpouring of the most beautiful quality prose, at a time when it was valued by quantity, and paid by the wordage. As Samuel Johnson prosaically put it: "No man but a blockhead ever wrote, except for money." Both Shakespeare and Dylan prove to be canny operators in the world of commerce. William Burroughs remembered meeting a young Dylan who described himself as having "*a knack for writing lyrics*" and that he "*expected to make a lot of money*".

Shakespeare and Dickens, now so justly academically revered, earned their living by producing hits for all of society. They did not write just for the privileged or especially educated elite. They were paid because they kept their audiences engaged and entertained. In this regard, it is clear that Bob Dylan has followed in their footsteps.

Over time, fashions change in both popular entertainment and what is deemed to be 'Art'. Drama was considered lowbrow compared to poetry, in turn the novel was seen as vulgar compared to drama and then cinema and TV, in turn, were seen as keeping people away from the more edifying novel. So it was that from Falstaff's Cheapside tavern, Shakespeare's work ascended to the peak of the ivory towers. Bob Dylan almost single-handedly has brought about the overthrow of the latest instalment of this 'genre snobbery'. Pop music was seen as so lowbrow by some as to be the work of the devil, as were plays in Shakespeare's day. Even those not inclined to such an extreme view were unlikely to grant that such music had any capability for serious expression of emotion, far less thought.

Popular music by its very nature was not to be taken seriously. This attitude toward song is not new. Robert Louis Stevenson complained that Robert

Burns should not waste his time on such trivia as folk music when there were serious poems to be written. Such a limited view, from a writer as full of discernment and grace as 'RLS', is a bitter thing to read. It also provides an insight into how deep the scorn was to be towards the 'even lower' form pop music, into whose arena Bob Dylan stepped in the heady mid-1960s. Almost the whole point of 'pop' was, surely, that it was to be consumed feverishly, quickly binned and replaced by 'The Next Big Thing'. It has taken some time for Dylan's genius to be widely recognised as a form of 'proper' or 'high' art due to the form his work takes. Similarly, Shakespeare originally was respected more for his poetry than his plays as that genre was not yet considered artistically respectable. The egalitarian nature of folk, country, rock, blues, country and gospel music should stand Dylan's work in good stead from ossifying into only academic acclaim. Similarly, Shakespeare has never been 'tamed' into a library or museum piece due in a significant degree to the popular cultural environment in which his creations flourished. The road his work has taken has been a rocky one, however.

The realisation of Shakespeare's towering genius and his pre-eminence as both dramatist and poet, led to a veneration of the latter yet not the former. Instead, that was for a long time comparatively downplayed as the stress on the written words as poetry had the deleterious effect of occluding it. An inspirational teacher, at the Perse School in Cambridge, Henry Caldwell Cook, rebelled against this state of affairs. Cook taught Shakespeare purely by having his pupils act the plays. This was part of his overall educational theories as published in his revolutionary 1917 book, *The Play Way*. When asked by a visitor to the Perse, 'What do you do with a play of Shakespeare?' Cook responded in two words that spoke volumes: 'Act it'. He then asked a question of his own: 'What else can you do with a play?' That all other Shakespearean teaching was via textual analysis of the printed word infuriated Cook. He saw the extraction of passages from the plays for study to be akin to mutilation before taking "thirty lines or so and proceeding to mince it into an unrecognizable slush"[31].

Following on from Cook, J.L. Styan propagated what he called "The Shakespeare Revolution" by stressing the primacy of performance. He and his followers extolled the virtue, indeed the necessity, of seeing the plays. Styan took it even further than that, and echoed Cook's injunction of 'act it':

"Hearing a lecture about painting is quite different from trying to do some painting oneself, and so it is with drama. Even going to see a play is not the same as trying to put it on. And the closest you will come, I take it, to understanding the nature of a play is to try to put it on, to try to get a response from an audience and thereby complete the creative act."[32]

It is unquestionable that Shakespeare's poetic and dramatic artistry were fused together in his plays. He surely would have been mystified to learn that we would separate our studies of his work so completely into differing, almost competing, areas and then take so long to start to bring them back together.

Similarly, we must not overlook the fact that Dylan is not solely literary: his art is a combination of music, voice and lyric, and his songs cannot be understood or appropriately appreciated in any other form than hearing him sing them. This last point is crucial, Dylan is esteemed as the master songwriter, but if all we had to go on were cover versions he would be diminished to an artistic standing of small import. The crucial relevance of his voice, as well as the music, is something we will soon be exploring.

It should be of significant benefit for Dylan studies that we have Shakespeare as an example of how a creator of performing art can still be justly appreciated for his words. Perhaps even more constructive will be the warning of pitfalls to be avoided. That is the hope, at least, but despite all that I have written above regarding performing art, Shakespeare is still studied by people reading his plays as poetry in far greater numbers than those who attend his plays live, even though the audience figures continue to rise. Additionally, many more people see the plays as films, or hear them as audio drama, rather than staged.

Even when Shakespeare is performed on stage now, this is almost always in very changed conditions from those Shakespeare envisaged for his audiences. Shakespeare would never have imagined performances where the stage was lit and the audience was in darkness. Even those staged nowadays, in the reconstructed Globe, which partly restores the balance back towards how the plays were meant to be viewed, are far from 'authentic recreations'. In Shakespeare's time the pronunciation would have been very different, and there may have been Seventies-football-crowd like throngs perhaps creating mayhem and much noise throughout the performances rather than sitting and following the poetry in rapt attention. Opinions on this vary, and, as with so many aspects surrounding the staging of plays in Shakespeare's lifetime, the situation was likely to have been highly fluid and different from performance to performance until the advent, late in his career, of candle-lit indoor theatres.

Interestingly, one can compare Sixties' Dylan audiences with later, much rowdier events for the reverse journey being made by Dylan's crowds. These began with the notion that theatres were places for quiet contemplation and enthusiastic applause was to be decorously delayed until the songs were concluded, perhaps as a consequence of how theatres had evolved after Elizabethan times. As the years passed, Dylan audiences 'rocked out' and became something more akin to those attending plays in the sixteenth century. In both cases the dynamic between people in the audience and performers on stage is crucial to the total effect.

No matter the manner in which his work is presented on stage, Shakespeare's words have been studied to a degree that seems almost unimaginable until you remember that those words more than bear the weight of said scrutiny, and that they then repay it a thousand-fold. It should also be stressed that even literary-focused commentators on Shakespeare's words do not ignore the dramatic spectacle completely and, correspondingly, neither need literary-inclined scholars writing on Dylan ignore the fact that his words are song lyrics. All one has to do is keep the performed drama and songs in mind. It is self-evident that one is not analysing poetry in Dylan's case but song-lyrics instead. Any time I write on Dylan's lyrics I either play the song or hear the relevant song being sung by him in my head. I recall multiple versions, at that, just as I remember various performances of Shakespeare scenes as I write about them. In both cases, I am looking at the words on the page but I am, internally, experiencing performances of them.

Critics such as Michael Gray, Christopher Ricks, and Stephen Scobie have proven that it is entirely possible to bring the tools of literary criticism to bear on Dylan's lyrics while simultaneously taking into account the musical performance heard. It is almost impossible not to, as the voice singing the songs is what brings us to the table for discussion in the first place.

The difficulties in encompassing the words of performing arts into written evaluations come clearly into focus in the academic literary critical world due to the dichotomy between words as the bases of perpetually evolving performances being read as fixed texts. When they are studied as the latter, the emphasis is taken away from the essential musical and vocal delivery. It is not the fault of literary departments that they take this approach, as it is this for which they were designed. Accommodating Dylan accurately would necessitate contorting the entire syllabus to feature lessons, lectures, demonstrations, research, including audio and video presentations, and appreciation of a single vocalist amongst centuries of poets, novelists and dramatists. And, to many people's ears, a singularly unpalatable vocalist at that.[33]

Interdisciplinary studies are, however, on the rise and cross-overs of media, literary, performance and cultural studies are perhaps more likely to flourish in the future and provide the environment for Dylan studies. Literary departments, in the aftermath of the 'Shakespeare Revolution' which insisted on the performative aspects being placed at the centre of appreciation may also be more flexible than I am imagining. The more that the methodologies and expertise surrounding performing and literary arts are entwined, the more hopeful will be the prospects for fruitful studies in the future.

A further concern may be receding somewhat since Dylan's work is being regarded in a more serious manner since he was awarded the Nobel Prize for Literature. Prior to this added gravitas, it was strikingly palpable that academic publications on Dylan, which were not by committed fans, were treating analysis of his work as something of a holiday from 'real literary studies'. Academic standards, such as documented dates, internal consistency, and verified quotes were forgotten in certain publications. The worry was, or is, that if academic books are going to ignore what is already well known and not apply the same level of rigour in their Dylan studies as those of say Coleridge, Wordsworth and Blake, then the future for such studies would be very bleak indeed. It has to be hoped, therefore, that this was a mere 'blip' at the outset of this field of academic study, when a new artist from a 'foreign field' edged his way into the canon and the syllabi of higher education. Even if such an optimistic vision prevails, however, there is a further problem, that of examinations.

While it is important to remember that what was once popular and looked down upon can later be held in such high esteem, it is also worth noting, warily, what can happen to the original excitement of the popular entertainment after it becomes entangled not only in the rarefied atmosphere of academia but also as grist to the mill for compulsory exam questions in education.

The risks for Dylan appreciation, here, are prefigured in the treatment of Shakespeare's plays. Shakespeare is not only often read rather than experienced, but his words are neatly dissected and packaged up by 'Spark/ Cliff Notes' for generations of bored-out of-their-wits teenagers to memorise and regurgitate at the appropriate part of examinations. Nothing could be further from the experience of watching a Shakespeare production than what is described here:

"It is doubtful whether there could be a more unsatisfactory way of approaching Shakespeare and his plays than the one suffered by generations of English-speaking people. Almost universally, our first experience at the man's work is in the classroom, where — often under the shadow of impending examinations — the once fair body is dismembered into forty-minute chunks of dreamy afternoons. It is hardly surprising that the vast majority of his compulsory readers never willingly open a text or go to see a play after they escape from the educational system."[vi]

The thought of the same being written about Dylan and his songs in the near future is a disturbing one. Approximately a century ago, the actor, director, producer, and playwright Harley Granville Barker mused with a wry bitterness that he was sure there were many critics of Shakespeare who had never witnessed the inside of a theatre. He is lucky he was not able to see into the future and learn how much this regrettable syndrome was to increase. It is already apparent that one is increasingly reading the works of 'experts' on Bob Dylan who have never witnessed him in any concert venue, nor, for another important example, heard a single Robert Johnson, Woody Guthrie or Chuck Berry song. It is a worrying trend that repeats the mistaken approach of literary critics who for so long ignored the 'business of the stage' when writing on Shakespeare.

It would sadly appear to be an innate part of human nature to stoutly defend whatever one sees as one's 'own space' and to simultaneously denigrate the perceived 'outsiders'. Such tribalism can infect even the loftiest of ivory towers, and hence Shakespearean literary studies sometimes seemed to regard the stage as something tawdry and an unseemly abode for the glittering and elaborate poetry of the Swan of Avon. In retaliation, performance based studies dismissed literary-critical contributions to Shakespearean studies as pretentious and divorced from the real world of the dramatist.

After the aforementioned Styan-led 'Shakespeare Revolution' swung things towards performance, after centuries of textual dominance, other trends and counter-currents have produced the present situation where nearly all literary critics will acknowledge up-front the theatrical settings for which the words were originally written. The wounding divide between Drama and Literary Departments has begun to heal in more recent times, to a degree at least, but is still far from being completely cured.

The above comments have been generalisations. As we will see, there was far more interchange happening than would appear from this surface view. Before looking at those cross-currents, however, we should examine the situation not just from the literary and performing art critics' perspectives but also that of the artist. We do not know Shakespeare's views on the matter, but Bob Dylan has lived his life with critics and academics passing comment on his every move. His views towards this, as they are with many things, have altered from time to time over the now nearly six decades of his career. In the main, though, his opinions have been strongly negative and very forthrightly stated. This is unsurprising, as it is customary for artists to be antagonistic towards critics.

Nonetheless, the situation is not necessarily as black-and-white as it first appears. You find yourself nodding along to Dylan saying in response to a question about the number of books written on his work:

> "....aren't there thousands of books written on Shakespeare's works? And Shakespeare too? How many do you need to read? I'll tell you, wouldn't you rather see a Shakespeare play than read a critical analysis on him? I know I would!"[ii]

Yet, you begin to mentally withdraw your 'nod of approval' when you think about it in detail. There is a limit to how many plays you can see in a day or week without being overwhelmed. You stop taking anything in. The same is true, for me at least, with all great art, such as paintings in art galleries, for example. Consequently, I find it far more rewarding to mix attendances at productions of Shakespeare's drama with enjoyable and enriching study, and I get more out of watching Shakespeare when I do this.

Dylan may have had in mind the increasingly prevalent negative criticism for its own sake. In his recent 'post MusiCares conversation with Bill Flanagan', Dylan said: *"Some seem to do a lot of griping for no reason."* He went on to, equally correctly, disdain those critics who lose sight of who is the creative artist and who the mere commentator. *"I particularly don't like the ones who talk down with that attitude of superiority, like they know and you don't."* [34] If this was all that criticism was about, then there would be no benefit in reading, nor pleasure in writing it. There is another side to it, though, and a highly beneficial one at that. This can be seen both in regard to Shakespeare and also to help alleviate what Dylan calls the 'struggle' to 'catch up' with the dynamic language of a Shakespeare play as it flies by you during a play.

There is a significant difference in thinking about 'artists v critics' with regards to our two Bards because Dylan is talking about critics of the art which he is still alive to produce and perform himself. Dylan can, therefore, reject or embrace anything that is written about him. Shakespeare on the other hand, while being produced ever more frequently, is not here to guide these productions. They are in the hands of others, who also face constant critical scrutiny. Yet, while most producers and directors of Shakespeare make Dylan positively benign in his attitude towards critics, their productions tell a different story.

Appealingly straightforward though their, and Dylan's, attitude of disdain may first appear, these same directors were influenced by the scholars and critics they professed to scorn. Peter Brook, whose kindest words for teachers and critics are "dullards" and "pedants" and who sees them as a pernicious influence on the theatre, had all but a creative collaboration of minds with the Polish critic, Jan Kott. Kott wrote the profoundly influential study: *Shakespeare Our Contemporary*. The existential, absurdist and sexual-psychoanalytic readings from Kott were visibly and movingly explored in Brook's celebrated productions of *King Lear* and *A Midsummer Night's Dream*. There are numerous other examples of critics influencing directors, and this happens in a continuous cycle of cross-fertilisation. Ultimately, then, the very shows Dylan is preferring to see rather than read a critical analysis of, will have themselves been inspired and influenced by critics, either directly or indirectly.

It should have been pointed out to Dylan, which is not to say he was unaware of it, that his was not an "either/or" question. One can both read studies of Shakespeare and read his plays before and after seeing them being performed, and by doing so you will find the experience of watching the play significantly enriched. Apart from the accumulated insight shared by centuries of solid scholarship, a basic understanding even of the vocabulary changes is necessary to appreciate the work fully. Were it not for a critic pointing out that in Shakespeare's time the word "doubt" meant "fear" rather than "uncertainty", I would still be misinterpreting Edmund's reply to Regan "*'Tis to be doubted, madam*" in *King Lear* in the way I did when I first saw it performed. The inference from my modern usage of "doubt" was that Edmund was, incomprehensibly, disagreeing with Regan's comment that the plan had apparently failed when, instead, he was merely agreeing with her. This is one single word example of plain matters of fact that can lead to increased understanding and thereby appreciation of a play; you can multiply it exponentially in all areas of knowledge be they philosophical, poetical, linguistic, historical, social, political and so forth to get an idea as to how and why both reading a critical analysis and seeing the play can be so very beneficial to enjoying the experience of the performance.

Interspersing attendance at Shakespeare plays with listening to knowledgeable teachers and reading insightful critics enhances the performances you next witness. The genius is all Shakespeare's, but appreciation increases with scholarly knowledge, not least because of the passage of time between Shakespeare's world and our own. That time distance is forever growing. I note that teenagers nowadays are considerably further from the Elizabethan language than I was in the Seventies. It is not only a matter of the forty-five years that have since elapsed, but also that the English language itself is evolving at an ever faster rate.

Such interpretative aid will be necessary if the study of Dylan's work is to survive and flourish in the future. Over and above any evaluative input, topical references and long-lost associations would need to be illuminated. While it may be that Dylan's antipathy to critical analysis is now so entrenched that he would prefer to sink out of our academic cultural heritage rather than have his work subjected to this, this seems unlikely. Instead, all the evidence points to the contrary and that he is extremely interested in his legacy surviving, to the extent of shaping how it will be viewed. The frequent recurrence of Shakespeare's name may also be partly influenced by thoughts of how the future may view his achievements; in addition to the unerring appropriateness of seeing Dylan's work in that light.

This partition between artist and critic, just like that divide between drama and literary studies, is based on a fallacy that it has to be 'one-or-the-other'; a fallacy that is demonstrably exposed as such by those who have excelled at both pursuits. For example, S.T. Coleridge and T.S. Eliot, poetic giants of the nineteenth and twentieth centuries respectively, were also leading critics.

Additionally, as Michael Gray observed in his book, *Song & Dance Man*, it was DH Lawrence's book of criticism, *Studies in Classic American Literature*, from 1923, that highlighted the worth of Walt Whitman to "American Letters". Consequently, without Lawrence's critical study being undertaken in the first place, Whitman would almost certainly not have been an influence on Dylan either directly or via Allen Ginsberg's poetry.

Dylan's antagonism towards critical opinion has never been complete. Naturally, he has thought of his work as being regarded as 'up there with the greats'. Talking to Robert Shelton, Dylan remarked that: "*Until* Bringing It All Back Home *song-writing was a sideline. I was still a performer. Then I knew I had to write songs... Get some of those literary people, some of those poetry people to sit down with my records ... that would be good.*" This was soon after declaring "*I never dug Pound or Eliot. I dig Shakespeare*", in Spring 1966.[35]

Even earlier than this we can see him on film, joking to Joan Baez, in a remark that echoes James Joyce, as he types a lyric, that he put bits in just to drive later scholars and professors mad. Also, in *No Direction Home* we hear Joan Baez recounting Dylan's expletive laden comments as he laughs about 'assholes' who will be writing about what his words mean far into the future, while he does not know what they mean himself. Such comments betrayed a clear sense of his perception of his own standing and future relevance and importance in the eyes of academia.

Additionally, Dylan remarked to Edna Gundersen in an interview after his Nobel Award, with regard to the meaning of his lyrics: "*The academics, they ought to know. I'm not really qualified. I don't have any opinion."*[36] It has to be remembered, though, that for Dyan interviews are also performance art and as ever, you would really need to hear the tone of that to get the intended message. The comments leading up to this suggest it may have been partly, if not wholly, ironic.

It could be meant in a straight-forward way and is, in an ideal world, a statement of fact. Also in that world, scholars and performers would co-exist in and cross-pollinate concepts and visions. J.L. Styan envisaged such a future for Shakespeare studies, eighty years ago:

"...both actor and scholar can render only what their sense of the dramatic medium will allow, for they see what they interpret before they interpret what they see. Their Shakespeare originates in the mind, in their reactions to Shakespeare rather than in Shakespeare himself. But as the style and idiom of their interpretation gain currency in each other's eyes, so they must with audiences and readers. Actor and scholar will teach each other, not what Shakespeare 'means', but what his possibilities are beyond logic. Nor will these be exhausted. The scholar will modify the actor's illumination, the actor will modify the scholar's, a process of infinite adjustment. Shakespeare remains uncharted territory waiting to be explored and articulated. But the object of all this earnest endeavour, the experience in some degree of Shakespeare's greater vision, cannot be reached without the humble services of both parties."[37]

Dylan and the Nobel Prize for Literature

How difficult it will be to find such a happy equilibrium when performing art meets literary academia again was highlighted when Dylan was awarded the Nobel Literature Prize in 2016. The announcement of the award, somewhat predictably, included an attempt, at one point, to misrepresent the essential nature of his art. It was also an extraordinarily cagey affair from beginning to end, on both sides.

The Nobel Literary Prize has always been regarded as of major import, and in receiving it Dylan became the first recipient to have been given the French Legion of Honour, and also have a Pulitzer citation, an Oscar, plus all those Grammies. Even George Bernard Shaw did not get all of these. Dylan, though, appeared unimpressed, as we will shortly witness.

Dylan's celebrity, the nature of his art, and the importance bestowed upon this award combined to guarantee extensive media coverage worldwide, and attendant controversy. Most of the planet, it appeared from the press coverage, was in a state of some agitation over Dylan having been awarded it in the first place. This was partly to do with questions over his worthiness and partly just a squabble over terminology.

The first I have no time for, as in terms of quality the breadth, depth and influence of Dylan's work stands as its own testimony. I do, however, have sympathy with the definition argument as the word literature refers explicitly to written works. The word itself is directly derived from the Latin word 'literatum' and meaning "writing formed with letters". That Dylan's songs have what we now call literary depth and range is undeniable, that the ancient songs which have survived do too is something everyone knows. The term literature itself is unyieldingly specific, however, and in certain cases inadequate. Dylan's art, like Shakespeare's, involves more than just the 'letters'.

There is however, a counter definition for the award itself. That is, there is a distinct mis-match between the award's title and its brief which specifically incorporates a far wider range of activities under the term of 'Literature'. This is why the award has previously been given to others who, while not songwriters, nonetheless did not produce work that you would find in a bookstore under the heading 'Literature'. Or at least not until after they had been awarded the Nobel Prize for Literature. They perhaps could and should have changed the award title some time ago.

Notwithstanding this, the announcement of Dylan's prize was initially exciting for those who have long extolled his quality. Even when you know the Academy's ways and history, there was still a certain magic in the name and the award brought with it a substantial increase in esteem. Most of us cannot resist that feeling. Dylan, though, and not unusually for him, may be an exception to the standard rule.

The wording of the announcement was distinctly underwhelming: "for having created new poetic expressions within the great American song tradition." Yes, that is true but there is so much more that could have been said without ceasing to be succinct. There was also the curious mention of one single work, 1966's *Blonde On Blonde*; curious because the Academy Award was formed and long known for favouring current work, not past glories.

The nagging concern over the delay there had been over the announcement of the 2016 winner, and for this to have been followed by the controversial choice of Bob Dylan recalled the award to John Steinbeck in 1962. On that occasion, not a single member thought Steinbeck worthy of the award, and nor did Steinbeck. When he was asked if he thought that he deserved it, Steinbeck answered, "frankly, no". This all seems somewhat hard on an author who created such significant work, but it is an interesting insight into the machinations of the Academy. With the award being limited to those living, and the presumed first choice being terminally ill and then passing away, the selection became mired in intrigues and in-fighting.[38] All this meant that, exhausted and embattled, they 'chose' Steinbeck because they could not agree on anyone else. This, or at least portions of this, were long rumoured and then finally corroborated with the release of the Academy's deliberation papers, fifty years after the award.[39]

Now they were selecting another American, not a common occurrence in itself, against all expectations. The thought kept nagging that Dylan, too, was a compromise choice of an academy unable to decide on anyone else. You wonder if the same thought passed through Dylan's mind as there was a delay of two weeks before he made any comment at all. This was a period filled with newspaper articles about Dylan, the award and his silence. Academy member Per Wästberg, whom one can safely discount from being in favour of the final choice, said: "One can say that it is impolite and arrogant. He is who he is," Wästberg as quoted in the Swedish newspaper *Dagens Nyheter* on October 22, 2016. When Dylan did finally speak he impishly explained away the gap in time by remarking that the award had left him "speechless".

Dylan did not attend the December banquet to honour the recipients, as is usually the case, saying that he had "pre-existing commitments" but not specifying what these were. Dylan not going to Stockholm in this December ceremony led to a plague of headlines where one could often find the words: 'arrogant' and 'snub'. A minority of others countered by portraying Dylan as a rebel against the establishment. This view of Dylan's behaviour had him re-enacting the stance of the highly principled Jean-Paul Sartre who refused the award in 1964 due to both personal and professional convictions.[40]

It is not known whether Dylan's hesitancy was due to doubts over the award itself, given its history and the delay in announcing their selection, or the fact that it specifically related to literature. We do not even know if he had doubts at all, though it seems as though he may well have had, and with good reason.

As always seems to be the case with Dylan, people rush to draw conclusions, positive as well as negative, without knowing anything factual on which to base those conclusions. No-one knew what his other commitments were, yet most implied that they were imaginary. Yet, they could have been real and perhaps deeply private, family or religious reasons, say, or medical. He may, as most seemed to assume, also have just not wanted to go, which was entirely his prerogative. When members of the Rolling Stones enthusiastically congratulated Dylan on the award, his response was decidedly lukewarm as he queried their expressions of it being a 'big deal'.

Dylan did write a speech for the banquet, which was delivered by Azita Raji, the United States Ambassador to Sweden and which was graciously grateful and managed to be both humble at the same time as aligning himself with Shakespeare, no small feat in itself. He also had not forgotten his "speechless" remark and extended it now to "truly beyond words": *"These giants of literature whose works are taught in the schoolroom, housed in libraries around the world and spoken of in reverent tones have always made a deep impression. That I now join the names on such a list is truly beyond words."* Patti Smith performed Dylan's song, "A Hard Rain's a-Gonna Fall" in his absence.

There was still the matter of Dylan's Nobel Lecture which had to be delivered by June 10, 2017 on which an approximately $900,000 bequest depended. Time passed, and the Swedish Academy's permanent secretary, Professor Danius wearily repeated in answer to the same question that the Academy had not been in touch with Dylan and they did not know what he was going to do. "What he decides to do is his own business", was how she put it.

Dylan left his Nobel Lecture until June 5, handily coinciding with his touring schedule which took him to Stockholm, before delivering it and it too provoked controversy as well as being insightful and highly pertinent to this book. The reasons for this are covered in the later chapters on 'Sources', including the section on plagiarism, because parts of Dylan's lecture came directly from exam crib-sheet books, and in the chapter on *The Tempest* and

Tempest, where some of the specific texts Dylan references are of significance.

Danius blogged that: "Now that the Lecture has been delivered, the Dylan adventure is coming to a close." She may have wished so, but it was far from over. Dylan's eleventh hour lecture delivery, followed by the fallout over its plagiarised portions, was again a fertile background for 'pro' and 'anti' newspaper articles. The continuing discussion brought us close to the point when the 2017 winner was due to be announced.

From there, this Nobel tale went down a strange path that almost begs for the title 'What the Academy Did Next'. 2017's recipient Kazuo Ishiguro gave his Lecture soon after receiving the Award and so it followed on from Dylan's. As we have seen, both here, and it should be added, in interviews, Ishiguro stressed how delighted he was to be following Dylan who had been his inspiration to write and whose win the year before made Ishiguro feel all the more honoured to win it in 2017. In his Lecture, Ishiguro also extended and deepened the debates surrounding songs and literature by passionately promoting the former as worthy of the standing of the latter. Dylan was still, therefore, very much in the Nobel Literature sphere of news.

Then came 2018, and the Literature Prize Committee imploded following a sexual scandal, with financial and procedural activities also being looked at in a negative light, including the leaking of winners' names. Many of the Academy, including Sara Danius, resigned and the Award for 2018 was cancelled and its future is currently uncertain.

Dylan, as a consequence, has dominated the end of the Nobel Literary Prize history as we knew it, and it was their adventure which ended soon afterwards, not his part in it. It remains to be seen if they begin a new adventure as Dylan continues on his own road, still touring the globe.

Interestingly, part of the Academy's campaign to 'clean-up' the literary jury's activities includes a new insistence on transparency over how the decision on the selection of the winners is made. If they were to backdate this new openness, then we would find out exactly why they came to select Dylan.

My main concern over this award, the highest for literature, is that it may cause Dylan's magnificent singing to be ignored or denigrated. This elevation of the words in isolation over performance is certainly something that Dylan has expressed concern over many times, the Musicares' Award speech from the year prior to the Nobel Award being the most recent example that springs to mind. Unfortunately, it only took a matter of hours following the Nobel Award announcement before I read an article, one that disturbingly thought of itself as a positive piece that was acclaiming the news, stating that it was only Dylan's words that mattered and that Dylan himself acknowledges cover versions are better than his own renditions. This extraordinarily misleading conclusion was reached by extrapolating one comment on a specific song into an erroneous overall view.

Meanwhile, the BBC opened their main website news page with an article[41] that began: "Bob Dylan is one of the greats of modern music - but he has never won any prizes for his voice." This is factually wrong, which is bad enough, but it was to deteriorate further. To compound matters the same article actually mentions him winning 'three Grammies' in one year. If they had looked at the titles of those awards, they would have noticed that one of them was the award for Best Male Rock Vocal which would have necessitated a rewrite of their opening sentence and general tone. Or perhaps they did read it and just decided to ignore it as it clashed with their poor attempt at humour. As a matter of record, Dylan has also won Grammy Vocal Awards in other years.

Part of the problem stems from the Nobel Literature Academy's announcement of Dylan's success. Sara Danius said, emphasis mine: "If you look back, far back, 2,500 years or so . . . you discover Homer and Sappho, and they wrote poetic texts that were meant to be listened to, they were meant to be performed, often together with instruments, and it's the same way with Bob Dylan. But we still read Homer and Sappho . . . and we enjoy it, and same thing with Bob Dylan. *He can be read, and should be read.*"

Starting with the pertinent, if slightly dubious for the terminologists, defence of pre-literate works as an example of literature, Danius then proposed something that is nonsensical. 'He can be read, but should be listened to' would have been a useful and true comment, rather than what is italicised above, which is neither useful nor true in any meaningful way.

This did not go unnoticed by Dylan, who concluded his Nobel Lecture by precisely and firmly correcting Danius:

"*...songs are unlike literature. They're meant to be sung, not read. The words in*

Shakespeare's plays were meant to be acted on the stage. Just as lyrics in songs are meant to be sung, not read on a page. And I hope some of you get the chance to listen to these lyrics the way they were intended to be heard: in concert or on record.'"

This redressing of the balance by Dylan himself came after much of the damage had been done. The BBC News Channel struggled, when the award was announced, to the extent of erroneously playing a clip of a Dylan impersonator rather than the real thing. The main BBC News TV coverage at least had the foresight to have musician, and Dylan author, Sid Griffin as a guest speaker on the subject. They were rewarded for this perspicacity as Griffin was suitably enthusiastic and eloquent, and he placed Dylan 'up with' Cervantes and Shakespeare. However, unfortunately, and obviously this was not the BBC's fault, Griffin went on to say that 'more than half of Dylan's songs could "stand as poetry"', which is simply untrue and more importantly, there is no reason why anyone, far less a musician, would wish to claim such a thing.

On the spot TV hyperbole is understandable, and Griffin re-adjusted himself, with admirably quick agility, into talking about a hundred Dylan songs, which is very many fewer than half. These he said could be 'put out as a poetry book' and 'they would make a marvellous collection of literature'. Again, though this is not true. This is a book about parallels between Shakespeare and Dylan but there is no parallel in the act of sitting down and reading their works. Shakespeare can be read and appreciated. It is not the same as witnessing a play but it is still an encounter with art at the highest level. With Dylan, you could certainly spot wonderful wordplay and profound poetic insights but his genius would not come across, as the lyrics are designed to be sung, not read, and as text only would seem poorly constructed, repetitive and often lacking coherence. They have none of these shortcomings in their natural environment of Dylan performing them. There are exceptions to this, songs in pure ballad form, most of *John Wesley Harding*, which Dylan has said is the only time he wrote the words before the music, and individual songs such as "Every Grain of Sand" can stand as poetry on the page. It is very far from the norm, however.

What you would have, in Griffin's scenario, is one hundred lyrics, which, especially when sung by Dylan, are wonderfully creative, and an awe-inspiring collection of songs. They are almost always seriously diminished when sung by others and diminished even further if treated as something that they are not. There is no need to reduce them by stripping away the music and voice and calling for them to be treated as a book of poetry. As I listened, my initial fears were all realised as what I viewed as the inevitable result of Danius's galling "he should be read" remark now unfolded.

***

On the other hand, perhaps this is too pessimistic and it would be better to look at the award as a tremendous breakthrough for song. This was something which the interviewer intelligently brought up and to which Griffin readily assented. Others wrote on the same point. Perhaps we were witnessing the first stage in a widening of the strictures of thinking in terms only of the written word when alluding to the power and majesty of 'literature'. If performing arts, which use other methods of communication, but retain the ability to convey that same power and majesty, are to be so esteemed in the wake of the 2016 Award, then this would form a highly significant step forward. Although a change in terminology would undoubtedly aid in this regard, presuming that is, the Award is re-instated and carries forward at least some degree of its former influence.

Kazuo Ishiguro was pushing for such an expansion in his 2017 Nobel Lecture. After speaking so movingly about the effect singers have on his writing and discussing a film, amidst his literary musings and remembrances, he ended with a plea that serves well as a conclusion to this Nobel Prize section with its comments on future generations, genre and form:

"... we must widen our common literary world to include many more voices from beyond our comfort zones of the elite first world cultures. We must search more energetically to discover the gems from what remain today unknown literary cultures, whether the writers live in far away countries or within our own communities. Second: we must take great care not to set too narrowly or conservatively our definitions of what constitutes good literature. The next generation will come with all sorts of new, sometimes bewildering ways to tell important and wonderful stories. We must keep our minds open to them, especially regarding genre and form, so that we can nurture and celebrate the best of them. In a time of dangerously increasing division, we must listen. Good writing and good reading will break down barriers. We may even find a new idea, a great humane vision, around which to rally."

This is an upbeat vision to end the chapter with and, were it to be heeded, would give hope that the ephemeral magic of performance is not downplayed when the value of song and play scripts are discussed as literature. This chapter has also stressed that Shakespeare and Dylan's work is grounded in popular entertainment and in pleasing audience. That 'work' is both business and artistic. Genius can exist, they prove, alongside commercial acumen and the highest artistry is not incompatible with widespread popularity and live shows.

NOTES

1 For example: ""Many of my records are more or less blueprints for the songs." Interview with Jon Pareles, *"A Wiser Voice Blowin' In the Autumn Wind"* in *The New York Times*:, September 28, 1997

2 Martin Scorsese *Bob Dylan - No Direction Home* 2006

3 Charles W. R. D Moseley, *Shakespeare's History Plays: Richard II to Henry V, the Making of a King* UK: Penguin, 1988

4 Mikal Gilmore, 'Bob Dylan Unleashed' Interview, *Rolling Stone*, 2012

5 *Guitar World* interview, published in March 1999 edition

6 Interview by Jon Pareles, *"A Wiser Voice Blowin' In the Autumn Wind"* Ibid.

7 https://www.rollingstone.com/music/music-news/bob-dylan-talks-a-raw-and-extensive-first-rolling-stone-interview-90618/ Accessed July 8, 2018

8 A good joke, given it was being read in neighbouring Sweden

9 Bob Dylan, Nobel Lecture, *Ibid*.

10 Or at least this was the norm in most if not all English speaking countries. Some non-English speaking countries have a history of printing lyrics on the album sleeves or as inserts

11 Bert Kleinman interview from October 30th 1984. Released on *Dylan On Dylan*, Westwood One, Radio Station Discs, Nov 17 1984

12 Bob Dylan, *The Uncut Interview* Robert Love *AARP The Magazine* Feb/Mar 2015

13 https://www.nobelprize.org/nobel_prizes/literature/laureates/2016/dylan-speech_en.html

14 There is both a book (Methuen Paperback, Anchor; 2001) and a highly recommended DVD set (Athena, June 2, 2009)

15 Interview with Denise Worrell, "'It's All Right in Front': Dylan on Life and Rock" in *Time Magazine* (November 25, 1985)

16 And there may have been others, including a play now referred to as the "Ur-Hamlet". This featured a character called Hamlet and a ghost urging him to enact revenge and is known to have been performed in 1587, though its authorship is unclear

17 Nicholas Hytner, Second Annual Stanley Wells Lecture — "Stand and Unfold Yourself — How to

do Shakespeare" https://www.youtube.com/watch?v=6olzcG2CF0U (accessed August 16th 2018)

18 https://www.halcyongallery.com/exhibitions/bob-dylan-mondo-scripto (accessed October 21, 2018)

19 Bob Dylan, to Edna Gundersen, *USA Today* September 1989

20 Bob Dylan interview by Kathryn Baker 1988 *Love Me Or Leave Me* September 4, 1988

21 Antony Scaduto, *Bob Dylan: An Intimate Biography* Abacus, London, 1972 (Quoting Richard Farina)

22 Quoted in Robert Shelton, *No Direction Home* Beech Tree Books, William Morrow, 1986

23 Robert Shelton, *Ibid.*

24 *Spin*, Volume One Number Eight December 1985

25 Telephone interview conducted by Bruce Heiman from the KMEX Radio in Tuscon Arizona on December 7, 1979, transcribed by Clinton Heylin

26 Nobel Lecture 2017 https://www.nobelprize.org/nobel_prizes/literature/laureates/2017/ishiguro-lecture.html

27 John Lennon: *The Rolling Stone* Interview By Jann S. Wenner Part Two: Life with the lions February 4, 1971
https://www.rollingstone.com/music/features/john-lennon-the-rolling-stone-interview-part-two-19710204

28 Paul Zollo, *Bob Dylan: The Song Talk Interview*, 1991

29 Edna Gundersen, *Bob Dylan Interview* for *USA Today* September 21, 1989

30 John Lennon defended Dylan against criticism on this very point in the mid-Sixties. "What's wrong with staying at the Savoy? Does starving in a garret make his points any more valid? They say to be ethnic as a *folker* you must also be poor and act the part. Absolute rubbish" (Quoted in Robert Shelton, *No Direction Home* Beech Tree Books, William Morrow, 1986)

31 Caldwell Cook, *The Play Way* 1917

32 J.L. Styan interview with Derek Peat

33 This is always a difficult thing for admirers of Dylan's singular art to comprehend as we find his voice capable of such mesmerising beauty that it convinces you in a heartbeat of the worth and depth of what he is singing.

34 Originally on the Bob Dylan official website. Now can be accessed at: http://rocknycliveandrecorded.com/from-bobdylan-com-a-post-musicares-conversation-with-bill-flanagan.html accessed June 13th 2018

35 Robert Shelton, *No Direction Home* Beech Tree Books, William Morrow, 1986

36 "Bob Dylan Acknowledges Nobel Prize" *The Washington Post* October 29, 2016

37 J.L. Styan *The Shakespeare Revolution* Cambridge University Press April 29, 1983

38 Alison Flood, *Swedish Academy reopens controversy surrounding Steinbeck's Nobel Prize* https://www.theguardian.com/books/2013/jan/03/swedish-academy-controversy-steinbeck-nobel

39 If you are already wondering about the true merits of receiving this award, I should add to your musing thusly, that the year before their released deliberations included the dismissal of Tolkien's *Lord of the Rings* because it "has not in any way measured up to storytelling of the highest quality". {Emphasis, mine}

40 http://www.lefigaro.fr/histoire/culture/2014/10/22/26003-20141022ARTFIG00081-prix-nobel-de-litterature-les-raisons-du-refus-de-sartre.php

41 http://www.bbc.co.uk/news/entertainment-arts-37645503

Chapter Four

OPPOSITION

So great an opposition

This chapter is concerned with the virulent opposition that theatres and rock music faced from both civic authorities and self-appointed cultural guardians in the sixteenth and twentieth centuries, respectively. These condemnations may have been separated by four hundred years, but their content and tone turn out to be disturbingly similar.

We begin by looking at what incensed the civic authorities before moving on to the cultural objections. There are many factors which propel both 'anti' camps, with those old perennials, money and sex, prime amongst these. This is due, to a significant degree, to the ever present distrust of the young by the old. Generational resentment is usually driven by the fear that current youth are enjoying an easier, better and more fun-filled time than they, the previous generations, had ever had, especially in the bedroom.

London expanded rapidly in the sixteenth century, and it is estimated that half the city's population would have been under twenty years old at the time Shakespeare is thought to have arrived. Teenagers were attracted by the possibilities of work and the excitement of the big city. The numbers

of servants, apprentices, cleaners and craftsmen of all kinds soared. After
their hard shifts, they had a little money, entertainment on their minds
and no patience with authority figures who attempted to curtail the small
opportunities for leisure that they had so well earned.

In twentieth century US, the birth-rate began to rise dramatically in 1941
and then climbed even faster following the end of World War II. This was
the beginning of what is called the 'baby boom' period. Inevitably, this led
to a huge increase in the teenage population from the mid-Fifties onwards
until the birth-rate began to decline. 'Teenage' was the latest popular
expression to describe adolescents and it is historically linked to that era
when the age group became numerically more significant, coupled, in the
affluent US, with hitherto unheard-of spending power. As a result, they, too,
had money in their pockets, entertainment on their minds and little time for
authority figures.

The backlashes this caused in both time periods were as ferocious as
they were predictable. They began the generation before Shakespeare and
Dylan hit their respective scenes and continued on throughout both artists'
careers. The ever thorny topic of sex was compounded by gender issues and
outright racism in the twentieth century.

At the University Library in Cambridge, there is a remarkable shelf of
books containing the many attacks, as well as the spirited defences, of the
playhouses in Queen Elizabeth I's time. The very first I opened had the
Reverend William Law warning sternly that playhouses were places of
"wanton amours, profane jests and impure passions" in his *The Absolute
Unlawfulness of the Stage-Entertainment*". [1]

John Stockwood, a puritan preacher of the time, described a newly
erected theatre, the first to be a significant success, and called,
unsurprisingly, The Theatre, as "a show place of all beastly and filthy
matters". This was somewhat more dramatic than the more common
complaint of 'lewd matters', a phrase used with depressing regularity. In a
short, but highly influential, chapter, "Of Stage-Playes and Enterludes, with
their wickedness", in his *Anatomy of Abuses* (1583), Philip Stubbes referred
to playhouses as "Venus palaces" and railed against their immorality to an
astonishing degree.

Stubbes proceeded to write: "I beseech all players and founders of plays and interludes to leave off that cursed kind of life, and give themselves to honest exercise." This call for 'honest exercise' evokes thoughts of the UKIP candidate who declared, in 2013, that 'homosexuality could be cured (sic) by physical exercise', which shows that such views are not mere historical foolishness.

In the US from the Fifties onwards, Rock and Roll and then Rock music were seen as leading the young into sexual misconduct and degeneracy. There is the stench of racism attached to the way the musical beat was described as stirring lustful and 'savage' passions. Bawdy lyrics, that had been disregarded when so-called 'race music' was listened to only by black audiences, suddenly became highly contentious when white ears started eavesdropping. The frank nature of the lyrics is partly what attracted disaffected white teenagers, who were on the hunt for thrills and spills and bored by the bland fare that was considered 'proper' for their delicate young minds and bodies.

Religious opposition was again ferocious and highly organised. Dylan would have been seventeen years old and going to St Paul and Minneapolis whenever he could, when it was reported that: "The Catholic Youth Center (CYC), high school students in Minneapolis, and jockeys around the country launched an anti-rock campaign in 1958 to combat records which lowered teenagers' moral standards. 'Secretly' and 'Wear My Ring Around Your Neck' were on their blacklist because they both advocated going steady. This group sponsored a contest for high school students to write "fresh and decent" song lyrics and submit them to local radio stations. They sent promotional material to jockeys across the country, addressed to "the most disk-criminating disk-ciminating, disk-jockeys' at your station." The CYC issued a newsletter to teens in Minneapolis and urged them to buy only the "wholesome" records that were listed weekly in the *Catholic Bulletin*. The group also advised its readers to "Smash the records you possess which present a pagan culture . . . Phone or write a disk jockey who is pushing a lousy record. Switch your radio dial when you hear a suggestive song... songwriters need a good swift kick. So do some singers. So do jockeys."[2]

Dylan's 'It's Alright Ma (I'm Only Bleeding)' comes to mind at this juncture:

Old lady judges watch people in pairs
Limited in sex, they dare
To push fake morals, insult and stare[3]

It appears that these 'old ladies' could be any age or gender. Elvis Presley's gyrations brought a slew of disapproval. He was infamously only shown from the waist up on TV, but he once had to endure worse than that when the police made him perform standing still. A small stream of the torrents of invective hurled upon Elvis will give you a flavour of what took place. *The New York Daily News's* Ben Gross was repulsed by Presley: "Elvis, who rotates his pelvis, was appalling musically. Also he gave an exhibition that was suggestive and vulgar, tinged with the kind of animalism that should be confined to dives and bordellos." That quote is taken from the book, *Anti-Rock: The Opposition To Rock 'n' Roll*, which has a chapter dedicated solely to the litany of abuse suffered by The King. It also informs us that: "Writing in the *Catholic Sun* William Shannon complained that "Presley and his voodoo of frustrations and defiance have become symbols in our country." While in Dylan's soon to be stomping ground of Greenwich Village in New York, the Reverend Charles Howard Graff called Elvis a "whirling dervish of sex."[4]

Note the words "voodoo" and "dervish" and add them to the "savage" mentioned earlier and you can see where this leads. Diatribe followed diatribe blaming the "jungle" rhythms for hypnotising impressionable white youth into acting out animalistic impulses. The combination of prudishness, prurience and racism displayed was utterly deplorable. Presley's movements were likened to an "aborigine's mating dance" by New York TV critic Jack O'Brien, and we had the manager of the Armory, in Washington, one Arthur Bereman, claiming that: "it's the jungle strain that gets 'em all worked up." Meanwhile, *The Pilot*, a newspaper from Boston, fulminated that: "The last few weeks have substantiated the worst fears of observers. And it is clear now that the disk jockey-ed dance is in notable instances, a menace to life, limb, decency and morals." The dance with the "tribal beat" and the songs with lyrics of 'race music' was far too much for those who saw themselves as the guardians of teen morality. Before we think that such racism only existed in the United States, over in the United Kingdom, Sir Malcolm Sergeant, conductor of the

BBC Symphony Orchestra, dismissed the teenage craze as 'nothing new' because "Rock 'n' Roll has been played in the jungle for centuries."

As the decades have passed, the claims have become ever more exaggerated. Johnny Marr has chronicled some of the writers who have continued to make a living out of pumping out opposition to popular music, and one of these is a certain Jeff Godwin, who seems to be teetering on the brink of a breakdown as he rants:

"The music encourages the use of "mind decaying, death-dealing drugs", frequently couched in slang only understood by teens. Not only is promiscuous sex promoted, but also abnormal sex as epitomized by David Bowie, the "limp wristed king of the abnormal world of Homo Rock". Jeff Godwin claims that all screamed rock vocals are actually inspired by the sound of the "homosexual penetration of the male" and whip crack drum beats are the first step on the path that leads directly to steamy homosexual S&M."[5]

The extremity of such views is more than matched by the denunciations against theatre and rock as being anti-Christian and the work of the devil.

***

Back at 'my' shelf in the University Library, I am faced with what Catherine Arnold called: "the incessant denunciation of the stage from the pulpits, and especially from the famous rostrum at Paul's Cross."[6]

The father of metaphysical poet Richard Crashaw spoke from that very rostrum. Or perhaps 'thundered' would be a more accurate verb: "The ungodly Plays and Interludes so rife in this nation, what are they but a bastard of Babylon, a daughter of error and confusion, a hellish device (the devil's own recreation to mock at holy things) by him delivered to the Heathen, from them to the Papists and from them to us."

He was far from alone. The seat of Shakespeare's towering achievements was seen as a source of unmitigated evil: "The infamous Playhouse, a place of contradiction to the strictness and sobriety of Religion; a place hated by God, and haunted by the Devil. And for such I have as great an abhorrence as any man."[7]

In the aforementioned, "Of Stage-Playes and Enterludes", Stubbes saw attendance at such a venue as a betrayal of Christ and that those who did so were "Heathen Gentiles" who worshipped false gods in Venus Palaces created by Satan himself. Like the anti-Rock and Roll denunciators that Johnny Marr describes, Stubbes made his way in the world on the back of his anti-playhouse stance. His original preface, which acknowledged some positives of the new theatrical experience, was swiftly dropped and the tone became shriller and one hundred per cent opposed.

There was, in at least two further regards, no small degree of self interest behind the attacks. Firstly, in any sense of a popularity contest, sermons were faced with the prospect of animated throngs of theatre aficionados passing by their doors and by-passing their services. "The actor's practice, also derived from medieval tradition, of performing on Sundays and holy days did not tend to soften the exasperation of the godly, who listened with indignant horror to the sound of the player's trumpet passing the open door of the church".[8]

One of the ingenious defences against the religious attacks on the theatre stressed that dramas could offer valuable Christian messages and instruction, particularly for those who could not read. This argument occasionally held some sway, but among the more extreme, or those that felt most threatened, preachers, it redoubled their fury and was seen as blasphemous. Interestingly there was a similarly split response to 'Christian Rock' in the late twentieth century. Some ministries embraced it as a way of reaching out to youth while others condemned it as a sacrilegious horror. Bob Larson in the revealingly titled, *The Devil's Diversion* warned against using what he saw as the enemy's tools to 'spread the Lord's message'[9]: "When used excessively, under proper circumstances, the beat of rock is a force accommodating demonic possession and therefore is not worthy as a vehicle to communicate the gospel".[10] Osmund Lake, from some four hundred and sixty years earlier, thought similarly with regards to acting as a vehicle for the Lord's word: "because he hath ordained the Preaching, and not the Playing of his word," [11]

The arguments continued after Shakespeare's death, and his name appears in another bout of jealousy when we read William Prynne bemoan that "Shackpeers Plaies are printed in the best Crowne paper, far better than most Bibles." This comes in his gargantuan, puritanical broadside against acting whose truncated title below is still revealing of its content and excessive nature:

Histrio-mastix: The players scourge, or, actors tragædie, divided into two parts. Wherein it is largely evidenced, by divers arguments, by the concurring authorities and resolutions of sundry texts of Scripture ... That popular stage-playes ... are sinfull, heathenish, lewde, ungodly spectacles, and most pernicious corruptions; condemned in all ages, as intolerable mischiefes to churches, to republickes, to the manners, mindes, and soules of men. And that the profession of play-poets, of stage-players; together with the penning, acting, and frequenting of stage-playes, are unlawfull, infamous and misbeseeming Christians. All pretences to the contrary are here likewise fully answered; and the unlawfulnes of acting, of beholding academicall enterludes, briefly discussed; besides sundry other particulars concerning dancing, dicing, health-drinking, &c. of which the table will informe you.

This tome was first published in 1632, and a decade later the puritans were closing down the theatres. Prynne himself suffered terribly for his labours as he attacked a 1629 appearance of French women on an English stage, where they were booed and pelted with fruit, and decried all women actors as "notorious whores". His timing was lamentable as the Queen chose around the same time to appear in masques herself. Punishments being severe in those days, the righteous Prynne found himself exposed to public abuse twice in the pillory, fined enormous sums of money, had his ears cut off and was imprisoned. This did not stop him writing nor getting into more trouble, and the small, remaining parts of his ears were later removed and he had his cheeks branded.

The God-fearing preachers saw karma of the opposite kind in 1583 when, on January 13, the wooden scaffolding at the Paris Garden collapsed resulting in eight deaths and many injuries at a bear-baiting show. As plays shared the same venues as bear-baiting 'entertainments,' and with the disaster happening on a Sunday, those so inclined jumped to the 'obvious' conclusion that this was God punishing the sinful who indulge in licentious and unholy pursuits in such arenas. God's judgement was pronounced as having taken place for all to see by preachers and balladeers. The ornate frontispiece to one publication opens with: "A godly exhortation, by occasion of the late judgement of God showed at Paris-garden, the thirteenth day of January'". It goes on to include the following: "where by estimation about a thousand persons whereof some were slain, & of that number, at the least, as is credible reported, the third person maimed and hurt." And that was just for starters, the author, one "John Field, Minister of the Word of God" goes on to give instruction, warning and dispense Biblical authority "concerning the keeping of the Sabbath Day" and all of this is is to be found merely on the opening, illustrated, page[12].

God's judgement against the playhouses was also given as the reason for the frequent outbreaks of plague by those determined to see the theatres closed. This is another ridiculous claim from the past that we might airily scorn from our more rational century, especially as we now know the cause of those plagues. Until, that is, we recall that hurricanes were being blamed on same-sex marriage 434 years after Mr Field's 'exhortation'.[13] Marlowe's death was also seen as divine justice, not least in the unforgettably titled: *The Thunderbolt of God's Wrath against hard-hearted and stiff-necked Sinners.*[14]

Similarly, in the twentieth century, the anti-rock Crusaders had no doubt who was behind the 'lewd' entertainments that the youth of the country were enjoying. The book titles alone make this clear, for example: "Bob Larson's *Rock & Roll: The Devil's Diversion*, plus Jeff Godwin's *The Devil's Disciples* and *Dancing with Demons.*"

Sex was part of the Devil's temptations and the two themes have oftentimes been intertwined. Minister Albert Carter, in 1956, proclaimed that: "The effect of rock and roll on young people, is to turn them into devil worshippers; to stimulate self-expression through sex; to provoke lawlessness; impair nervous stability and destroy the sanctity of marriage. It is an evil influence on the youth of our country." [15]

Frank Garlock, once a professor at Bob Jones University, had his anti-rock fulminations published by his alma mater, in a publication entitled *Big Beat - A Rock Blast*. In those pages, you find all manner of accusations. Of particular interest is the one that folk-rock, in particular, causes 'neurosis' and that Garlock described Dylan as the "filthy minded king of pop" and was particularly exercised by Dylan's mention of John the Baptist on "Highway 61 Revisited".

This is Garlock in idling mode, however, and he often builds up a head of steam before letting fly with stentorian declamations: "...many Christian parents who are too spineless, weak-kneed and timid to control their children will let their youngsters play the sensual, filthy, suggestive music of the devil's disciples..."; "Rock music will only bring slavery to the devil and his deceitful laws" and "Rock music is the devil's masterpiece for enslaving his own children." Declaring that "not one person" he knows "loves the Word of God" and "likes Rock music", Garlock further asserts that: "Adherence to the standards of the Bible and devotion to decency is about to be inundated by animal behavior unless we can root out the corruption that is associated with and inherent in rock 'n' roll."[16]

Christian rock became fashionable and, therefore, lucrative but, as we've seen, the more extreme anti-rock critics thought that this was just a satanic trap, just as the sixteenth century preachers had denounced even the theatre that was promoting a Christian message. Consequently, shows like *Godspell* and *Jesus Christ Superstar* were labelled as 'blasphemous' and 'satanic' respectively. The redoubtable Frank Garlock went so far as to describe the latter as being, "obviously an assault on the deity of our Saviour".

Garlock, you might have thought, had taken the Christian opposition to Rock as far as anyone could: "Bringing racism into his attack, Garlock noted that rock had its roots in the music of Africa, South America, and India, places he said where voodoo, sex orgies, human sacrifices, and devil worship abounded. Garlock linked some rock performers with Satan." [17] Yet, even further excesses of abuse on the theme of Rock-as-Satanic have followed as the years have passed. Possibly the craziest is Jacob Aranza's claims that "75 percent of the rock and roll today (top 10 stuff!) deals with sex, evil, drugs, and the occult." And that this is all part of a decades' long, four step plan, "Satan's Agenda", to "pronounce rock stars as messiahs".[18]

Jeff Godwin took this even further: "The Lord has also revealed to some Christians that incarnate demons from the netherworld actually are members of some of the most popular bands."[19]

Converts are famous for their zeal, and as early as 1957 one celebrated rock'n'roller turned on the music that had propelled him to fame when he found religion. Richard Wayne Penniman, better known as Little Richard, stopped playing rock'n'roll and began to preach against it:

"I was in the eighth grade at San Diego Adventist Elementary School, his conversion touched my life. Little Richard arrived at our school with an entourage of about three black limousines and a staff of personal assistants in black suits. He spoke in chapel, then preached Sabbath morning in a local church (probably San Diego 31st Street), then spoke and sang in the afternoon for a standing-room-only Associated MV (AY) meeting at the old San Diego Broadway church.

The point of his presentations was that Rock and Roll was from the devil and that we kids should destroy our records and not listen to the devil's music. He made it clear that he was not asking us to make sacrifices he would not make, recounting how he had recently tossed his diamond rings into the ocean to make a clean break from sin."[20]

It seems that there is something about particular branches of religious sects that insists on intolerance to others' beliefs and fidelity to a sexual dictatorship that controls others' bodies and what they should be allowed to do with them. Sadly, therefore, we find Dylan himself portraying these same tendencies when he was in full 1979 Christian evangelising mode. Amidst some unhinged rants, he included a homophobic speech in San Francisco and an attack on rock 'n' roll after one audience member, tired of hearing only the new Christian material, shouted for some. Dylan's scornful reply made that old, familiar connection to the Devil:

"If you want rock 'n' roll, you go down and rock 'n' roll. You can go and see Kiss and you can rock 'n' roll all the way down to the pit!"[21]

Thankfully, Dylan later evolved into playing rock 'n' roll again without 'losing his religion'; nor, one trusts, sending himself "all the way down to the pit". Also, in 2018 Dylan, now the father of a same-sex married daughter recorded a cover of '(S)he's Funny That Way' for the same-sex promoting compilation, *Universal Love*.

As another balance to the above outburst, it is comforting to recall that fifteen years prior to his remarks in 1979, Dylan was the one with a keen insight into the lack of real spirituality in his society:

Make everything from toy guns that spark
To flesh-colored Christs that glow in the dark

It's easy to see without looking too far
That not much is really sacred

There is, in both sixteenth and twentieth centuries, a hysterical tone to the rabid denunciations and you wonder how much is real and how much is posture. The Lord Mayor of London, James Hawes, in 1574 prefigured the various extreme anti-rock comments above, in his proclamation against the 'Sundry great disorders and Inconveniences'. These 'Inconveniences' allegedly included: 'sundry robberies by picking and cutting of purses, and many other corruptions of youth'; 'evil practices in Great Inns, having chambers and secret places where chaste maids and good citizens' children might be corrupted." He also maintained that: "sundry slaughters and maimings of the Queen's subjects have happened by ruins of Scaffolds, frames and stages, and by engines, weapons and powder used in play". He had not forgotten the 'God's judgement' card, either: "In times of God's visitation by the plague such assembles of the people in throng and press have been very dangerous for the spreading of Infection."[22]

Political careers have been made by writing censorious proclamations of a sensationalised nature. From Stubbes dropping his preface, to Godwin and Aranza's insane claims, you are left wondering how much of it is for show and how much for book sales.

Tabloid newspapers and other mass media outlets are another area where anti-rock statements have a long history of boosting sales, and especially by the reporting of 'rock and roll riots'. It seems that for many, there's nothing more satisfying on a suburban Sabbath than tut-tutting over reports of urban youth riots on the previous night. Again, as we turn to look at riots, subversion and censorship, the sixteenth century got there first.

Riots, Subversion and Censorship

It is difficut to gauge from this distance how serious the riots associated with Elizabethan theatre-going actually were. It was in the interests of the religious and civic authorities who were intent on eliminating all playhouses to exaggerate any disturbances. As Catharine Arnold has written:

"It would not be fair, however, to ascribe to plays alone all the disturbances which are on record. Such incidents as those which took place outside the Theater in 1584, when 'one Browne, a serving man in a blew coat, a shifting fellowe,' attacked an apprentice with a sword, were due rather to the fact that the neighbourhood of this house was the 'ordinary place for all maister-les men and vagabond persons . . . to meet together and to recreate themselfes'."[23]

Those very authorities had pushed the playhouses out of the city limits and into areas rife with crime and prostitution, and the playhouses were surrounded by taverns and brothels. Similarly, when the film *Rock Around the Clock* was shown in the UK in the Fifties, every fight and disturbance in the hosting city was attributed by the tabloid press to 'juvenile delinquents' at the film, which was seen to promote violence. It was as though Glasgow, Liverpool and the East End of London had never known trouble on the streets on a Saturday night prior to the distinctly non-threatening and chubbily wholesome Bill Haley appearing on a local screen.

Apprentices in the mid-to-late 1500s and teenagers four hundred years later were also pre-judged as trouble-makers intent on creating mayhem. Their love of theatre and rock'n'roll respectively meant those activities were often damned in advance or by association.

A riot was linked to a performance of *Harry VI*, probably Shakespeare's *Henry VI part one*, at the Rose Theatre. This was only an indirect connection, though, as feltmakers' apprentices went to the area in order to protest against the jailing of a feltmaker's servant and disguised their intent by pretending to be on their way to the theatre to watch the play. This vague connection was enough for the Mayor of London, William Webbe, to rail against the playhouses for 'providing the opportunity' for 'suchlike disorders'.

This is not to deny that there were any riots at all during or after plays. There are eyewitness reports of trouble in Cambridge, far less London:

"... there was a similar riot at Cambridge, when there was 'foul & great disorder committed at the time of a comedy in King's College,' probably a lost play by Phineas Fletcher. In the same month, four years later, there was a yet more serious disturbance at Cambridge, when the St John's men, angry at being excluded from a comedy acted at Trinity College, began an affray outside the Great Gate, which led to proceedings in the vice-chancellor's court."[24]

Some outbreaks of trouble are known to have taken place in the capital; there was, for example, one in 1592 after a performance of *A Knack To Know A Knave* at the Rose Theatre. This led the Mayor to demand of the Queen, via a letter to her principal secretary, Francis Walsingham, that "those playhouses that are erected and built only for such purposes shall be plucked down namely the Curtain and the Theatre near to Shoreditch, or any other within that county". The letter went on to demand that owners of the theatres must be sent for "and enjoin them forthwith to pluck down the stages, galleries and rooms that are made for people to stand in, and so to deface the same as they may not be employed again to such use; which if they shall not speedily perform, you shall advertise us that order may be taken to see the same done, according to her Majesties pleasure and commandment."

Thankfully, no such thing happened and although theatres were closed until Hallowe'en the shows carried on afterwards. 'To be plucked down', though, was a phrase that was to rear its head again in 1596-7, as we shall see a little later, after a performance at the Isle of Dogs.

In both the US and the UK, the rock'n'roll explosion was seen as the catalyst for teenage delinquency even though that 'social malaise', hardly a new phenomenon, had taken on a distinctly modern tinge in the generation growing up after World War II. As with World War I, society in the succeeding decade was shaken and shaped by the global conflicts which had changed so much of community life and of people's perceptions of their places in it.

Everything was soon swept up into the 'rock' basket, however, and the alliteration of 'rhythm', 'rock'n'roll' and 'rioting' was irresistible to newspapers. That there were riots is again undeniable, though their extent and number were unquestionably over-hyped by the hyperbolic opponents of the new music. They were also virtually inevitable because the young people who went to concerts in the US, and US rock'n'roll films in the UK, wanted to dance and clap along to the music they were hearing. The police and civic guardians were of the opinion that music should be listened to quietly, in your seats, and politely applauded at the end of a piece, song or concert as appropriate.

Report after report of so-called "out of hand disturbances" repeat the same story: kids go out to dance and have fun, then stewards and/or police try to force them to sit still. Youths resist, the enforcers get heavy-handed, youths respond. It becomes a metronomic sequence when you read through the coverage of the time.

There was a fundamental misunderstanding of the nature of the music and between the generations. Rock music was for dancing to, but not everyone understood this. Add the customary over-reaction that can demand a cancellation before there is any reason for it, and you have a recipe for mayhem:

"March of 1956 saw a "teen riot" at the Massachusetts Institute of Technology (MIT) in Cambridge, Massachusetts. The event was a live rock concert emceed by local disk jockey Bill Marlowe ... Many thought there was going to be a dance. However, the event was exclusively a concert with no room for dancing. After two acts had performed, the audience crowded closer and closer to the stage. The seven police who had been in attendance all evening, fearing problems, ordered Marlowe to bring the concert to a halt. The crowd then commenced to smash tables and generally trash the place. Twenty additional police were called in to quell the disturbance which lasted for about ninety minutes."[25]

Close, relatively speaking, to Dylan's territory, there was a fight after a rock dance in St Paul and a banning of all such dances throughout the Twin Cities on the grounds that they 'incited riots'. These were scenes and reactions repeated nationwide and reported on with salacious glee.

Over in the UK, similar scenarios unfolded as *Rock Around the Clock* hit the cinemas there. Again the problem was movement, the audiences wanted to dance, clap their hands and stamp their feet in time to the music. Any who tried to do so were swiftly ejected by hired bouncers or police. The trouble that followed was inevitable, and again the music got the blame for all of it.

Over and above everything else, Elizabethan and Jacobean playhouses staged performances where boys played females and commoners portrayed nobility and even royalty. This was seen by the theatres' opponents as the ultimate in subversion. There were practical links to actual subversion, too. In 1571, the Queen issued a proclamation severely restricting how many men her Lords could keep on retainer. This move was inspired by the fear that hired soldiers were being listed as actors in attempts to build up undetected private armies. It was a time of considerable paranoia; often with considerable justification.

Back in the US of the late nineteen-fifties, the subversion of rock was still viewed primarily in moral terms. Here are the editors of *Music Journal* on the music's 'threat to civilization' and effect on the youth of the day:

"... influenced in their lawlessness by this throwback to jungle rhythms. Either it actually stirs them to orgies of sex and violence (as its model did for the savages themselves), or they use it as an excuse for the removal of all inhibitions and the complete disregard of the conventions of decency ... it has proved itself definitely a menace to youthful morals and an incitement to juvenile delinquency. There is no point in soft-pedaling these facts any longer. The daily papers provide sufficient proof of their existence. . . It is, however, entirely correct to state that every proved delinquent had been definitely influenced by rock 'n' roll. "[26]

America in the nineteen-fifties saw the spectre of Communism everywhere and this became the latest stick with which to beat the young and their music. The full titles of two books by professional rock denouncer, David A. Noebel, give you an insight into this mindset. *"Rhythm, Riots, and Revolution:An Analysis of the Communist Use of Music, the Communist Master Music Plan"*. This was published, unsurprisingly, by Christian Crusade Publications in 1966. Noebel is also responsible for *The Marxist Minstrels: A Handbook on Communist Subversion Of Music*, among others. This effort, which includes disparaging passages on Dylan, was, again unsurprisingly, published by the American Christian College Press, in Tulsa, Oklahoma in 1974. One shudders to think about what Noebel made of the University of Tulsa's decision to host the Bob Dylan archives some forty years later. Everything Noebel hears in rock music is part of a vast conspiracy controlled from Moscow, the endgame of which is that "degenerated Americans will indeed raise the Communist flag over their own nation".

Dylan, the young folkie who hung around with the likes of Pete Seeger, is a natural target: "It has perhaps never occurred to Mr Dylan ... that the single greatest threat to world peace is atheist Communism's intent on total world conquest. He may not be able to stomach "professional anti-Communists," but for reasons known only to him it is quite obvious that he can stomach "professional Communists."" In an inventive leap, Noebel then goes on to describe photographs of Dylan in *Life* magazine as being those of an "unwashed Bob" being protected by "bearded bodyguards (Castro style)".

There was a lot more where that came from in the States, but to call someone a communist in the UK carried little of the weight it did for the Christian Crusaders and other professional 'Red bashers' in the US. As a result, the reporters in Britain used a different term altogether and this, and Dylan's response to it, were captured for posterity in an amusing scene at the end of D.A. Pennebaker's documentary on Bob Dylan's 1965 UK tour, *Dont Look Back*.[27] Dylan is leaving a concert and waving to fans from the back seat of a car. Dylan's manager Albert Grossman tells him, as they are departing, "They've started calling you an anarchist". Dylan asks who and Grossman continues, "the papers, that's the word now" Dylan replies, "Anarchist? Which paper said that?" Grossman: "oh two or three, yeah, just 'cause you don't offer any solution." Dylan: "You're kidding, anarchist?" (in a disbelieving tone). Dylan then removes his glasses and laughs, saying "Give me a cigarette, give the anarchist a cigarette". The film ends with Dylan wondering how long it took them to come up with the name and there's a discussion over why 'communist' is not used. The conclusion they come to is that being a communist is cool in Britain and consequently the denigrating papers would not use that.

Censorship in Shakespeare's career

The opposition to Shakespeare and Dylan's primary areas of artistry, on the grounds of sexual, religious and riotous behaviour demonstrate illuminating and relevant similarities. Such opposition naturally leads to censorship. However, censorship is something that artists have to put up with, work around or fight against in nearly all times and societies. Therefore, only two examples from the early careers of both parties are discussed below, beginning with Shakespeare.

OPPOSITION

You may well be wondering how the early modern theatre ever survived at all with the full and vigorous weight of the civic authorities and clergy so implacably opposed to it. The answer lies in royal protection. Although 1559 saw the mayor and the city authorities gain control over theatrical performances, Queen Elizabeth, and then King James, wanted plays as part of the court entertainment over the festive period. A curious game of 'cat, mouse and protective dog' developed and was played out annually. The city authorities harassed theatres beyond distraction, and to the point of extinction. When things got desperate, the theatre owners would appeal to the Lords and the Crown for protection. Such aid would usually be forthcoming under the claim that to ensure the plays were ready to be performed before the court in the Christmas period, and other special occasions, the acting companies must first perform them in public.

Everyone knew that this theory of 'live rehearsals' was a front, as there were far too many plays being performed for them to be justified by this reasoning. Things could get very heated, but the plague often came along to make all arguments moot for a long cooling off period. As a result, the game continued and for those who did play at court, protection was obviously much stronger than for the others, who led a very perilous existence indeed. For Shakespeare, royal patronage was to come back with considerable vigour when James ascended the throne and Shakespeare's company became The King's Men.

For a variety of reasons, the relationship between Crown and playhouses was fraught with its own tensions and subject to its own game of the theatre pushing boundaries until the powers that be retaliated. Back in Elizabeth's reign, the Crown had its own worries over the theatre and the content of the popular dramas. As a result, playhouses went from one kind of censorship (barring everything, in effect, within the city walls) to another, that of being under the censorious eye of the Privy Council, ever alert for the slightest hint of sedition, conspiracy and so forth. The theatre companies, accustomed to ignoring and/or outwitting the mayor's proclamations, tried to more or less continue as they pleased. They very often sailed close to the wind and ignored the Privy Council's dictates. This could move the Queen from one side of the chessboard to the other, and to line up with the mayor. In 1597 the Privy Council and City authorities prohibited the public presentation of plays within the city limits for a year, again with the fearsome phrase 'be plucked down':

"Her Majesty being informed that there are very great disorders committed in the common playhouses both by lewd matters that are handled on the stages and by resort and confluence of bad people, has given direction that not only no plays shall be used within London or about the city or in any public place during this time of summer, but that also those playhouses that are erected and built only for such purposes shall be plucked down."

Again, mercifully, that last threat was not carried out. The root cause of the Queen joining in the suppression of the theatre here is customarily attributed to a performance of a play called *The Isle of Dogs* by Ben Jonson and Thomas Nashe at the Swan theatre in 1597. It would appear that the performance went too far and it was roundly condemned for its 'lewd' and 'slanderous' content. The play was immediately suppressed, and unsurprisingly it survives in legend and reports only. The theatre owner's licence was revoked, and imprisonments followed; both these punishments were a constant threat to the acting community.

Still, poking fun at authority always pleases audiences and is an irrepressible part of live performances. As a result, it continued both onstage and in print and, although it was enjoyable and meaningful, this was a dangerous game to play, as the Privy Council had fearsome powers. This was demonstrated again in a 1599 proclamation which became known as 'The Bishop's Ban.' This prohibition was targeted at all writing, not just that for theatre, and earned its name because it was signed by the Archbishop of Canterbury and the Bishop of London. The most severe of four such declarations under Elizabeth's rule, it included the following commands: "That no Satires or Epigrams be printed hereafter. That no English histories be printed except they be allowed by some of her majesty's Privy Counsel. That no plays be printed except they be allowed by such as have authority."

Some of Shakespeare's fellow playwrights fared particularly badly. The erratic, sometimes brilliant, Thomas Nashe was singled out as one whose work should be destroyed. Of the nine individual books listed, to be collected and burnt, were two by John Marston, one by Thomas Middleton and Christopher Marlowe's translation of Ovid's *Elegies*.

Satires and erotic verse seemed the prime targets, but both the banning of the printing of plays unless approved by the Privy Council, and the focus on English history made life very uncomfortable for the Playhouses.

Shakespeare responded to this ban in his play *As You Like It*. The title could indicate that he was giving his audience what it wanted, a light, airy, pastoral romance. It could also be taken to mean that this, mere escapism without any troublesome reflections on real life, is how the censors like it. Except, under that beguiling surface, pointed references occur and this delightful play is full of hidden depths.

Celia's words, *By my troth, thou sayest true. For, since the little wit that fools have was silenced, the little foolery that wise men have makes a great show* directly confront the fall-out from that ban. Shakespeare includes more than one nod to Marlowe in the play. The most touching and famous is a reference to the report of Kit's death in a small chamber, allegedly over the reckoning (bill): "*it strikes a man more dead than a great reckoning in a little room*".

Mapping the complex character of the real life Thomas Nashe with that of the fictional Jacques, and Shakespeare's view of both would provide more than enough material for a book all on its own. It is suffice to say here that Jacques parallels Nashe in a number of aspects. Perhaps this is most clearly seen in a speech that, however perceptive and beautifully written, is not particularly necessary in a plot sense. In the Forest of Arden exile, Duke Senior's First Lord quotes Jacques on seeing a hunted deer:

"'*Sweep on, you fat and greasy citizens,*
'*Tis just the fashion: wherefore do you look*
Upon that poor and broken bankrupt there?'
Thus most invectively he pierceth through
The body of the country, city, court,
Yea, and of this our life, swearing that we
Are mere usurpers, tyrants and what's worse,
To fright the animals and to kill them up
In their assign'd and native dwelling-place."

(Act II Scene i)

These, and other comments attributed to Jaques, remind us of Nashe's perceptive passages against meat eating in *Pierce Penniless: His Supplication to the Devil.*[28] Here are two which you can easily envisage Jacques voicing:

"It is not for nothing that other countries, whom we upbraid with drunkenness, call us bursten-bellied gluttons, for we make our greedy paunches powdering-tubs of beef, and eat more meat at one meal than the Spaniard or Italian in a month. Good thrifty men, they draw out a dinner with salads, like a swartrutter's suit, and make Madonna Nature their best caterer. We must have our tables furnished like poulters' stalls, or as though we were to victual Noah's ark again (wherein there was all sorts of living creatures that ever were), or else the goodwife will not open her mouth to bid one welcome. A stranger that should come to one of our magnifico's houses, when dinner were set on the board, and he not yet set, would think the goodman of the house were a haberdasher of wild-fowl, or a merchant-venturer of dainty meat."

And:

"Whatsoever he could rap or rend, he confiscated to his covetous gut. Nay, we are such flesh-eating Saracens that chaste fish may not content us, but we delight in the murder of innocent mutton, in the unpluming of pullery, and quartering of calves and oxen. It is horrible and detestable; no godly fishmonger that can digest it."

The speech above, from *As you Like It*, accomplishes far more than merely a possible connection to Nashe. It is an elaboration on the theme of usurpation which the Duke himself had instigated shortly before with the telling thought:

Come, shall we go and kill us venison?
And yet it irks me the poor dappled fools,
Being native burghers of this desert city,
Should in their own confines with forkèd heads
Have their round haunches gored.

(Act II Scene i)

The Nashe connection seems deliberate, however, and is indicated as such, perhaps, by the use of the word "pierceth" which may have been an allusion to *Pierce Penniless*. As a satirist, Jacques longs unrestrained in his witty commentary on the fallen world he sees all around. He makes an impassioned plea, in other words, for satire to be free from all censorship:

> *That I am wise. I must have liberty*
> *Withal, as large a charter as the wind,*
> *To blow on whom I please: for so fools have.*
> *And they that are most gallèd with my folly,*
> *They most must laugh.*

(Act II, Scene vii)

It does not require a stretch of imagination to think that Shakespeare had the notorious Bishop's ban, the subsequent book burnings plus the plays being refused licences in mind here. Katherine Duncan Jones certainly hears it that way. She has speculated that *As You Like It* may have been written to open the recently built Globe Theatre "or it may have been designed primarily for performance at the mansions of dissident young courtiers such as the Earls of Southampton and Essex."

She continued: "Either way, the play was daringly topical. Pleas for freedom of speech and writing are both explicit and implicit. Jaques requests, and receives, "as large a charter as the wind" to inveigh against human folly and corruption. At different points both Celia and Touchstone allude to a recent act of state censorship, the Bishops' Ban of June 1599 ... In its Elizabethan context the play was haunted by the dead, and now silenced, Marlowe. The relaxed freedom of Duke Senior's woodland realm, where even such an annoying poseur as Jaques is cheerfully tolerated, offered a pointed contrast to the brittle, dangerous court of the ageing Elizabeth I.[29]

'Dangerous court' is where the next example of Shakespeare's brushes with censorship takes us; that is, to the curious case of his *Richard II* and a palace rebellion in 1601. *Richard II* depicts the fall of the King and his replacement by Henry Bolingroke who takes over the throne as Henry IV. It starts the magnificent tetralogy that continued with *Henry IV Part I*, *Part II* and *Henry V*. After relinquishing his throne, Richard is murdered while in prison. The play debuted in or around 1595, and the Quarto text first appeared, as far as we know, in 1597. This was reprinted in 1598. These editions did not include the notorious deposition/abdication scene. It has long been assumed this was due to other censorship or self-protecting prudency on the part of the printers, and that they were dropping the highly, politically charged scene from the play from fear of persecution for promoting treasonous material.

Jonathan Bate has queried this generally accepted assumption:

"...there is no evidence of active censorship. The idea that it must have been censored is an enduring misapprehension even among some distinguished Shakespeareans. The scene appeared as a 'new addition' in the 1608 reprinting of the quarto and again, in a better-quality text, deriving from the theatre promptbook, in the 1623 Folio version of the play."[30]

The supposition that it had been censored, a very reasonable assumption, had hitherto become widely accepted as fact. On closer examination, proof of it as such is seen to be lacking.

The first point is that Richard is not merely deposed; instead, he abdicates in typically grand style. Everything Richard does is a dramatic act in front of an audience. He is forever, or at least until his final moments away from the spotlight and spectators, an actor in the central drama that is his life. It is impossible to tell for sure when Henry Bolingbroke moves from fighting to restore his own stolen birthright and deciding that he should aim to take Richard's birthright, the throne.

Richard, to a considerable extent, propels Bolingbroke along what increasingly seems, but never necessarily was, an inevitable path. Richard, astutely or self-defeatingly, depending on how the play is performed, seeing where it will all probably end , throws himself into his role as The Usurped, and hands, though only after a mighty internal struggle, the crown to Bolingbroke.

It is difficult to see how the inclusion of this scene makes the play more seditious. If anything the opposite is true. Without it we have a play where a monarch is forcibly removed by a usurper, which would surely have been apprehended as an even more disturbing scenario.

Bate's speculation, already alluded to, is that the scene may never have been censored but that it was, instead, added after the Essex "rebellion":

"This raises the possibility, generally neglected by scholars, that Shakespeare may have written it as an addition after the real-life drama of February 1601, in order to give the impression of a formal, stately handing over of power, as opposed to the presumption and hugger-mugger of the original version that was now tarred by association with the trial of Essex and his accomplices."[31]

With or without this scene, the tale of Richard II's loss of the crown and subsequent death in such times of plots and treason was highly contentious, not to mention potentially dangerous. Added to this, Richard, just like Elizabeth, was notorious for relying too heavily on favoured advisors. And on top of that, Richard, as with the Virgin Queen, had produced no heir. The lack of forward dynastic certainty engendered by this was the central concern of the time. When you put all of this together, you can see just how thin the ice was that the play skated upon.

However, as a counterpoint to some extent, we should remember that Richard's despised advisors were also presumed by many to be his homosexual lovers, thus giving the added twist that it was his bed-fellows who were being unjustly favoured. This, at least, was part of the comparison that was not analogous to the situation with Elizabeth.

Nonetheless, there was more than enough going on in the play to make it hazardous. It clearly held special significance for the Earl of Essex and his close confidants and when, it seems all but proven now, they requested it to be played on the eve of staging a rebellion, the risk factor increased exponentially.

Another story, so oft repeated as to be generally accepted as 'fact' regarding this play, is that Queen Elizabeth is reported to have asked: "I am Richard, know ye not that?" Unfortunately for all lovers of this story, it is most likely to be apocryphal. The written remembrance of the conversation comes so many years later that it cannot be trusted. Additionally, when all the reported comments are read in context they become far more ambiguous than how they are often presented.

The rebellion I mentioned occurred on February 8, 1601. Its aim was to replace the advisors and government officials who surrounded the Queen. It was ill advised, ill planned and shambolic in planning and execution. It quickly collapsed, and the ringleaders were all arrested, tried and convicted.

Part of the trial involved questions regarding what the conspirators had done in the lead-up and this included paying over the odds for Shakespeare's company, The Lord Chamberlain's Men, to put on a special performance of the by now dated play, *Richard II*. This was meant to boost the morale of the plotters and perhaps also, though this would have been a wildly over-ambitious aim, to encourage the London population to rally around Essex.

Shakespeare's company tried to demur when the proposal was put to them. Whether this was due to realising its inherently hazardous nature, or merely fearing its lack of appeal as a 'past it' production for the novelty-hungry London theatre audiences is something we shall almost certainly never know. In the end, they accepted what was a generous over-payment to do as they were bid by powerful and influential backers.

Consequently, it came to pass that on the eve of what is known as 'the Essex Rebellion', the Earl and his men witnessed a private showing of Shakespeare's *Richard II* at the Globe Theatre. 'On the eve of ...' means the day before, not the evening, far less the night. Plays had to be performed in daylight and February in London would mean that it would be dark before even the more standard finishing time of around five in the afternoon. A play about the overthrow of the monarch the day before a palace coup meant that it was inevitable that when the coup failed, and investigations started, the authorities would have to be satisfied that they did this in all innocence.

Augustine Phillips, giving evidence for The Chamberlain's Men at the trial, testified as follows: "He says that on Friday or Thursday, a week ago, Sir Charles Percy, Sir Jocelyne Percy and the Lord Montague with some three more spoke to some of the players in the presence of this *Examinate* to have the play of the deposing and killing of King Richard the Second to be played the Saturday next, promising to get them forty shillingsmore than their ordinary to play it. Where this *Examinate* and his fellows were determined to have played some other play, holding that play King Richard to be so old and so long out of use as that they should have small or no Company at it. But at their request this Examinate and his fellows were Content to play it the Saturday and had their forty shillingsmore than their ordinary for it and so played it accordingly."[32]

As no charges were brought against the actors, their seemingly flimsy defence that they were merely playing for a paying request and saw no political significance in what they were acting, apparently was successful. Nothing happened to the author of the play, one William Shakespeare, despite one of Essex's closest companions being The Earl of Southampton, the very patron to whom Shakespeare had dedicated his poems, *Venus and Adonis* and *The Rape of Lucrece*.

Part of the reason for this might be that everyone knew that Essex's rebellion was not aimed directly at the Queen. Although his enemies certainly portrayed the rebellion in that light at the hearing, Bate assures us that:

"The deposition of the queen was the last thing on their minds: the project was to rescue the queen from bad advisers. The notion, parroted by Shakespearean biographers and critics (including, it has to be confessed, me), that there was a conscious attempt to prepare the London public for a deposition is wildly implausible."[33]

Even more importantly, in tracing the events of the day in detail, Bate demonstrates that the play itself was not the cause or start of any untoward actions:

"The trigger for Essex's march into the streets came only after the show, with the evening summons from the Council. Nowhere in the subsequent investigations was it explicitly claimed by Cecil and his team that this was how they regarded the performance."

Nonetheless, one might still be justified in wondering quite how Shakespeare emerged unscathed when Cecil directly blamed Essex for: "Making this time seem like that of Richard II, to be reframed by him as by Henry IV." Cecil continued that, like Bolingbroke, Essex, after having "removed Her Majesty's servants" then would have "stepped into her chair".[34]

However, while Essex was executed and the Lord Southampton cast into The Tower (his death sentence having been transmuted after appeals by his wife and mother) the players and author of the play were not pursued on any charges. Nor were they in any disfavour at all, it would seem, because the Queen requested that they perform for her on Shrove Tuesday, February 24, which just happened to be the night before Essex and other plotters were executed.

It is becoming more common to see it asserted that the Queen requested *Richard II* as the play to be performed on that occasion. It would be marvellously pointed of her to have done so. However, although this would make a good story, there is no evidence for it. The registrar for the night's proceedings at Whitehall records the acting company name but does not mention which play was performed. What follows is from a facsimile copy of 'Feb 24, Privy Council to the Constable and Lieutenant of the Tower':

'Richard Coningsby, Usher of the Black Rod for the Order of the Garter, is appointed...to disgrade and deprive the late Earl of Essex, being attainted of high treason, of that honourable Order in pulling off the George and Garter, and therefore it is her Majesty's pleasure you shall admit him to the person of the said Earl to execute this office in your presence'.

At the Tower the Works had been 'making a scaffold for the beheading of the Earl of Essex'. Feb 24, Chamberlain to Carleton: 'His execution was expected on Saturday, then yesterday, now tomorrow or on Thursday...The general opinion is there will be no great executions, for the Queen is very gracious and inclines much to mercy'.

'We have continual watch and ward day and night in arms through the city'.

Also Feb 24, Shrove Tuesday play, by Lord Chamberlain's Men.'[35]

The "mercy" refers to the execution being straightforward rather than being hung until nearly dead, then cut down, tortured, then drawn and quartered.

Censorship in Dylan's career

Bob Dylan has had his own run-ins with censors though thankfully nothing as physically threatening as that last one could have been for Shakespeare.

'Talkin' John Birch Paranoid Blues', originally titled 'John Birch Society Blues' is a humorous little piece about those John Birchers who were paranoid about the "red menace" and who saw Communists hiding everywhere they looked. Dylan hones in on the absurdity of it all as the narrator discovers to his horror that *"they wus red stripes on the American flag!"*.

Dylan planned to play this as the one song on his scheduled appearance on the Ed Sullivan Show in May 1963. This TV show was of considerable importance. It commanded large viewing numbers and the cultural impact commensurate with those. Elvis's appearance on the show was legendary, as would be the first of the Beatles', the following year. There would have been a particularly apt verse of the song for TV, though, one which would have comically drawn his audience in on the act where Dylan sings: *"Well, I wus sittin' home alone an' started to sweat, Figured they wus in my T.V. set."*

That aside, however, it seems a slightly strange choice for Dylan to have made as he had many more accomplished songs that he could have showcased, whether making a social protest or not, and he had evolved considerably as an artist since writing this talking blues number.

Dylan biographer Clinton Heylin leans towards the choice being deliberately confrontational on Dylan's part:

"All the evidence points to a decision by Columbia's lawyers to replace 'John Birch' being forced on Dylan some weeks prior to the Sullivan show. ... Such a chronology puts a whole different slant on Dylan's non-appearance on *The Ed Sullivan Show* on May 12. If Dylan had already been instructed by Columbia lawyers to pull 'Talkin' John Birch' before the April 24 session, then the fact that he attempted to perform it on a CBS TV show three weeks later suggests a very deliberate act of confrontation. If he had managed to get it past the head of program practices, as he might well have, Columbia Records and CBS-TV would have been made to look very stupid, and Dylan would have succeeded in publicly ridiculing the John Birch Society."[36]

It was not to be, because, as one of Dylan's earliest biographers reported: "During rehearsals on a Sunday afternoon in May, hours before the show, Dylan was told by Stowe Phelps, editor of program practices for the CBS network, that he could not sing the song because there was a possibility it libeled members of the Birch organization."[37] The lines which most bothered the internal censor(s) were the ones that linked the John Birchers to the views of Hitler:

Now we all agree with Hitler's views
Although he killed six million Jews
It don't matter too much that he was a Fascist
At least you can't say he was a Communist!

Early Dylan biographer, Anthony Scaduto describes a highly excitable Dylan that raged against the decision at the time and for weeks afterwards: "Are ya out of your fuckin' mind?" Dylan shouted, according to one who was there. "What the hell can they sue about?" Phelps said: "I'm sorry, Bob, but that's the order from the lawyers. They won't let us use it." Precht and Sullivan both apologized, asked Dylan to sing something else. "Bullshit," Dylan almost screamed. "I sing that or I sing nothing." And he stalked off."[38]

Years later, and with considerably more research behind him, Clinton Heylin, reports a very different scenario:

"As it was, during the afternoon rehearsal Dylan was informed that his satirical blues about the John Birch Society might upset those he was seeking to satirize, and that he couldn't perform it. His response was remarkably calm and measured. He was asked if he wanted to do something else and he apparently replied, `No, this is what I want to do. If I can't play my song, I'd rather not appear on the show.' It was almost as if it had all come down as he expected."[39]

Dylan was not without backers in the immediate row over the decision. He had, after all, previously rehearsed the song for Sullivan and the show's producer and no objections had been raised then. According to Scaduto: "Sullivan later told TV columnist Bob Williams: "We fought for the song. We pointed out that President Kennedy and his family are kidded constantly by TV comedians. Governor Rockefeller is also kidded, among others. But the John Birch Society — I said I couldn't understand why they were being given such protection. But the network turned us down. They told us they understood and sympathized with our viewpoint, but insisted they had previously handled the Birch Society and their lunatic behavior on network news programs and couldn't take the subject into entertainment. We told CBS, 'It's your network, but we want to state that the decision is wrong and the policy behind it is wrong.' "[40]

The network was unmoved, the song was not to be broadcast, and so Dylan walked away and lost his chance of a debut on nationwide TV. Furthermore, the issue inevitably spread from CBS TV to CBS records and Dylan was ordered to drop the song from his forthcoming album, *The Freewheelin' Bob Dylan*. Again there were some in the CBS organisation who argued against the censorship, saying that it was wrong and overly cautious in any case. Again the censorship stood. Dylan bowed to the pressure, but, instead of being criticised for going along with these ridiculous demands, he instead rode a wave of approval over his principled stand regarding the TV show. Heylin documents that: "As it was, the *New York Times* and *Village Voice* both ran stories on the furore, while *Time* and *Playboy* referred to the incident in articles on the folk-music revival, emphasizing Dylan as the most promising up-and-coming folksinger. Nat Hentoff's profile in *Playboy* even included an account of Dylan's original audition for *The Ed Sullivan Show*, at the time his first album was released."

The story was a perfect boost for Dylan's rebellious image; that of the folksinger up against the big, bad corporations, and the radical against the conservative establishment. Dylan kept the song in his live set for longer than would otherwise have been the case, it is safe to assume. He drew rapturous ovations when he introduced it and added short prefatory comments, such as "....and there ain't nuthin' wrong with this song." He sharpened the lyrics up, and it became officially known as "Talkin' John Birch Paranoid Blues."

Dylan benefitted in other ways, too. He took the opportunity afforded by having to replace one song on *Freewheelin'*, to make the album more representative of his current output by changing four of the cuts. Out went not only 'John Birch' but also: 'Let Me Die in My Footsteps', 'Ramblin' Gamblin' Willie' and 'Rocks and Gravel'. In their places came: 'Masters of War', 'Girl from the North Country', 'Bob Dylan's Dream' and 'Talkin' World War III Blues'. Much as I enjoy the original tracks and admire the excellent 'Let Me Die in my Footsteps', in particular, there is no doubt that the album was strengthened overall by these four substitutions.

Censors were to attack another Dylan song in 1966. Similarly to *As You Like It*, Dylan's 'Rainy Day Women #12 and 35' appears light, fluffy and full of fun. It also superficially appears superficial, you might say, as it, too, is all of these things but is also much more besides.

The title, music and lyrics all tread two paths simultaneously, the obvious one of intoxicated partying and another that hints at social and religious persecution. There's no doubt that fun predominates, but both are ever present. 'Rainy Day Women #12 & 35' is so compellingly infectious that it reached number two in the singles chart, which was extremely unusual for Dylan who was and is more known as an 'album artist.' In that realm, with its party atmosphere and glorious punning, it provides a perfect *aperitif* for the sumptuous banquet that is the *Blonde on Blonde* double album.

There is more to the music than just party sounds; it comes across almost like a New Orleans jazz band marching down the street or an unholy mixture of intoxicated players at a religious walk. Producer Bob Johnston has spoken of his attempts to capture a 'Salvation Army' sound in amongst the bedlam. He succeeded brilliantly, and so the song gives us musical, as well as verbal, puns.

The song's central pun, of course, is that of 'being stoned'. 'Being stoned' as in being high on dope, or 'being stoned' literally and metaphorically by those entirely too quick to judge, as in the famous Bible episode when Jesus is asked to pronounce sentence on 'the woman taken in adultery':

So when they continued asking him, he lifted up himself, and said unto them, He that is without sin among you, let him first cast a stone at her.[41]

The non-numerical part of the title, meanwhile, is a slang name for a marijuana joint as well as, potentially another allusion to the Bible: "*A continual dropping in a very rainy day and a contentious woman are alike.*" [42]

There is no doubt that, whatever else is felt about the song, the repeated refrain of "Everybody must get stoned' makes the biggest impact on every listener. So much so that in America, this became the song's *de facto* title. Also, this is what brought censorship down upon its head:

'Rainy Day Women #12 & 35' ... triggered a drug-song controversy so feverish that ... " it was banned by American and British radio stations. *Time*, July 1, 1966: "In the shifting multi-level jargon of teenagers, 'to get stoned' does not mean to get drunk but to get high on drugs... a 'rainy-day woman', as any junkie [sic] knows, is a marijuana cigarette." [43]

Other elements of Dylan's work of the decade are also swimming just beneath this hazy surface, however. There is a nod to the ongoing scourge of racism in the line: *They'll stone ya when you're tryin' to keep your seat*. That may come across as innocuous nowadays, but in the nineteen sixties, and especially from the mouth of Bob Dylan, who had skewered institutionalised racism in a number of masterly songs, it brought to mind those black women who had refused to give up their seats on buses to whites after the 'whites only' seats were all taken. Rosa Parks was not the first, but she was by far the most famous of these, and it is she who springs to mind here. Everyone should be able to take a seat on a bus without fear of persecution, of 'being stoned', regardless of one's skin colour. An obvious point, you would think, but it needed to be made then and sadly perhaps still does in many places even now.

Dylan had sung out against racism, and he had also sung out against those who send young men off to die in battle. In 'Rainy Day Women #12 and 35' there are also references to young soldiers dying:

They'll stone you and then say you are brave
They'll stone you when you are set down in your grave.

These lines conjure up memories of Dylan during his so-called 'protest phase' and especially songs such as 'Hero Blues' and 'Masters of War', songs that lamented the terrible waste of young men being sent off to be maimed or killed. As was often the case with his seemingly nonsensical, surrealistic responses to interview questions in the mid-sixties, Dylan hinted at these aspects to the song while simultaneously pulling the interviewer's leg. Replying to a question seeking the meaning of this song at a press conference in Stockholm on April 28, 1966, Dylan ended his 'explanation' with: *"It's a sort of Mexican thing, very protest... and one of the protestiest of all things I've protested against in my protest years."*[44]

In other interviews, such as this one with Jonathan Cott in December 1977, Dylan has shown that he consciously created the multi-levelled meanings of this seemingly innocuous novelty song, stressing alienation and persecution for standing up for what one believes in:

JC: You can't really dance to one of your songs.
BD: *I couldn't.*
JC: Imagine dancing to 'Rainy Day Woman #12 & 35'. It's kind of alienating. Everyone thought it was about being stoned, but I always thought it was about being all alone.
BD: *So did I. You could write about that for years...*

You can easily hear why Jonathan Cott's interpretation rings so true. The repeated 'alone's in the opening and closing verses drive home his point about isolation. Yet it is not the sadness associated with this lonely, closing 'homecoming' that one feels on first coming across the song. It is true that there is a resigned tone to the lyrics that acknowledges all-pervasive persecution, but at the same time the most immediate message is, still, 'Hey, it's party time – let's get stoned'.

As with all of his songs, it also depends on where one hears it and, live, how Dylan chooses to perform it. In concerts, the crowds roar back "everybody must get stoned" in delirious, Dionysian celebration. There, it is all about getting high. This is probably mostly true regarding the single, too, and when first heard as the opening track of *Blonde on Blonde*. Perhaps after repeated listens to the pun-strewn double opus, you start to also listen to the song as being about persecution. *"They'll stone you when you're playing your guitar"* sings a man who has been touring the world to boos, catcalls and demonstrations against how he chose to pursue his art.

Dylan never forgot this aspect of the song:

'Everybody must get stoned' is like when you go against the tide. ..you might in different times find yourself in an unfortunate situation and so to do what you believe in sometimes, people, uh, some people they just take offence to that. You know, I mean, you can look through history and find that people have taken offence to people who come out with a different viewpoint on things. And ' being stoned' is like...it's just a kind of way of saying that.[45]

Nonetheless, he too, even while emphasising that that there are 'lots of meanings' in the song has no doubt as to which 'precise' meaning this other interviewer is alluding to, a dozen years later:

PA: Knowing the influence that you exercise over millions of young people, don't you think it is dangerous to go on singing "Everybody Must Be Stoned"?
BD: But that song has lots of other meanings.
PA: Maybe, but it does have a precise one.
BD: Marijuana isn't a drug like the others (a pause). Today there are drugs that are a lot more dangerous than in my time.[46]

There were other analogies amongst all this repression. Both actors and rock stars were repeatedly attacked on grounds of personal hygiene. Both Marlowe and Dylan have been described in books as, 'unwashed' while slovenly, unshaven, dishevelled and unkempt are other favourites. That was, to be fair, an image the young Dylan carefully cultivated for a brief period.

As is ever the way, the more the theatres and concerts were attacked as centres of lewd and licentious behaviour, the more appealing they became to young people. Those who were ostensibly attacking the various entertainments were more or less running advertising campaigns for them: "Roll up, Roll up – get your thrills here: sexual excitement and intoxicating pleasures guaranteed." There came a time in the US when no self respecting youth would want to own a disc that did not have a "Parental Advisory Label" attached to it. This was seen as a handy guide to material guaranteed to contain explicit content.

***

In the areas of condemnation on the grounds of sex, religion and social politics, the more you read, the more you begin to see 1596 and 1965 as interchangeable. I have yet to touch on one of the leading causes for angst and antipathy towards both of our bards. I am referring to money and its attendants, commercial success and envy. In moving on to the subject of commercialism replacing free communal entertainment, we hear Pistol from *Henry V* ask:

'*Art thou base, common, and popular?*"
(Act IV Scene i)

Commentaries decrying the commercial aspects of acting were common in Shakespeare's time:

"One of the greatest causes of indignation against the Elizabethan theatre was that what had been a natural social activity, the recreation of the people, should have become a sordid money-making commercial concern. Playing was not one of the professions or trades of society, it was an activity anyone and everyone could share. To leave one's recognised trade and to take money for acting was behaving like a prostitute, who made a profession out of sexual intercourse."[47]

The words here are reminiscent of Scottish poet and folk-singer Hamish Henderson's defence of Dylan's 'move from folk into commercial pop'. Henderson was responding to the same condemnatory language, and the same charge of "sordid money making":

"And before we start reaching for stones to chuck at Bob Dylan, as if he were a sort of folk-song equivalent of the woman taken in adultery, and before we join the hooting chorus when his 1965 Newport "image" comes up for discussion, let us for heaven's sake remember that an unmistakable vein of genuine poetry runs through the best of his work. If the American success machine is currently giving him the treatment, it is our loss as well as his."[48]

In both cases, the arguments were the same, that something which should be given freely out of pure love and communal spirit was now being 'prostituted' to provide fame, success and – shock, horror – money. In both cases, the outrage seems to have been propelled more by envy than the purist love of the folk process, though it is hard to disentangle the two.

This is made clear in a series of plays put on by students between 1598 and 1601 at St John's College in Cambridge. These satirical plays took aim at a host of targets, but prominent among them was Shakespeare and his company of actors. The savaging they receive is evidently clearly the product of envy and a fear of losing out on making a living that was all too real. It was not a new charge against Shakespeare. Infamously, in his 1592 pamphlet, *A Groatsworth of Wit* the jealous Robert Greene[49] complained:

"Yes, trust them not, for there is an upstart crow[50], beautified with our feathers, that, with his tigers heart wrapped in a Player's hide, supposes he is as well able to bombast out a blank verse as the best of you; and being an absolute Johannes Factotum, is in his own conceit the only Shake-scene in a country."

We will look at this attack in the chapter of sources and plagiarism, but for here the vital point is its revolt against the idea of Shakespeare the actor becoming a playwright also. This field had hitherto been seen as a private fiefdom for University writers, men like Christopher Marlowe, Robert Greene, and Thomas Nashe from Cambridge and Oxford's John Lyly, Thomas Lodge and George Peele. Things were changing and some of the group known as the "University Wits" had trouble adapting to the new ways of the world.

The three plays in Cambridge over the turn of the century are collectively known as *The Parnassus Plays* and were written and performed by students for students. These scholars were facing uncertain futures, and the plays concern themselves with the seemingly insoluble problem of how they will survive when they leave university. The trilogy is filled with episodes bemoaning their wasted youth in studying when no gainful employment is to be found at its conclusion. The success of the likes of Shakespeare's company shuts off one more potential revenue stream. There's a lot of snobbery involved as well. Shakespeare is middle class and never went to University, and this seems to add insult to injury in the eyes of the anonymous author(s) of the plays.

Shakespeare may have been a target they were particularly keen to pillory as *Hamlet* was played in Cambridge around this time, though we do not know the exact dates of either that or the Parnassus performances. You can imagine how galling a successful play written by a 'non-educated commoner', as they would have viewed Shakespeare, would appear to them. Especially so for a drama whose central character was a university student and which was being performed at their university. There is real trepidation in the plays, too. Unless you were the inheriting son, the world was beginning to seem a shifting and uncertain place in which to make a living. There was an intense nervousness among the established, landed upper classes over the dynamic new world of innovation and exploration with its broader education that was being eagerly embraced by a strongly emerging middle class. The world was rapidly changing, and the old order felt itself on very unsure ground.

Shakespeare and Dylan's careers coincide with times when youth from 'lower classes' made their voices heard and expressed a desire for new entertainment forms that they could think of as their own. Workers wanted to enjoy themselves at performances and careers were made on the back of this, and made by the 'wrong people', as far as those whose place was usurped were concerned. Furthermore, Shakespeare's acting company and Dylan, especially once he added rock musicians to back him, were seen to have sprung from folk art that was practiced on a free, or at least pay-as-you-please, basis but who were now charging and making money through the same entertainment.

Like the would-be next generation of 'University Wits' above, the professional songsmiths of 'Tin Pan Alley' (the name given to the companies who churned out hit after hit) were horrified by the rise of the singer-songwriters who followed in Dylan's wake. Dylan was quite aware of what he had done to them: *"Tin Pan Alley is gone, I put an end to it. People can record their own songs now."*[51]

Prior to this, the singers of standards in the Forties and early-Fifties had felt similarly threatened by the rise of rock 'n' roll. Frank Sinatra fulminated: "Rock 'n' roll smells phony and false ... written for the most part by imbecilic goons... lewd, in fact plain dirty lyrics. It was lapped up by "every sideburn delinquent on the face of the earth" and was "brutal, ugly, desperate and vicious"[52]. You can hear in these words just how threatened the old establishment was feeling at the time.[53]

Both Shakespeare and Dylan were lambasted for ensuring that their artistic efforts generated money. The more perceptive peers of both Bards would have been intimidated by the quality of the work even as they decried it as worthless, as well as envious of the success. Such jealousy and resentment breeds the same language of denunciation that is mirrored across the centuries. All classes were annoyed at the actors' successes in Elizabethan time, and they were attacked as being not worthy of the money they earned. The same criticism was launched upon pop stars in the Sixties. The argument then appeared to move from the 'purity of the communal folk art' to 'anybody can do this folk art stuff, so it is not worth paying anyone for doing so'.

The furore over Dylan's notorious move from acoustic to electric guitar was, initially, at its core more about the move from the communal to the commercial. The electric guitar was symbolic of the latter and for many 'commercial' was a dirty word. A similar argument would develop soon after this between single and album artists and AM and FM radio when the former were dismissed as commercial, popular and therefore superficial, and the latter were considered important and meaningful. Again, 'commercial' was a term of disparagement. Back in the mid-sixties, the abuse that followed Dylan around the world became legendary in its intensity. Two of the post show comments caught in the film *Eat The Document* give you the picture and the antipathy towards success and money:

"Any pop group could produce better rubbish than that; it was a bloody disgrace, it was... He wants shooting. He's a traitor."

"You know, he's always pretending he's for the person in the gutter. Well, if that's how he walks in the gutter, I'd rather walk with my head up in the gutter rather than, like he is, crawling through the bloody gutter, just making a pile out of it: yeah, he's making a pile out of people he pretends he's for."

With a similarly felt grievance to the disgruntled fans in that film, the authorities from centuries earlier lined up to complain over the playing companies that had supplanted the traditional troupes around the country. Troupes that were also being systematically wiped out by puritanical and council disapproval, it should be added. Nonetheless, the upshot of the twin attack, from authorities and competition from professional players, meant that, during the time of Shakespeare's career, the old wandering minstrels who played 'interludes' around the country were wholly usurped by the new professional acting companies. These, in turn, were confined to London for their base, although often forced out to tour, by outbreaks of plague in the city, boys' companies or on orders to spread the Government line on religious and political issues of the day. They were also subject to the harassment I have been documenting and the complaints again focused on the making of money.

In 1580, the Lord Mayor of London wrote that 'the players of plays . . . are a very superfluous sort of men' while four years after that, the Corporation of London came out strongly against the idea that acting was in any way a proper profession, and proclaimed that it was strictly supposed to be unpaid for entertainment.

"It hath not been used nor thought meet heretofore that players have or should make their living on the art of playing; but men for their livings using other honest and lawful arts, or retained in honest services, have by companies learned some interludes for some increase to their profit by other men's pleasures in vacant time of recreation."

Philip Edwards noted this line of attack in the 1599 satiric play, attributed, by most, to Marston, called *"Histriomastix"*. In this, workmen leave their trades to set up a company of players in time of peace; clearly it was felt that war would have kept them in their proper place in society.

Incle: *This peace breeds such plenty, trades serve no turns.*
Belch: *The more fools we to follow them.*
Posthaste: *Let's make up a company of players, For we can all sing and say, And so (with practice) soon may learn to play.*
Belch: *Pray sir, what titles have travelling players?*
Posthaste: *Why proper fellows, they play lords and kings.*

Again the fear of the social order being overthrown is evident, in addition to the attack on people being paid for something that should not take the place of 'real work'. Interestingly, from the point of view of this book, the workmen who here decide to become a company of strolling players entered the scene singing a folk song, 'The Nut Brown Ale.'

This neatly parallels what was viewed as Dylan's move from folk to commercial pop. That is, from the folk process ('our') to copyrighted property of the individual ('mine'). Again the question arises as to whether the negative views were adopted out of purism or purely jealousy. Hamish Henderson, himself a dynamic spirit in the folk revival in Scotland, had little doubt at the time:

"I think the time has probably come to take a cool unhurried look at the identity and motives of some of the people who are doing their best to hash Bob Dylan out of the ring — in so far as one can see past their pseudonyms. The folk scene has been bedevilled not only by the cynical money-grubber — and the witless bonehead — of the commercial revival, but also by the phoney purist: the bloke who poses as the cleaner out of an Augean stable into which he himself has tipped a goodly amount of muck, Not all the evidence makes particularly pleasing reading. The phoney purist just can't stand it if he's not right in the middle of the picture; far from discouraging his personality cult, he's likely to be its most assiduous promoter and actor-manager. There's usually little anyone can teach him about the money angle. Furthermore, he can do any God's amount of folk-faking himself, when he feels inclined."

OPPOSITION

As Henderson writes in the same article:

"...Not long back, Folk Music's Jack Speedwell took a slap at Bob Dylan. He quoted Pete Seeger's remark, "Bob Dylan is a great poet," and professed bafflement. Valery, Rilke, Lorca were widely regarded as among the greatest twentieth century poets — yet Speedwell could see little in common between their work and the songs of Bob Dylan. This being the rather depraved scene we are faced with, let us be grateful, at any rate, for the creators, the makars[54], the composers, those with a spark of the divine fire — if anyone can leaven this unholy lump, they will."[55]

***

Our two writers, then, had to overcome opposition on a personal level as well as attacks upon their chosen professions. Attitudes towards sex, politics, religion, distrust of boisterous enjoyment and financial envy all contributed to the opposing forces. Uncanny parallels are apparent in the harassment and censorship both Shakespeare and Dylan faced and in the ways they confronted and overcame, or circumnavigated, all of them so admirably.

NOTES

1 I have modernised the spelling for ease of reading here, and I will generally continue to do so, although I will also include some in their original form as that better conveys the feeling and tone

2 *Anti-Rock: The Opposition To Rock 'n' Roll* by Linda Martin and Kerry Segrave Da Capo Press; New edition, 1993

3 'It's Alright, Ma (I'm Only Bleeding)' Bob Dylan Copyright © 1965 by Warner Bros. Inc.; renewed 1993 by Special Rider Music

4 *Anti-Rock: The Opposition To Rock 'n' Roll op. cit.*

5 Johnny Marr: *Christ, Communists and Rock'n'Roll: Anti Rock'n'Roll Books* https://wfmu.org/LCD/18/antirock.html

6 Arnold, Catherine *Globe: Life in Shakespeare's London* Simon & Schuster, UK April 5, 2016

7 Didacus de Tapia, as cited by Collier, quoted in A *Select Collection of Old Plays: Historia histrionica; God's promises* edited by Robert Dodsley, John Payne Collier, Isaac Reed and Octavius Gilchrist. Septimus Prowett, London 1825-27

8 *The Cambridge History of English Literature, Volume 6* Sir Adolphus William Ward, Alfred Rayney Waller. Originally, The University Press, 1910. CUP reprint 1969

9 Bob Larson's book *Rock & Roll: The Devil's Diversion* went through various versions as Mr Larson updated it with fresh allegations of Satan's corruption of the youth of America, as rock music continued to flourish down the years

10 He was later to do a u-turn on this and embrace Christian rock, "even if it had a beat to it."

11 *A Probe Theologicall*, 1612. Quoted in The Cambridge History of English Literature, *op. cit.*

12 "Printed by Robert Walde-graus, dwelling without Temple-barre, for Henry Carre in Paules Churchard. 1583"

13 http://www.independent.co.uk/news/world/americas/gay-people-hurricane-harvey-blame-christian-leaders-texas-flooding-homosexuals-lgbt-a7933026.html accessed October 17, 2017

14 This is all reminiscent hurricanes being blamed on same-sex marriage, 434 years after Mr Field's 'exhortation'

15 https://www.wired.com/2006/04/war/ accessed October 17, 2017

16 Garlock, Frank *Big Beat — A Rock Blast* Bob Jones University Press, Greenville SC, USA 1971

17 *Anti-Rock: The Opposition To Rock 'n' Roll op. cit.*

18 *Anti-Rock: The Opposition To Rock 'n' Roll op. cit.*

19 Jeff Godwin *The Devil's Disciples* and *Dancing with Demons* Chick Publications Inc., U.S. Oct. 1988

20 *https://spectrummagazine.org/article/jared-wright/2009/09/08/little-richard-rock-and-roll-star-adventist-minister* Accessed October 28, 2017

21 This exchange occurred during a 1979 concert in Tempe, Arizona

22 Arnold, Catharine *op. cit.*

23 Arnold, Catharine *op. cit.*

24 *The Cambridge History of English Literature, Volume 6. Op. cit.*

25 *Anti-Rock op. cit.*

26 Music Journal *Editorially Speaking* (February 3, 1958), as quoted in *Anti-Rock op. cit.*

27 The missing apostrophe is tediously deliberate. Pennebaker took the blame for this, saying that he did it to try and simplify the language

28 Nashe, Thomas *Pierce Penilesse: His Supplication to the Devil.* London Imprinted by Richard Jones, dwelling at the sign of the Rose and Crown near Holborn Bridge. 1592

29 Duncan-Jones, Katherine *The Times Literary Supplement, Arts & Commentary, As You Like It* July 8, 2005

30 Bate, Jonathan *Soul of the Age: The Life, Mind and World of William Shakespeare* Penguin, 2009 (first published October 2008)

31 *Ibid.*

32 Originally quoted by Chambers, Sir Edmund Kerchever, *William Shakespeare*. Here recast in modern spelling.

33 Bate, Jonathan *op. cit.*

34 From Chambers, *op. cit.*

35 https://folgerpedia.folger.edu/mediawiki/media/images_pedia_folgerpedia_mw/3/39/ECDbD_1601.pdf Accessed October 24, 2017

36 Heylin, Clinton *Behind The Shades: The 20th Anniversary Edition* Faber & Faber, London, UK 2011

37 Scaduto, Anthony *Bob Dylan* originally 1972, Re-published by Helter Skelter, London, UK, 1996

38 *Ibid.*

39 Heylin, *op. cit.*

40 Scaduto, Anthony *op. cit.*

41 *John: 8.7* King James Version

42 *Proverbs: 27:15* King James Version

43 Shelton, Robert *No Direction Home: The Life and Music of Bob Dylan* Beech tree Books, New York, US, 1986

44 Dylan, Bob. Klas Burling interview, Stockholm April 28, 1966

45 Dylan, Bob. Bob Fass Radio Phone-in, May 21, 1986

46 Dylan, Bob Philippe Adler interview for *L'Expresse* June 16, 1978

47 Edwards, Phillip. *Threshold of a Nation: A Study in English and Irish Drama* (Cambridge University Press. December 30, 1983

48 Hamish Henderson http://www.mcgonagall-online.org.uk/articles/william-mcgonagall-and-the-folk-scene accessed May 5, 2019

49 There is some debate as to whether the dying Greene was the actual author of the piece accredited to him

50 It is from here that the popular BBC comedy series about Shakespeare, *Upstart Crow,* get its title. The sitcom features Robert Greene as a recurring character, and is gloriously portrayed by Mark Heap

51 Colin Dwyer Bob Dylan, Titan Of American Music, Wins 2016 Nobel Prize In Literature NPR 'Breaking News' October 13, 2016. http://www.npr.org/sections/thetwo-way/2016/10/13/497780610/bob-dylan-titan-of-american-music-wins-the-2016-nobel-prize-in-literature accessed October 29, 2017

52 Sinatra quoted in *New York Times*, ('Why they rock 'n' roll') January 28, 1958 and Frith, Simon *Sound Affects* Constable, London, UK 1983

53 Frank Sinatra and Bob Dylan were later to become very much closer with Sinatra requesting Dylan sing the little-known, and previously unheard live, 'Restless Farewell' at Frank's eightieth birthday celebration. In the second decade of this century Dylan has released, so far, five discs of covers of American Standards, nearly all of which are strongly associated with Sinatra.

54 Makars is the Scottish word for 'bards', fittingly as the word poet stems from the greek for 'maker'

55 Hamish Henderson *op. cit.*

Chapter Five

RELIGION

I see you have some religion in you

The religious leanings of both our bards have long excited fevered speculation. The Bible has, inescapably, infused both of their writings. Debates over denominational leanings are one thing, but it is assumed that Shakespeare was always a believer in Christianity, as was common in his society. Though it is perhaps worth noting that his contemporary playwriting genius, the ever reckless Christopher Marlowe, was reputed to be 'Godless' in his own time. Indeed, if the infamous "Atheist Lecture" contains Marlowe's own words then one marvels, when added to his other activities, how he quite managed to survive until he was all of twenty-nine years old.

Notwithstanding Marlowe's example, which is itself a contested point, Shakespeare is presumed to be a believer, and unlike in Dylan's case, there can be no debate over whether this was in Christianity or Judaism. There has been very fierce debate, however, over which of those two confessions of Christianity, which were so central to the politics and society of his time, Shakespeare favoured, namely, Protestantism or Catholicism. Dylan, meanwhile, has always believed, as he puts it, *"in a God of time and space"*[1] and in the afterlife. The debate that swirls around his convictions are to do with whether these are Christian or Judaic or an amalgamation of the two.

Shakespeare lived in a Christian society that was fully imbued with its outlook, traditions, rituals and holiday celebrations. A basic Christian mindset was taken for granted as a shared backcloth to his plays by his first audiences. Dylan had a Jewish upbringing and family but in his late thirties experienced a Christian conversion and his marriages and children either side of that time followed Jewish and Christian paths, respectively.

What is clear amongst all the often divisive debating that surrounds these facts is that *The Bible* provides a source of symbolism throughout both artists' entire canons. It is one of the central bedrocks in both of their art. This chapter looks into these areas after first exploring both writers' approaches to those associated concepts of death and the apocalypse.

***

Even given the ubiquity of death as a central topic in artists' work, it is a strikingly persistent and prevalent one throughout both Shakespeare's and Dylan's writing.

Dylan's focus on death was evident from the very beginning of his career. It was the dominant theme of his first album. It is not unusual for the young to be concerned with such thoughts, but Dylan seemed remarkably preoccupied with them on that disc. This was all the more notable because the album was housed in a sleeve adorned by a photograph of a cherub-faced Dylan which was very much at odds with the contents of the songs inside. On the other hand, his voice told a different story to the face on the cover. Instead of a startling contrast with his material, his voice provided a perfect match, sounding as old, hard-travelled and aware that the end was approaching. All but two of the songs were cover songs and so reflected the genres they came from as well as Dylan's own predilections. Nonetheless, it is striking that his selections were overwhelmingly of death-related songs.

In title and theme, three of the tracks: 'In My Time Of Dyin', 'Fixin' To Die' and 'See That My Grave Is Kept Clean' would alone ensure that death's pallor hung over the album, but there is also much more contributed in this vein on the other tracks, as can be demonstrated by the following quotes studded throughout them.

The opening track, 'You're No Good' ends with the line: *"You give me the blues, I wanna lay down and die"*, 'Man of Constant Sorrow' contains, *"Perhaps I'll die upon that train/I'll see you on God's golden shore"* while 'Pretty Peggy-O' tells us that: *"Well, our captain he is dead, died for a maid. He's buried somewhere in Louisiana-O".* In 'Highway 51' we hear: *"And if I should die before my time should come/Won't you bury my body out on the Highway 51."* And on 'House of the Rising Sun': Dylan sings: *"I'm going back to New Orleans, my race is almost run/I'm going back to end my life down in the rising sun."*[2]

Added to the above, one of only two self-penned tracks on the album, 'Song To Woody' is a homage to the dying folksinger who was languishing in Greystone Park Psychiatric Hospital, where Dylan had visited him, in the final throes of his inevitably losing battle with Huntington's Chorea.

When albums followed, filled with Dylan's own lyrics, death did not leave the scene. His early songs concerning wars and the threat of nuclear destruction were necessarily filled with images of death, as were the personal stories of death through poverty and racism.

In the grimly comical post-nuclear scenario of 'World War III Blues', only two people are left alive. 'A Hard Rain's A-Gonna Fall' and 'Let Me Die in My Footsteps' were among his other responses to the threat of annihilation as the world held its breath over the USA and Soviet Union's acts of nuclear brinkmanship. Older wars are also covered and 'With God On Our Side' presents the story of the US as one of slaughter.

His 'civil rights songs' tell a sad story of blacks killed, including Emmett Till, Medgar Evers and Hattie Carroll. Additionally, the distraught farmer at the end of 'Ballad of Hollis Brown' is driven to kill his starving family and then himself while the un-named Hobo dies uncared for on the sidewalk in 'Only A Hobo'. The litany of the departed grew long in all directions. *"How many deaths will it take"*, 'Blowin' in the Wind' asked, before the realisation dawns that *"too many people have died."*

By the middle of the Sixties, Dylan was in a different space, but death was always in the air historically, personally and metaphorically. That turbulent decade was shattered by the assassinations of John and Robert Kennedy as well as Martin Luther King. As the decade progressed, so did the death toll from rioting and from that nightly horror show on the TV news, the Vietnam War.

Meanwhile, on a personal level, people either felt that Dylan was likely to be assassinated or that he was driving himself to an early grave with his workload and lifestyle. One of Dylan's 1965 backing musicians, Al Kooper, decided not to go on a leg of a tour because "we were scheduled to play Dallas. I thought: 'If that's what they did to JFK, can you imagine what they have in store for Dylan?' I'll just stay home'."

Anyone viewing the wasted mannequin figure in the film, *Eat The Document* on the 1966 world tour sees a man on the brink of self destruction. There was a widespread feeling that Dylan would not be around for long. Partner for a crucial period leading up to this time, Joan Baez said that: "Bobby may be on a death trip ... I always pictured Bobby with a skull and cross-bones on his head.[3]" And an unidentified Australian actress spoke of a widespread apprehension, in 1966, when she remarked that: "I came to believe that Dylan was Christ revisited ... communication with people was the truest, most honest and most Christ-like thing I've ever heard. I began to feel that Dylan was sacrificing himself in his whole philosophy, his thinking. That he would eventually die or that something horrible would happen to him. I felt it physically, I felt it strongly ... I know that other people felt that Dylan was Christ revisited, sacrificing himself. Adrian Rawlings came to that conclusion the same time I did. Other people felt it."[4] The martyred prophet is a role that Dylan has portrayed on numerous songs.

Christ was one of those who died young, with whom Dylan both identified and was identified with. Dylan was seen as being akin to one of those wild rebels who died from the 'rock 'n' roll lifestyle', a situation which could include film stars (James Dean), comedians (Lenny Bruce) and many musicians who pre-dated rock 'n' roll, such as Hank Williams. Back at the time this unnamed actress made her announcement, Dylan was following up on statements about 'lifelessness' being the big 'sin' and espousing both verbally and in his actions, that famous line from 'It's

Alright, Ma (I'm Only Bleeding)', "*He not busy being born, is busy dying*". For the Dylan of the classic mid-Sixties period, everything it seemed was about the struggle for individual survival in the face of concerted opposition from those who wished to take this away, be they lovers, racists, the over-thirties, the military-industrial complex or society at large.

When interviewed about him seemingly leaving folk music behind and in the face of accusations that he had 'killed it', Dylan responded with a passionate and insightful defence of the invulnerable form: "*It comes about from legends, Bibles, plagues, and it revolves around vegetables and death...*" he told Nat Hentoff in his 1966 interview with *Playboy* and then went on to describe traditional music as "*the one true, valid death you can feel today off a record player*".[5]

Dylan's later move into an overtly evangelical branch of fundamentalist Christianity, with its obvious focus on death and the afterlife, may have been intimately bound up with the same fear of death that Hamlet meditates on so eloquently and which Claudio brings so vividly to the listener's mind in *Measure For Measure*:

Ay, but to die, and go we know not where,
To lie in cold obstruction and to rot;
This sensible warm motion to become
A kneaded clod; and the delighted spirit
To bathe in fiery floods, or to reside
In thrilling region of thick-ribbed ice,
To be imprison'd in the viewless winds
And blown with restless violence round about
The pendent world, or to be worse than worst
Of those that lawless and incertain thought
Imagine howling; 'tis too horrible.
The weariest and most loathed worldly life
That age, ache, penury and imprisonment
Can lay on nature is a paradise
To what we fear of death.
(Act III, Scene i)

This was certainly the view of Howard Alk, the film-maker who had known Dylan since 1963 and had worked with him on three films, with the latest being 1978's *Renaldo and Clara*. Alk informed the late critic Paul Williams that he had missed this theme, fear of death, out of his otherwise excellent book, in response to Dylan's conversion, *Dylan – What Happened?*[6] Dylan certainly found the answer to his questions and his fear, if Alk was correct in his analysis of Dylan's state of mind, in the Christian Vineyard Fellowship. This was to be Saved, with the capital "S" very much intentional, and 'chosen' to be 'among the few' who would be raised to heaven after Judgement Day.[7]

The 1997 album *Time Out Of Mind* was released after, though written prior to, a brush with mortality for the singer himself when he contracted histoplasmosis whose symptoms range from being flu like to being life threatening. Dylan was seriously ill and, upon returning to public view from his recuperation, wryly remarked that: "I really thought I'd be seeing Elvis soon."

Death was very much on Dylan's mind on *Time Out Of Mind*, including one of its key songs, 'Not Dark Yet'. "*It's not dark yet, but it's getting there*" was a phrase that seemed to sum up much of the mood of the time. It harks back to the lines on 'Knocking On Heaven's Door', "*It's gettin' dark, too dark to see/I feel like I'm knockin' on heaven's door*", which in turn are recalled in another core track from *Time Out of Mind*, 'Tryin' To Get To Heaven' where the singer is "*Trying to get to heaven before they close the door*". By 2009's 'Forgetful Heart' things are sounding even more forlorn:

All night long
I lay awake and listen to the sound of pain
The door has closed forevermore
If indeed there ever was a door

The fascination with death that began with his first album continues throughout Dylan's career, up to and including his last, at my time of writing, self-penned album, 2012's *Tempest*, which has an alarmingly high body count.

Shakespeare's writing also features death throughout his work, starting from its very beginning. In Shakespeare's day, death was ever-present in both life and, consequently, the theatre. Disease, particularly the plague, regularly ravaged the population, as did famine. The knowledge of this led Elizabethan and Jacobean artists to stress the transience of life, and, therefore, characters in Shakespeare's plays are not only forever contemplating death; but also stressing how important it was to grasp what little experience of life that you might be given and to wring the most out of each passing day.

It was a period when mutilation, torture, executions, putrefying disease, rotting carcasses, human and otherwise, and starvations were all regularly to be witnessed. If you walked across Tower Bridge to the Globe, you would see heads on spikes on your way. You may even pass an actual execution in progress before you saw one on the stage; and, if so, you would struggle to decide which were the more theatrical. This was reflected in the audience's taste for extreme violence. Death was often staged in a particularly grisly fashion. On-stage deaths of all kinds were expected, if not demanded. A list of ways in which Shakespearean characters meet their ends would be very long. It would include poisonings, executions, stabbings and war deaths among its most recurrent and at the other end of the spectrum, the singular instances of such as being torn to pieces by rioters, being baked in a pie and served to your mother or, perhaps most famously of all, being eaten by a bear.

Actually, that list omits one other very popular method, that of self-killing. There are a considerable number of suicides in Shakespeare's plays. Suicides are inherently dramatically compelling. They take the artistic and philosophical concerns of certain plays to the very limits of what can be presented on stage.

You would expect Shakespeare's Histories and Tragedies to be filled with death, but it is highly significant that death is also featured throughout his comedies. Even when the death is not real, but only imagined, main characters spend much of the plays missing people that they think are dead and wishing that they were alive instead. Such wishes are often granted at the end of Act 5, in the earlier comedies. At the end of the early play, *Love's Labour's Lost*, though, we have a comedy with a very different ending. There the comic resolution is not attained; instead, it is, at best, postponed. This is due to the sudden intrusion of death, which brings the play to a shuddering conclusion and *"interrupt'st our merriment."* Biron's penitential task for the forthcoming year is to attempt to cheer up the sick and the dying with his wit. He first balks at this as being impossible before agreeing to *'jest a twelvemonth in a hospital'*. His initial reaction is to say:

To move wild laughter in the throat of death?

It cannot be, it is impossible.

Mirth cannot move a soul in agony.

(Act V Scene ii)

His quickly following acceptance is doubly apt in the play because 'moving wild laughter in the throat of death' is exactly what it and Shakespeare's other earlier comedies do. In the face of prevalent fatalities, causalities and with a common belief that the Apocalypse was relatively imminent, there is a fitting meta-theatricality here. Cast and audience alike are sharing joy despite wars, plagues and the habitual loss of life that surround them, and are trying to capture the good times while they can. Palfrey and Smith have commented insightfully on this aspect:

"...death is the spur to life, the necessary counter that gives tension and energy to the action. Death provides a formal frame establishing the boundaries of the game. Without it the action would be lax, there would be too much choice, too much time, like tennis without a net. It gives the story and jokes their compulsion, edge and timing. Comedy must always be up against it, harried and pressed and working in tiny circles, the threat of loss or failure ever present. The clock is running out on festivity."[8]

Clocks are always running out, and endings are forever getting closer. Dylan sings, on "Cross The Green Mountain':

I look into the eyes

Of my merciful friend

And then I ask myself

Is this the end?[9]

That question, and the worry about what may lie on the other side of death, is a perennial one in both Shakespeare and in Dylan's work. Both the idea of personal salvation or damnation and, by extension for all humankind, feature throughout both writers' careers. The envisaged Apocalypse or "the promised end" as the loyal Kent puts it in *King Lear* when the old King enters with Cordelia dead in his arms. Dylan, too, is intensely concerned with endings and their finality or not, as phrases such as "the finishing end", and "the final end" attest. However, it is 'The End', itself, that most concerns him and not only in his evangelising period. Eschatological matters not only predate Dylan's 'born again' period but have been present from the very beginning of his song writing and have remained a theme throughout his entire career.

Dylan sounds quite gleeful while imagining others facing the judgement of their eternal souls as he sings the early songs, 'I'd Hate To Be You On That Dreadful Day' and 'Whatcha Gonna Do', and yet, the same questions he posed there come back to haunt him regularly until he 'meets his Maker' and is "*Saved/By the blood of the lamb*" as he sings on the title track of his 1980 album *Saved*, whose original cover showed a hand descending from Heaven to select the few Elect among the many damned. "*I don't deserve it, but I sure did make it through*" sings an exultantly relieved Dylan, on 'What Can I Do For You' from the same album.

Dylan's reading of *The Bible* is a frankly literal one, as he has made clear in numerous interview comments such as this one from 1984:

> "*Sure, I believe in it. I believe that ever since Adam and Eve got thrown out of the garden, that the whole nature of the planet has been heading in one direction – towards apocalypse. It's all there in the book of Revelation, but it's difficult talking about these things to most people because most people don't know what you're talking about, or don't want to listen.*" [10]

***

The date of that quote is relevant as many, probably a majority, prefer to dismiss Dylan's Christian faith as merely 'a phase' that only lasts from, approximately, 1979 to 1981. His faith continued, however, as Dylan has made clear, time after time in the years since then. How, one wonders, whatever one's own beliefs, could such a thing as being visited by Jesus, which Dylan clearly felt is what happened to him, be the instigator of just 'a phase'. That experience profoundly affected and altered Dylan. As he put it in a 1980 interview with Karen Hughes: *"Jesus put his hand on me. It was a physical thing. I felt it all over me. I felt my whole body tremble. The glory of the Lord knocked me down and picked me up. Being born again is a hard thing. You ever seen a mother give birth to a child? Well it's painful. We don't like to lose those old attitudes and hang-ups."*[11] And, as he expounded in the same year to Robert Hilburn, *"Most of the people I know don't believe that Jesus was resurrected, that He is alive. It's like He was just another prophet or something, one of many good people. That's not the way it was any longer for me."* Furthermore, in answer to Hilburn's question of why Dylan had played no songs from before 1979 on his tour of that year: *"I truly had a born-again experience, if you want to call it that. It's an overused term, but it's something that people can relate to. It happened in 1978. I always knew there was a God or a creator of the universe and a creator of the mountains and the sea and all that kind of thing, but I wasn't conscious of Jesus and what that had to do with the Supreme Creator."*[12]

There was a period where Dylan played no concerts on a Sunday and it has often been pointed out that when Dylan has played 'Masters of War' since 1979, he has not included the sixth verse. That stanza contains the line *"even Jesus would never forgive what you do"*, a comment that would be doctrinally inadmissible to a believer in Christ. It is never commented that Dylan did not play this verse, nor the ones mentioning 'Judas' and 'soul' during his World Tour of 1978, either, so the reasons behind such decisions may sometimes be performance related rather than anything else. As is customary, multiple interpretations can present themselves. Dylan, however, was crystal clear on what Christianity and Christ mean to him. The Karen Hughes interview above found him laying it out in very specific terms:

"Christianity is not Christ and Christ is not Christianity. Christianity is making Christ the Lord of your life. You're talking about your life now, you're not talking about just part of it, you're not talking about a certain hour every day. You're talking about making Christ the Lord and the Master of your life, the King of your life. And you're also talking about Christ, the resurrected Christ, you're not talking about some dead man who had a bunch of good ideas and was nailed to a tree. Who died with those ideas. You're talking about a resurrected Christ who is Lord of your life. We're talking about that type of Christianity".."It's HIM through YOU. 'He's alive', Paul said, 'I've

been crucified with Christ, nevertheless I live. Yet not I but Christ who liveth in me'."

There have been many testaments to Dylan's continuing belief in Christ as the Saviour in numerous interviews and in the lyrics to his songs. Additionally, Dylan made very specific choices for cover songs in his concerts at the end of last century and the beginning of this one, with one of them usually the opening song in the set-list. These traditional readings of the Gospels included: 'I Am The Man, Thomas', 'Hallelujah, I'm Ready To Go', and Roy Acuff's 'This World Can't Stand Long' with its intimations of imminent Judgement Day: "A long time this world has stood/It gets more wicked every day/The maker who created it/Will never let it stand this way."

These, and other similar songs were performed as set openers while we also got to hear 'Rock of Ages' and 'A Satisfied Mind', all hymns with particular and pointed Christian messages. Dylan also used these as the basis for his own writing. As he remarked to Robert Hilburn, in 2004: *"My songs are either based on old Protestant hymns or Carter Family songs or variations of the blues form."*[13] People who dismiss these covers as evidence of continuing faith in Christ presumably think that the content of these cover choices is irrelevant and that Dylan chose a consistent set of songs at random. It was always quite clear, as the twentieth century gave way to the twenty-first, what Dylan was nightly testifying to, as yet another opener, 'Somebody Touched Me', put it: "Glory glory glory somebody touched me/ Must've been the hand of the Lord". This imperative conclusion chimes very much with Dylan's comments, in various interviews, regarding his experience. In the Hilburn 1980 one for example, Dylan's description stressed that: *"There was a presence in the room that couldn't have been anybody but Jesus."*

Additionally, there is one of his songs from the *Saved* album that Dylan has much played, loved and praised, 'In the Garden'. In the sixteen years after its 1979 live debut, Dylan played it 328 times and brought it out again for a concert in 2002. The song is based on the Gospel accounts of Jesus in the garden at Gethsemane and its drumming, rhetorical questions build up an intense pressure over classical sounding chords. Clinton Heylin said its persistence in the set-lists, long after people claimed Dylan had turned away from Christianity, as evidence that Dylan had not done so: "Unless Dylan is the most appalling hypocrite, I do not see how an apostate can sing that song."[14]

Quite so, and the song was self-evidently of prime importance to Dylan not only during the evangelising tours but also after it. It featured as the show closer in his 1986 tour[15], the place normally reserved for a 'greatest hits' rock-out crowd-pleaser such as 'Like A Rolling Stone'. Dylan prefaced 'In The Garden' with a sharp message to his audience:

> "All right. Yeah, we gonna get out of here now. Yeah. We got to go. It's way past my bedtime, I don't know about you. Anyway we always sing this last song here. It's about my hero. Everybody's got a hero. Some people got a hero, lots of different heroes. Money is a hero, success is a hero. To lots of people Michael Jackson's a hero. Bruce Springsteen, John Wayne, everybody's got a hero. Shut up you! Well, I wanna sing about my hero, I don't care about those heroes. I have my own hero."

Two years later he was still introducing it with barbed messages for those he knew did not want to hear what he was saying. At the Tower Theatre, Upper Darby in Pennsylvania on October 14, 1988, Dylan remarked by way of prefacing the song:

"You know an Amnesty Tour's going on, and I was very honoured that last year they chose a Bob Dylan song to be their theme song, 'I Shall Be Released'. This year they surprised me again by doin' another Bob Dylan song as their theme song, they used 'Chimes of Freedom'. Next year the Amnesty Tour, I think they're gonna use 'Jokerman'. Anyway, I'm trying to get them to change their mind. Trying to get them to use this one!" He repeated a similar introduction to the song for the following three nights, which brought the 1988 tour to its conclusion.

Paul Williams, in his book *Dylan – What Happened?*, which Dylan ordered copies of to give to friends, described a concert at San Francisco as being like "a stage production, carefully planned and orchestrated". Williams added that Dylan "climaxes the show with a musical enactment of (what else?) scenes from the life of Christ". Following on from a musical description of "In The Garden", he continued by proposing, intriguingly from this book's perspective, that, "It all reaches back to the mystery plays of the middle ages, the religious dramas that are the starting point of modern theater."

RELIGION

After Dylan recorded an album of Christmas songs in 2009, Bill Flanagan remarked to Dylan, in an interview that Dylan sang 'O Little Town Of Bethlehem', 'like a true believer'. Dylan's reply: "Well, I am a true believer" should have come as no surprise. Six years later, in his MusiCares' award acceptance speech Dylan yet again made his position crystal clear:

"The Blackwood Bros. have been talking to me about making a record together. That might confound expectations, but it shouldn't. Of course it would be a gospel album. I don't think it would be anything out of the ordinary for me. Not a bit. One of the songs I'm thinking about singing is "Stand By Me" by the Blackwood Brothers. Not "Stand By Me" the pop song. No. The real "Stand By Me. The real one goes like this: "When the storm of life is raging / Stand by me / When the storm of life is raging / Stand by me / When the world is tossing me / Like a ship upon the sea / Thou who rulest wind and water / Stand by me"

Dylan recited the whole song and then added: *"That's the song. I like it better than the pop song. If I record one by that name, that's going to be the one."*

Given the above, it is surprising that there has been such a lot of controversy over Dylan's beliefs. This stems from his re-awakened interest in Judaism from the early Eighties onwards and the popular and partisan views that you have to be 'one or the other'. Whatever the precise nature of his personal beliefs during the Eighties, Dylan undoubtedly demonstrated a renewed interest in Judaism. This has been credited to family pressures, the arguments of the Jewish scholars and leaders he was urged to meet, and presumably his inherently questioning nature.

Reputedly disillusioned by infighting and personal promotion within certain Christian churches[16], Dylan backed off from overt evangelising and distanced himself from the Born Again label. As a man who hated labels this was not too surprising, but although it was delivered with a degree of reluctance, his 1984 comment to *Rolling Stone*'s Kurt Loder, *"I've never said I'm born again"* is somewhat contradicted by the quotes above. A number of connections with his Jewish heritage began to be noticed. Pressure had been brought to bear by Dylan's family for him to listen to Jewish leaders and thinkers. His friendship with the ever rebellious Allen Ginsberg remained strong, in spite of Ginsberg being the antithesis of all the Vineyard Fellowship believes in, and Ginsberg introduced Dylan to a Rabbi with whom Dylan reportedly spent some time. Dylan was seen at Jewish feasts, attending synagogues and a spirited defence of Israel appears on 1984's *Infidels* album on the track "Neighbourhood Bully". Dylan appeared on the fund-raising Chabad Telethon in 1989 and 1991 live on TV. On the first of these appearances, Dylan sported a yarmulke and sang a traditional Jewish song that he had made the topic of a comic talking blues number over a quarter of a century earlier, "Hava Nagila". At the latter, he implored the audience to: *"give plenty of money to Chabad. It's my favourite organization in the world. Really, they do nothing but good things with the money. The more you give, the more it will help everybody"*.

None of this, however, meant that he had stopped believing in Christ. As in the organisation "Jews for Jesus", Dylan seemed perfectly able now to balance the two faiths. He has studied Jewish and Biblical texts, and has refused, much like he did back in the early Sixties' folk scene, to be drawn into sectional infighting and, it looks from the outside, at any rate, moved from being the property of one clique and gone on to forge his own path. The interview with Loder continued in the following vein:

KL What is your spiritual stance, then?

BD: *Well, I don't think that this is it, you know – this life ain't nothin'. There's no way you're gonna convince me this is all there is to it. I never, ever believed that. I believe in the Book of Revelation. The leaders of this world are eventually going to play God, if they're not already playing God, and eventually a man will come that everybody will think is God. He'll do things, and they'll say, "Well, only God can do those things. It must be him."*

KL: You're a literal believer of the Bible?

BD: *Yeah. Sure, yeah. I am.*

KL: Are the Old and New Testaments equally valid?

BD: *To me.*

KL: Do you belong to any church or synagogue?

BD: *Not really. Uh, the Church of the Poison Mind [laughs].*[17]

Membership of a specific church may not have remained constant, but it is evident that Dylan's belief in Jesus has never wavered and nor does he see this as contradictory to other things he has said and done in those decades. In his 1965 opus 'Desolation Row' people were crying out *"Which side are you on?"* and they are crying it out to Dylan still, albeit in a different context. You imagine that Dylan's answer would be: 'neither and all' and that he would wish, as always to be free from that thinking and at liberty to believe simultaneously that the Jews are the Chosen People and that Jesus, a Jew himself, was and is the Messiah.

As a final example of what we can know amid the speculation, claims and counter claims, we can note Dylan's comments in his *Rolling Stone* interview, in 2012, when he said:

> *"These are the same people that tried to pin the name Judas on me. Judas, the most hated name in human history! If you think you've been called a bad name, try to work your way out from under that. Yeah, and for what? For playing an electric guitar? As if that is in some kind of way equitable to betraying our Lord and delivering him up to be crucified. All those evil motherfuckers can rot in hell."*

Despite the distinct lack of Christian forgiveness on show, that *"our"* is surely crucial.

The Merchant of Venice

We have all these interview comments from throughout his life from Dylan but we have none from Shakespeare. Even if interviews were available, Shakespeare lived at a time when one was cautious to the point of reticence or subterfuge in regard to one's beliefs, on pain of death.

We do have a play from Shakespeare that looks at the Christian-Judaic divide, however. Here was a religious topic he could explore without straying into the minefield of the sectarian conflicts surrounding him. Jews were suddenly box-office despite being rarely seen in England following earlier persecution and banishment. This came about due to the enormous popularity of Marlowe's *The Jew of Malta* and the, quite likely manufactured, hysteria over the Jewish origins of the Queen's doctor, a converted Christian by now, found guilty of attempting to poison her.

Shakespeare's *The Merchant of Venice* is a difficult play for directors and audiences in the modern world. It has become inevitably altered and forever shadowed by the horrors of the attempted genocide of Jews around eighty years ago. After centuries of persecution and pogroms, the abhorrent disgrace of 'The Final Solution' placed the Christian-Jewish dynamic in an unforgiving light that should never be dimmed.

After this, Shylock took over the play and turned it from comedy to tragedy. No longer could we put on stage a caricature villain of black-hearted enmity to Christianity whose overwhelming love of lucre was the only character trait that was stressed. This was how the Nazis saw the character and why this was their favourite Shakespeare play. It was played purely as anti-Semitic and, as such, was most likely much closer to how the Elizabethan audiences probably viewed it than we seem willing to admit. In Shakespeare's time, in this folk infused play, a Princess is a fairy-tale Princess and a Jew is a figure to laugh at, ridicule and scorn.

While our sympathetic portrayals of Shylock are clearly more necessary now than ever, and it is to Shakespeare's great credit that his multi-viewpoint text means they are possible, our modern post-Holocaust productions would surely puzzle Shakespeare. After World War I a similar thing happened with *Henry V*. It was felt after the horrors of that war that it would be wrong to portray it as a glorious tale of war and conquest in French fields. *Henry V* was reinvented as a play that was protesting for peace and against war. Similarly after World War II and its attendant atrocities, *The Merchant of Venice* became a play protesting against the victimisation of Jews by Christians. In both cases the play in question is recast in a way which is demanded, out of sheer decency, by the historical situation in which they find themselves.

One reason it is possible to convincingly stage Shakespeare in different ways in different historical periods is related to the uses of paradox and ambiguity which we look at in Wordplay. Paradox writ large, as it were. The questioning nature of his art provides us with the ability to always see things from different points of view. Like Dylan, like all bards, he, in Whitman's words 'contains multitudes' and all their attendant attitudes. Problems, concepts and controversies can be posed without dogmatic stances being ascertained or personal convictions revealed.

Such attributes allowed Shakespeare to discuss religious questions without anyone being able to pin him down on a particular point or charge him with any specific offense.

***

Inevitably, given all of the preceding comments on their religious backgrounds and biblical allusions they form a core of symbolism that runs throughout both Shakespeare and Dylan's work.

With Dylan, there remains a mistaken apprehension that such tropes entered his work only in the late Seventies, along with his conversion experience. On the contrary, they are in evidence from his earliest songs at the start of the Sixties and all the way through to 1978. Clearly, the albums of 1979 and 1980 consisted entirely of biblical lines and messages, but you can also find them recurrently in his prior lyrics, going all the way back to his first batches of live performances and demo songs.

One of the most striking, in the light of later developments, was 'Long Ago, Far Away' where Dylan's seeming self-identification with Christ received, perhaps, its first expression:

To preach of peace and brotherhood
Oh, what might be the cost!
A man he did it long ago
And they hung him on a cross

In 'Long Time Gone' Dylan comes close to quoting *Amos 7:14*, "I was no prophet, neither was I a prophet's son" when he sang: *"But I know I ain't no prophet/An' I ain't no prophet's son"*.

Even a fun song such as 'All Over You' has references to *"Little David when he picked up his pebbles/Even Sampson after he went blind"* in Dylan's comic tale of waiting for his chance with his girl.

In the years that followed, Dylan continued to use the biblical allusions, proverbs and stories in his songs. Including the dramatic conclusion to 1963's 'When The Ship Comes In':

And like Pharoah's tribe

They'll be drownded in the tide
And like Goliath, they'll be conquered

By 1965, no longer the prince of the protest movement, Dylan was the coolest star in the rock firmament. Notwithstanding this, he sang of 'Gates of Eden' on 1965's *Bringing it All Back Home* and on the same year's *Highway 61 Revisited*, the title track's opening verse retells a famous biblical passage in modern street language: *"Oh God said to Abraham, "Kill me a son" / Abe says, "Man, you must be puttin' me on""*

So suffused with biblical imagery, especially from *Isaiah* was the 1968 album, *John Wesley Harding*, that Robin Witting wrote a study of it entitled, *Isaiah On Guitar*. It was this same year that Dylan's mother visited him at his Woodstock retreat. She recalled that: "... there's a huge Bible open on a stand in the middle of his study. Of all the books that crowd his house ... that Bible gets the most attention, he's continually getting up and going over to refer to something" [18] As his attention to the Bible increased, so its symbolism seeped further into his writing. Around this same time, Noel Paul Stookey, of Peter Paul and Mary, the first group to have a hit with a Dylan song ('Blowin' in the Wind'), was having some trouble visualising what the true meaning of his life was or should be. Noel thought Dylan was so insightful that he should seek his advice. He travelled to Woodstock to do so, and Dylan suggested that Noel revisit the haunts of his youth and that he should read through the Bible. This is exactly what anecdotal evidence and Dylan's forthcoming albums, *New Morning* and *Planet Waves* indicate that Dylan was doing himself. Paul Stookey, incidentally, became a committed, practising Christian shortly afterwards, in 1968.

New Morning was an interesting case as it could have been taken as 'coming out' in religious terms but was never treated as such despite its title and the closing songs, 'Three Angels' and 'Father of Night'.[19] 1975's *Blood On the Tracks*, written in 1974, contained Dylan's most extraordinary Christ-identification song where he, or the narrator of the song at least, sings: *"In a little hilltop village, they gambled for my clothes/I bargained for salvation an' they gave me a lethal dose"* In retrospect, the album immediately prior to Dylan's encounter with the figure he takes to have been Christ, *Street Legal* can been heard to contain clear intimations of the coming Christian conversion.[20]

Dylan's albums immediately following that conversion experience were explicitly proselytising and the Biblical imagery, which had always been prevalent in his work prior to that, inevitably has become even more prevalent in the decades following it. Biblical stories, metaphors, proverbs and language stand as an ever-present backdrop to his work as it always had for Shakespeare and Shakespeare's original audiences.

Shakespeare's symbolism and themes often stem from Christian sources. There are far too many to quote from here, as over two thousand biblical allusions have been discovered in Shakespeare's plays. These can range from common sayings, proverbs and allusions to universally known stories, or the deep and intricate weaving of a Biblical backdrop to a scene he is creating that gives the action added resonance and gravitas. Shakespeare would have started off mainly using *The Bishop's Bible* but for the bulk of his career would have been immersed in the popular and dynamic, 1560 *Geneva Bible*. In 1611 the *King James Bible* came out and was promoted, with the Geneva being suppressed because its popularity did not wane. *The Geneva Bible* informed the *King James Version*, which is Dylan's most favoured, though not sole, version of choice. *The Geneva Bible*, as well as being the basis for the biblical language of John Bunyan's *The Pilgrim's Progress*, informed the work of Shakespearean contemporaries such as John Donne, as well as Shakespeare himself. All of these, in turn, influence Dylan's language. Linguistic connections are at the heart of these artists' works even with their emphasis on performance, but for many commentators it is presumed religious links from their lives to that art take precedence.

***

As with certain other critical approaches, the experience of interacting with the art tends to be subsumed into either dogma or an attempt to read biographical, spiritual, authorial intent and to change that experience into a message. Perhaps unsurprisingly it is also an area where impartiality is rarely found. Attempts to label Shakespeare a Protestant or a Catholic and Dylan a Christian or a Jew mostly turn out to be exercises in 'claiming him for our side.' Once the claim is made the play and lyric scripts that are meant to come alive in performance, are pored over in a search for reasons to read these claims back into the text. In such exercises, the qualities of the performances and the art involved in creating them, and moving us, are bypassed in favour of agenda-driven investigations with an emphasis on authorial intent, which is a matter of guesswork, bias and conjecture from those proposing such a thing. Shakespeare's life-story is then invented by reading backwards from his work. This is a path so fraught with dangers as to be instantly recognisable as an impassable one. Notwithstanding these clear "Dead-End" signs, drivers still progress down this road in large numbers believing there is a way through to their imagined destination.

This particular example is further confounded because Shakespeare could not have avoided being influenced, no matter what camp he was in, by the others. Even as a Protestant, let alone an atheist, the Catholic religious tradition that Protestants had eagerly, or grudgingly, shuffled off was embedded in the nation's psyche. At the same time, Catholicism is more showy, more theatrical and symbolic. Crudely put, it stages better, which is why TV and Hollywood so often use priests even when the flock of the relevant production is more likely to be Protestant, hence the priest, Father Mulcahy, in the long-running TV series *MASH*, for example.

The country had been Catholic recently enough for the language still to be infused with its associated terminology. As a result, characters in Shakespeare's plays use Catholic terms and refer to Catholic rituals. Additionally, in a post-Reformation state, such language and customs can be used as a distancing effect. They immediately historicise the action and place it at a safe distance from everyday political reality the play may really be addressing.

These factors aid those pro-Catholic writers, who have been particularly vocal in recent times, in endeavouring to 'claim Shakespeare as one of our own'. They begin from the solid foundation of Shakespeare's mother belonging to a traditionally strong Catholic family from Warwickshire and build from there. The edifice then constructed becomes so expansive that I once watched a TV documentary where the case for this culminated in a dramatic holding aloft of a book, claimed disingenuously as 'this book' as though it were that very one, of spiritual testament to the old faith, that Shakespeare's father had left hidden in the house in Henley Street, Stratford, and which was later found in the mid-eighteenth century by workmen. If Shakespeare's father's alleged illiteracy is true, then a signed version seems impossible, but the theory went that his 'cross marked the spot' and sealed the claim that all the Shakespeare family members were adherent to Catholicism. All the leaps of assumption inherent in that string of 'logic', aside, the book was potentially an exciting find regarding his father's convictions. Edmund Malone saw this document and was initially excited by it, though he was later to come to the conclusion shared by most modern scholars, that is, the whole thing was almost certainly a hoax. It has never been tested, as it conveniently disappeared when doubts were raised. Colin Burrow picked up on this some years ago:

"There is at present a large industry surrounding this ... together with the belief that Shakespeare was a Catholic, which is often supported by the apparent discovery in 1757 of a will in the roof space of John Shakespeare's house in Henley Street. This followed a Catholic formulary by Cardinal Borromeo, and was signed by Shakespeare's father. Malone transcribed the will, but then it vanished. No one knows if it was forged or real, and Malone publicly expressed doubts about its authenticity in 1796. Shakespeare may or may not have been Catholic, but generally if a document that sounds too good to be true is found exactly where you'd hope to find it and then goes missing in mysterious circumstances it is indeed too good to be true."[21]

One of the problems with such over enthusiastic 'deductions' is that once the misrepresentation becomes clear, you automatically begin to doubt everything that is claimed in the same argument. Other sides of the same debate over Shakespeare's beliefs can also be guilty of the same tunnel vision and much previous writing on the subject, drew quite the opposite conclusions.

This is because the few facts we have are open to different interpretation or are contradictory in nature. Much, for example, is made of Shakespeare's daughter Susanna still refusing to take Protestant communion even after the failed gunpowder plot of 1605. This apparently very brave action is taken as an expression of one of Shakespeare's closest tenaciously clinging on to the Catholic faith. Were the father's testament accepted as fact despite the numerous reasons to doubt it, then Susanna's actions become part of an overall case for complete family conviction in the old beliefs. Yet, not only can the 'testament' just be accepted as fact only because it fits a pre-determined narrative, but Susanna herself married the physician John Hall in 1607. John Hall was not only a Protestant but one strong enough in that to have been referred to as a Puritan, and a staunch supporter of the local Puritan vicar who was enduring vigorous opposition.

Shakespeare appeared to be friendly with Hall, as far as we can tell. We know, for instance, they worked together on the same side in the local Stratford debates over land enclosures, and there is a record of them travelling together. Certainly, there is no record of Shakespeare being in any way against the marriage nor that Susanna marrying a Protestant was anything but positive. One imagines that, coming two years after the gunpowder plot was foiled and so many of its instigators found to have a Staffordshire connection, it was a prudent move. Whether Shakespeare's support for the marriage came out of fatherly care for her safety, personal inclination, or lack of denominational concern, we shall never know for certain. The first would seem the most reasonable to assume with any degree of confidence.

As a woman of her time, Susanna would be expected to follow her father's instructions on such matters. However, in the 'dedicated to her faith in the face of all external pressures' biography of her, she had withstood the dictates of the Crown and State and risked heavy punishment in refusing the Protestant Communion, and therefore there is a seeming contradiction between these stories. Or at least there is from our perspective but from an Elizabethan and Jacobean perspective perhaps there is not. Outwith matters of statehood, people had become very used to the two different expressions of Christianity living side by side.

Partly this is because it was sensible to play both sides. Shakespeare clearly was canny enough to do this as well as artistically inclined, as Dylan is, to raise questions and look at topics from multiple viewpoints. Catholic rulers had killed Protestants in gruesome fashion before Protestants took power and did the same to Catholics. No-one knew what denomination the next rulers would be. The sensible approach would clearly be to keep your head down, nose clean and your ears on the side of your head, rather than sliced off in punishment for any perceived infractions.

Even some priests, far less playwrights, were known to move from being Catholic to Protestant and were probably ready to go back again if need be. They, too, 'rolled with the times' which comes as quite a refreshing thought when compared to the wars, murders and tortures ostensibly waged in the name of one confession or another of the same religion.

In daily life, it was probably difficult to know what anyone then was thinking, as not only was it wise to keep your own counsel and muddy your own tracks, but, to add to the confusion, conspiracy theories were as happily and illogically embraced in those days as they are in our own. It was thought by some, for one example of this, that Christopher Marlowe was killed on the instructions Elizabeth's spy service because his plays were written to secretly promote Catholic ideology. This is the same Marlowe who was regarded by others as a notorious atheist, and those same plays which were decried by certain Catholics for being 'anti-Catholic' propaganda. To be fair, with Marlowe you can feel that virtually anything was possible, and, consequently, I quote this only as an example of the mixed signals we receive from the time.

The eponymous hero of *Hamlet* and the play as a whole are examples of where the author has been claimed to be supporting both Catholicism and Protestantism by divergent commentators. What we get in the play is a beguiling mixture which is a reasonable reflection on the times. It is surely no coincidence that Hamlet studies at Wittenberg, famed for its associations with Martin Luther. When Hamlet conducts his famous monologue meditating on death, he does so in distinctly Protestant tones.[22] Hamlet's father, on the other hand, could hardly be more classically Catholic, suffering as he is in Purgatory because his sins were not cleansed prior to his murder.

As Stephen Greenblatt put it: "Shakespeare's plays provide ample evidence for doubleness and more: at certain moments – Hamlet is the greatest example – he seems at once Catholic, Protestant and deeply skeptical of both."[23]

Shakespeare's writing, overall, is remarkably free from any set doctrinal message. The characters in *King Lear* call out to all manner of Gods, be they pagan, Classical or Christian and the overall tone is one of comic cosmic absurdity and universal, existentialist angst. It is no surprise that Gloucester's line from Act 4 Scene 1, is so often quoted to sum up the play's ambience: "*As flies to wanton boys are we to th' gods. They kill us for their sport.*" George Orwell noted that:

"The morality of Shakespeare's later tragedies is not religious in the ordinary sense, and certainly is not Christian. Only two of them, Hamlet and Othello, are supposedly occurring inside the Christian era, and even in those, apart from the antics of the ghost in Hamlet, there is no indication of a 'next world' where everything is to be put right.... We do not know a great deal about Shakespeare's religious beliefs, and from the evidence of his writings it would be difficult to prove that he had any."[24]

***

Syncretism, the merging of divergent beliefs, was perhaps a natural development for our two writers, with both being masters of paradox, as we see in their thought and wordplay,. Certainly, it was a necessary way of life for Shakespeare, depending on whom he was talking to and where he was at any given moment and for Dylan, coming from a Jewish family and later having 'a truly born again experience' it is a way of marrying the two faiths of his life.

Listening to songs and watching plays is enjoyable and fulfilling. There is a danger when one turns to analysing the content that the rational mode of thinking necessary for this can lead you to forget the pleasure and particular insights that live performances give you. Religious interpretations have the added difficulty that they bring with them scriptural direction and moral concepts that are laid down in advance of the artistic performance being experienced. In the years when Dylan was actively and directly evangelising, the two certainly came together, and it can be argued in both artists' cases that they come together at other times, too. However, it is a particularly difficult route of critical interpretation given that by its nature it has to impose a fixed reading on dynamic art and one that accords with factors outside reception of the art itself.

In Shakespeare's case, this is all linked to the misconception that fuels the lucrative Bard biography industry. This contends that if we knew the person, then a magic key to understanding (as in, 'explaining away') his art would be ours. This is an illusion and a particularly foolish one to adhere to in a case when so little is known of the person in question. For all that we know so much more about Dylan, it is still illusory to think that we know him now, or ever could, in a way that would 'explain' his art as though it were a puzzle seeking a solution.

The joy is in what the writers open us up to while often using Biblical imagery; the alternative vistas they present to our minds the questions they make us ask, while, never let it be forgotten, entertaining us as they do so.

NOTES

1 In Jon Pareles *A Wiser Voice Blowin' In The Autumn Wind* New York Times, Sept. 27, 1997 as one example

2 Bob Dylan album, *Bob Dylan*, 1962 https://www.bobdylan.com/albums/bob-dylan/

3 Anthony Scaduto: *Bob Dylan*, W.H. Allen & Co. Ltd. 1972. Reprinted 1996, Helter Skelter Publishing, London

4 *Ibid.*

5 Nat Hentoff, *Playboy interview*, 1966.

6 Paul Williams, *Dylan – What Happened?* Entwhistle Books, 1980

7 Alk himself faced death a few years later and passed away from a heroin overdose that was deemed accidental by the coroner but many, including Alk's first and second wives, contend he committed suicide

8 Simon Palfrey and Emma Smith *Shakespeare's Dead*, The Bodleian Library 22 April 2016

9 https://www.bobdylan.com/songs/cross-green-mountain/ No information as of August 25, 2018

10 Mick Brown "DYLAN 'Jesus, who's got time to keep up with the times?'" *Sunday Times*, July 1, 1984

11 Karen Hughes Interview, Dayton, Ohio, May 21, 1980 (printed in the New Zealand newspapers *The Star* on 10 July 1980 and *The Dominion* on August 2 1980 and is widely available online.

12 Robert Hilburn, *Bob Dylan's Song of Salvation Los Angeles Times* November 24, 1980

13 Robert Hilburn, *Rock's Enigmatic Poet Opens a Long-Private Door Los Angeles Times* April 4th 2004

14 This was mentioned by Heylin in various talks and in conversation with Derek Barker, editor of *ISIS* magazine, who reported it there

15 It was moved out of sequence for the video recording, *Hard To Handle*, though it was still in a "prime" slot as it was placed there as the opener

16 This was foreshadowed, a decade earlier, when Dylan had been put off by the behaviour of organisation of Jewish groups according to Antony Scaduto's 1972 biography.

17 Kurt Loder, Bob Dylan Interview *Rolling Stone* June 21, 1984

18 Toby Thompson, *Positively Main Street* Coward-McCann, New York, 1971

19 This was perhaps because some of the songs were originally intended for an Archibald MacLeish play. Though, on the other hand, this was rarely mentioned in reviews and the album is

generally taken as a statement from Dylan himself.

20 There have been two studies of the Bible in Dylan's lyrics: *Tangled Up in the Bible* by Michael J. Gilmour and *The Bible in the Lyrics of Bob Dylan* by Bert Cartwright

21 Colin Burrow, *Who wouldn't buy it?* (on Stephen Greenblatt's *Will in the Word*) London Review of Books Vol. 27 No. 2, January 20, 2005

22 Or at least he does in the Folio version; whereas, interestingly, in the first quarto, whether in Shakespeare's words or not we cannot be sure, the verse takes on a Catholic hue

23 Stephen Greenblatt, *Will in the World: How Shakespeare Became Shakespeare* W. W. Norton & Company, May 3, 2010

24 George Orwell, *Lear, Tolstoy and the Fool*, 1947. Reprinted in *King Lear: Crirical Essays*, edited by Kenneth Muir

Chapter Six

SHAKESPEARE IN DYLAN

Dragon clouds so high above

The bulk of this book concerns parallels between Shakespeare and Dylan but the following two chapters, instead, investigate those moments when their work intersects. Firstly, when Shakespeare appears in Dylan's work and then when Dylan's songs are used in productions of Shakespeare's plays.

Shakespeare references, from the passing allusion, embedded quotation, or resonant echo occur throughout Dylan's lyrics, prose and film scripts. Prior to looking at these, it is worth reiterating that Shakespeare and Dylan have much 'source material' in common because they share significant cultural backdrops to their lives and works. Moreover, Dylan studied Shakespeare at school as well as many later poets, themselves inevitably influenced by Shakespeare. Consequently, when you hear an echo between the two in their words, there is always the possibility of a common source such as the *King James Bible*, the *Book of Common Prayer*, nursery rhymes, the classics, and the balladeers who preceded both. There are other writers in common, too, from the Classical age and from closer to Shakespeare's own time.

Printing of quarto versions of Shakespeare's plays took place alongside those of traditional ballads many of which Dylan has sung in one form or another, referenced in his songs and used as the basis for his own work. Furthermore, so popular were these traditional songs that new ones were written, again including a number that Dylan has sung over the years, including 'The Golden Vanity,' 'Barbara Allen' and 'The Roving Blade'. The term used for them was 'broadside ballads', and this is where the mimeographed magazine in the early Sixties New York folk world got its name. Lyrics and music to topical songs were disseminated in *Broadside*, with Dylan the star contributor. It would be here that songs like 'Masters of War' would first appear with the lyrics and music accompanied by small drawings. The language of these Elizabethan ballads had crossed the ocean with the songs and was absorbed into Dylan's linguistic core as part of the direct link from Elizabethan broadside ballads to the *Broadside* ballads in the magazine of that name.

Even lines and phrases in Dylan, which we take to be from the folk and blues, can be found in Shakespeare despite sounding relatively modern. "Kill me dead" is a tautology that worries some critics, but Dylan, before writing his own version, sang it early (and later) in his career as part of 'Cocaine Blues'. It appears straight, as those three words, in Shakespeare's *Titus Andronicus* and in variants elsewhere, most notably, given Dylan's frequent recourse to that seminal play, in *Hamlet*.[1] We will be looking at the language of Dylan's *Tempest* in detail in the final chapter, but it is fitting here to quote one of Anne Margaret Daniel's notes on 'Early Roman Kings': "That 'Gonna shake 'em all down' sounds contemporary, or at least twentieth century; automatically, we associate shakedown with the Grateful Dead, yet, it too is Shakespeare's. Merriam-Webster lists its first use in 1859, but Shakespeare riffed on it in *Coriolanus*."[2] A connection which immediately made me think of the line *"I been to Sugar Town, I shook the sugar down"* in Dylan's 'Tryin' To Get To Heaven'.

The classics are discussed in a separate chapter. Here, I should make mention of Geoffrey Chaucer, the 'Father of English Literature', whom Dylan has made allusions to and quoted quite extensively on 2006's *Modern Times*.[3] Even a writer contemporaneous with Shakespeare, John Donne, would appear to have had an impact on the writing of both; Dylan especially,

Shakespeare perhaps more speculatively, though I do think a strong case can be made for this.

Further to that, Shakespeare can come to Dylan directly or refracted through the consciousness of any of a myriad of creative artists who came before him. T.S. Eliot provides a striking example of this, particularly with regard to *Hamlet*, *King Lear* and *The Tempest*.

The connections to Shakespeare's writing throughout Dylan's art, in various fields, range therefore from the coincidence of shared culture and vocabulary through the far-fetched and the speculative all the way to reasonably reliable and firmly certain. These links are numerous, as you would expect from someone who declares that: *"I've been trying for years to come up with songs that have the feeling of a Shakespearean drama, so I'm always starting with that."*[4]

There are times when connections are unsustainable, even though others have claimed it. For instance, just because Dylan's 'incest verse' on the track 'Highway 61 Revisited' includes the title of a Shakespeare play, hardly suggests that he is making an allusion to that drama: *"Now the fifth daughter on the twelfth night/Told the first father that things weren't right."*

The title 'twelfth night' here being in lower case is probably not too noteworthy a point given Dylan's iconoclastic approach to punctuation, and his emphasis on oral rather than written art. However, there is not, in any case, anything in the verse or the song to convey a connection to the Shakespeare play. It is a notable date in the calendar, marking the Epiphany for many and predates not only both our writers but also Christianity itself, although the date it was celebrated in the Julian calendar would be January 17 in current almanacs. Shakespeare's title is often thought to have come from it being performed on that last night of the Christmas season. This would explain why the much more suitable, *What You Will*, is relegated to a mere sub-title.

There are times when echoes are heard that increase my pleasure and appreciation, although they are not necessarily intentional references. I have written before on 'Don't Think Twice, It's Alright'[5] and pointed out a similarity of use of the word 'light' with a celebrated line from *Othello*. It occurs in a verse which is of particular interest as it changes in the different

Dylan versions we have of the song.

Dylan sings the following lines in the version from *The Gaslight Tapes 1962*:

Well, it ain't no use in turnin' on your lights, babe
Lights I never knowed
And it ain't no use in burnin' your lamp, babe
I'm on the dark side of the road.

While on the later *Freewheelin'* album version, we hear, in addition to slight improvements to the first two lines, the stanza concluding with:

An' it ain't no use in turnin' on your light, babe
I'm on the dark side of the road

By changing the third line, Dylan makes this verse consistent with all the others in the song, where the third line repeats the first. In the first version, the "burning" image is redolent of ashes, of 'burning out' and interestingly, of 'burning your bridges' in addition to its primary meaning of 'shining' which puts the lamp in opposition to the dark. *"Turning on your light"* in the *Freewheelin'* version suggests something much more forceful and active, and Dylan has changed the word from the plural in both the first and (now) third lines. The phrase *"turning on your lights"* simply suggests lighting up her home to make it a welcome place for the singer in contrast to the 'dark side of the road'. *"Turning on your light"* is much more personal. It reminds you of the phrase 'to hold a torch for someone', and has an intimate appeal, though it is a forlorn one in this case. The light here is now both a physical thing, and also the woman's inner being. The song's line now shares the same two meanings of light that we hear in Othello's chilling statement as he murders Desdemona: *Put out the light, and then put out the light.*[6]

This could well just be my familiarity with both the song and the play bleeding into each other. Not that this makes it irrelevant or unworthy of note. Echoes can be just as illuminating when coincidental as when intended. They can be working at a subconscious level for artist and audience alike. Nonetheless, the avoidance of jumping on every shared phrase or theme is to be strongly advised. For example, although the term 'time out of mind' is the title of a Dylan album and it appears in Mercutio's renowned 'Queen Mab' speech, in *Romeo and Juliet* Act I, Scene iv: *Made by the joiner squirrel or old grub,/Time out o' mind the fairies' coachmakers*, we have to recall that it existed prior to Shakespeare using it and could have come to Dylan's mind from anywhere. Interestingly, though, it appears in the play only twenty-one lines after the words Romeo says 'I dreamed a dream', a phrase which occurs in 'Bob Dylan's Dream' as well as, with the addition of the adjective 'monstrous, in "Cross The Green Mountain', decades later. Moreover, 'lovers' brains' being driven to 'dream of love' is highly relevant to the *Time Out Of Mind* album. "*Give me your hand and say you will be mine*" in Dylan's 'Mississippi' (written at the time of *Time Out of Mind* but released on "*Love and Theft*") may merely be the use of a common phrase or it may be recalling the same line in Shakespeare's *Measure for Measure* (Act V Scene i).

Almost inevitably, all natural phrases of common origin soon begin to take on the hue of a deliberate allusion, if you wish it to do so. However, that way madness lies and one gets excited by the possibility of the line, "*And the poet and the painter far behind his rightful time*" in 'Chimes of Freedom' referring to the poet and the painter in *Timon of Athens*.

Still, this reverberation demonstrates how it is impossible not to make such direct connections at times, especially when something chimes so well in your mind. For example, a possible connection to *Macbeth* occurred to me once as I listened to 'Knocking on Heaven's Door'. It is not just the words but the rhythm and the meaning in both play and song; albeit that in the play the 'knock knock knocking' is on Hell's door, as the imagery repeatedly makes clear. The acoustic drumming effect of the knock goes back to those medieval cycle of plays which Dylan says his 'songs are like'. In this case to the the *Harrowing of Hell* whose story of Christ banging at the doors of Hell, Shakespeare uses for a variety of layered messages. Speak this scene aloud, and you will find yourself slipping into a familiar groove:

SCENE III. The same.
Knocking within. Enter a Porter

Porter: *Here's a knocking indeed! If a man were porter of hell-gate, he should have old turning the key.*

Knocking within
Knock,
knock, knock! Who's there, i' the name of
Beelzebub? Here's a farmer, that hanged
himself on the expectation of plenty: come in
time; have napkins enow about you; here
you'll sweat for't.

Knocking within

Knock,
knock! Who's there, in the other devil's
name? Faith, here's an equivocator, that could
swear in both the scales against either scale;
who committed treason enough for God's sake,
yet could not equivocate to heaven: O, come
in, equivocator.

Knocking within

Knock,
knock, knock! Who's there? Faith, here's an
English tailor come hither, for stealing out of
a French hose: come in, tailor; here you may
roast your goose.

Knocking within

Knock,
knock; never at quiet! What are you? But
this place is too cold for hell. I'll devil-porter
it no further: I had thought to have let in
some of all professions that go the primrose
way to the everlasting bonfire.

Inevitably individual listeners will make different connections. To return to Queen Mab, for example, Kees de Graaf sees a Shakespearean analogy with a Dylan song that we will be looking at later in this chapter, 'Soon After Midnight':

"Queen Mab is portrayed by Mercutio as a sort of miniature creature who drives her chariot into the noses and brains of sleeping people, forcing them to have dreams in which their wishes and wildest dreams are fulfilled. At one time Mercutio says about Queen Mab: 'And in this state she gallops night by night, through lovers' brains, and then they dream of love'. This is exactly what happens in this song. The poet hasn't got her yet, he has to wait for her, the woman or bride is very much a promise for the future, yet he knows for sure that she will be his and he is now fantasizing on how great and wonderful the prospect will be of being with her forever."[8]

Tales and images from the fecund folk-store of fairy stories, ballads and legends can appear in the output of both and so a direct connection is only a possibility. For example, the famous phrase: "Fee, fi, fo fum" appears in Dylan's 'All Over You' and 'I Shall Be Free No. 10' as well as in Shakespeare's *King Lear* but I think we can safely discount this as being significant. Likewise, I would find it astonishing if Dylan sang 'Seven Curses' as an acknowledgement of Shakespeare's play concerning the same theme, *Measure for Measure*. It almost certainly came to Dylan in the form of a song popular on the folk circuit he was part of at the time he wrote his own version. It is a very old tale, and was the plot behind songs, poems and plays long before Shakespeare, far less Dylan, was born. This is not to say that it is not enlightening to consider the two together. Professor Ricks does just that over seven illuminating pages in his book, *Visions of Sin*,[9] after acknowledging that Dylan's likely source is Judy Collins singing 'Anathea'.

Sometimes a seeming coincidence gathers further strength from adjacent quotes. Two phrases appearing close together in *Romeo and Juliet* that happen to be found in Dylan's lyrics, do not convince me, however, a triplet of seeming references in *Together Through Life* begins to do so. Dylan sings a potential *Hamlet* reference on 'Forgetful Heart', *The door has closed forevermore*, perhaps referring to Hamlet's line: "*Let the doors be shut upon him that he may play the fool nowhere but in's own house."* This occurs in Act III Scene I, just after the *"get thee to a nunnery"* outburst. Dylan source sleuth, Scott Warmuth, pointed out the *Hamlet* allusions in the closing song from the same album. This was a song to which I had paid insufficient attention, having thought it a mere formulaic, throwaway 'list song'.

Warmuth writes: "I've come across a similar pairing of references in the song 'It's All Good'. Here's the first verse:

Talk about me babe, if you must
Throw on the dirt, pile on the dust
I'd do the same thing, if I could
You know what they say, they say it's all good
All good, It's all good"

I suggest that this verse references *Hamlet* Act V, scene i. When Laertes jumps in Ophelia's grave he exclaims, *"Now pile your dust upon the quick and the dead."*

The final verse of the song shows why it is probably Shakespeare's dust:

I'm gonna pluck off your beard and blow it in your face
This time tomorrow I'll be rolling in your place
I wouldn't change a thing, even if I could
You know what they say, they say it's all good
All good, Oh yeah

In Act II, scene ii Hamlet's soliloquy includes:

"Who calls me villain, breaks my pate across,
Plucks off my beard and blows it in my face?
Tweaks me by the nose, gives me the lie i'th'throat,
As deep as to the lungs? Who does me this?"[10]

The close proximity of the second *Hamlet* reference in the same song not only markedly strengthens both this first allusion but also gives me pause over disregarding the possible reference in the earlier 'Forgetful Heart'.

There could be no delay in recognising that the early Dylan piece, 'Percy's

Song' closely parallels 'Feste's song' from Shakespeare's *Twelfth Night:*
  When that I was and-a little tiny boy,
  With hey, ho, the wind and the rain,
  A foolish thing was but a toy,
  For the rain it raineth every day.

Feste's second and fourth lines are repeated in each verse until the final
one, which goes like this:
  A great while ago the world begun,
  With hey, ho, the wind and the rain,
  But that's all one, our play is done,
  And we'll strive to please you every day.

In the Dylan song[11], the second and fourth lines are again repeated in each
verse:
  Bad news, bad news came to me where I sleep
  Turn, turn, turn again
  Sayin' one of your friends is in trouble deep
  Turn, turn to the rain and the wind

And again the only stanza to deviate from that is the final one. The
Shakespeare song has been adapted and appropriated so many times over
the centuries, that this parallel between the two bards, striking as it is, is
not necessarily a direct one.

Other allusions grow more evident. In the song, 'Dirge', which opens with
a quatrain replete with theatrical imagery, *"The stage was set ...the lights went
out ... the curtain fell"*, Dylan offers the disturbing observation: *"You were just a
painted face on a trip down Suicide Road."* This recalls the most famous character
to contemplate suicide, Hamlet, and his misogynistic outburst to Ophelia,
who was indeed on the road to suicide: *"I have heard of your paintings well
enough. God hath given you one face and you make yourselves another"*. The male
insecurity in Shakespeare's day saw 'a painted face' as witchcraft designed
to seduce and beguile men. To slightly defend their indefensible attitudes
and desperate desire to shift responsibility away from themselves, it was true

that the 'recipes' for cosmetics were remarkably similar to those for witches' potions. It is not much of a defence, though, especially as witches make us think of *Macbeth* and there Lady Macbeth was linked to the demon world because she read aloud a letter. Females being literate was another thing that frightened men, and made them call out "witch!", as being able to read and write confirmed an ability to understand and create spells. Whatever women did, it appears, led to the same accusation.

An even clearer connection between our two artists' works can be made when Dylan refers to one of the most beautiful and deepest passages of *Antony and Cleopatra*. Mark Antony philosophises:

Sometimes we see a cloud that's dragonish,
A vapour sometime like a bear or lion,
A towered citadel, a pendent rock,
A forkèd mountain, or blue promontory
With trees upon't, that nod unto the world
And mock our eyes with air. Thou hast seen these signs;
They are black vesper's pageants.

(Act IV Scene xiv)

In a love song to his then girlfriend, Ellen Bernstein, 'You're Gonna Make Me Lonesome When You Go'[12], Dylan sings: "*Dragon clouds so high above*" before continuing a beautiful paean that weaves personal details of his own romance around many lines which reflect on Antony's situation in the play: "*You might be spoilin' me too much, love*", "*Never been so easy or so slow.*" Antony, too, had never previously 'known careless love' as his marriages and relationships were dictated by political, Roman, necessity and he too was made by a lover who left to 'give himself a good talking to'.

It is not only the crickets in the song who speak in rhymes, but also the lovers in Shakespeare's play. Antony sits by the Nile when he should be addressing the turbulent times in Rome: "*Blue river runnin' slow and lazy/I could stay with you forever and never realize the time*". This intertwining of Dylan's own romantic affair with one of the greatest love stories ever told makes it an outstanding tribute. It came as no surprise to read that an early draft of the song included the lines: *"But now we're in the 2nd Act, / More real, less abstract."*[13] Dylan's rewritten song-lyrics for 2018's *Mondo Scripto* exhibition continue the theatrical allusions as they include many references to the stage and acting, including the lines: *"the play was over before we knew it, my part was easy..."* and *"I wear the magic actor's mask"*.

***

Moving on from firm to direct references, we find that various Shakespeare characters appear in Dylan's songs and prose. Moreover, the dramatist himself features in 'Stuck Inside Of Mobile With The Memphis Blues Again', from 1966's *Blonde on Blonde*:

Well, Shakespeare, he's in the alley
With his pointed shoes and his bells

However, nothing of significant import can be read into this. Shakespeare, dressed much like one of the court jesters from his plays, appears as just yet another persona to join a whole range of cultural and historical names that populate the phantasmagoria of Dylan's mid-sixties lyrics: Ma Rainey, Einstein, Robin Hood, T.S. Eliot, Ezra Pound and so on. Nonetheless, along with other interview and private comments, it does show that the Bard was on his mind. As were images of Shakespeare's times. An eye-witness to Dylan in Australia that same year, remembered that it "was amazing to watch him work on a song. He would have the poetry of it worked out in his head, and he would say to Robbie [Robertson, guitar player]: '...just imagine this cat who is very Elizabethan, with garters and a long shepherd's horn and he's coming over the hill with the sun behind him. That's the sound I want.'"[14]

***

Fictional characters appear in the same magical mix; sometimes seemingly just a 'name', while at others a 'name' that reverberates meaningfully in its new and unlikely context. Certainly, there are layers attached to the appearance of Ophelia in 'Desolation Row'.

Now Ophelia, she's 'neath the window
For her I feel so afraid
On her twenty-second birthday
She already is an old maid
To her, death is quite romantic
She wears an iron vest
Her profession's her religion
Her sin is her lifelessness

Shakespeare is not, however, the writer most on Dylan's mind in this song. Kerouac's *Desolation Angels* stands squarely behind Dylan's 'Desolation Row', to the extent that the phrase *'the perfect image of a priest'* makes its way from one to the other, unaltered, while the shadowy, anti-life authorities in the novel are said to "sin by lifelessness".

Nonetheless, Dylan pointedly uses a character here from Shakespeare's *Hamlet*, a play which would appear to have been much on his mind in the mid-Sixties, and to which he has often returned in succeeding decades. The first thing to note is how apt an image 'lifelessness' is in terms of Dylan's songs of the period. Lifelessness being a sin perfectly chimes with Dylan's writing at the time. The hip, visionary Dylan was constantly contrasting the vibrant young with the stagnant and decaying old, and the vital against the lifeless. *"He not being busy born, is busy dying."* sang Bob in 'It's Alright Ma, (I'm Only Bleeding')' in perhaps the most famous of these assertions. It is not, however, a fair depiction of Ophelia as she appears in the play. The Ophelia in Dylan's song is portrayed as a wrongdoer rather than the victim she is in *Hamlet*.

The 'iron vest' reference is intriguing. TV documentary producer Mick Gold pointed out to me that Grigori Kozintsev's film of *Hamlet*, where Ophelia appears in what could reasonably be described as an iron vest, could have been seen by Dylan, prior to him writing the song. The film was completed in June 1964 and shown at the New York Film Festival on September 19, 1964. The commonly quoted debut date of March 1966 is instead the date of the general release in the USA.[15] It is a landmark film and essential viewing if you are interested in cinematic adaptations of Shakespeare. With music by Shostakovich and the adaptation written by

Boris Pasternak, you would perhaps expect nothing less.

In the film, after Polonius's murder, Ophelia is dressed in black by old lady attendants. Before the outer clothes, they put her in an 'iron vest'. First there is a breastplate, and then her ribs are covered and finally an extravagant iron structure which makes her dress billow out into a large bell shape. During this and in the following scene, Ophelia seems almost as though in a trance:

"The grisly farthingale that she is strapped into when dressing for her father's funeral suggests an instrument of torture and, as she finally loses her reason she strips off her dress to reveal the iron corset beneath as she pushes her way through fawning lackeys into the maw of the castle. Her last scenes are poignant as she wanders in her shift – free of the cage but insane."[16]

It is possible that Dylan saw this cinematic adaptation before writing 'Desolation Row'. He might have caught it at one of the many art movie houses operating in Greenwich Village at that time. The 1965 *Inside Guide to Greenwich Village*, describes it as "a film-lover's paradise". Dylan writes in *Chronicles* that: *"There was an art movie house in the Village on 12th Street that showed foreign movies—French, Italian, German. This made sense, because even Alan Lomax himself, the great folk archivist, had said somewhere that if you want to get out of America, go to Greenwich Village. I'd seen a couple of Italian Fellini movies there—one called* La Strada, *which means "The Street," and another one called* La Dolce Vita."[17]

On a more general point, in addition to his primary meaning, that of the sin of not being engaged in life, what Dylan writes about Ophelia is also literally true of the character in Shakespeare's play. Making herself lifeless was her sin. Suicide was, and still is by many, looked upon as a terrible crime. Our societies have developed in such a way that what the Church once declared a sin, the State often decrees a crime.

It could be thought that there is not much religious or civic authorities can do to punish a suicide victim, or, in their eyes, 'suicide perpetrator'. However, a suicide's last moments can be tortured by fears over whether their loved ones will be plagued by the thought of the unchristian after-life suicides were supposedly condemned to endure, and whether those thoughts are correct. In different cultures, at different times this mattered greatly. Consequently, it is highly significant in the play.

If Ophelia has deliberately committed the sin of suicide, then burial on consecrated ground should be impossible, with all the dire implications that flow from that. Let us not forget the play starts with the appearance of a spirit that is not allowed to rest. Much debate, therefore, ensues on the issue with both the passive nature of her death and her madness being suggested as ways 'around' the Church's clear decree which the priest is adamant should stand. Meanwhile, the attempt to give her a Christian burial is scoffed at as a rich man's evasion of the law by the 'lower orders'. A compromise of sorts, of 'maimed rites', leaves, as compromises almost invariably do, all sides unsatisfied. We are left to ponder that a hip comment, deriving directly from Kerouac, and so befitting of the 1965 Bob Dylan, turns out to also be faithful to the Shakespeare character in a way that seems surprisingly literal, whether or not this was part of his intention.

***

There is also a hint in this passage of Dylan having already noticed that referencing more than one play, explicitly or implicitly, cheek by jowl, can have impressive effects. It is something he knows all about from an earlier strand of American popular song, minstrelsy, as is made clear in his 2001 album, *"Love and Theft"*. Dylan commented on minstrel shows in an interview just before the album came out:

"...And 'Desolation Row'? That's a minstrel song through and through. I saw some ragtag minstrel show in blackface at the carnivals when I was growing up, and it had an effect on me, just as much as seeing the lady with four legs."[18]

And the album title, enclosed by quotation marks, appears to be alluding to a 1993 book by university professor Eric Lott, about minstrelsy, entitled: *Love and Theft: Blackface Minstrelsy and the American Working Class*. The connections of minstrelsy to *"Love And Theft"* is an extensive subject which myself and others have pursued elsewhere[19], but here we are focussing on the Shakespearean connections to both.

One of these is evidenced in 'Po' Boy' where the poisoned wine appears to come straight from the last scene of *Hamlet* to appear in a rewritten

Othello where killer and victim are reversed:
> *Othello told Desdemona, "I'm cold, cover me with a blanket,*
> *By the way, what happened to that poisoned wine?"*
> *She said, "I gave it to you, you drank it."*

Drinking poisoned wine is how Gertrude dies in *Hamlet*, while
Desdemona is choked to death by Othello. The writers of the burlesques
knew this, but enjoyed conflating more than one Shakespeare scenario
with another, and Dylan enjoys doing the same. In these short lines, with a
deft twist, the slain women here emerge in triumph. Romeo also dies from
drinking poison, and Juliet attempts to do so before stabbing herself. Those
star-crossed lovers also appear in another song, 'Floater (Too Much To Ask)'
on *"Love and Theft"*, where we have the marvellously colloquial:
> *Romeo, he said to Juliet, "You got a poor complexion*
> *It doesn't give your appearance a very youthful touch!"*
> *Juliet said back to Romeo, "Why don't you just shove off*
> *If it bothers you so much"*

There is a rich musical and dramatic history to the blending of
Shakespeare and blackface minstrelsy and one that is also steeped in
the history of America, of 'the South' and the tortuous and tortured Afro-
American experience. Writing on 'Po Boy', Richard Jobes stated that:

"The same song borrows its opening verse directly from an 1866 minstrel
performance of *Othello*, written by George Griffin. 'If for my wife – your
daughter – you are looking,' Othello says to Brabantio, 'you'll find her in the
kitchen busy cooking.' Dylan takes these lines, and with very little variation,
transports them into 'Po' Boy' ... Productions of *Othello* were highly popular
amongst blackface minstrelsy's audience, unsurprisingly because of the
play's racial themes. Jobes also quotes relevant passages from William J.
Mahar: "Having transformed the dramatic elements into comic situations,
Griffin replaced Shakespeare's text with the rhyming couplets typical
of popular verse and introduced every scene or action with melodies
borrowed from contemporary American and Irish song." And: " Rather
than transforming the principal characters of *Othello*, *Hamlet*, or *Macbeth*
into plantation workers or urban characters living in social margins, the

Ethiopian sketch writers reduced royalty to common folk and translated the grand tragedies of life into short sketches about courtship, mixed-race marriages, or conventional domestic life. Minstrel shows were mass entertainment, and were 'America's first new form of non-elite culture.'"[20]

Scott Warmuth follows the same trail as Richard Jobes and adds, regarding George Griffin's *Othello: a Burlesque*, that "The full play, and other Shakespearean parodies, can be found in the book, *This Grotesque Essence: Plays from the American Minstrel Stage*."[21] This, I discovered, is also available online[22] and noted, among other things, that for Act 1 scene ii the characters enter to the melody of "Dixie" which Dylan performs in his film, *Masked and Anonymous*. The lyrics they sing to this are a burlesque of Shakespeare's *Othello*. I reproduce them here, with a warning that the language of the time is most offensive to today's eyes and ears. However, they give you an important taste of how Shakespeare's scripts were re-cast in these extraordinary blackface minstrel shows that form one of the many tributaries that contribute to the mighty river of song that is *"Love and Theft"*.

The opening scene ends with Desdemona's father moaning: "Just as I tink dat Barnum would take her/Dis nigger comes, and mit her runs away." Then Scene 2 begins like this:

SCENE 2. A *Room.*
Enter OTHELLO and DESDEMONA, L., singing and dancing a walk around.—Air, " Dixie."

OTHELLO *Oh, Desdy, dear, now you're my wife,*
I mean to pass a happy life—Away, away, &c.
I'll never more be melancholy,
But be happy, gay and jolly.—Away, away, &c.
I love my Desdemona, away, away—
And hand in hand we'll take a stand,
To spend Brabantio's money.—Away, away, &c.

DESDEMONA *For you I've run away from pap,*
But I don't care a snap for that. —Away, away, &c.

I love you and you love me,
And all our lives we'll merry be.—Away, away, &c.
With you I'll sport my figure, away, away—
I'll love you dearly all my life,
Although you are a nigger.—Away, away, &c.

You can hear a snatch of this segment, on a radio documentary[23] that Scott Warmuth also tracked down and quotes, in the opening minute or so, the 'looking/cooking' couplet with which Dylan kicks off his song. As Warmuth writes:

"The radio documentary "Shakespeare in American Life" includes an episode by Richard Paul on the African-American experience with Shakespeare called "Shakespeare In Black and White." It asks the question "Who 'owns' Shakespeare?" and Paul begins his piece by contrasting a straight reading of *Othello* with actors doing the very same lines from *Othello: a Burlesque* that Dylan uses in *"Love and Theft."*[24] This is a rewarding listen and is of relevance to both Dylan and Shakespeare scholars as well as to anyone interested in the social history of the United States.

***

Michael Gray, after also noting the Shakespeare references in 'Po' Boy' and 'Floater (Too Much To Ask)', proposes a less obvious third Shakespeare presence on *"Love And Theft"*. This time it is straight from a Shakespeare play rather than via a minstrelsy show:

"As so very often, Dylan's skill with literary allusion is such that if you don't happen to pick up on the echo, it doesn't obtrude, distract or bother you; but if you do pick up on it, it deepens the resonance of the song. In this instance, it occurs in 'Bye and Bye', when Dylan sings that lovely line 'I'm not even acquainted with my own desires'. The delivery, on the track, is modest, reflective, personally confessional, but at the same time, the language itself is of Shakespearean eloquence. It comes from Rosalind, the heroine of *As You Like* It, in Act One, Scene iii, when she has been exiled and accused of treason by the duke..."[25]

The passage that Gray refers to is a dark one in that song-filled play:

DUKE FREDERICK   *You, cousin.*
                   Within these ten days if that thou be'st found
                   So near our public court as twenty miles,
                   Thou diest for it.

ROSALIND   *I do beseech your grace*
                   Let me the knowledge of my fault bear with me:
                   If with myself I hold intelligence,
                   Or have acquaintance with mine own desires,
                   If that I do not dream or be not frantic,
                   (As I do trust I am not) then, dear uncle,
                   Never so much as in a thought unborn,
                   Did I offend your highness.

Dylan's song also has dark moments despite him singing '*sugar-coated rhymes*'. This threatening hue is first introduced in the song by the phrase '*I'm walking on briars.*' It is worth noting at this point that, just before the above dialogue, Rosalind exclaims: "*O, how full of briers is this working-day world!*"

Dylan's song ends with a verse far removed from the earlier: "*singing love's praises in sugar-coated rhyme*", instead we are now presented with a father gone insane, a depressed mother and the ringing declaration:

> *Well, I'm gonna baptize you in fire*
> *So you can sin no more*
> *I'm gonna establish my rule*
> *Through civil war*

Then comes the final line of the song: "*Gonna make you see just how loyal and true a man can be*" This makes me think of the character, Adam who followed "To the last gasp, with truth and loyalty" in *As You Like It*, though only because the play is now in my thoughts. The song itself has by now shifted its focus onto matters of civil war, both Roman and American, a topic we will examine in this book's final chapter. It is also worth noting that *As You Like It* was directly quoted in Dylan's film, *Masked And Anonymous* and on his *Theme Time Radio Show*.

This same movement, from light and frothy pop to something more sinister, can be found in yet another *"Love And Theft"* song with possible Shakespeare connections, 'Moonlight'[26]. In this song the lyrics tell one story while the music and vocal delivery tell another. We listen to 'the songbird's sweet melodious tone', as the song puts it, but we have grown used to the agreeable turning nasty on this album. The same thing happens again here, starting with 'earth and sky that melts with flesh and bone'. The disturbing signs then pile up until mid-song we hear:

> *The clouds are turning crimson*
> *The leaves fall from the limbs an'*
> *The branches cast their shadows over stone*

The baleful touches in the lyrics keep accumulating and they belie the pre-war, romantic sounding song to which we initially appeared to be listening. This culminates in: *"For whom does the bell toll for, love? It tolls for you and me."* The inevitability of love leading to death had already been prefigured by the movement from 'orchids' to 'cypress trees', that is from flowers symbolising love, to trees denoting death. This mirrors the way the same conceit at the heart of *Romeo and Juliet* is foreshadowed in the prologue and in the language from the beginning of their brief relationship. The menace in Dylan's lyrics becomes overpowering as it becomes clear why he wants to meet her *alone*. That is, he wants her to be alone, with him, and vulnerable. He boasts that *"I know when the time is right to strike"* and that he will then take her across the river. That river surely is the river Styx and he is, as the imagery of the song repeatedly tells us, going to ferry her to her death.

Despite noting all these signs of danger, and linking them to *A Midsummer Night's Dream* and Oberon's warning: "Ill met by Moonlight, proud Titania", Professor Ricks sees it very differently:

"...the song, on the face of it, makes much of things that suggest, as against levity, gravity. A groan, and tears, and a funeral bell, for a start. But then the song achieves its sense of relief and release by incorporating within itself reminders of all those things in life that cast shadows, those weights that make us seek relief and release in the first place and in the last place. Moonlight achieves light-heartedness not in spite of but because of the many intimations of mortality, of sadness and loss, that it touches upon or that touch it."... It was a funeral bell, no doubt about that, but how unfunereal it all feels on this occasion, how much more like marriage bells for you and me. A bit like those cypress trees, freed from their dark associations." [27]

It is striking that our feelings about the song are so divergent despite noting the same points. Having written extensively on the primacy of performance, I am more than open to the claim that how a song sounds and makes you feel should be key. Yet, for me, Dylan's achievement is in deliberately cloaking the bitter intent of the words in *'sugar-coated rhymes'*. After all, sometimes, as he warns us, *"Satan comes as a man of peace"*, or one can *"look like the innocent flower,/But be the serpent under't"*, as Shakespeare's Lady Macbeth puts it in *Macbeth* Act V scene i.[28]

An opinion by a critic as worthy as Christopher Ricks was not something to be overlooked, and so I asked a number of Dylan fan acquaintances how they viewed the song. Intriguingly, there was an even divide between those who saw it as a sweet song and those who saw it as a solemn warning of danger disguised as a sweet song. Each person in both camps was astonished at the others' understanding of the song, as it had never previously occurred to them as being a possibility.

"Moonlight" is the younger sister to a track on Dylan's 2012 album, *Tempest*. This song is called: 'It's Soon After Midnight'. Again we move, in what sounds like a beautiful love-song of beauty, from "singing praises" to something much darker, in this case killing floors, dining in blood and dragging corpses. The Shakespeare connection here, if any, comes in the lines: *"It's soon after midnight/And I've got a date with the fairy queen"* which were taken by many to refer to Titania as the fairy queen in *A Midsummer Night's Dream*. This is tempting, particularly in the light of the song's affinity to 'Moonlight'. Dylan plays in the song with the idea of love and madness being two versions of the same thing. As the moon symbolises both, he brings this together very succinctly in the narrator's claim that *'the moon is in my eye'*[29]. This kinship of madness and love is something that is central to *A Midsummer Night's Dream*.

Notwithstanding this, there is no particularly apparent correspondence between the song and the play that I can see, although this song boasts Shakespearean phrases[30]. While, therefore, Shakespeare is an influence on part of Dylan's creativity, it seems to me that the likeliest fairy queen on Dylan's mind here, if there is a particular one, is Edmund Spenser's *The Faerie Queen*. Given that Dylan quotes both Shakespeare and Chaucer, it would be fitting if he also tipped his hat to the outstanding poet who came between those two giants. This particular song is thematically closer to Spenser's poem than to *A Midsummer Night's Dream*. The themes Spenser is writing about come from an older source, that source to which Shakespeare and Dylan so often return, *The Bible*.

Kees de Graaf feels similarly about Spenser's *The Faerie Queen* seeming to be a more likely reference than Shakespeare's Titania, and also points out the Biblical backdrop. Dylan's *Tempest* is steeped in Biblical themes and imagery, and consequently, it is natural for de Graaf to make the following connections:

"The idea that Christ will return at midnight – as bridegroom to meet his bride, the church, – is wide-spread within the Christian tradition and is based on *Matthew. 25:6* where it says: 'At midnight they were roused by the shout, 'Look, the bridegroom is coming! Come out and meet him!' ... in this song, in the quest to find the perfect bride, there is a struggle going on between lust, infidelity, and disloyalty on the one hand and chastity, fidelity, and loyalty on the other hand. ...God (Jesus) is the groom and his people (the church) are the bride.[31]

Dylan and King Lear

Decades earlier, as with many listeners, my first experiences of Dylan alluding to Shakespeare came when listening to *The Basement Tapes* with its many echoes of Shakespeare's most piercing and complete vision, *King Lear*. The instigator of all the mad, bad, magnificent, desolate things we experience in *King Lear* is the single word: "nothing". Everything comes from nothing and returns to it, but the route to recognising this is, for Lear and others, the most painful of journeys.

LEAR ...	*Now, our joy,*
	Although our last and least, to whose young love
	The vines of France and milk of Burgundy
	Strive to be interested. What can you say to draw
	A third more opulent than your sisters? Speak.
CORDELIA	*Nothing, my lord.*
KING LEAR	*Nothing?*
CORDELIA	*Nothing.*
LEAR	*Nothing will come of nothing, speak again.*

Cordelia's refusal to play along with the charade of pandering to the old king's vanity sets in motion a play in which the word "nothing" assumes, along with the companion negatives of "no", "not" and "never", greater and greater significance until they embrace all of reality as perceived by humanity. Everything from the simple "no" to the terrors of 'the void' of Sartrean "nothingness" is evoked. These themes and feelings, and key words, echo throughout a particular set of Dylan songs from the sprawling collection collectively known as *The Basement Tapes*.

'Nothing Was Delivered', 'You Ain't Goin' Nowhere', 'I'm Not There', 'Too Much of Nothing' and other titles, reflect that nothingness/emptiness is a major, recurring theme in these songs. Similar concerns to *King Lear* are embedded in many songs: "*life is brief*", or 'Goin To Acapulco's', "*It's a wicked life but what the hell/Everybody's got to eat/And I'm just the same as anyone else/When it comes to scratchin' for my meat*'" And even in that modern nursery rhyme,[32] 'Quinn The Eskimo (The Mighty Quinn)' where the titular character, Godot-like, is also not there.[33]

Cordelia's initial statement is echoed throughout the play "*No, I will be the pattern of all patience; I will say nothing*", says Lear, in the storm subconsciously, one presumes, reiterating Cordelia's words that set everything in motion. In Act I, scene iv, the Fool castigates the fallen Lear in lines that begin with a comment that is akin to Dylan's song title, "Love Minus Zero/No Limit': "*Now thou art an O without a figure. I am better than thou art now: I am a fool, thou art nothing.*" Earlier in the same scene, they had shared this exchange:

LEAR: *This is nothing, fool.*

FOOL: *Then 'tis like the breath of an unfeed lawyer; you gave me nothing for't. Can you make no use of nothing, nuncle?*

LEAR: *Why no, boy; nothing can be made out of nothing.*

(Act I scene iv)

Lear has yet to learn that insight and wisdom come from a proper grasp of the deeper meanings of "nothing". Edgar realises it and Lear and Gloucester learn it via the harshest of lessons, as do we, the audience, as we watch on in pity and horror.

All the other major characters also whirl around the multifaceted meanings of the key word. In Act II Scene III, in a short monologue, Edgar concludes it by stating: "*Poor Tom! That's something yet: Edgar I nothing am.*" Even as Edgar is, or seems to be obliterated, Poor Tom stands there as a symbol of at the very least, and it is the very least, *something*.

Edgar also embraces the 'wheel of fortune' tenet, so neatly summed up by Dylan's line in "Like A Rolling Stone": "*When you ain't got nothing, you got nothing to lose*"[34]:

EDGAR: *To be worst,*
              The lowest and most dejected thing of fortune,
              Stands still in esperance, lives not in fear.
              The lamentable change is from the best;
              The worst returns to laughter.

(Act IV Scene i)

This trope is central to many a play by Shakespeare and to a number of central songs by Dylan. One immediately thinks of *"you'll find out when you reach the top you're on the bottom"* from 'Idiot Wind' which was to 1975 what 'Like A Rolling Stone' was to 1965. In turn that brings to mind: *"She knows there's no success like failure/And that failure's no success at all"*. 'Like A Rolling Stone' is more purely Learian, though, and irresistibly so in the quatrain:

"Ah you never turned around to see the frowns
On the jugglers and the clowns when they all did tricks for you
You never understood that it ain't no good
You shouldn't let other people get your kicks for you"

Cordelia's sisters also wield the 'nothing' stick. In a callous duet, they whittle the old king's retinue down from one hundred to zero, in Act II Scene iv. It is a literal countdown to the end of all empathy, and Lear spirals downwards, wildly out of control, following it. Goneril says she will only take him with half the original one hundred. Regan had already declared that she would only accept twenty-five. Lear, distraught at such barbarous treatment and having given the two vipers his kingdom on the understanding he would have one hundred knights, is batted back and forth like a table tennis ball and quickly reduced to, yet again, to nothing.

LEAR   *What, must I come to you*
        With five and twenty, Regan? said you so?

REGAN   *And speak't again, my lord; no more with me.*

LEAR   *Those wicked creatures yet do look well-favour'd,*
        When others are more wicked: not being the worst
        Stands in some rank of praise.
To GONERIL
        I'll go with thee;
        Thy fifty yet doth double five and twenty,
        And thou art twice her love.

GONERIL   *Hear me, my lord;*
What need you five and twenty? ten? or five?
To follow in a house where twice so many
Have a command to tend you?

REGAN   *What need one?*

(Act II Scene iv)

The numerous references throughout the drama end, almost, in the terrible lines wrenched from Lear after he has been healed and then broken again. Here, in the final scene, with Cordelia reduced to nothingness, "no" and "never" are relentlessly drummed into us, the listeners. The old king wails:

No, no, no life!
Why should a dog, a horse, a rat, have life,
And thou no breath at all? Thou'lt come no more,
Never, never, never, never, never!

(Act V Scene iii)

Yet even then, we are not quite finished with "nots" and "nos" because we then have the heroically loyal Kent's final statement. This takes the form of a noble reversal to so much of what has gone before: "I must not say no".
Dylan sings, in 'Tears of Rage':

And now you'd throw us all aside
And put us on our way
Oh what dear daughter 'neath the sun
Would treat a father so
To wait upon him hand and foot
And always tell him, "No?"

The opening two lines encapsulate Goneril and Regan's refusal to house his retinue as promised and send him out into the storm while the next four summarise his relations with Cordelia. To *"wait upon him hand and foot"* is what Cordelia is always willing to do and actually does when they are re-united. Yet she would not play his game of enforced flattery and denied his request for an expression of her obvious love. Her negative response completely confused him when he had his wits, far less after he lost them. It may be worthy of note that Dylan played this song, in a truncated summer festival setlist of only ten songs, when he appeared at The Phoenix Festival in 1995, less than six miles from Shakespeare's birth and resting place.

This sudden concentration of Shakesperean imagery may have had something to do with the books Allen Ginsberg brought to him as Dylan recuperated from a motorcycle accident, the accounts of which range from 'fell over while walking it' to 'came off it while riding it'. Whatever is the case, Dylan was undoubtedly recovering from the 1966 world tour that nearly killed him and probably would have, had he carried on with it, as originally scheduled. Instead, he was lying low in Woodstock and reading voraciously. Ginsberg says he took the following for Dylan to read: "a box full of books of all kinds. All the modern poets I knew. Some ancient poets like Sir Thomas Wyatt, Campion. Dickinson, Rimbaud, Lorca, Apollinaire, Blake, Whitman and so forth." Although Ginsberg does not list Shakespeare among the 'ancient poets', I am inclined to think he was included in the 'and so forth', or at least that Dylan used some of his reading time re-acquainting himself with Shakespeare because we do know that Ginsberg was talking to Dylan about Shakespeare on the phone soon after this visit.[35]

As an aside, for a moment, from *The Basement Tapes*, it is worth pointing out that Christopher Ricks sees a connection between Cordelia and Dylan's song 'Love Minus Zero/No Limit'. That song is from from the *Bringing It All Back Home* album which I have already made reference to in regard to this seminal Shakespearean drama. Ricks wrote:

"At the beginning of *King Lear*, Cordelia does not know how she will be able to reply to her father's insistence that his three daughters announce their love for him. She has an aside (an aside being a combination of speech and silence, as speaking to oneself is): *"What shall Cordelia speak? Love, and be silent."* Her love, it speaks like silence. Or she hopes it will. But this, in the unjust upshot, does not satisfy Lear. Her silence, which becomes her refusal to placate him (let us not talk falsely now), moves him to violence.

"What can you say to draw
A third more opulent than your sisters?
Speak."
"Nothing, my Lord."
"So young and so untender?"
"So young, my Lord, and true."

True like ice, like fire, and true moreover as love. When Dylan puts a question and answer, the exchange may find itself harboured within parentheses, themselves carrying a suggestion of the unspoken, the silent."[36]

Professor Ricks also brings together the song's line, *"my love she speaks softly"* with Lear's comment *"her voice was ever soft,/Gentle, and low, an excellent thing in woman."* (Act V Scene iii), while acknowledging, in a witty Dylan re-write, the perils of generalisations. A further note on those perils is to stress that it is Lear speaking, not Shakespeare; and also that, in the context of the Dylan canon, his love is clearly being laudably contrasted with the noisy and judgemental stances which Dylan has gladly left behind as illustrated in his song, 'My Back Pages':

Half-wracked prejudice leaped forth
"Rip down all hate," I screamed
Lies that life is black and white
Spoke from my skull. I dreamed

Returning to *The Basement Tapes*, we also have 'This Wheel's on Fire', which has a Learian ring to its chorus and final verse as well as sharing, as do so many other Dylan songs of this and other periods, the same apocalyptic tone. Additionally, there is the unmistakable echo in its very title, which puts the play in our mind even before we first hear the actual song. This comes from when Lear is re-awakened from his death-like slumber in Avt IV scene vi, and itself refers back to Greek myth:

KING LEAR: *You do me wrong to take me out o'th'grave:*
Thou art a soul in bliss, but I am bound
Upon a wheel of fire, that mine own tears
Do scald like moulten lead.

With all that has gone before, we feel that "Too Much of Nothing" , too, is imbued with the ethos and vocabulary of *King Lear*. However, there are two other sources which also stand behind this Dylan song. One of them also shares Shakespeare as a contributory source while the other was a source for the dramatist himself.

Firstly, there is T.S. Eliot and in particular his poem, *The Waste Land*. I believe that Matthew Zuckerman[37] was the first to observe that the chorus referred to Eliot's wives, Vivienne Haigh-Wood and Esmé Valerie Fletcher, notwithstanding an alternate spelling of 'Vivian' (which is not necessarily unusual in printed lyrics of aural art). Death by water is a recurring theme in all three artists. However, to return to our main track here, Michael Gray, in his *Dylan Encyclopaedia*, quotes Zuckerman, as writing:

"Vivien Haigh-Wood was Eliot's first wife, Valerie Fletcher his second." And that Zuckerman also writes: "'too much of nothing" is a fair précis of . . . [one theme of] The Waste Land'. These lines illustrate the point: 'What is that noise now? What is the wind doing? / Nothing again nothing. / You know nothing? Do you see nothing? Do you remember / "Nothing"?' ".

Still, even behind all three cases: Shakespeare's *King Lear*, Eliot's *The Waste Land* and Dylan's "Too Much of Nothing" stands a primary source. Dylan points this out in his lines: *"Now, it's all been done before/It's all been written in the book"* where the word 'the' alerts us to the fact that this could be more usefully written: "Now, it's all been done before/It's all been written in The Book."

Shakespeare's *King Lear* is founded upon the book of Ecclesiastes as Kirsch illuminated in his 1988 article "The Emotional Landscape of King Lear":[38]

"In this regard, as in others, *King Lear* is very reminiscent of Ecclesiastes. The depiction of suffering in *King Lear* has often been compared to the Book of Job,' ... but in its overall conception as well as in much of its ironic texture,

King Lear is closer to Ecclesiastes, the book of the Old Testament that is most nearly pagan in its outlook and that treats human life almost exclusively in terms of the immanence of its ending... His announced theme is "vanity," a word whose principal connotation (and whose translation in the New English Bible) is "emptiness," and he speaks of man's identity in this life as "a shadow" (7:2) and his achievements as "nothing" (5:14; 7:16). Lear-like, he likens men to beasts:

"For the condition of the children of men, and the condition of beastes are even as one condition vnto them. As the one dyeth, so dyeth the other: for they haue all one breath, and there is no excellencie of man aboue the beast: for all is vanitie. (3:19)"

Kirsch goes on to point out a number of directly relevant quotes from the Geneva 1560 version of *The Bible*, including:

"And I gaue mine heart to knowe wisdome & knowledge, madnes & foolishnes: I knewe also that this is a vexacion of the spirit."(1:17)

"Better is a poore and wise childe, then an olde and foolish King, which wil no more be admonished" (4:13).

"As he came forthe of his mothers belly, he shal returne naked to go as he came, & shal beare away nothing of his labour, which he hathe caused to passe by his hand" (5:14).

The play's persistent imagery of seeing and blindness in general, and the Gloucester subplot in particular, are traced back by Kirsch to "For the wise mans eyes *are* in his head, but the foole walketh in darkenes: yet I knowe also that the same condition falleth to them all" (2:14) and, as the King James Version has it: "Better *is* the sight of the eyes than the wandering of desire. (6:9)". While *King Lear*'s pre-occupation with injustice can be seen as growing from 7:17: "I have sene all things in the daies of my vanitie: there is a iuste man that perisheth in his iustice, and there is a wicked man that continueth long in his malice."

Michael Gray[39] sees the same backdrop to Dylan on both in the 'Tears of Rage' conclusion: . . . *you know we're so alone / And life is brief* and in, as he continues:

"...the contemporaneous *Basement Tapes* song (a title that in itself summarises the gloomy end of the Ecclesiastes meditative spectrum) Dylan worries away at other parts of the Preacher's text. The song's opaque second verse seems to follow a line of thought prompted by the beginning of Ecclesiastes 8, which advises people to be circumspect and at least appear obedient in front of a king, to be safe: and goes on immediately to the thought that no-one knows anything about anything much, and certainly not about when they will die. Here is Ecclesiastes 8:2 & 5–9 in the ploddingly unmemorable *Good News* version: 'Do what the king says.... As long as you obey his commands, you are safe, and a wise man knows how and when to do it. There is a right time and a right way to do everything, but we know so little! None of us knows what is going to happen, and there is no one to tell us. No one can keep himself from dying or put off the day of his death . . .'

Dylan's meditation boils this down to 'Too much of nothing / Can make a man abuse a king. / He can walk the streets and boast like most / But he wouldn't know a thing.' ('Curse not the king . . . ', as Ecclesiastes says again in 10:20)—after which Dylan adds at once, echoing Ecclesiastes far more plainly: 'Now, it's all been done before, / It's all been written in the book.'"

It has, and that is the Book of Ecclesiastes from *The Book*. The passages surrounding the one quoted here are also echoed in Dylan songs from the beginning of his career (in 'The Times They Are-A-Changin', for one of the more famous examples) to his latest album of original lyrics at the time of writing, *Tempest*.

There is also a later, seemingly apt and precise, reference to *King Lear* in Dylan's lyrics. This occurs in an album steeped, like the play, in nonsense verse, fairy tale and *The Bible*. That album came out in 1990 and was titled then, all in lower case, *under the red sky*[40]. It included a track called, 'Handy Dandy' which conjures up a passage from *King Lear*: *justice rails upon yond simple thief. Hark, in thine ear: change places; and, handy-dandy, which is the justice, which is the thief?*

However, this could be merely coincidental, as 'Handy Dandy' is part of an old nursery rhyme based on a 'hand game' for children that is part of the wider Anglo-American culture that Dylan and Shakespeare share.

One final point on Bob Dylan and *King Lear* is that film director and Dylan fan Jean-Luc Goddard tried to get Dylan involved in his 1987 experimental film version of *King Lear*. A sharper contrast to the dismal 1986 movie,

Hearts of Fire, in which Dylan did appear could hardly be imagined. At least, however, one of his co-stars there was another Dylan fan, Mark Rylance, one of the greatest Shakespearean actors of our time, as well as being the first artistic director of the reconstructed Globe Theatre.

***

It is not only in his lyrics that Dylan echoes to the Swan of Avon. He also does so in his prose, films and on his radio show[41]. This happens most numerously in the pages of *Tarantula*[42], Dylan's book that has been variously described as an 'experimental novel', 'a long prose poem' and many things too rude to reprint.

Direct references include: "someone's coming to tame my shrew" (page 24) "hanging out at the press room & shelling out to the day crew & merchants of venice" (page 29). There are also various allusions to clowns and fools that cross-refer to Dylan songs and their connections to Shakespearean characters and plays. Most extendedly we get a fictive actor playing with celebrated lines from *Macbeth* and *Romeo and Juliet* on page 45:

"*i work for the city. before i swat you, you'd best tell me your occupation*" "*i'm an actor. tomorrow & tomorrow & tomorrow lights this petty grace from blow to blow like a poor stagehand pounding fury signifying nothing. oh romeo, romeo, wherefor fart thou? pretty good huh?*" "*i work for the city, i'll trample you with my horse*" "*wanna hear some oedipus?*"

Hamlet is referred to most frequently, but, as with *King Lear* and 'Too Much of Nothing', T.S. Eliot seems a likely intermediary to some of the mentions here. "*Prince hamlet of his hexagram*" appears in the middle of page 133 and is in dialogue with Obie for a page or so. In the chapter on *Tarantula*'s textual allusions in *Bob Dylan's Words*[43] it is noted that:

"Since Hamlet is important to this chapter, as well as to the novel, and in light of Dylan's demonstrable use of the work of T.S. Eliot, it is likely that the line (*you're a phoney, you're no prince*) is derived from T.S. Eliot's *The Love Song of J. Alfred Prufrock*, "No, I am not Prince Hamlet nor was meant to be."

Other lines appear to be more directed at Shakespeare's play. Hamlet, as a character, is a major touchstone throughout the book and the references are compunded by adjacent ones to mothers, the oedipus complex and ghosts.

***

Dylan looked to *Hamlet* for inspiration when editing *Renaldo and Clara*. One of three quotes Dylan wrote on the wall of the studio where he edited this film, came from the opening scene: *"For this relief, much thanks, for 'tis bitter cold and I am sick at heart"*.[44]

Dylan's underrated film, *Masked and Anonymous* contains yet another trove of Shakespeare references in a film whose plot is reminscent of many of Shakespeare's works: a ruler dying, a brutal succession, betrayal, political, familial and dynastic intrigue. With a mixed genre style and generic character parts such as mistress, soldier, drunk; as well as metaphorical names such as Bobby Cupid, Tom Friend and Pagan Lace and a plot of civil and familial turmoil, it is no surprise that Larry Charles described the film as "Shakespeare meets Cassavetes".[45] We also have a character named Prospero, and in the film script, at least, a Hotspur and a Blunt, plus that familiar pair from *King Lear*, Edgar and Edmund. Edmund here is also a son who is not a 'full' son and perhaps for similar reasons, power-crazed and driven to dominate. Edmund assumes control in Dylan's film, in contrast to the play. Although, what he has control over seems to be built on extremely shaky ground.

Ed Harris, who plays the titular character in Michael Almereyda's film of *Cymbeline*, which features Dylan's 'Dark Eyes', here performs the part of Oscar Vogel, a character who takes us back to the blackface minstrelsy of *"Love And Theft"* and the mintrels' burlesques of Shakespeare. Vogel also quotes, almost straight, from *As You Like It* when he comments that "The whole world's a stage." Co-director Larry Charles talks about this on the DVD commentary track: "... 'the whole world is a stage' – quoting Shakespeare referring to the stage. It's all play, playing with the reality; the Rastafarian janitor – was it real, was it not, was it a dream?"

Dylan himself cited the speech that this is excerpted from, in episode 52 of his *Theme Time Radio Show*. The theme was "Young and Old", and Dylan opened the show by reciting the play's most quotable speech, Jaques' *"All the world's a stage"*, written it is suspected, very much with an eye on the Commonplace books so prevalent and influential at the time it was written. Dylan then added that *"... as usual, Willy the Shake said everything that you need to say, so for the next hour we'll just be presenting footnotes of a musical variety... "*.

In his 2018 hand-written lyric with accompanying drawings exhibition, *Mondo Scripto*, Dylan copied Laurence Olivier as Shakespeare's Richard III for the drawing to accompany 'Song to Woody'. This is turn brings to mind Christopher Ricks's description of meeting Dylan: "Shortly before the concert I received word to come backstage, so my wife and I went half an hour before the show. And Dylan said: "Mr Ricks, we meet at last." My reply was: "Have you read any good books lately?" Dylan wasn't at all surprised by my question and he really did want to talk about *Richard III*. I think it was partly because there had been some films of it and partly because I'd mentioned *Richard III* in something I'd written about his song 'The Lonesome Death of Hattie Carroll'.[46]

****

Every now and again you come across quotes from Dylan that are useful as tips for Shakespeare appreciation. *"... tragedy ... no deeper than comedy"* from *Tarantula* and *"you can't be wise and in love at the same time"*, from the *No Direction Home* documentary being two of my favourites.

From at least as far back as B.J. Rolfzen's class, over sixty years ago, Shakespeare has played a part in Dylan's thoughts and work. In every decade, up to and including until Dylan's last album, thus far, of self-penned material, 2012's *The Tempest*, Shakespeare appears in Dylan's songs. The Bard of Avon appears in parody, in allusion, in burlesque, as a touchstone, in quotes and intertextuality that ranges from a light touch to being central to a song's meaning. The same is true of Dylan's prose and film scripts and, with increasing frequency as the years have passed, Shakespeare has been used by Dylan, in interview, to offer revelatory insight into his own working practice.

NOTES

1 Albeit this occurs in the melodramatic lines of the play-within-a-play: *"A second time I kill my husband dead"*

2 Anne Margaret Daniel *Tempest,* Bob Dylan and the Bardic Arts, in *Tearing the World Apart: Bob Dylan and the Twenty-First Century* , Eds. Nina Goss, Eric Hoffman. University Press of Mississippi 2017

3 Something that was immediately picked up on by Scott Warmuth and then expanded with regard to the song "Thunder on the Mountain", in particular, by Tony Attwood, here: https://bob-dylan.org.uk/archives/5344

4 Robert Love "Bob Dylan: The Uncut Interview" Feb-Mar 2015 (from AARP Magazine)

5 Muir, Andrew *Troubadour,* chapter two, Woodstock Press, UK, 2013

6 Christopher Ricks draws attention to Dylan and Shakespeare's joint fascination with "light" imagery when discussing the song 'Moonlight' in his book *Visions of Sin.* Published by Ecco, HarperCollins, 2004

7 In Dylan's official lyrics, this line is presented as: 'An' the unpawned painter behind beyond his rightful time'

8 http://www.keesdegraaf.com/media/Misc/6632p17vcu230mpne1itf4o31h851ug1.pdf accessed September 13, September 2017

9 Ricks *Visions of Sin Op. cit.*

10 Posted 21st April 2009 by Scott Warmuth http://swarmuth.blogspot.com/2009/04/together-through-life-dispatch-8-human.html accessed September 7, 2017

11 "Percy's Song" Bob Dylan Copyright © 1964, 1966 by Warner Bros. Inc.; renewed 1992, 1994 by Special Rider Music.

12 The song is on *Blood On The Tracks.* Bernstein was born in Ashtabula, living in San Francisco and going to Honolulu. She also told Dylan about Queen Anne's lace (all of these are mentioned in the song). http://www.a-muir.co.uk/Dylan/Judas/J2.pdf

13 Anne Margaret Daniel *There Will be Blood* Hot Press Annual 2019. Additionally, the 2018 *Mondo Scripto* Exhibition rewrite, has the singer wear his lover's coat. It may be stretching things too far to connect this to Cleopatra dressing Antony in her clothes, but is worth noting

14 Antony Scaduto, *Bob Dylan: An Intimate Biography* Abacus, London, 1972 (Quoting "an Australian Actress")

15 http://www.imdb.com/title/tt0058126/releaseinfo?ref_=tt_ql_dt_2 accessed September 12, 2017

16 *Bird Droppings from Estonia: Narva as Elsinore* March 1, 2010 Hilary Bird http://www.eesti.ca/bird-droppings-from-estonia-narva-as-elsinore/article27357 accessed September 12, 2017

17 Bob Dylan *Chronicles: Volume One* Simon and Schuster 2004

18 Bob Dylan interviewed by Edna Gundersen *USA Today,* August 2001

19 For more on Minstrelsy and *"Love and Theft"* see Muir, Andrew *Troubadour,* Woodstock Press, UK, 2013; Jobes, Richard http://www.a-muir.co.uk/Dylan/Judas/J3.pdf accessed September 12, 2017; Warmuth, Scott through https://www.pinterest.com/scottwarmuth/a-bob-dylan-bookshelf/?lp=true and various blog, including: http://swarmuth.blogspot.com/2009/04/together-through-life-dispatch-3.html where he also posits a minstrelsy source for the title of Dylan's *Masked and Anonymous* movie

20 William J. Mahar "Ethiopian Skits and Sketches", published in *Inside The Minstrel Mask,* ed. by Bean, Hatch and McNamara

21 http://swarmuth.blogspot.com/2013/03/april-fools-day-2013-bob-dylan.html accessed September 7, 2017

22 https://babel.hathitrust.org/cgi/pt?id=osu.32435054621529;view=1up;seq=3 text of play accessed September 7, 2017

23 https://beta.prx.org/stories/10311 accessed September 7, 2017

24 http://swarmuth.blogspot.com/2013/03/april-fools-day-2013-bob-dylan.html accessed September 7, 2017

25 Michael Gray *Bob Dylan Encyclopaedia* Continuum; Updated, Revised ed. edition July 21, 2006

26 'Moonlight' Bob Dylan Copyright © 2001 by Special Rider Music

27 Christopher Ricks, *Visions of Sin Op. cit.*

28 Which in turn brings to mind Dylan's "Paying attention like a rattlesnake does/ When he's hearing footsteps trampling over his flowers" from a version of 'Caribbean Wind'

29 There's a Hamletesque touch to this, too, a sense of 'to put on an antic disposition'

30 Two alone in the one line: "*It's now or never, more than ever*"

31 Kees de Graaf http://www.keesdegraaf.com/media/Misc/6632p17vcu23ompne1itf4o31h851ugl.pdf op. cit.

32 Dylan comments in the liner notes to *Biograph*: "I don't know what it was about. I guess it was some kind of nursery rhyme." For an extensive look at Dylan's use of nursery rhyme see Muir, Andrew *Troubadour op. cit.*and Gray, Michael *Song and Dance Man III: The Art of Bob Dylan* Continuum International Publishing Group Ltd.; New Ed edition (July 4, 2002)

33 To underline the point, and drive a generation of fans to distraction, Quinn of said mightiness was pictured on the cover of the heavily compromised 1975 double LP release of *The Basement Tapes* but was, aptly if infuriatingly, nowhere to be found

34 Dylan, having experienced some three decades more of life sang instead, on *Time Out Of Mind's* 'Trying To get To Heaven', that: "*When you think that you lost everything/You find out you can always lose a little more*"

35 See later section on *The Tempest* and *Tempest*. Their conversation is recalled here: Allen Ginsberg, Teaching class, http://www.openculture.com/2014/03/hear-allen-ginsbergs-short-free-course-on-shakespeares-play-the-tempest-1980.html accessed November 11th 2017

36 Christopher Ricks, *Visions of Sin op. cit.*

37 Matthew Zuckerman: 'If There's an Original Thought Out There I Could Use It Right Now: The Folk Roots of Bob Dylan', *Isis* no.84, Bedworth, Warwickshire, UK, Apr–May 1999

38 *The Emotional Landscape of King Lear*, Arthur Kirsch, *Shakespeare Quarterly*, Vol. 39, No. 2 (Summer, 1988), pp. 154-170 Published by: Folger Shakespeare Library in association with George Washington University Stable URL: http://www.jstor.org/stable/2870627 Accessed: September 18, 2017

39 Gray Encyclopaedia *op. cit.*

40 The title song of the LP was, contrastingly, in initial caps

41 http://www.themetimeradio.com/ accessed December 25, 2018

42 My quotes are all from the Macgibbon & Kee hardback, first published in Great Britain 1971, © 1966 Bob Dylan and © 1971 The Macmillan Company

43 Richard Wissolik and Scott McGrath, *Bob Dylan's Words: A Critical Dictionary and Commentary.* Greensburg, PA: Eadmer Press, 1994

44 "A Draft of an Introduction to Renaldo and Clara" by Allen Ginsberg, *Telegraph 33* Manchester, UK Summer 1989. (The other two were: Milton's "Peace of mind, All passion spent" from *Samson Agonistes* and Emily Dickinson's "Tell all the Truth but tell it slant, Success in Circuit lies", a line from an untitled poem, number 1129 in *Collected Poems*)

45 Larry Charles was the film's co-writer as well as director. He is here referring to the director

and actor, John Cassavetes
46 *A Lesson in Dylan Appreciation*: https://www.eurozine.com/a-lesson-in-dylan-appreciation/
accessed November 4, 2018

Chapter Seven

DYLAN IN SHAKESPEARE

The present will now later be past

G iven Shakespeare's omnipresence in culture generally, and his tendency to appear in popular song,[1] it is almost inevitable that he would appear in Dylan's writing. It may come as more of a surprise to find Dylan turning up in works of Shakespeare; however, this is something that is beginning to be experienced, as evidenced by various productions in recent years.

I thought that I was going to witness my first live, as opposed to film, occurrence of a Dylan song being played in a Shakespeare production in 2016. This was at St John's College, Cambridge, where *Henry V* was being performed at the annual Cambridge Shakespeare Festival. The cast all appeared, with stringed instruments, playing what I took to be 'Restless Farewell'. When the singing began, I realised that they were, in fact, playing 'The Parting Glass', an old Scottish/Irish folk song whose melody Dylan had appropriated for his hastily written retort to press attacks.[2]

I only had a year to wait, however, before I was sitting in a London audience, watching a performance of *Hamlet* at the Harold Pinter Theatre, directed by Robert Icke, in the second consecutive sold out run of a production featuring a variety of Dylan performances from a wide range of his albums. Before that, however, I saw two films by Michael Almereyda that featured Dylan songs, although not sung by Dylan. The first was, again, *Hamlet* and at a pivotal moment a snatch of 'All Along the Watchtower' was played that has been much discussed.

It is fitting that we start with *Hamlet* as Dylan has been compared to the eponymous hero of the play and has referred to the play himself on numerous occasions. This association inevitably comes to mind when you view photographs of Dylan taken at Elsinore Castle in 1966.[3] In his recent book, *Invisible Now*[4], John Hughes acknowledges this: "Hamlet, a figure similarly burdened by people's intrusions and expectations, has always haunted my perceptions of Dylan since I first saw the pictures of Dylan at Elsinore castle taken on 1 May 1966." Hughes proceeds to draw a number of parallels between Dylan's created persona and the fictive prince of Denmark; most tellingly, here: "Dylan's best work always has this theatre and tension of a self who is illegible, caught between a discarded, rejected, or superseded version of who he has been, and a future self that he has not yet become. Indefiniteness and obscurity are internal to this transitional subjectivity, in motion between the no longer and the not yet."

Mr Hughes also formulates a correlation between Dylan's inventive and table-turning performances in his mid-Sixties interviews with, probably, Shakespeare's most famous character: "Many of Dylan's comments in interview or press conferences – witty, barbed, enigmatic, fleet-footed, retaliatory, gnomic, unfathomable – are certainly reminiscent of Hamlet, as in the memorable remark in the February 1966 *Playboy* interview that 'People have one great blessing – obscurity – and not really too many people are thankful for it.' It would not be an overstatement to say that Dylan's career and work perpetually cultivate, in the face of world fame, this need for remaining, as it were, imperceptible in plain view."

It is perhaps, therefore, not so surprising that Dylan has been used as a touchstone by more than one director/producer of *Hamlet*. Michael Almereyda's *Hamlet* film, from 2000, in an explosive start to the new millennium's productions of Shakespeare, featured a brief but telling nod to the bard of the end of the preceding century.

Dylan in Michael Almereyda's Hamlet 2000

The movie has a number of Dylan resonances, not least Sam Shepard playing the part of the ghost of Hamlet's murdered father. Actor and director Sam Shepard has a long history with Dylan. The highlights of their association include the co-written song, 'Brownsville Girl', Shepard's observations on those involved in Dylan's mid-Seventies touring in the book, *The Rolling Thunder Logbook;*[5] and the 'play' by Shepard titled *True Dylan (A Play)*. The blurb for the last of these proclaimed: "A one act play that features only two characters – Sam and Bob. It was first published in *Esquire* in 1987 and can be seen as a dramatised short 'interview' between Sam Shepard and Bob Dylan, focussing mainly upon Dylan's early days in New York, his meeting with Woody Guthrie, what constitutes 'truth', the greatness of James Dean, his musical influences and his motorcycle crash." It is a curious piece, being neither an interview nor a play and not wholly fictional nor fully factual. It shines a bent and fractured light on many of the myths that circle around the Dylan legend and thus provides a new and revealing perspective on them.

As you can tell from the blurb, James Dean features prominently in this 'play'. Dylan, like so many teenagers of his time, was mesmerised by Dean's legendary appearance in the films *East Of Eden, Rebel Without A Cause,* and *Giant*. The famous cover of Dylan's *Freewheelin'* album sees Dylan in a pose strikingly similar to an iconic photo of Dean in Times Square, their jackets being similar enough to inspire one of Don McLean's lines about Dylan in 'American Pie': 'in a coat he borrowed from James Dean'. Dean's films spoke to the yawning chasm between parents and children that we have seen Shakespeare and Dylan so adroitly address in their respective centuries. Dylan inherited Dean's mantle both literally and metaphorically when he sang of this division.[6]

Dean appears in Almereyda's film precisely as a reference to the disconnection between generations. As Hamlet watches TV and constructs his video diary, scenes from *East of Eden* and *Rebel Without A Cause* show Dean being the character that Hamlet wanted to be, as Dylan similarly wished when watching those 1955 releases. Hamlet looks on at his 'film within a film' and wonders at Dean's ability to perform in a fictional scenario how he himself should be acting in 'real life':

Is it not monstrous that this player here,
But in a fiction, in a dream of passion,
Could force his soul so to his own conceit
That from her working all his visage wanned,
Tears in his eyes, distraction in's aspect,
A broken voice, and his whole function suiting
With forms to his conceit?
(Act 2 Scene ii)

Dean provides an immediately recognisable reference point to Hamlet's struggles and one that at the same time underpins the Dylan connections to the film. In *True Dylan (A Play)* we read:

Sam Shepard: So you didn't have any big burning desire to get to New York or anything?
Bob Dylan: Naw. The only reason I wanted to go to New York is 'cause James Dean had been there.
Sam Shepard: So you really liked James Dean?
Bob Dylan: Oh, yeah. Always did.
Sam Shepard: How come?
Bob Dylan: Same reason you like anybody. I guess. You see somethin' of yourself in them.[7]

That Dylan was very much on Almereyda's mind is further indicated by a quote from the original screenplay, though not the one subsequently published. I have Douglas M Lanier to thank for pointing out that: "In the original shooting script the multiple deaths were followed by the entrance of Fortinbras, described as "a scruffy young man ... a bit like a young Bob Dylan," strongly resembling Almereyda himself."[8]

The scene featuring the opening of Dylan's song, 'All Along the Watchtower', being sung is brief[9]. However, typically for this fast-paced and connotation-heavy movie, it represents an entire mode of thinking in a compressed, fleeting but image-drenched scene. As such, a number of writers who have written at length on Michael Almereyda's *Hamlet*[10] have paid close attention to the 'gravedigger scene', here truncated to the digger at work, singing Dylan's 'All Along the Watchtower' to himself, unaccompanied.

Fittingly, given our discussion of Ophelia in 'Desolation Row' in the previous chapter, this occurs in a passage in the film which serves as a replacement for the gravedigger scene. It provides, as all commentators, including Almereyda himself, stress, the only respite from the claustrophobic surroundings of hi-tech[11] corporate life in the soulless city. Set in autumnal sunlight with bright leaves falling around children playing in Hallowe'en costumes, it is a welcome novelty after all the closed rooms, concrete, glass and steel. A breath of fresh air, literally as well as metaphorically. It comes too late, alas, for Ophelia. She instinctively knew that she should be in and with nature, but the only nature she had was artificial. She did not have real plants. Instead, she only had photographs of flowers. She dies in an artificial pond, which was visually heartbreaking, especially when you compare it, as you instinctively do, with the famous and glorious description of where she dies in Shakespeare's words, via Gertrude:

> There is a willow grows askant[12] a brook,
> That shows his hoar leaves in the glassy stream.
> There with fantastic garlands did she make
> Of crowflowers, nettles, daisies, and long purples,
> That liberal shepherds give a grosser name,
> But our cold maids do dead men's fingers call them.

(Act IV Scene vii)

In this film the only time she is with nature is in her grave. And, although it may be claimed that she reaches salvation through death, as she lies now 'in nature', it does not feel that way. The only emotions are ones of poignant loss and a wasted life.

The scene is much reduced from what was first envisaged:

"I think it was Harold Goddard who pointed out that no character in the play can match Hamlet when it comes to verbal sparring, no one is his intellectual equal – except the nameless Clown (as he's designated in the text) digging Ophelia's grave in this famously mordant wild-card of a scene. I liked the idea of the gravedigger being a kind of uncrowned prince and purposely cast the part young, tagging Jeffrey Wright, a dazzling actor, expert at conveying wiley intelligence. We shot in a vast cemetery, Halloween day, autumn leaves flickering in the sun. Jeffrey was primed; the scene seemed to fly. But in the editing room it became clear that I'd failed to get it right. The tone and timing were off, and the whole episode seemed to sidetrack Hamlet's response to Ophelia's death. The movie worked better with the prized scene cut out. But we kept a vestige of Jeffrey's performance, a chorus (sic) from the Dylan song, as a wistful souvenir."[13]

It is altered even from the official screenplay, though this following excerpt is close to what is shown. It is worth keeping in mind, however, that the words to the song fade quickly and are hard to catch after 'Businessmen they drink...':

EXT. GRAVEYARD – DAY
Among the stones and crypts, kids are playing in Halloween outfits. They scatter as Horatio's bike rounds a bend, slowing alongside an embankment.
Over this we hear the grinding sound of a backhoe, and the gravedigger's voice, a gravelly growl, singing.

GRAVEDIGGER (off-screen)   'There must be some way out of here,'
                                 Said the joker to the thief.

The Gravedigger is young, close to Hamlet's age. The backhoe, operated by another man, finishes clawing at the earth. The Gravedigger moves to the grave, shovelling out broken roots.

'There's too much confusion, I can't get no relief.
Businessmen, they drink my wine, plowmen dig my earth,
None of them along the line know what any of it is worth,'

Hamlet and Horatio dismount the bike and remove their helmets.
*[The Gravedigger, seeing them approach, chooses to ignore them.]

'No reason to get excited', the thief he kindly spoke,
'There are many here among us who feel that life is but a joke
But you and I, we've been through that, and this is not our fate"[14]

Although the only clearly decipherable lines are the song's opening two, they have been taken by critics to connote, via allusion and intertextuality, extremely wide resonances. Those radiate out from the opening verse and through the largely absent gravedigger scene, the play as a whole, the song as a whole, the character of Hamlet and Dylan himself.

Douglas M Lanier noted in *The Shakespeare Quarterly*[15]: "In the film's much-truncated funeral scene the Gravedigger merrily sings Bob Dylan's 'All Along the Watchtower' as he works: "There must be some way out of here, said the joker to the thief." In many ways, that throwaway allusion epitomises Almereyda's desire to find "some way out" of the wraparound media system to which his Hamlet and Shakespeare's *Hamlet* have been subjected, some cinematic mode of escape, evasion, or resistance that is not always already appropriated by that system."

While Mark Thornton Burnett[16] interestingly, if somewhat far-fetchedly, linked the presence of a Dylan song to the once widely-held conspiracy theory that the CIA was hoping to eliminate Dylan in much the same way as Claudius tries to do to Hamlet. Burnett traces connections between Dylan's "protest" phase and Hamlet and their analogous 'celebrity status':

" ... aural snatches of the song 'All along the Watchtower,' as sung by the Gravedigger (Jeffrey Wright), recall its composer and first performer, Bob Dylan, and his involvement with the burgeoning civil rights movement; once again, Hamlet is vitalised by the association. As the Gravedigger philosophizes about "too much confusion," "businessmen" who "drink my wine," and "plowmen" who "dig my earth," one is reminded of the original circumstances of the song and, in particular, the rumor that Dylan, following a protracted withdrawal from public life, was the victim of a CIA assassination attempt. It therefore seems as if Hamlet (who returns to Elsinore/New York having frustrated the murderous designs on him) is conceived of as a latter-day folk celebrity; however, because it is the Gravedigger and not the prince who intones Dylan's lyrics, a complicating dimension is added to the comparison."[17]

These and other interpreters are all quoted and commented on by Marie Gerzic who has written more extensively and in more depth than anyone else on this.[18] One of Gerzic's contentions is to see the song's line being picked because "businessmen they drink my wine" refers to Dylan's career and is in context of his manager Albert Grossman having exploited him. A similar view is often taken to be the main meaning behind the song 'Dear Landlord' from the same album. I find these analyses of the songs to be very reductive.

On the other hand, it is known that Dylan has used personal grudges as starting points for songs. The most often quoted story illuminating this trait is that the prophetic anthem 'When The Ship Comes In' with its biblical language, allusions and 'Pirate Jenny' analogies was triggered in response to the somewhat mundane occurrence of Dylan, as scruffy as Aldemeyera imagined Fortinbras-as-Bob, being rebuffed by receptionists in a hotel or motel where Joan Baez had made a reservation. He was only allowed in when she requested it and, as she recounted in confessed disbelief, 'he was so pissed' he wrote the song in one evening 'to get back at those idiots'. This tale provides an object lesson in how the 'trigger' itself may bear little relation to the finished artistic achievement that it ignites.

Commenting on Burnett's views, outlined above, Gerzic proclaims contrarily that: "...the words are sung by the gravedigger (who is played by Jeffery Wright – an African American actor) and not by Hamlet himself. Therefore, the connections to Dylan's celebrity are tenuous at best and ignore the "meaning" behind the song's lyrics. The allusions to a period of social change, especially with regards to the civil rights movement, are much more applicable. These connections to ideas of race are further punctuated by the fact that the song 'All Along the Watchtower' was later recorded and made famous by Jimi Hendrix (an African American musician)."

However, Maria Gerzic's main emphasis comes when she equates her own distillation of the song's core message with that of the (missing) grave-digger scene in particular, and the play as a whole:

"The song is basically about what is valuable, human life, and what is not, the more material things associated with a consumer society."

That this is the view to be found at the heart of Almereyda's adaptation of *Hamlet* is clear, but the crucial line: "none of them know what any of it is worth" is all but inaudible in the scene under discussion. Granted you can still take it as an implied reference and, unquestionably, the film is saturated with images of and references to a consumerist society. Money reigns supreme, and we are bombarded with brands and company names. Still, what you actually hear clearly is only the opening couplet of the song. This is, I think, important in a way that none of these commentators, whose detailed observations are illuminating in many other aspects, have mentioned. Much has been made of 'All Along the Watchtower's' curious narrative structure. It seems to tell the story out of sequence and by doing so creates an endless circle of either repetition or determined fate, or both. Dylan's deliberate decision to begin the 'story' of the song where he does means that the opening lines, when first heard, can surely only bring one incident to mind; that of Jesus on the cross talking to the thief.

Mythologically and symbolically speaking, the joker in cards is the successor to the Fool in the Tarot pack and both are connected to the Trickster figure. All three are linked to and antecedents of Christ in iconography. As Nick De Somogyi puts it:

"As such, as Shakespeare emphasises in *King Lear's* Fool, he may also be a figure for Christ. The unnumbered Tarot card, the Fool, according to Paul Hudson, derives from representations of Dionysus: "Like his successor Jesus, Dionysus was also an overturner of hidebound traditions and restrictive tyranny. He was the incarnate power of spiritual revolt and rebirth." The Fool of Tarot Cards is the ancestor of the joker in latterday cards. Dylan uses the image with an earthy familiarity, as his song envisages a conversation between Christ and thief on the cross, an interpretation strengthened by line three: the "wine" of His blood is depicted consumed by capitalist businessmen rather than by faithful disciples"[19]

After hearing the whole song, other views may present themselves. However, here in Almereyda's *Hamlet*, you only hear the opening lines and so this re-evaluation of what might be going on is not open to you unless you bring the remainder of the song, unheard in the film, into play. Even if one does, though, any divergent meanings and interpretations can only be laid beside the initial impression. Which means that when we reach the end of the song, we feel an accumulated impact. De Somogyi describes this:

"In retaining the "couple of horsemen" but omitting the "chariot of men" and the shield, Dylan draws attention to the more celebrated image of the Apocalypse, and along with the implicit situation of the Crucifixion, condenses Old Testament prophecy, with New Testament fulfilment and Revelation: all Biblical events "focused on a single episode", the single episode upon which Christianity pivots. Furthermore the substitution of "wildcat" for "lion" and "riders" for "horsemen" makes the location of the song the more contemporary and, like Christ's speech, the more American."[20]

As we watch Hamlet and Horatio approach Ophelia's burial plot, we are listening to Christ in dialogue with the most famous of thieves who describes Christ as 'this man who has done nothing amiss' and to whom Christ promises 'Today shalt thou be with me in paradise'. (Luke 23:43-43) Dylan was to return to this scene in a 1981 song, called 'Thief on the Cross', which opens with the lines: "There's a thief on the cross, his chances are slim/There's a thief on the cross, I wanna talk to him." He has played that song in concert, once, on November 10, 1981 in New Orleans.[21]

The lines seem almost as particularly apt for Hamlet's situation as they are for Christ's. Hamlet too is looking for a way out and can find no relief. Hamlet is also feeling bewildered by his father's demands and worries that he is incapable or unworthy of carrying out his mission. In their respective stories, both 'jokers' are doomed to die imminently.

Dylan in Michael Almereyda's Cymbeline (Anarchy: Ride or Die)
Almereyda returned to using a Dylan song for his 2014 film adaptation of *Cymbeline*, sometimes bearing the title *Anarchy: Ride or Die*[22]. Dylan's song 'Dark Eyes' is beautifully sung by Milla Jovovich, who plays the evil queen, as a centrepiece in the movie. Critics were divided over this. Peter Sobczynski found that: "... the action stops for a minute for a scene featuring co-star Milla Jovovich singing Bob Dylan›s 'Dark Eyes'." Speaking as an enormous fan of both of them, I thought this union of two favorites

in the pop-culture firmament would be worth the price of admission all by itself. Alas, it is not...[23]" However, it was not the song's performance or placement that disappointed him but the rest of the film.

Alan Stone, however, was singularly unimpressed by the song itself, describing it as an "an indigestible lump in the bowels of his Shakespeare adaptation."[24] Quite what is 'indigestible' in this strong and moving performance is difficult to comprehend. Also, the word 'lump' suggests something hard to get over, and something long and arduous. Given that his review also, incorrectly, states that the whole song is sung, it would certainly appear that it felt overly long to this particular reviewer. That is doubly surprising as 'Dark Eyes' as a complete song is only sixteen lines long and is reduced here to twelve, due to the unfortunate omission of the crucial second verse. That verse links to a Biblical passage to which Hamlet also refers and thus would have provided another apposite connection between the two Shakespeare films where the director utilises Dylan songs.

Justin B Hopkins, on the other hand, remarked: "(The Queen)... His mother, another arguably less-than fully fleshed-out figure in the text, receives completely sufficient interpretation from Milla Jovovich, most of all in an extra-textual scene in which she serenades Cymbeline and his gang with a superb rendition of Bob Dylan's 'Dark Eyes.'[25] David Rooney seems to me to also hit the right note when he describes it as "a nice smoky rendition"[26].

The music begins immediately following Iachimo's request for storage of his supposed present. The vocals kick in just as he leaves the room and Imogen, stressed by their strange meeting, flops down wearily. We cut to the Queen performing to an audience of bikers, some wearing glitter eye masks, with Ed Harris[27], a magnificent Cymbeline, looking on with love. The Queen is both in and out of character. Partly she is in a bubble for this scene, being a nightclub singer commenting on the world outside as *"they're drinking up"* as the second line of the song puts it. Yet she is also in character at various times, such as at the end of the first verse when Cornelius states of her, before passing drugs on to Cloten: *"I will not trust one of her malice with/A drug of such damn'd nature."* That drug looks the same as at least part of the consignment which we soon see the police handling as they simultaneously count the money they have taken from a biker. That sorry individual is meanwhile being beaten to death by other cops, with golf clubs, for the entertainment of their leaders.

Before that, still in the opening verse, as we hear: "*I live in another world where life and death are memorized*" we see Imogen, dressed for bed and looking sad and nervous, as the trunk containing Iachimo is rolled by. The closing of the couplet "*and all I see are dark eyes*" plays over an aerial shot of Posthumus sprawled desolately on a distant floor.

When the second verse here, the third of the song proper, plays, the camera pans across the audience in which we see a skeleton, an image which is seen elsewhere in the film. Cornelius supplies Cloten with drugs and Jovovich then sings "*I feel nothing for their game where beauty goes unrecognized*" as we witness Cymbeline, flanked by two of his mob, looking like a mixture of cowboys and gangsters and striding forward with serious intent. You just know that this is going to end badly for somebody.

With the verse ending, we cut to the beginning of the biker being battered with golf clubs. The poor man seems to have already been through a rough time before they drag his body in for this ordeal. Curiously they now concentrate on his head which is still protected by his biker's helmet. We cut back and forth from this scene to Ed Harris and his crew shooting up two policemen who have stopped their car for a coffee break. The recently sung line: "*They tell me revenge is sweet and from where they stand, I'm sure it is.*" seems irresistibly apt at this juncture.

As the song approaches its close we see that Imogen is suspicious about Iachimo's trunk. It is as though she intimates that Iachimo is planning something underhand. If we know the play, we are aware that the flimsy, long shirt she is wearing as night attire will soon be lifted by Iachimo's hand while she sleeps. It is as though she, too, knows that something is badly awry. As she, seemingly reluctantly, heads to bed, the song reaches the words: "*passion rules the arrow that flies.*" At the very end of the song, the singer pauses between the last recitation of "dark" and "eyes", and then, on the final word, the camera moves to enact the Queen looking directly into Cloten's drug addled eyes. And then we cut back to Imogen's house and immediately after the last notes of the song play, the lock of the trunk springs open. In a very rushed production, Dylan's song, albeit truncated, paradoxically affords some breathing space despite all the vital action that unfolds as it is performed.

Dylan in Robert Icke's Hamlet

Our final 'Dylan in Shakespeare' production takes us back to live theatre but this time to Dylan himself singing. Robert Icke's London stage production of *Hamlet* in 2017 first ran at the Almeida Theatre. It was so popular it later transferred to the Harold Pinter Theatre. Echoing Almereyda's film; screens, video technology, and CCTV featured prominently.

The Almeida run was very successful. Tickets were very hard to come by, and the returns snapped up instantly by those at the head of long queues. This was doubtless helped by the celebrity status of the actor in the lead role. Hamlet was played by Andrew Scott, most famous for his portrayal of Moriarty in the BBC TV series *Sherlock*.[28] The widespread audience acclaim was reflected in reviews which were mainly positive if not downright adulatory. Unsurprisingly, however, there was more of a split when it came to the liberal use of so many Dylan songs, chosen from throughout his career, and, crucially, sung by the man himself. This development dovetails so neatly with this book that it is worth noting the range of opinions and detailing how the songs were employed in the production.

Although many aspects of the production were lauded, the primary focus of the praise fell on the chosen method of delivering Shakespeare's lines, and this was softly and as close to normal conversation as could be made possible. Pauses, fittingly enough for this play, dominated. Here are some of the comments this elicited:

"In Andrew Scott he has an actor capable of making the verse feel like tip-of-the-tongue stuff, the words clean and new ... He splits open the lines and gets at the sweet, ripe stuff inside. It is a performance of wit, delicacy and clarity, with silences that are equally as eloquent."[29]

"The originality is a question of pitch and pace and breath. It is as if the lungs of the play are different. ... It has extraordinary conversational ease."[30]

"Aspects of the staging and sound design are ambitious, and the success of these parts of the production ensures this modern setting fits the text effectively. The production did not in any way disappoint, as neither did Andrew Scott's captivating performance of a softly spoken, frequently sarcastic Hamlet."[31]

While admiring this 'conversational style' in theory, and enjoying it in certain passages, I felt it brought with it a problem, especially for a play of this length. Firstly, the positive benefits; these came from transforming those speeches that we are overly used to hearing declaimed in familiar oratorical styles. The effect of this, familiar words appearing in a different light, was not dissimilar to Dylan's re-interpretations of his own songs. The way in which Dylan expresses meaning by changing pitch and tempo, and by his voice inserting new pauses, stresses and elongating or contracting phrases over the new melodic arrangements. In *Hamlet* all the speeches are famous, but in the most celebrated even of these, the style was a triumph. It is so difficult to hear the soliloquies, in particular, anew, but one did so hear them here.

However, although Icke's *Hamlet* was not as long as often quoted, because those timings included the duration of the two intervals, it was still generously over three hours of playing time. I found that the downbeat style, over such a stretch, drained the play of much of its energy. For long stretches, there was no light to the shade; so much so that I must confess that the declamatory and bombastic visiting players came as something of a relief, just by the nature of the contrast. Much of the multi-layered meanings and frissons of the text were lost, and the relationship of the words to the action was often not present due to the casual delivery.

On the other hand, it worked superbly well at other times, and especially when the insertion of considerable pauses made the experience of hearing Hamlet "talk to himself" fresh and natural. In "To be or not to be..." and many other passages, you really felt as though he was thinking these things through for the first time.

The conversational approach also threw the songs into high relief. Dylan's music and voice boomed around the previously subdued stage in a suitably theatrical manner. This drew a mixed response. Some reviewers were unsure, though leaning to the negative: "I was less sure about the use of Bob Dylan songs"[32], while others were firmly against: "If this *Hamlet* gets so much right, it's not perfect. I found the occasional use of Bob Dylan's music incongruous and intrusive, loudly jarring."[33] At the other end of the receptive scale came comments, such as: "Tom Gibbons' cinematic sound design was wonderful. The Bob Dylan soundtrack was intricately woven into the show and subtly challenged the absolute modernity of the setting".[34] Plus David Nice from *the arts desk*: "quietly remarkable, Hildegard Bechtler's sets work in tandem with Natasha Chivers' lighting and the best of Tom Gibbons' sound – I'm not so keen on its ambient omnipresence, but the use of Dylan songs is superb – to change scenes with cinematic ease. It's good to have the Norwegian threat played out on Danish television, and the fencing filmed, too, with some of the crucial lines purposefully drowned out by Dylan".[35]

It is not entirely clear if this next comment is praise or condemnation, but it certainly catches an element of the experience very expressively: "Dylan songs thread through the action like the voice of a goblin damned."[36] Perhaps it is a mixture; another who had mixed feelings was John Stokes, writing in *The Times Literary Supplement*. Mr Stokes worries not about the quality of Dylan's songs but whether their own "unignorable pulse" will interfere with, rather than augment, the play's message. This gets to the nub of the matter. Mr Stokes asks: "The immediate issue, though, is whether there can be room on a single stage for two writers of "literary" stature but contrasting timbre. Do we hear those well-known lyrics as annotations, corroborations, or alternatives, more or less ironical?"[37]

The answer to this would vary, though 'corroborations' and 'more or less ironical' are the predominate ones for those familiar with both the songs and the play. In effect, however, all the songs can be taken in a whole range of ways; by turn: whimsy, instrumental break, ironic, underscoring, oblique or literal to the point of blunt connectivity.

This production was later shown, slightly altered for TV, by the BBC in 2018, and although this has drawbacks, as already discussed, compared to seeing the actors in the flesh, it will be the most watched and re-watched version. Consequently, I shall use the present tense to describe it and remark on any major differences between stage and film in the use of Dylan material.

The audience is greeted, prior to the play commencing, with Dylan singing 'One More Cup of Coffee (Valley Below)'. This song was presumably felt to be apt because we know that Hamlet is destined to die (to "go to the valley below") after taking revenge upon his uncle. Also, before going, he spends his time procrastinating, always finding something else to do. His continuous delays perhaps equating to the song's "one more cup of coffee before I go...". At the start of the play, if you did not know the song, you would need the chorus to pick up on this. All we hear at this point are the opening lines. After that, a blaring horn, which we come to learn is the production's way of signalling the ghost's imminent presence, sounds, and is followed by the question "Who's there?" As a result, the performance opens with Shakespeare's words coming immediately after Dylan's. In the TV production, the viewers' screen is filled with the images from what was shown on the stage TV in the theatre, as the song plays.

The second quatrain of Dylan's song could be read as having pertinence to Hamlet's situation as he cannot 'sense affection or love' from Ophelia, nor most others he encounters in the play, and he is, often rightly, doubting the loyalty of those around him:

> But I don't sense affection
> No gratitude or love
> Your loyalty is not to me
> But to the stars above.

One of the more oblique uses of a song comes after just six minutes into the production when we get the opening minute of Dylan's song 'Spirit on the Water'. This comes just after the discussion of the ghost as a spirit. We hear the opening two and a half verses, including the instrumental beginning, but the relevance seems tenuous other than the closing line of the first verse "*I can't hardly sleep*". The song starts: "*Spirit on the water/ Darkness on the face of the deep*". This a clear invocation of the opening lines of *The Bible*:

> 1 In the beginning God created the heaven and the earth.
> 2 And the earth was without form, and void; and darkness was upon the face of the deep. And the Spirit of God moved upon the face of the waters.[38]

Perhaps this was in the director's mind, or alternatively, maybe this song was chosen here more for its atmospheric quality. On TV the song can be heard for some time, faintly in the background, as Claudius holds forth. The same song re-emerges soon afterwards with a more literal connection to the play in the lines we hear. This occurs some half an hour into the production, in Act II Scene ii, when Rosencrantz and Guildenstern are welcomed by the King and Queen.

I'm pale as a ghost –
Holding a blossom on a stem
You ever seen a ghost? No
But you have heard of them

The opening line is appropriate because we have just heard how Hamlet is "ailing", while the closing two lines could hardly be a straighter link between song and play when experienced together. This is underlined as the song is interrupted a few words thereafter by the now familiar blare to signify the approach of the ghost. The second line in that verse, like so many lines in both play and song, is a direct reference to *The Bible*. In this case, *Isaiah 11:2:*

"There shall come forth a rod out of the stem of Jesse, and a blossom shall grow out of his root; and the Spirit of God shall rest upon Him, the spirit of wisdom and understanding, the spirit of counsel and of might, the spirit of knowledge and of piety; and He shall be filled with the spirit of fear of the Lord."

On TV, the song played while Ophelia and Hamlet shared a dancing embrace. It was an intimate passage before everything started to unravel for them. The production has still not finished with 'Spirit on the Water'. It re-appears as an instrumental passage some ten minutes later, where it acts as a bridge between a textual jump in scenes.

Prior to that, we have a song with, in context, some obvious textual parallels to the play in progress. "Something is rotten in the state of Denmark" segues, aptly enough, into *"Everything went from bad to worse"* the opening phrase from Dylan's 'Up To Me'. *"Death kept followin', trackin' us down"* and *"Time is an enemy"* soon follow, and are words very pertinent to how Hamlet is feeling. The same is true of: *"Now somebody's got to show their hand... I guess it must be up to me."* The opening to the second verse serves as a sardonic commentary on the sweet prince: *"If I'd a-thought about it I never would've done it, I guess I would've let it slide"*. You also cannot escape hearing the relevance of, *"I was just too stubborn to ever be governed by enforced insanity"* or think of Ophelia as we jump in the song to a verse where Dylan sings: *"She's everything I need and love but I can't be swayed by that."* The song cuts abruptly soon after.

'Up To Me' is the most intriguing of the songs chosen. It is not well-known, relatively speaking. It was omitted from the *Blood on the Tracks* album, presumably because it shared too much of the melody and themes of 'Shelter from the Storm', 'Tangled Up In Blue' and 'A Simple Twist of Fate'. As a song, it achieves the same superlative standard as those three. However, it did not appear, officially, until the 1985 compilation box set *Biograph*. It was also effective in the TV production, although more truncated there than in the theatre performances, in two revealing dumb shows. As Dylan sings, the camera homes in on Claudio and Gertrude cavorting, full length on the floor, followed by Ophelia lying in a bath and surprised by Hamlet appearing and kissing her, and then holding her throat with a manic look on his face.

Soon after this scene, Hamlet exclaims: *"O heavens! died two months ago, and not forgotten yet? Then there's hope a great man's memory may outlive his life half a year"*, and a pipe starts playing the melody to Dylan's 'One Too Many Mornings'. Later, the music comes in, and then the vocal. It is all beautifully timed amidst the initial dumb show and then the play-within-a-play dialogue. On TV, the close-ups afforded of the dumb show and the music knit together perfectly, with Hamlet and his family looking on as the actors and Dylan's song play.

'One too many mornings', as a phrase, is almost ironically literal to Hamlet's procrastination, but the song of that name hints most forcefully at the break up of Hamlet and Ophelia's relationship. We hear Dylan as the dumb show precedes *The Mousetrap* and as we hear, in Shakespeare's words:

OPHELIA   *'Tis brief, my lord.*
HAMLET   *As woman's love."*

There is a male viewpoint towards the end of an affair in the song, too. However, it does not have as bitter, nor anti-female, a perspective as some of Dylan's earlier and later songs which would have more exactly matched Hamlet's demeanour and outlook at this point in the play's proceedings. Despite having clear links to 'Don't Think Twice, It's Alright', there is no *"You just kinda wasted my precious time"* here. Instead, Dylan sings: *"You're right from your side/I'm right from mine."*

Still, the songs keep coming, 'All Along the Watchtower' partly works in a similar manner to the snippet of it in Almereyda's film. The shared imagery and theme of "worth" strikes home when the song begins, soon after we hear Hamlet declaim: *"My thoughts be bloody, or be nothing worth!"*. This time we are not constricted to a snippet, and we have the communicative power of Dylan's own delivery to open up the song's depth. The same connections mentioned previously are therefore palpably more present in this production, while the line *"So let us not talk falsely now, the hour is getting late"* captures precisely the state of play on stage.

The song ends with a sense of foreboding so intense as to be apocalyptic:
Outside in the distance a wildcat did growl
Two riders were approaching, the wind began to howl

From the song's shared biblical imagery and figures from *Isaiah*, we take this ending to be the beginning of the fall of Babylon, but we also sense the devastating final days that are foretold in similar imagery in the Bible Eschatological visions which suffuse Dylan's work and are of obvious import to Shakespeare, too, throughout his work. 'All Along the Watchtower' here also leads up to the later playing of 'Not Dark Yet' and that song's even closer proximity to what Kent in *King Lear* refers to as "the promised end".

Before that, however, we have a snippet from 'Sugar Baby'. The surrounding of the gravedigger scene is an apt place to hear Dylan clearly sing the opening line of the fourth verse *"Every moment of existence seems like some dirty trick"*. The following lines would also resonate, especially the end of the verse, but only if you already knew them as Dylan was played very softly by then[39]:

Try to make things better
For someone, sometimes, you just end up making it a thousand times worse

During the fateful sword-fighting scene, Dylan's 'Not Dark Yet' rings around the theatre. It is introduced only instrumentally to begin with, as Hamlet speaks the biblically infused lines (Act V, Scene ii):

HAMLET *Not a whit, we defy augury. There's a special*
providence in the fall of a sparrow. If it be now, 'tis not
to come; if it be not to come, it will be now; if it be not
now, yet it will come – the readiness is all. Since no man
has aught of what he leaves, what is't to leave betimes?

This in turn suggests one of Dylan's masterpieces that drew on the same source, his 1981 song, 'Every Grain of Sand':

I hear the ancient footsteps like the motion of the sea
Sometimes I turn, there's someone there, other times it's only me
I am hanging in the balance of the reality of man
Like every sparrow falling, like every grain of sand

Wissolik and Mcgrath also see the second to fourth lines of the above *Hamlet* quote reflected in Dylan's '11 Outlined Epitaphs'[40]:

(if it rhymes, it rhymes
if it don't, it don't
if it comes, it comes
if it won't, it won't)

To return to Ickes' play, both in the theatre and the TV version, the music frames the conversations leading up to the sword fight, playing beneath them instrumentally until Dylan's vocals are fully manifest as the rigged contest fight begins. Again we are reminded of that enemy, time: "time is running away...." and the overall connection of the song to the play is so direct at this point as to be blunt. It is a figurative dig in the ribs and a voice whispering "see what he did there?"

On the other hand, there are also particular resonances, and the following verse is immensely fitting as Ophelia's ex-boyfriend and brother fight:

"Well, my sense of humanity has gone down the drain
Behind every beautiful thing there's been some kind of pain
She wrote me a letter and she wrote it so kind
She put down in writing what was in her mind"

As with 'Sugar Baby', this song has strong religious overtones and allusions to Shakespeare's contemporary, John Donne. As we muse these connections, Dylan's voice sings:

"I just don't see why I should even care
It's not dark yet, but it's getting there"

Then his vocals are cut, and it does 'get there', it *is* dark, as Laertes, the Queen, Claudius and Hamlet all die one after the other in quick succession. After Horatio implores: *"flights of angels sing thee to thy rest!"* 'One More Cup of Coffee (Valley Below)' starts to play again and following Fortinbras' concluding speech, booms around the auditorium over the sustained applause. During this all the actors on the corpse-strewn stage 'rise from the dead' to take the acclaim, connecting us back to the theme of resurrection and the questions of what comes after death in both Dylan's songs and the Shakespeare play they have been entwined with over the preceding hours.

***

The inclusion of Dylan songs in productions of Shakespeare is a new occurrence. It remains to be seen whether it is a trend that will continue. Given Icke's major development in this regard, it may be more likely than not. The adaptability and suitability of Dylan's lyrics to the stage has been further underlined by Conor McPherson's musical-play *Girl From The North Country*. An emotional and triumphant staging, McPherson's production, based around songs from throughout Dylan's career, has moved to America's

Broadway after winning awards, acclaim and sold-out runs in London. Mr McPherson's comments about how Dylan's songs always seemed to fit, wherever he placed them, speak to the probability of their future use in more drama:

"Sometimes I would wake in the night with a Bob Dylan song going round in my head. The next day I would come into rehearsals and we'd learn the song and put it in the show. Did it fit? Did it matter? It always fit somehow ... It strikes me that many of Mr Dylan's songs can be sung at any time, by anyone in any situation, and still make sense and resonate with that particular place and person and time. When you realise this you can no longer have any doubt you are in the presence of a truly great, unique artist ... Many books have been written in an attempt to explore this universal power. Even though Mr Dylan will say he's often not sure what his songs mean, he always sings them like he means them. Because he does mean them. Like Philip Larkin, like James Joyce, Mr Dylan has the rare power of literary compression. Images and conceits are held in unstable relations, forcing an atomic reaction of some kind, creating a new inner world."[41]

Endnotes

1 See *Shakespeare and Popular Music*, by Adam Hansen, Continuum, November, 2010

2 'The Parting Glass' is more commonly attributed as a traditional Irish song nowadays after its modern popularisation by the Clancy Brothers by whom Dylan almost certainly was introduced to it. The song's long genealogy takes in much of the intermingled history of Scottish and Irish folk. It was the standard Scottish parting song until Robert Burns partially re-wrote 'Auld Lang's Syne'

3 https://www.gettyimages.com/detail/news-photo/folk-singer-bob-dylan-contemplates-kronborg-castle-the-news-photo/514679348 accessed January 17, 2019

4 Invisible Now: Bob Dylan In The 1960s (Ashgate Popular And Folk Music Series) by John Hughes, Routledge; July 4, 2013

5 "Brownsville Girl": https://bobdylan.com/songs/brownsville-girl/Copyright © 1986 by Special Rider Music

The Rolling Thunder Logbook; original publication by The Viking Press, NY – 1977

Sam Shepard was also in a relationship with Patti Smith, herself with many a Dylan connection, and co-wrote a play with her, *Cowboy Mouth*, with the title taken directly from Dylan's lyrics to "Sad-Eyed Lady of the Lowlands"

6 In July 1988 Dylan took a detour and visited Fairmount, Indiana, Dean's hometown and resting place at around 01:30. The police opened up the James Dean Gallery for him soon thereafter. David Loehr, the owner of the gallery was quoted in a BBC website 50th death anniversary tribute as saying: "In 1988 Dylan even visited the farm where Dean lived, and walked around the fields at

02:00, which must have been a cosmic moment."

7 Sam Shepard, *True Dylan (A Play)*, Vintage (2012) originally Esquire magazine, 1987

8 *Shakespeare's Noir* by Douglas M Lanier. *Shakespeare Quarterly Vol 53 No. 2 Screen Shakespeare* (Summer 2002) Published by the Folger Shakespeare Library in association with the George Washington Library. Stable URL: http://www.jstor.org/stable/384407

9 It is curious that the subtitles have the wrong lyrics for the clearest of the few lines heard. It is sung correctly as "said the joker to the thief" but is transcribed as "send a joker to your king"

10 Released December, 2000 in the UK, sometimes referred to as *Hamlet 2000*

11 Hi-tech for 2000, that is. Technology very quickly dates and what was filmed as cutting edge now looks quaint

12 More commonly given as 'aslant', but New Cambridge argues for "askant"

13 *Shakespeare's Hamlet* Michael Almereyda, page 140, Faber and Faber, London, 2000

14 *Ibid.*

15 Douglas M. Lanier *Ibid.*

16 Mark Thornton Burnett, "I See My Father' in 'My Mind's Eye': Surveillance and the Filmic Hamlet', in *Screening Shakespeare in the Twenty-First Century,* ed. by Mark Thornton Burnett and Ramona Wray (Edinburgh: Edinburgh University Press, 2006), pp. 31–52; and Mark Thornton Burnett, "'To Hear and See the Matter": Communicating Technology in Michael Almereyda's *Hamlet (2000)',* Cinema Journal 42.3 Spring (2003), 48 69 (52–3)

17 "To Hear and See the Matter": Communicating Technology in Michael Almereyda's Hamlet (2000)" *Cinema Journal*
Vol. 42, No. 3 (Spring, 2003), pp. 48-69

18 *Gerzic, Marina (*First sent to me by Stephan Pickering): *When Dylan Met the Bard: Fragments of Screen (Sound) in Michael Almereyda's Hamlet* University of Western Australia http://research-repository.uwa.edu.au/en/publications/when-dylan-met-the-bard(a2774b41-b2e1-4ae8-a98a-25911903cd20)/export.html accessed 18th October 2017. Accessed 18th October 2017
BA Thesis 2008, *The Intersection of Shakespeare and modern culture; an intertextual examination of some millennial Shakespearean film adaptations (1999-2001) with special reference to music.* Presented for the degree of Doctor of Philosophy, University of Western Australia

19 De Somogyi, Nick *Jokermen & Thieves: Bob Dylan and The Ballad Tradition* (and here is quoting Paul Hudson, *The Devil's Picturebook: The Complete Guide to Tarot Cards* (London, 1972), p. 113) Wanted Man, UK, 1986

20 De Somogyi, Nick, *Ibid.*

21 Released on *The Bootleg Series Vol. 13: Trouble No More 1979–1981* Legacy Records, November 2017

22 Released in 2015 in most countries, including the USA and the UK

23 http://www.rogerebert.com/reviews/cymbeline-2015 Accessed July 1st 2017

24 http://bostonreview.net/film/alan-stone-michael-almereyda-cymbeline August 17, 2015
LITERATURE & CULTURE *Park that Lark* Alan A. Stone Accessed July 1st 2017

25 Justin B. Hopkins, *Early Modern Literary Studies: Cymbeline,* a film directed by Michael Almereyda (2014) Franklin and Marshall College

26 http://www.hollywoodreporter.com/review/cymbeline-venice-review-729713 9/3/2014 by David Rooney Accessed July 1st, 2017

27 Ed Harris also appears in Dylan film, *Masked And Anonymous,* playing the character Oscar Vogel

28 Intriguingly the actor who played Holmes in the same series, Benedict Cumberbatch, had preceded Scott in playing the lead role in Hamlet on the London stage

29 The Stage, review by Natasha Tripney – March 1, 2017 https://www.thestage.co.uk/reviews/2017/hamlet-review-almeida-theatre-london/

30 *The Observer Hamlet review – Andrew Scott is a truly sweet prince* https://www.theguardian.com/stage/2017/mar/05/hamlet-almeida-review-andrew-scott-robert-icke accessed September 1, 2017

31 A Younger Theatre Review: Hamlet, Almeida Theatre By Hattie Pierce on March 9, 2017. Accessed September 1, 2017 https://www.ayoungertheatre.com/review-hamlet-almeida-theatre/

32 Progressive Geographies: Some thoughts on Andrew Scott as Hamlet at the Almeida https://progressivegeographies.com/2017/02/25/some-thoughts-on-andrew-scott-as-hamlet-at-the-almeida/

posted February 25, 2017 accessed September 1st 2018

33 Broadway World Review: *HAMLET, Almeida Theatre* by Gary Naylor March 1, 2017

34 A Younger Theatre Review: *Hamlet, Almeida Theatre* By Hattie Pierce on March 9, 2017 in Theatre accessed September 1st 2017 https://www.ayoungertheatre.com/review-hamlet-almeida-theatre/

35 Andrew Scott, predictably unpredictable, is subject to Robert Icke's slow-burn clarity by David Nice Wednesday, 01 March 2017 theartsdesk.com http://www.theartsdesk.com/theatre/hamlet-almeida-theatre

36 *The Observer Hamlet review – Andrew Scott is a truly sweet prince* https://www.theguardian.com/stage/2017/mar/05/hamlet-almeida-review-andrew-scott-robert-icke posted February 25, 2017 accessed September 1st 2017

37 There must be some way out of here by John Stokes, *The Times Literary Supplement* March 15, 2017 From https://www.the-tls.co.uk/articles/private/tom-stoppard-shakespeare-bob-dylan/

38 Genesis 1-2 King James Version (KJV)

39 Dylan's voice was never played over the speeches, 'purposefully drowning them out' as one reviewer of the Almeida Theatre run put it, when I saw it at the Harold Pinter theatre

40 *Bob Dylan's Words – A Critical Dictionary and Commentary*. Richard David Wissolik and Scott McGrath. Eadmer Press, Greensburg PA, 1994. Bob Dylan's '11 Outlined Epitaphs' in *Writings and Drawings* Jonathan Cape Ltd; 1973

41 Conor McPherson, *Girl from the North Country* Theatre Communications Group November, 2017

Chapter Eight

WORDPLAY

Words, words, words

The double attraction of both Shakespeare and Dylan is that as well as being masters of performing art their words shine like beacons and speak to everyone. Their work is so compelling as to have circulated in unauthorised, bootlegged and pirated formats, and their writing away from published sources, was passed privately from hand-to-hand. We have observed the Bardic quality of their writing in chapter two. In this chapter we explore other aspects of their literary mastery such as paradox, punning and hendiadys; as well as investigating their examinations of the nature of language.

Unsurprisingly, both Shakespeare and Dylan portray intense interest in the nature of language in their work. They probe at the limits and possibilities of both the word and the Word. Shakespeare lived through a time when the printing press began to change the world and when English as a language began to step out of the shadows of Latin, the language of religion and law, and French, the language of politics and war. As such, the language itself was at the forefront of writers' thoughts. Charles Moseley has written forcefully about the effect this had on the speech of Shakespeare's characters:

"I would argue that Shakespeare has been exploring the very speech itself that identifies men as English, its resources, its relation to truth and reality, the way the individual creates in it the world he inhabits – and the ironies of the clash of those individual worlds. He is not in the least unusual in this, for at the end of the sixteenth century and throughout the seventeenth, English was being self-consciously 'discovered' as a language, and the analysis of words attracted practically everyone's attention in one way or another ... The demonstrable interest in language *qua* language of Shakespeare and his contemporaries has profound implications for the styles and utterance Shakespeare gives his creatures."[1]

A large part of the ever-beguiling struggle of prince Hamlet is his battle with the translating the imprecision of slippery speech into direct action. He is somewhat akin to the scholars trying to 'translate' Shakespeare and Dylan's poetic words into literal prose. The tortured prince is another who 'is so good with words and at keeping things vague' as Joan Baez described Dylan in her beautiful song looking back on their relationship.[2]

Yet, it is from that very 'vagueness' that expressions of underlying truth emerge. Every time we use language a play on words can suggest itself, while puns and striking correlations spontaneously arise. Master writers instinctively corral these into use as they produce enduring works of art. By interlacing their narratives with these and adding them to the cumulative effect of chains of imagery, they produce in us, their audiences, a heightened sense of reality. We feel this when we witness Shakespeare's plays, and it is a similar apprehension that inspired the old joke that 'Bob Dylan knows the secrets of the universe, it's just that he's not telling anyone.' It was a telling joke but it missed the point entirely. It was felt that Dylan knew the secrets because of the very way his songs spoke to listeners and so he was, in fact, opening up new worlds for us to experience and learn from, in the only way possible. As with Shakespeare, a welcoming embrace of opposites is a major element in how this is achieved. It is through paradox, punning, oxymorons and a yoking together of antithetical tropes and concepts that their art communicates to us on a level that is difficult to describe without using similar techniques. It is also why Shakespeare and Dylan can appear, through their art, as 'all things to all men'.

Ambiguity in the lyrics and play scripts is exploited in performance. Dylan's different musical and vocal delivery from performance to performance, or even of the same chorus line repeated in the same performance, can, in "Don't Think Twice, It's Alright", for example, move from anger to regret to wistful remembrance to exultant leave-taking. Directors and actors can decide how to play a line replete with potential readings in a Shakespeare play.

Macbeth is predicated upon reality-bending paradoxes. From opening comments such as *"When the battle's lost, and won"* and *"Fair is foul, foul is fair"* through all the witches' prophecies, the language equivocates, confuses and misleads while simultaneously opening up marvellous insights into the world as we apprehend it.

There is a connection here to the perennial theme of all artists and philosophers, that of appearance and reality. One thinks of Feste in *Twelfth Night* and how his debunking of language's referential powers raises questions about *"what is real and what is not"*, as Dylan archly sings in 'Gates of Eden'.

The investigation into language in Shakespeare's era was intensified by the religious background to the nature of language. *The Bible* tells us that: 'In the beginning there was the Word'. From this Creation myth, we move on to the time when the universal language, which brought with it a full comprehension of true reality, was lost. Adam's immediate descendants would have spoken the one language, which equated with reality, but man's hubris was punished by the creation of multiple tongues and a confusion between words and the objective reality that they were supposed to describe.

Dylan's song, 'Man Gave Names To All The Animals', thus dramatises one of the leading questions of Shakespeare's age that exercised all the leading minds of the time, including the brightest mind of all. What, they all wondered, could be done to repair this 'Fallen nature of language'? Milton tells us in *Paradise Lost* that Adam 'readily could name, what e'er he saw' and, crucially, when he named them he 'understood their nature'. However, that, as Dylan sings, was *"in the beginning, a long time ago"* before the Word was lost. The story of the Tower of Babel haunted the Renaissance. As Moseley asked, after his passage above: "For how can the Fall be undone when language itself is fallen?" He continued by observing that:

"The issue is not a small one: how could language and words not be a central and conscious concern, in the front of all thinking men's minds in an age when the crux of the Reformation theological debate lay precisely in the *meaning* and *utterance* of the words in the Gospels and in St. Paul's writings? Did the language of the Bible relate to real things existing independently of their description, or was language merely a convention among human beings that, ultimately, could only discuss itself? ... The number of books on language, its theories, forms and uses published between 1500 and 1700 is huge, and there is not the slightest doubt that no one of even the most minimal education could have avoided stubbing their toes on the issue. At the heart of the way men thought about these things are the notions of the creating Word of God (Genesis i), uttering all that is into being, the language of Adam and the myth of the Tower of Babel (Genesis xi). It is only when we grasp this fact and its implications that the significance of the vast number of medieval and Renaissance engravings and paintings – for example the one by Bruegel – of the Tower of Babel becomes clear."[3]

Babel was on the mind of Henry Miller, a writer whom Dylan admired, when he was contemplating Arthur Rimbaud, a poet Dylan also admired and to whom he felt an affinity, given the legacy left by the French poet. Miller surveyed the position of poetry in the middle of the twentieth century and was filled with despair: "To be a poet was once the highest calling; today it is the most futile one. It is so not because the world is immune to the poet's pleading, but because the poet himself no longer believes in his divine mission. He has been singing off-key now for a century ... When the poet stands at nadir the world must indeed be upside down. If the poet can no longer speak for society but only for himself, then we are at the last ditch. On the poetic corpse of Rimbaud we have begun erecting a tower of Babel."[4]

Miller saw poetry as having devolved into a small clique of writers writing only for their own circle and bemoaned that in it there was no "longer art but the cipher language of a secret society for the propagation of meaningless individuality. Art is something which stirs men's passions, which gives vision, lucidity, courage and faith."

Enter Bob Dylan to supply that very art and rescue poetry from being a 'secret society' and, by tying it back to its historical musical and oral roots, ensure that, as song, it once again communicated widely and resonated deeply throughout society at large.

In a prodigious bout of creativity in 1965 and 1966, Dylan produced,
amongst other things, a trilogy of albums that each scaled new peaks of
artistic heights: *Bringing It All Back Home*, *Highway 61 Revisited* and *Blonde
on Blonde*. One of his themes and concerns was language itself. In a
characteristically modernist way, he was trying to capture in words that
which cannot be captured in words. This inevitably ended up by becoming
a struggle with language itself. By the time of 'Visions of Johanna' on *Blonde
on Blonde* Dylan had pushed his words, melded invisibly into his music, to
the edge of all that could be communicated. It was difficult to see how a
song could be any more illuminating, but still Dylan pushed on, and when
he completed 'Sad Eyed Lady of the Lowlands' to round off that double
album's fourth side, he ecstatically acclaimed it as the best thing he had ever
written. Dylan was initially convinced he had captured his visions perfectly.
That feeling passed. Beautiful though the music, his voice and much of the
imagery is, the song teeters over the brink of intelligibility for the listener.
Given the luxurious, sensuous nature of the melody and performance it
can still be enjoyed, but it does not communicate as fully and deeply as
'Visions of Johanna' does. Fragments flow by and parts momentarily cohere,
the Steinbeck references, images of America, the same sexual imagery as
elsewhere on the album, and even a piece of personal history, "magazine
husband", yet it all seems like a mirage and a song that never quite gets its
message across.

Even Dylan in the mid-Sixties, it would appear, could push language too far.
He also did so in his prose-poetry novel, *Tarantula*. Again, sections, a whole
chapter or two indeed, cohere into something meaningful, but for the most
part we feel we are drowning under the curse of Babel again as Dylan almost
deconstructs the very language he is using.[5] The next album Dylan released
would be stripped down, plain words and straightforward folk, and even
country, music. This particular experiment with language was over, for now,
and a new one, beguiling in its own way, took its place.

Dylan was to have future experiments with language, and more attempts
to express the seemingly inexpressible. The co-writer of Dylan's ambitious
and illuminating 2003 film, *Masked and Anonymous*, Larry Charles, explained
that: "We were making American Civil War references, Bible references,

Shakespeare references, modern music references, all synthesised into some sort of new type of language. That's a big part of what the movie is about, sort of experimenting with language."[6]

Back in the mid-sixties, in *Tarantula* and 'Sad Eyed Lady of the Lowlands' we are left, in Dylan's words, trying "to shovel the glimpse". All these years after Milton was faced with the conundrum of describing Eden in English, a language from after the Fall and after the Tower of Babel, the same struggle still affects all poets as the ending to Dylan's 'Gates of Eden" makes clear:

At times I think there are no words
But these to tell what's true
And there are no truths outside the Gates of Eden

Language, then, is a very serious business for both our Bards. However, it is also part of their lifeblood, a major component of their works that have brought so much joy and insight to so many. Moreover, it is fun; it brings endless, joyous, uproarious fun into their writing, and our lives. Not least in what seems at times, and on the surface, the most throwaway form of wordplay, the pun.

***

We appear to have a national obsession with puns in the UK. Earlier this evening, I was listening to a weekly satirical show on BBC Radio Four called *The Now Show* and it opened with this punning joke: "Why is the EU Brexit transition offer like someone tried to get hold of your on-line data? Because they both involve fishing (phishing) scams". This was greeted with a few laughs but mostly groans, and their joint reaction brought the audience together. A similar thing happens with families when reading aloud the traditional, terrible, punning jokes from inside our Christmas crackers. The worse they are, the more they seem to add to the festivities. One example of these will more than suffice: "Where can you find a cow? In a *moo*seum."

Our daily newspapers, especially, but not solely, our tabloids, seem to aim for something similarly groan-inducing. Although these can be deftly inventive, the incessant daily need to produce so many punning headlines inevitably means that most over-reach or have become repeated so often as to go unnoticed. Shops and businesses are quick to employ puns in their names, and if you ask Amazon's Alexa for a joke, then there is a good chance that 'she' will answer with a lame pun.

Dylan seems to love these 'grandad jokes'. More than once he has said it is time to go, and so he has 'put an egg in his shoe and is going to beat it". On stage, referring jokingly and separately to both an ex-wife and an ex-girlfriend, he has said: "She was so conceited I used to call her Mimi", or that *"She's a tennis player. Love means nothing to her."* Nothing is too corny for him; *"I almost didn't make it tonight, we had a flat tire, there was a fork in the road"*, he once announced. At another show, when introducing his drummer, David Kemper, Dylan remarked: *"He had a job as a waiter, but he never took any tips. He was a dumb waiter."* Trust me, there are many more from where these came. It is not just on stage, either. 2001's pun-filled album, *"Love And Theft"* features a number of corny examples amongst other jokes. There, we hear, embedded in separate songs: *"Calls down to room service, says, "Send up a room"*. *"I'm sittin' on my watch so I can be on time"*, *"I'm stark naked, but I don't care/I'm going off into the woods, I'm huntin' bare"* and, even, a knock-knock joke: *"Knockin' on the door, I say, "Who is it and where are you from?"/Man says, "Freddy!" I say, "Freddy who?" He says, "Freddy or not here I come"*.

There is also a just-for-the-fans pun on that album's 'Sugar Baby' when he sings: *'some of these bootleggers, they make pretty good stuff'*. 'Bootleggers' may primarily refer to moonshiners; however Dylan is obviously well aware that he has a core audience who listen to bootlegs of his music. So much so that his own record company had already begun releasing some of these under the series title "The Bootleg Series".

Dylan's love of puns, however, is as nothing compared to Shakespeare's whose work features, it has been estimated, over three thousand. Punning was one of the leading literary devices of the time. Shakespeare's contemporary, that man who so often uses language in a similar way to both Shakespeare and Dylan, John Donne, was also expert in the use of them. Donne's *A Hymn to God the Father*, in which he begs forgiveness for his earlier life of promiscuity, is a *tour de force* of punning. This includes playing on both his and his wife Anne More's surnames as well as gaining much mileage from one that reverberates through Shakespeare and Dylan's work, that is Son/sun: "at my death thy Son/Shall shine as he shines now."

Punning is a literary device that has enjoyed wide patronage from eminent writers throughout the centuries, yet many people seem to dislike and scorn them. Perhaps this is partly because they feature so strongly in weak bawdy humour, such as "Carry On" films and seaside postcards. Samuel Johnson accounted puns as the lowest form of humour and Shakespeare's addiction to them he viewed as a kind of diabolical mental affliction. This is regrettable as Johnson missed out on so much that is valuable in the Bard's work, because any full appreciation of Shakespeare's work has to glory in his masterful use of puns and their integral part in his overall art. Perhaps Alfred Hitchcock was thinking of this when he stated, on the Dick Cavett show in 1972, that puns were "the highest form of literature." They certainly seem that way in Shakespeare's hands.

Another reason that may count against puns for some people is their aforementioned prevalence in all walks of daily life. However, it is natural for writers to particularly love puns; words are their tools, and puns are both powerful and fun, and therefore provide a hugely rewarding resource. Shared sources for Shakespeare and Dylan, including Virgil, Ovid, Chaucer, Spenser and ballad writers all enjoyed employing them. Our two bards share with the last of these, and the poetry when recited, the added benefit of aural puns, untethered from the printed sheet and thereby unfixed and inherently indeterminate.

Wordplays appear throughout the work of both, not just in the comedy plays or the lighter songs. Puns in both writers work is often integral to mood, theme, character and even plot. They are not merely added decoration but central to the plays and songs. Simon Palfrey, in his study, *Doing Shakespeare*, explains why this is for the dramatist, and the same holds true for Dylan's song-writing:

"If we unfold each aspect of the pun then the impact and significance of the moment is almost always enhanced. To argue this is to maintain a simple but powerful premise: rather like a gifted ball-player, Shakespeare 'sees' things early, finds space where others cannot. This gives him time to play, and therefore his delivery is at once more complete and more substantial. It means that the most common arguments against wordplay, that it is trivial and self-indulgent, are pre-empted. For Shakespeare's most characteristic wordplay is not about dazzling display. It is simply about the spoken moment bearing multiple lines of possible unfurling. This implies a series of simple but profound things: that we can say one thing while thinking something else; that the mind can hold more than one option at a time; that the addressor and addressee may agree on a meaning that a third party - the overhearing reader or audience - may not agree on; ..."[7]

***

Not only do our two artists delight in giving voice to those who 'can say one thing while thinking something else' but they take special pleasure in embracing opposed concepts in oxymorons and paradoxes. This is so central to their mode of creation that when introducing Dylan at the 1991 Grammy Awards, Jack Nicholson pronounced that the 'fairest word' to describe Dylan was 'paradox' because it meant: 'a statement seemingly self-contradictory but in reality possibly expressing a truth.'

Describing the fundamental value of 'my love' in 'Love Minus Zero/No Limit' Dylan sings that she seems like *"like ice/like fire"*. Albeit in a satirical vein, Shakespeare utilises the concept of "hot ice" in *A Midsummer Night's Dream* (Act V scene i). Another striking use of contradiction appears in *Cymbeline*. After his long journey into self-knowledge, the wiser and chastened Posthumus declares: *"O Imogen, I'll speak to thee in silence."* (Act V, Scene iv). In 'Love Minus Zero/No Limit' Dylan also signifies the wisdom of the same contradiction when he describes his love as one who *"speaks like silence"*. Dylan follows this up with the unforgettable double paradox of: *"She knows there's no success like failure/And that failure's no success at all"*. A decade later, he was to remind us of those lines when he sang on "Idiot Wind" that: *"What's good is bad, what's bad is good, / you'll find out when you reach the top. / You're on the bottom"*.

In the play that *A Midsummer Night's Dream* connects with, in so many ways, *Romeo and Juliet*, oxymorons also lead to full-blown paradoxes in Juliet's reaction to hearing that her beloved Romeo has slain Tybalt, her kinsman. In an astonishingly compact speech of contradictory descriptions, we are confronted with the following: *"Beautiful tyrant, fiend angelical"*, *"Dove-feathered raven, wolvish-ravening lamb*" and "*A damnèd saint, an honorable villain!*". These are intermingled with longer expressions such as: "*O serpent heart, hid with a flow'ring face! / Did ever dragon keep so fair a cave?*" and "*Despisèd substance of divinest show, / Just opposite to what thou justly seem'st.*" The speech then culminates in:

> *O nature, what hadst thou to do in hell*
> *When thou didst bower the spirit of a fiend*
> *In mortal paradise of such sweet flesh?*
> *Was ever book containing such vile matter*
> *So fairly bound? O that deceit should dwell*
> *In such a gorgeous palace!*

(Act III Scene ii)

The poet Allen Ginsberg, while teaching a course on Shakespeare's *The Tempest*, told his class that, in a telephone call with Dylan in the Sixties, Bob had remarked that "*to live outside the law you must be honest*" was the favourite of his own lines. Dylan had described it as his 'supreme Shakespeare shot'. Ginsberg linked the paradox in the Dylan line with Shakespeare's characteristic mode of expression. He brought it up while discussing Shakespeare's "constructions of paradoxical phrasing" and the "polarity of opposites", which Ginsberg describes as an "automatic poetry" of "yoking opposites" together but which have "got to make sense, though". This prompted Ginsberg to quote the famous Dylan line and recount the telephone call. Allen said of Dylan's line: "The contradiction is so apt, so perfect, so simple – it's the simplicity that does it."[8]

Not only do both often express themselves and their characters through paradoxical statements, but Dylan's conception of his art-form often seems based on the paradox of the artist forever straining to achieve perfection while constantly being aware that perfection is deadly to creative art. You can trace this in such songs as 'Lay Down Your Weary Tune', 'Farewell Angelina', 'Mr Tambourine Man' and 'Gates of Eden'[9]. He reiterates the same view with piercing clarity when discussing his songs' true habitat as that of being sung by him onstage in ever-changing live performances. They are fluid, dynamic and unstable and forever bursting with the potential of new embodiment, as opposed to the art that has been perfected and which may as well be hung up in museums, 'where infinity goes up on trial'. Throughout the spring of 1995, Dylan played a wonderful, new version of 'Mr. Tambourine Man'. It continually improved as he strove to capture the new vision of the song in its entirety. Then, one night he did just that, after which this new arrangement was promptly dropped. The striving to embody a new work had been at the root of the creative forces unleashed in the new take on the old classic. Once this was perfectly realised, it left the set to be replaced by another old favourite dressed in new musical clothes.

As with Shakespeare, Dylan's love of paradox continues throughout his career. As one of numerous examples 'Pay in Blood' from 2012's *Tempest* album boasts the lines: *"The more I take the more I give / The more I die the more I live"*.

Both artists enjoy having fun with words and use them to make 'in-jokes' against the very mediums that convey them. Dylan sang, as the vinyl era was giving way to the CD age, *"Has the record been breaking / Did the needle just skip"*[10] while *Twelfth Night*, in Act 3 Scene iv contains the wonderful observation that: *"If this were played upon a stage now,/ I could condemn it as an improbable fiction."* Part of all this punning and playing with paradoxes is just that – playing. Both artists have an infectious, exuberant and nearly uncontainable delight in playing with words and, naturally, rhyme. They can take rhyming to extraordinary lengths. One thinks of Shakespeare's early plays, such as *Love's Labour's Lost*, written at the end of a tradition for heavily rhyming poetic drama, and, for one Dylan example, of his 'Angelina' with its bravura list of rhymes for the title name: 'concertina', hyena', 'subpoena' 'Argentina' and 'arena', all of which appear as the last line of four in verses where they are preceded by rhyming triplets.

The sheer fun in the dazzling wordplay entrances us and draws us into the works as a whole. Fun for its own sake is very much on the table, too. Once, when discussing rap, Dylan remarked upon the attractiveness of 'rhyming for rhymes' sake'. As Dylan aficionado Stephen Rendell noted: "On *Street-Legal* ... His fascination for rhyme and wordplay are given free rein. I've said before that Dylan's intoxication by the possibilities of rhyme is like

Shakespeare's addiction to quibbles (playing on words), they're both happy to follow wherever the compulsion leads them and if the larger work that contains it ultimately loses out they shrug and think it's well lost. Fortunately, given how good both of them are at what they do it isn't often that the larger work suffers – and personally, if it does I tend to shrug along with them and think, "So what, the rhyme's so brilliant and unexpected. The punning is so superbly funny, sly and dirty, it's worth it." [11]

Through this element of playfulness, we also link to my chapter on use of source material because playing with the words of those who have gone before, in parody, mockery or in the knowledge of shared exposure, can all be part of the fun. As Ruth Finnegan writes:

"We should not forget, either, the playfulness that at times colours all these forms. Parody, puns, satire, and clever twists on known wording have roots in the fertile ground of quotation, mimicking and echoing established texts in amusing, sometimes devastating, ways. This frame again has a long history. The very word 'allusion' derives from the Latin *alludere* (to mock, play with), suggestive of its ludic, game-like dimension. Parody was cultivated as a fine art in classical Greek literature, with mock imitations of others' words and styles in many settings, from epic and drama to Plato's dialogues and Aristophanes' comedies, famous for the burlesque parodies which at the same time functioned as subtle literary comment through their comic allusions, exaggerated imitations and satirising of other playwrights' words and styles." [12]

Puns lead us down many interlacing pathways of verbal wit, and we should not let the fun element distract us from the important weight that puns, rhymes and paradoxes can lend to spoken art. Their compact nature opens up into so many potential meanings that it can become dizzying, and both of our artists know this and often push it to, perhaps even beyond, the limits of our ability to comprehend in their pursuit for capturing as much of reality as they can in their art. Puns may appear small, but it would be a considerable error to underestimate their significance.

Simon Palfrey illustrates one example of this insightfully, when writing of these famous lines in *Macbeth*: "*They have tied me to a stake. I cannot fly, / But, bearlike, I must fight the course.*" (Act V scene vii). Palfrey comments that:

"Clearly, 'bear' as a noun is a referential battlefield. But flanking puns reinforce this multiplicity. So, 'bear' can be a verb, meaning to endure, or to undress. If we take this to be the sense, then Macbeth is imagining himself as an authentic tragic survivor, experiencing the limits of existence like an Oedipus or Lear. In turn, 'stake' means more than the post to which the bear is tied. It also refers to the money laid on the game by the eager crowd: Macbeth here is the contemptible object of public entertainment. But then 'stake' can equally evoke crucifixion: perhaps Macbeth briefly (irreverently, consolingly, sarcastically?) identifies with a very different kind of tragic martyr. Similarly, the word 'course' can be the predestined end, the rabbit hunted by the dogs, or the dead 'corse' or corpse at which the game aims (his enemies' or his own). With punning referents shooting out at all angles, the speech proffers all sorts of Macbeth-bodies or Macbeth-attitudes in one: it is like a battle, as his words animate his inward alternatives and situational antagonisms. To add to the difficulty, the basic intent of Macbeth's speech-act is paralysed with ambiguity. 'I cannot fly' might equally express pride. panic, fear, boastfulness, fatalism, or even strategic military logic ...

... And, importantly, Macbeth sees it all. This is where his puns come in: they tell us that he knows himself to be a sort of fraud. In other words, Macbeth's words are looking two ways at once: with a defiant sort of stare, out to the audience or over the battlements, he invokes splendid if suicidal bravery; but in the same motion he 'peeps' back into himself and sees something like a contemptible clown, caught in flagrante in a stolen bearskin."[13]

***

There are different kinds of puns, and for the purely literary writer a main division occurs between those that look alike and sound alike, such as "lie" (homographic) and those which sound alike, but have different spellings "sail/sale" (homophonic). As writers for performance, Shakespeare and Dylan have the added benefit of being able to fully exploit homophonic puns as though they were homographic. Due to his distinctive Minnesotan pronunciation there can be some uncertainty as to when and if this is deliberate with Dylan or if it is sometimes just a happy coincidence.[14]

To take two examples, just two lines apart, from one song, 'Shelter from the

Storm', the words 'mourning' and 'futile', as printed in the official lyrics, are difficult to distinguish from 'moaning' and 'feudal'. [15]

And the one-eyed undertaker, he blows a futile horn
"Come in," she said, "I'll give you shelter from the storm"

I've heard newborn babies wailin' like a mournin' dove
And old men with broken teeth stranded without love

As both 'moaning' and 'feudal' would be apt in context, it is tempting to view these as aural puns. Perhaps, indeed, they are and that was very much how I embraced the latter when I first heard the song. However, many years of listening to Dylan inclines me now to the view that here it is merely a matter of pronunciation. Naturally, though, I can never lose the nuance of the ghostly 'feudal' that I first heard.

An interesting double-hearing occurs in the opening song of Bob Dylan's *Self Portrait* album. This was an album of covers of others' songs and re-workings of his back catalogue. It was released at a time of national importance and at an absolutely pivotal moment of the counterculture that looked to Dylan as its leader if not its Messiah. Dylan, however, 'wrote' next to nothing new on this double album which was, in context, so provocatively titled. Or, as the couplet that comprises the total lyrics of the introductory, mainly instrumental song, seem to put it: *"All the tired horses in the sun / How'm I supposed to get any writin' done?"* In the lyrics and in the logical sense it was not 'writing', instead it it was 'ridin'' which he couldn't do because the horses were tired. Logic aside, many people took the meaning as "writin'" and the more drug obsessed noted that horses was slang for heroin. Such games of interpretation are second nature to Dylan's followers, just as they are amongst writers on Shakespeare.

A more significant, and dexterously superb, example of aural punning occurs in a line from Dylan's majestic song: 'Chimes of Freedom'. In this song, which encompasses the downtrodden and outcasts while highlighting wide-ranging and deep-rooted injustice, this line brilliantly illuminates the plight of those eternal scapegoats for societies' failings, unmarried mothers: *"For the mistreated, mateless mother, the mistitled prostitute"*. Before looking at the pun, it is worth pausing to admire the dazzling use of alliteration, a feature throughout the song. Here, the mixture of the soft, comforting 'm' sounds, forever associated with the maternal – ma, mama, mummy, mammaries - with the harsh, sibilant 's's, the sound of scorn, perfectly encapsulates the line's meaning. So, too, does the pun of 'mistitled prostitute' or 'miss, titled prostitute' which in their combined meaning provided another perfect summary of the mistreatment being sung about in the line.

There are numerous examples such as these where, as with Shakespeare, the aural pun is no mere embellishment but instead at the core of the meaning being conveyed. In 'It Takes A lot To Laugh, It Takes A Train To Cry' Dylan presents us, at the end of the highly sexualised song, with a vision of the difficulties of communication and an image of a seer whose words are ignored. He claims that he is unable to get 'across', thus signalling the first theme but when he sings it he stresses the other possibility of 'a cross', giving the alarming suggestion that without crucifixion a prophet's warnings go unheard. It is worth noting, too, that the song's title holds a potential Biblical pun and that, not for the last time, Dylan uses the trope of 'die' for orgasm, an image beloved of Shakespeare and other Elizabethan writers, as discussed in chapter eight.

As with so many things, Shakespeare is the indisputable master of the pun. Consider the title to his comedy: *Much Ado About Nothing*. Attractive in itself in the same whimsical way as other titles like *As You Like It* or *What You Will* (themselves containing puns), this title boasts a pun on "nothing" that is open to multiple interpretations and these potential interpretations set the scene for the key language and themes of the play. The title achieves this through a number of simultaneous puns. Firstly, 'nothing' happened between Hero and any man prior to her marriage and yet there was 'much ado about' the mistaken apprehension that something had. Secondly, in Shakespeare's day, 'nothing' was pronounced the same as 'noting' and the play prominently features people 'noting' other people, often mistakenly, and consequently this 'noting', too, causes a big fuss. Thirdly, and as a precursor to dipping our toes into the steamy bath of sexualised puns, which, as in many Shakespeare plays, permeate nearly every scene of *Much Ado About Nothing*, there is the pun on a word for female genitialia. Crudely put, a man has a thing between his legs and a woman has nothing. The 'much ado' is all 'about' Hero's 'nothing'. It is always worth noting that nothing entered her nothing and so there is nothing to bar her wearing Claudio's ring. That last word opens up another deep layer of genitalia related punning in the play. 'Nothing', in this sense, was a very common pun in Elizabethan England and as such appears elsewhere in Shakespeare, and nowhere more famously than during one episode of Hamlet's terrible treatment of Ophelia, where he also puns on what we euphemistically call nowadays, the "C-word" after beginning with the ambiguous 'lie':

HAMLET   *Lady, shall I lie in your lap?*

OPHELIA   *No my lord.*

HAMLET   *I mean, my head upon your lap?*

OPHELIA   *Ay my lord.*

HAMLET   *Do you think I meant country matters?*

OPHELIA   *I think nothing my lord.*

HAMLET   *That's a fair thought to lie between maids' legs.*

OPHELIA   *What is, my lord?*

HAMLET   *Nothing.*

(Act III scene ii)

Although propriety insists that Ophelia, in public in the court, has to act as though such puns are lost on her, such language was not regarded as offensive or shocking by either gender. Female characters are often more sexually explicit and daring in their language than the male characters on Shakespearean stages. Margaret's extraordinary performance of lewd suggestions to Benedick late in *Much Ado About Nothing*, alone, can attest to that.

We are yet to mine the depths of the punning from that one word in the title, however. Nothing, orally, can be punned with no thing as well as noting. Benedick notes that Beatrice has said she loves him but no such thing occurred; while Beatrice notes that Benedick has said he loves her but again no such thing has yet occurred. While, centrally to the main plot, Don Pedro and Claudio note Hero being unfaithful, yet no such thing occurred.

Unsurprisingly given their shared love of puns, our two writers have a number in common. Some of them will pop up in my section on bawdy puns but, before that, I want to look at two others; one being 'eye/I', but firstly 'sun/son'.

On *Time Out Of Mind*'s 'Not Dark Yet', Dylan sings *"I've still got the scars that the sun didn't heal"*. It works well enough on a straightforward, descriptive level, but it operates in deeper ways, too. In his later albums, Dylan often sends us back to his earlier work, just as Shakespeare does in his late Romances, and this is a fine example of that trait. The word 'scars' takes us back to 'Where Are You Tonight? (Journey Through Dark Heat)' and its line *"If you don't believe there's a price for this sweet paradise/ just remind me to show you the scars"*. "Sweet paradise" takes on extra meaning when you recall that the song was the last one Dylan released before his conversion and the evangelical, Christian albums and tours that followed that transformation.

Returning to the song 'Not Dark Yet', this has already raised questions regarding religious faith in the listener's mind and so this line strengthens that to the point where it is hard not to hear the line as a despairing cry of wavering faith: *"I've still got the scars that the Son didn't heal"*. That, in turn, sets us up perfectly for the closing couplet of: *"Don't even hear the murmur of a prayer / It's not dark yet, but it's getting there."*

The final song on the same album, 'Highlands' ends with both 'eyes' and the 'sun' playing prominent roles.

The sun is beginnin' to shine on me
But it's not like the sun that used to be
The party's over and there's less and less to say
I got new eyes, everything looks far away

After listening to 'Not Dark Yet', you may hear the sun/Son pun as explicit here, too, and in other songs on the album. We are told that the titular characters in the simultaneously serious and uproarious 'Tweedle Dee & Tweedle Dum' are *"Living in the Land of Nod/Trustin' their fate to the hands of God"*. This is closely followed by a use of the word 'sun', which is immediately succeeded by the double pun of *"His Master's voice"*. The capitalisation of 'Master' is surely intentional, despite my continuing misgivings over any edition of the official lyrics, matching as it does, the same punctuation as in 'Every Grain of Sand's' *"In the fury of the moment I can see the Master's hand"*. The puns would exist aurally, in any case:

Neither one gonna turn and run
They're making a voyage to the sun
"His Master's voice is calling me"
Says Tweedle-dee Dum to Tweedle-dee Dee

This particular pun has become quite a frequent one in Dylan's work. The third line of 2012's 'Pay in Blood' can be heard and appreciated in both meanings simultaneously: *"I'm drenched in the light that shines from the sun* (Son)."

Some have read Shakespeare's "Sonnet 33" as punning on sun and son. Not as in the Son of God but in Shakespeare's own, lost, child Hamnet.

Ev'n so my sun one early morn did shine
With all triumphant splendor on my brow;
But out alack, he was but one hour mine;
The region cloud hath masked him from me now.
Yet him for this my love no whit disdaineth.
Suns of the world may stain when heav'n's sun staineth.

As is ever the case with such Shakespearean biographical interpretation, it is all speculative. In contrast to that, we have the opening to *Richard III* where a sun/son pun is most certainly made. The famed soliloquy, with which Richard, then Richard of Gloucester, opens the play, begins:

Now is the winter of our discontent
Made glorious summer by this sun of York,

And all the clouds that loured upon our house
In the deep bosom of the ocean buried.

(*Richard III* Act I scene i)

The speech that follows was the first incontrovertible sign that here was a writer far beyond anything that had gone before; or has ever been since. The ascent of Richard's brother Edward to kingship had dispelled winter gloom and brought summer sun. This sun of York, though, is also a son of York literally speaking, as Edward is heir from the white-rosed, Yorkist side who have just gained the upper hand on the red-rosed Lancastrians. An added resonance to the pun is that this "sun and son" of York's crown was emblazoned with an emblematic sun.

Another celebrated Shakespearean sun/son play on words occurs in *Hamlet*. This time the clouds have not been dispelled, much to Claudius's annoyance. He asks of the Prince: "*How is it that the clouds still hang on you?*" Hamlet's answer is another multi-layered one, "*Not so, my lord; I am too much i' the sun.*" Hamlet manages to employ 'sun' in a variety of meanings all at once. Most pointedly he feels too much now the 'son' of Claudius, after Claudius has married his mother. Secondly, he is too much the son of the slain King Hamlet to be happy and have a 'sunny' disposition. Thirdly, he is complaining that there is too much 'sunshine' in the Court which he thinks should be in mourning for his father. Additionally there could be the inference that he finds Claudius's company too ever-present, that is if we take 'sun' in one of its primary symbolic meanings, that of royalty, now that Claudius is King.

Shakespeare was far from alone in utilising the sun/son pun in his own time. John Donne, as we have seen, was a contemporary who gained golden mileage from this and Donne's direct influence on George Herbert, and Donne and Herbert's subsequent influence on Henry Vaughan ensured that this traditional pun was retained in high poetic profile for years to come. Writing of *The Taming of the Shrew*, Ruth Vanita remarks that:

"In Elizabethan poetic rhetoric, the sun and the moon retain some of the divine qualities attributed to them by the Greeks and are among the most important visible signs of God's power ... and the sun in particular was also a trope associated with Christ. These associations with royalty and divinity are found in other plays: thus, Cleopatra compares Antony's face to the heavens and his eyes to the sun and moon, and in *Henry VIII*, the dying queen has a vision of angels whose faces cast a thousand beams upon her, 'like the sun'. (Act IV scene ii) Petruchio pits himself against the natural and the sacred order of things when he tries to control the meaning of the sun: 'Puns by my mother's son, and that's myself / It shall be moon, or star or what I list' (Act IV scene v). The near-blasphemous nature of this claim and of his arrogation of the son/sun pun normally used to glorify Christ, is highlighted by his reference to God in the opening line from this scene. 'Come on, a God's name, once more toward our father's' (Act IV scene v)."[16]

In *Richard II*, we have a spectacular confluence of Christ identification, the divine right of kings and an English king with all the trappings of a Sun God. This reaches a crisis point when Bolingbroke challenges Richard. Adrian Streete writes that:

"Richard makes one last attempt to co-opt the eschatological force of Christ's second coming when faced with Bolingbroke's assault. Drawing upon the metaphor of the sun (complete with its implied pun on sun/ son), the king summons the 'searching eye of heaven' that 'lights the lower world' (Act III scene ii). Richard is, quite literally, invoking a process of revelation here. The idea is further developed when he says of the sun:

But when from under this terrestrial ball
He fires the proud tops of the eastern pines
And darts his light through every guilty hole
Then murders, treasons and detested sins,
The cloak of night being plucked from off their backs,
Stand bare and naked, trembling at themselves?
So when this thief, this traitor, Bullingbrook,
Who all this while hath revelled in the night
Whilst we were wandering with the Antipodes.
Shall see us rising in our throne, the east
His treasons will sit blushing in his face,"[17]

(Act III scene ii)

There is a hint in that passage that Bolingbroke's claim has a divine blessing and that he, not Richard, is the Christ figure. By having Richard compare Bolingbroke to a 'thief', 'in the night', Shakespeare sets up a link with the various times in the Bible we read prophecies regarding 'the day of The Lord will come as thief in the night' or, as Dylan puts it in his song, 'When He Returns': *"Like a thief in the night, he'll replace wrong with right"*.

Sun/Son puns are often close by another favoured pun of both writers, that of "I" and "eyes". Dylan has often talked about the moment he read Arthur Rimbaud's phrase, "I is another," as being a revelatory one. Certainly, it is a message he has seemed to take to heart over much of the following half century. Punning on 'eye', with all of its inherent imagery and multiple leanings, and "I", he probed in the mid-sixties at the very bases of individuality, perception and identity. In the liner notes to his *Highway 61 Revisited* album, Dylan wrote: *I cannot say the word eye, anymore...when I speak this word eye it is as if I am speaking of somebody's eye that I faintly remember...there is no eye'* . In *Tarantula* the 'eye' and 'I' feel similarly beyond his control. So much so, that Bob Dylan writes Bob Dylan's epitaph and in doing so discovers that, when you 'interrogate', that is, look into it with your eyes, even a ghost has multiple identities or multiple "I"'s:

here lies bob dylan
murdered
from behind
by trembling flesh...

...bob dylan - killed by a discarded Oedipus
who turned
around
to investigate a ghost
& discovered that
the ghost too
was more than one person.[18]

You wonder if there is still a hint of all this conflation of "I" and "eye" in the quote from 'Highlands' that we looked at earlier, which closes the *Time*

Out of Mind album. The narrator's distance from everyday life that has figured throughout the song becomes explicit. And just as the sun (or Son) does not shine for him in the same way as it did previously, so his perspective and being have changed: *'I've got new eyes'*.

Eyes are a similarly dominant image in Shakespeare's work and nowhere more so than in *A Midsummer Night's Dream*. From the first scene to the last, the play teems with references to eyes, and vision. Again, here, amongst other things, eyes are the gateway, in both directions, to identity and also to perception both of the world and outward objects and inner world of the individual imaginations. This latter connection is made physical in the play by the love juice that is applied to the eyes of Titania, Lysander and Demetrius.

The related imagery builds to an unforgettable climax in a speech by Theseus on how the poet, the lunatic and the lover are all alike deceived by their eyes and how they are defined by this deception. Their "I"s (the identities of poet, lunatic, lover) are constructed from these illusions:

Lovers and madmen have such seething brains,
Such shaping fantasies, that apprehend
More than cool reason ever comprehends.
The lunatic, the lover, and the poet
Are of imagination all compact:
One sees more devils than vast hell can hold;
That is the madman. The lover, all as frantic,
Sees Helen's beauty in a brow of Egypt.
The poet's eye, in a fine frenzy rolling,
Doth glance from heaven to earth, from earth to heaven;
And as imagination bodies forth
The form of things unknown, the poet's pen
Turns them to shapes, and gives to airy nothing
A local habitation and a name.

(Act V, scene i)

Perception and identity are main themes from the opening of the play.

214

WORDPLAY

Between Demetrius and Lysander, there is no real difference and they are deliberately portrayed as interchangeable. It is how they are seen in the eyes of others that defines them. Their "I"s are only in the eyes of the beholders:

THESEUS   *What say you, Hermia? be advised fair maid.*
          To you your father should be as a god,
          One that composed your beauties; yea, and one
          To whom you are but as a form in wax
          By him imprinted, and within his power
          To leave the figure or disfigure it.
          Demetrius is a worthy gentleman.

HERMIA   *So is Lysander.*

THESEUS   *In himself he is;*
          But in this kind, wanting your father's voice,
          The other must be held the worthier.
HERMIA   *I would my father looked but with my eyes.*

THESEUS   *Rather your eyes must with his judgment look.*

Shakespeare extends punning on ways of seeing, in the play, to include not only 'eyes' but all manner of vision. When Helena pleads to Hermia, *O, teach me how you look* in Act I scene i, both ways of hearing the line are equally valid and pertinent.

Shakespeare combines the eye/I and sun/son puns in *King John Act II scene i*

DAUPHIN
I do, my lord, and in her eye I find
A wonder or a wondrous miracle,
The shadow of myself formed in her eye,
Which being but the shadow of your son,
Becomes a sun and makes your son a shadow.
I do protest, I never loved myself

Till now enfixèd I beheld myself
Drawn in the flattering table of her eye!

Frank Kermode provides a masterly gloss on this passage: "Other poets, including John Donne, made use of the conceit that lovers could see their own images in the eyes of the beloved, and others had punned on "son" and "sun," but here the two ideas are combined: the lady's eyes are so bright that he, the son, becomes a sun. He has never admired himself so much as when he sees himself as a picture drawn on the "table" of her eye. The picture is so wonderful that from being a shadow it becomes a sun, while the sitter, a son/sun because the son of the King, is reduced to mere shadow."[19]

***

As can be seen from the example of the pun in the title of *Much Ado About Nothing*, above, the 'lofty Shakespeare' was far from averse to the language of the body and the bawdy. Such puns permeate all his writing. There are entire critical studies devoted to this one area of Shakespeare's language, such as Stanley Wells' *Shakespeare, Sex, and Love* and Pauline Kiernan's *Filthy Shakespeare: Shakespeare's Most Outrageous Sexual Puns.* [20] Furthermore, there are glossaries and dictionaries dedicated to this sole area.

Shakespeare easily moves from the physical to the spiritual or philosophical. As in their forebears, the Mystery Plays, crude jokes about bodily functions are mixed in together with the sublime. The plays of the time reflected all of human nature from the most elevated to the lowest. This mix of elements, combined with the variety of presentation in rhyme or prose, ranging from elevated poetic flights to demonstrations of rhetorical excellence to puns and insults based on genitalia and toilet humour, contributed to the vitality, popularity and enduring appeal of early modern theatre. Elizabethan and Jacobean writers and audiences did not split life into boxes of decorum. Instead, they embraced it all. As Raymond Chandler put it:

"If some people called some of Shakespeare's work cheap (which some of it is), he wouldn't have cared a rap, because he would know that without some vulgarity there is no complete man. He would have hated refinement, as such, because it is always a withdrawal, and he was much too tough to shrink from anything."[21]

The numerous jokes about young ladies' 'rings' were working on numerous levels, from the most basic to the most sophisticated. Shakespeare was not only capable of giving us the most poetic exploration of the human condition and the smuttiest of innuendoes within the same play, but he was sometimes even up to combining the two in one dazzling piece of wordplay. John Donne is a similar connection once again here. Donne wrote, in his pre-ordination days, a lovely passage of poetry that combined a surface meaning with a thinly disguised description of cunnilingus, much like Dylan does in a *Blonde On Blonde* song.

Later revisionists, however, were so shocked by these aspects of his work, which they considered beneath Shakespeare's dignity, that they tried to re-write his work by taking out what they considered as 'low'. However, this cannot be done without destroying the plays, as it is built into their foundations. Nonetheless, many have tried and various campaigns have been waged over the centuries, and still continue, to denude Shakespeare's texts of words, expressions and imagery that self appointed guardians of morality have deemed 'too low' for the Great Man.

It seems that this has long been the case. In the Restoration it was decided that the saintly Shakespeare was forced, against his better sensibilities, to include 'low humour' to please the 'groundlings'; that is, the 'lower sort' who stood in front of the stage. This is patently incorrect as such language and imagery appears in every aspect of his work. Kiernan has estimated that there are over four hundred puns for reproductive organs in the collected plays. Consequently, you will find it in the most exquisite scenes as well as in those of vulgar farce. Characters from all social classes indulge in it. It occurs in all plays, not just the comedies. In Shakespeare's time, this was unremarkable, and the plays of his contemporary dramatists are similarly packed with puns carrying sexual innuendo and coarse interchanges. Everyone, except that figure of fun, the slow-witted Sir Andrew Aguecheek in *Twelfth Night,* understands them; which is why it is so amusing that he needs the following line explained to him: *'this is my lady's hand these be her very C's, her U's and her T's and thus makes she her great P's'.*

There were many who would continue to work at prohibiting the public from the pleasures and enlightenment of appreciating Shakespeare's plays in their full glory, however. Two of the most prominent, and, regrettably, hugely successful people in this regard were Thomas Bowdler and his sister, Henrietta Marie. We have derived the verb 'bowdlerise' from Thomas's surname, and it means to cut offending material from a text, and often takes on the added meaning of 'and thereby weakening the original'. This added inflection is because this is precisely what the brother and sister team did to Shakespeare. Their edition, *The Family Shakspeare*, in 1807 proudly proclaimed that it 'omitted words and expressions which cannot be expressed in the Family' and Bowdler stated, with astounding hubris, in the introduction that: "My great objects in this undertaking are to remove from Shakespeare some defects which diminish their value".

The verb we should use might well be "marie-ised" rather than bowdlerised, as the sister did the editing work. However, her name had to be kept quiet as to do otherwise would be to acknowledge that a female actually understood the expurgated material. The hypocrisy of their actions did not affect their zeal, and this zeal immediately found an audience. Their edition was extraordinarily popular and by 1850 there had been no fewer than eleven editions of their redacted Shakespeare. These were to have a considerable impact on how Shakespeare and his plays came to be regarded.

Such things do not belong to a prim past that we can laugh at from a modern perspective. Into the twentieth century and still, I am told, into this century in the United States, heavily censored versions of the plays are taught in schools. So much so that a play such as *Romeo and Juliet* is left making little sense as so much material has been excised. A more adult approach is favoured by more enlightened schools, but many thousands of young adults are kept from reading saucy exchanges in Shakespeare even when they have access to all manner of pornography at their fingertips on computers and smartphones.

Many problems arise when the plays are edited in a ham-fisted manner for reasons of prudency. Their individual use of bawdy language is crucial to the characters' identity and essence, and it has a significant bearing on how we apprehend them. The way a couple flirt by bantering with sexualised puns and the extensive Shakespearean sub-genre of crude insults are vital in communicating insights into his characters and how we come to see them in terms of their social roles, gender and power relationships, social mobility and so forth. We see, in such exchanges, Beatrice's power in her relationship with Benedick and both their characters laid bare, so to speak, through them. Similarly we see Prince Hal's ease in moving from court to tavern and back again and that Mercutio's entire character depends upon his lewd jests. Such examples of characters being revealed via their mastery, or lack of same, in rude punning, proliferate though the plays.

Simon Palfrey demonstrates how important these bawdy puns are in defining character when he discusses this passage in *Romeo and Juliet*:

ROMEO   *Why then is my pump well flowered.*

MERCUTIO   *Well said: follow me this jest now till thou hast*
           worn out thy pump, that when the single sole of it
           is worn, the jest may remain after the wearing sole singular.

ROMEO   *O single-soled jest, solely singular for the singleness.*

As Palfrey notes, Mercutio finds himself compelled, by its very appropriateness, to pursue the pun further and further:

"Romeo has picked up on previous banter to pun on "pump" as slipper and penis. Mercutio cannot help himself from delving deeper into the pun ... the jest for him really has a defining significance. If sex is a jest, then a jest is sex: both can be everything and nothing. So, the 'pump' is a slipper, appropriate for dancing, courtly games, seduction; this suggests both a condom and a cock. In turn, 'pump' is a verb as much as a noun. It is both *full* and self-emptying; both conical force and effluent swill. In this it fits a sexualised penis, moving from inflation to deflation. But it equally fits Mercutio's wit – tragically ditto."

As Palfrey goes on to elucidate, it goes much deeper than that: "For Mercutio, a jest would be both proof *and* proxy of his masculinity. But then the joke is that one must take from the other: if his manhood is a joke then it can hardly count … So, he recommends a self-mutation into a 'solely singular' joke. It might be understood as a call to arms, a challenge directed precisely to his conceited imagination. It is then almost a kind of secret soliloquy. Can I go still further? Can I take wittiness so far that nothing will be left standing except this murderous joke? Mercutio wants to strain meaning so fine that no one else can get it. But he doesn't so much survive his joke as he becomes it. Mercutio's thought is therefore strangely self-dissolving: certainly it anticipates the way he dies through (and as) a 'grave' sort of joke gone wrong. Hence the further pun on 'pump', which in Mercutio's projection is worn down to a 'sole': that is, to a single layer of material that he then equates with a human soul. To be 'worn' also means to be worn out: Mercutio is then imagining a life run dry, or a frayed 'soul' that has nothing left to it but the earth into which it is dissolving."[22]

Unsurprisingly, given the sheer range of Shakespeare's sexually-based play on words, Dylan employs some of those that Shakespeare did. While Dylan, too, is adept at multilayered puns that can include spirituality and sex, amongst other meanings, simultaneously, his use of "pump", in the following example, is straightforward: *"Well, sometime you know when the well breaks down/I just go pump on it some"*. Those lines come from 'Goin' To Alcapulco' and, as is often the case in the laid back *The Basement Tapes*, which were originally recorded for private use only, the words might well be about the body and not much else. Similarly, little or no imagination is needed to work out what the 'pumphouse' refers to on the scabrous 'Don't Ya Tell Henry' from the same collection. This is not to say that multi-levelled and highly evolved lyrics do not co-exist in that treasure-trove of songs.

Other shared sexual puns may include 'die'. This was a staple pun in Elizabethan times for orgasm, which was known as 'the little death', and occurs as such throughout the literature of the period. It is possible Dylan is using it in the same way in 'Cold Irons Bound' when he sings: "my love for her is taking such a long time to die". It is also possible that the aforementioned meaning of 'nothing', as referring to female genitalia, was in Dylan's mind even as the T.S. Eliot and *King Lear* connotations of 'nothing' played out in the song 'Too Much of Nothing', also from *The Basement Tapes*. We are, after all, given an intriguingly descriptive list of the things 'too much of nothing' can do to man: *"Can make a man feel ill at ease"*, *"Can make a man abuse a king/He can walk the streets and boast like most"* and it *"Can turn a man into a liar"*.

More on Dylan's sexual punning in a moment, but returning to Shakespeare, two points are worthy of note regarding genders and society at large. It is striking that both males and females indulge in extensive bawdy banter on the Shakespearean stage and that the women normally come out on top, as it were. Women, although barred from being on the stage, did attend the performances and their number amazed visitors from Europe. While females were unlikely to go to the theatres alone for reasons of safety, or because they might have been assumed to be prostitutes working the audience, this does not mean they were absent.

There are social reasons, too, as to why standards of propriety were so different from some later eras, including, at times, our own. Life was shorter, more brutish and considerably less private. As such, topics from which we shy away, especially sex, death, disease and toileting, were not as taboo in the sixteenth century. Contemporaneously with the birth of what we would recognise as a 'secret service', and with conspiracies, spies and plots abounding, code-breaking was part of the zeitgeist.

Dylan's songs went, and go, out to a different society with different restrictions on what can be said and where. Radio, and TV, in particular had to operate under very restrictive moral regulations. Musicians and the young have forever taken delight in circumventing such regulations. As such, Dylan inherited, from various musical streams, a rich vein of puns that speak ambiguously, if only just, of taboo subjects, especially sex. Blues music has a rich terminology of images and puns for sexual parts and activity. Early rock 'n' roll and pop songs had to adopt a code to by-pass the censors. At its lowest level this was just 'coded smut' but it developed into extensively witty and inventive lyrics. The ambiguity of puns fitted songwriters' needs perfectly. As such, it was the censors themselves who caused an epidemic of sexual puns in popular music by encouraging the need for ambiguity and informed slang. As noted in the chapter on opposition forces, the impact of rock and roll was crucial in this regard, as white youngsters were now listening to such material.

The explosion in automobile ownership was intimately tied to blues and then rock 'n' roll lyrics. This was partly, but not only, for the freedom they provided, like the railways before them. Everything to do with cars and driving them became a source for innuendo and double-entendres. The extended treatment given to such stock blues imagery by Dylan, in songs on *Blonde on Blonde*, shows off a wit worthy of the Metaphysical poets in one of their more bawdily playful moods. Puns and other wordplay lead to a web of inter-connecting imagery. The same traditional trope of the eye as a window into the soul appears in Dylan's writing. He also uses window-as-aperture, that is, an opening for a man to enter. This trope is compounded by the centuries old song tradition of featuring the associated idea of the woman opening her window to let in a secret lover. Thus, it works on both the physical and metaphysical levels as an entry both to the body and the soul.

I have written extensively on Dylan's use of this image elsewhere,[23] and I commented then that: "The particular power of window as a figure of speech is that it can always work in at least two basic ways. You can see in through a window and you can also look out. A window can be opened to let you in, but it can also be closed to deny you access" Consequently, I was gratified when Dylan said the following when discussing gates: "Gates appeal to me because of the negative space they allow. They can be closed but at the same time they allow the seasons and breezes to enter and flow. They can shut you out or shut you in. And in some ways there is no difference." This comment was made as part of an exhibition of iron gates that Dylan welded, at Halcyon Gallery from November 2014 to January 2015. The exhibition was punningly titled *Mood Swings*. 'Gate', incidentally, was also employed as sex imagery on *Blonde on Blonde*: "*Well, your railroad gate, you know I just can't jump it /Sometimes it gets so hard, you see/I'm just sitting here beating on my trumpet*" and "*my Arabian drums/Should I leave them by your gate/ Or, sad-eyed lady, should I wait?*"

That is not surprising as *Blonde On Blonde* positively drips with salacious innuendo and 'Temporary Like Achilles' is the epitome of this. Dylan here depicts the frustrations of '*kneeling beneath the ceiling*' of an unresponsive hoped-for lover. The narrative perspective is everything in this extended *tour de force* of double entendres. *The Basement Tapes* as mentioned above have a very different tone and feel from *Blonde on Blonde* but also features songs replete with sexual undertones and overtones. Into this century and *2001's*

"Love And Theft" shows that Dylan has not lost the taste for this wordplay. As befits the album as a whole, he employs it by looking back and reinvigorating old traditions. In this case, it is back to automobile terms: *"Well, I got eight carburetors and boys, I'm using 'em all / I'm short on gas, my motor's starting to stall.* This is quickly followed by another traditional sex image: *"I got my hammer ringin', pretty baby, but the nails ain't going down"*. *"Love and Theft"* is an album with a unique ambience in which puns, bawdy, and corny jokes all play an important role in the overall atmosphere of the album.

***

Both of our artists are also drawn to the creative uses of what can be considered the opposite of puns. Here, instead of two or more meanings being compacted into one word, you get one concept or word split into two words, and joined by the conjunction 'and'. This splitting can cause multiple nuances, inflections and extended meanings.

As well as being a literary technique, it is, as with punning, one much liked and widely used in daily speech. Known as binomials, these sometimes express mere repetition. Phrases such as 'ranting and raving', 'trials and tribulations', plus 'prim and proper', link two words that have come to mean almost the same, for purposes of emphasis.

The similarity between the two conjoined words can become gradually more extended, in sayings such as 'born and bred' and 'peace and quiet' where the two, slightly divergent meanings combine to create a third. When the original terms become completely different, as in 'wine and dine' the specific yoking together of disparate words creates a phrase with the distinct meaning of treating someone to a lavish meal.

In literature, the same thing happens with examples ranging again from doubling for emphasis to the combining of disparate terms to create dynamic new thoughts and concepts. Again, examples of such effects abound in Shakespeare and Dylan's shared sources of ballads, The Bible, and the Book of Common Prayer. In Act IV, scene iv of *Hamlet* we hear of *'a delicate and tender prince'* which is an inversion of the biblical 'woman that is so tender and delicate'. Dylan has the further sources of Shakespeare himself and other past poets influenced in this regard by Shakespeare, most notably major influences Robert Burns and Allen Ginsberg. Furthermore, Dylan inherited the Blues vernacular of 'tired and weary', 'rolling and tumbling' plus their phrases refracted through 'rock 'n' roll' which is itself a doubling term for copulation.

Dylan would naturally be attracted to this figure of speech. Even without the connecting, and sometimes distancing, conjoining 'and', Dylan is fond of saying the same idea in two almost identical words: 'killed dead, 'finishing end' and 'rich wealthy' parents. As with puns, some people seem to have a low tolerance for doubled expressions. One of these from Dylan that attracted criticism was *'bring me my boots and shoes'* in "Workingman's Blues". This is not, however, an example of doubling but rather a realistic description of working men leaving home in the morning with shoes for leaving and re-approaching home and boots to change into for their work in grimy, muddy or soot-filled surroundings. The term would be instantly recognisable in many working man's communities, such as mining, and the songs that came from them and, so could hardly be more apt for the song in question.

Shakespeare's doubling on the other hand attracts praise, not criticism. Frank Kermode has a much praised chapter in his book, *Shakespeare's Language*, in which he documents how doubling occurs all the way through Hamlet. His examples include: "book and volume", "rank and station" "sanctified and pious", "pith and marrow" and, my favourite, "Angels and ministers of grace "

A standard dictionary definition of the term hendiadys is: "The expression of a single idea by two words connected with 'and', e.g. nice and warm, when one could be used to modify the other, as in nicely warm." [24] As with daily sayings, the expressions can vary. Sometimes the same idea is repeated, with the two words only being slightly different causing a tension to build upon the 'and' conjunction and producing new and different meanings, often disturbingly so, as Kermode notes: "Hendiadys is a way of making a single idea strange by splitting an expression in two, so that it calls for explanation as a minute and often rather sinister metaphor".

A key point about these verbal constructions is that their combination produces a unique meaning and by taking one away that new meaning is lost. A Dylan example that immediately springs to mind, even with the two words being reasonably close in meaning, is *"your needless and pointless knowledge"* from 'Tombstone Blues'.

Kermode, still on *Hamlet*, notes that: "In the sequence *'Forward, not permanent, sweet, not lasting, / The perfume and suppliance of a minute; No more'* simple antithesis gives way to hendiadys: *'perfume and suppliance of a minute'* means something like 'a pleasant, transitory amusement,' but the two nouns interlocked; one can't remove either of them without destroying the sense."

Ginsberg, as we will return to in the final chapter, was most taken with this technique and his musings over the endlessly intriguing phrase from Prospero regarding Miranda's memories from the 'dark backward and abysm of time' led him to recall Horatios' words about Hamlet's father's ghost being first encountered in *"the dead vast and middle of the night"*.

The creativity bound up in phrases such as *"backward and abysm"* and *"vast and middle"* is akin to the compacted meaning of the most powerful puns. As with that form of word play, hendiadys range from the thrillingly creative to the merely sweet confection of things, or, as Dylan sings in one on 'Handy Dandy', *"just like sugar and candy"*. However, every bit of it, at every stage is integral to their plays and songs and to take any of it away would be to diminish the whole.

Before leaving this chapter on wordplay, it is worth noting Shakespeare and Dylan's use of the rhetorical power of repetition. In Shakespeare's *Henry VI Part 3* we hear:

How many make the hour full complete,
How many hours bring about the day.
How many days will finish up the year,
How many years a mortal man may live.
When this is known, then to divide the times:
So many hours must I tend my flock;
So many hours must I take my rest;
So many hours must I contemplate;
So many hours must I sport myself;
So many days my ewes have been with young;
So many weeks ere the poor fools will ean;
So many years ere I shall shear the fleece:

And in Dylan's "Blowin' in the Wind" we hear:
How many times must a man look up
Before he can see the sky?
Yes, 'n' how many ears must one man have
Before he can hear people cry?
Yes, 'n' how many deaths will it take till he knows
That too many people have died?

Shakespeare is drawing on his rhetorical training and classical models, while ballad and other song traditions are at play in Dylan's creativity. One thinks of the use of repetition in 'A Hard Rain's A-Gonna Fall' and the ballad which informs that song, Lord Randall, with their repeated questions of "Oh where have you been...".

***

Both Shakespeare and Dylan delight in such wordplay and rhetorical flourishes throughout their careers. Puns still appeal to Dylan to this day. He recently contributed a recording to a collection that transforms classic tracks into same-sex wedding anthems, called *Universal Love*. The six-track compilation producer, Rob Kaplan reported that Dylan eagerly agreed to the proposal: "It wasn't just 'yes, I'll do this'. It was 'hey, I have an idea for a song.'"[25] The song on Dylan's mind was made famous by Frank Sinatra and Nat King Cole, "She's Funny That Way" which Dylan has changed to "He's Funny That Way", with such pronoun changes being the norm over the selections. Dylan, in this tender and moving rendition, thus also has a pun on 'he is funny that way' which, in the time from which the song comes, was used euphemistically for a man being gay.

Puns, then, still attract Dylan, just as they never ceased fascinating Shakespeare, and for both artists, they and other glittering wordplay contribute to an underpinning mesh of imagery that holds together and invigorates play after play and song after song. Dylan plays with language in much the same ways as Shakespeare did. As Anne Margaret Daniel has written:

"The Shakespearean flipping of word order, the loose and easy play of subjects, objects, verbs, adjectives, and adverbs upsets subject-object-verb, with modifying words clinging to the main ones. In this sense, Dylan clearly loves the Renaissance freedom of linguistic inversion and unconstraint".[26]

Both artists have a natural facility for language that seems magical in its ease and unerring accuracy. They speak to us all in what seems to be our own words, and articulate our own innermost thoughts. Time and again they tell us "what oft was thought, but ne'er so well expressed" as Alexander Pope, a writer from a very different context, put it. Even further, they seem to express what we have not yet thought, but feel we would have, eventually, given time enough. In reality, we always need a touch of their genius to help us on our way.

NOTES

1 Charles W. R. D. Moseley, *Shakespeare's History Plays: Richard II to Henry V, the Making of a King* UK: Penguin, 1988

2 Joan Baez "Diamonds and Rust" © Downtown Music Publishing www.joanbaez.com/Lyrics/diamonds.html

3 Moseley *Op. cit.*

4 Henry Miller *The Time Of The Assassins: a Study of Rimbaud* New Directions 1962

5 I discuss this struggle with language at length in chapter nine of my book, *Troubadour* Woodstock Press, UK, 2013

6 Bob Dylan and Larry Charles, *Masked and Anonymous* Sony Pictures Classics July 2003

7 Simon Palfrey *Doing Shakespeare* The Arden Shakespeare London *2005*

8 http://www.openculture.com/2014/03/hear-allen-ginsbergs-short-free-course-on-shakespeares-play-the-tempest-1980.html Accessed March 28, 2018

9 I investigate this theme in these songs in detail in my book *Troubadour op. cit.*

10 Bob Dylan "What Was It You Wanted" Copyright © 1989 by Special Rider Music

11 Stephen Rendell writing as 'charlesdarwin' on *Expecting Rain* Discussion Forum. Post subject: Re: rating Street Legal (1978) Posted: Sat June 17th, 2017, 10:27 GMT http://www.expectingrain.com/discussions/viewtopic.php?f=6&t=84284&sid=ddd07b186a4a4ceeb656db17c9c51a9b&start=50 Accessed March 24, 2018

12 Ruth Finnegan, *Why Do We Quote?: The Culture and History of Quotation* Open Book Publishers, Mar 1, 2011

13 Simon Palfrey *op. cit.*

14 Dylan's official lyrics are a guide but do not, as things stand, provide definitive answers to such questions. Perhaps it is not possible to ever do so. For Shakespeare, too, editors of print versions must make a choice and then explain multiple possibilities in footnotes.

15 To complicate matters further many people hear 'morning' for the former

16 Ruth Vanita, *'When Men and Women are Alone': Framing the Taming in India; Shakespeare Survey 60* Edited by Peter Holland, Publisher: Cambridge University Press 2007

17 Adrian Streete, *Protestantism and Drama in Early Modern England* Cambridge University Press 2009

18 Bob Dylan *Tarantula Op. cit.*

19 Frank Kermode *Shakespeare's Language* Farrar, Straus and Giroux, 2001

20 Wells, Stanley, *Shakespeare, Sex, and Love* Oxford University Press, Oxford 2012 and Kiernan, Pauline *Filthy Shakespeare: Shakespeare's Most Outrageous Sexual Puns* Quercus London 2006

21 Raymond Chandler, 1949,from *Raymond Chandler Speaking*

22 Simon Palfrey *op. cit.*

23 Andrew Muir *Troubadour*, Woodstock Press, UK, 2013

24 The Oxford English Dictionary

25 http://www.nme.com/news/music/bob-dylan-hes-funny-that-way-gay-love-anthem-2282939

26 Anne Margaret Daniel *Tempest*, Bob Dylan and the Bardic Arts, in *Tearing the World Apart: Bob Dylan and the Twenty-First Century* , Eds. Nina Goss, Eric Hoffman. University Press of Mississippi 2017

Chapter Nine

SOURCES

To sing a song that old was sung

B oth Shakespeare and Dylan make extensive use of source material throughout their careers. This manifests itself in numerous ways. These range from major thematic, stylistic and linguistic importing, through verbatim quotes and both direct and diffuse allusions, to inspired transmutation of material that ranges, in its original state, from the mundane to the already highly artistic. Given that their art is rooted in live performance, it is only natural that they developed a heightened ability to integrate elements of others' creations into their own.

They often refer themselves to the practice. Shakespeare has a contributory predecessor to his *Pericles* act as the chorus and tell us that he is going to "*sing a song that old was sung*". In addition to the relevant Dylan quotes below, he sang, on 'Too Much of Nothing': "*It's all been done before, it's all been written in a book*" and on "*Love And Theft*", a patchwork album of thefts that he loves, he incorporates a line that encapsulates his mode of composition: "*My grandmother could sew new dresses out of old cloth*".

There is wide range of vocabulary to indicate what particular form of copying is taking place in any given situation. These range from the positive, particularly in artistic contexts, terms of; allusion, interleaving, *imitatio*, acknowledging, through the more neutral referencing, recycling and quoting to a sliding scale of the judgemental; imitation, copying, plagiarism, copyright infringement and theft.

These last two categories can only be applied to Dylan, in any meaningful sense. Like all the dramatists of his era, Shakespeare almost always built his work on stories written by others, and this was seen as both natural and the basis of creativity. Due to cultural and legal changes over time, there would be no place for much of the early modern artists' brilliant output in the current world, given their mode of creation. This chapter inevitably, then, has more to say about Dylan's far more complex situation over a much longer career, now beginning to approach its sixtieth year, than the more straightforward situation in Shakespeare's span of just over two decades in the theatre, at a time that pre-dated any copyright laws.

I also restrict myself, in Shakespeare's case, to borrowings that are very clearly utilised or are from sources that are referenced on multiple occasions. This is because, as Jonathan Bate has perspicaciously warned:

"... verbal parallels can be coincidental and shared ideas can be derived at second-hand, especially in a culture that encouraged the recycling and amplification of *sententiae* and commonplaces. I suspect that Shakespeare skimmed many a new volume at the bookstalls outside St Paul's, but closely read fewer books than is often imagined by bookish scholars, who (like everyone who writes about Shakespeare) have a subliminal desire to make him more like themselves than he really was."[1]

This is very true, too, for Dylan; although Dylan has had a longer and more convenient access to material than Shakespeare. Shakespeare and Dylan gratefully accept and put to use anything that helps create a song or a play. Both artists clearly had minds that picked up on and stored the rhythm and imagery of things they heard and read and moulded these into their own work with graceful ease. Nonetheless, they both are also renowned as literary craftsmen, and by dropping in quotes from other literary figures, as well as referencing their dramatic and musical forebears and peers, they encourage us to follow up on these borrowings. Sometimes their works seem to almost insist upon us doing so and are considerably enhanced when we do. This is as true for many literary references as it is, for example to Shakespeare playing, on more than one occasion, on Christopher Marlowe's line "Is this the face that launched a thousand ships"[2] or Dylan answering John Lennon's 'Norwegian Wood' with 'Fourth Time Around'. Our two artists have produced their work in eras with very divergent views of, and laws on, originality and creative ownership.

***

The idea of authorship was very different in Shakespeare's time, so much so as to be unrecognisable to modern eyes. The dramatist was an almost unacknowledged presence in the time of Shakespeare's theatre. The Bard's name did not appear on the front of the first printed editions of his plays and Shakespeare had nothing to do with these publications.

Most plays during this extraordinary period of drama were collaborative efforts. In a sense all were inherently so, as you would expect from companies putting on popular performances at a time of high competition and constantly changing fashions. The quantity of theatrical performances, and tight timescales within which they were staged, is truly astounding. Consequently, most plays were written by a variety of hands and, in any case, we have to assume that all were transformed to a greater or lesser degree during performances by the casts of the acting troupes who performed them. Similarly, one has to also presume that Shakespeare as a shareholder and actor in The Chamberlain's (later King's) Men company also partly modified the plays from others that his company put on stage. As John Jowett writes:

"The dramatist working for the commercial theatre in the early 1590s potentially had little or no status as an author. He (for women did not write for the professional theatre) would work for a fee, often in collaboration with other dramatists. Only a small proportion of plays appeared as printed books. The title pages of published plays almost always named the theatre company that had performed the play, and it was the theatre company that usually would have released the manuscript for publication. The dramatists' names were often not recorded in the printed texts of their plays, and there was no Copyright Act to recognize and protect their interests. Anonymity, collaboration, and the absence of authorial rights were the typical circumstances of dramatic writing."[3]

Shakespeare appears to have been one of the most solitary of the writers of his time, but that is still a relative description. By today's standards, the extent of Shakespeare's collaboration would doubtless be viewed as extensive. Centuries of Bardolatry turned a blind eye to this, and it is becoming increasingly apparent that he collaborated more than was first acknowledged. Collaboration was, after all, the norm for the drama writing of the time, as was recycling stories. It would be wrong to think this demeans him as it would be an anachronistic standard by which to judge him. As we shall see later, it may well be an unsupportable standard to attempt to uphold in any age.

For now, though, it is important to note, that, in the sixteenth and seventeenth centuries, there was no legal protection for authors. The first act on the way to modern copyright statutes was still a century or so away and that was designed to safeguard publishers rather than authors. This was all in the future, and for Shakespeare's plays it was The Worshipful Company of Stationers, commonly referred to as The Stationers' Company, who controlled all printing and publications. The first rights to the works, such as they were, were maintained for publishers, not playwrights. This could be a reason why Shakespeare never oversaw his own plays being printed.

With no existing copyright act, nor the concept of plagiarism being an unsavoury custom, it was inevitable that plots, characters and themes were taken wholesale from others' stories and retold in a new fashion. Furthermore, to imitate and re-use the words of established authors, and in particular one from the Classical Era, was considered the very essence of creativity.

Sir Philip Sidney, in his massively influential *An Apology for Poetry* describes poetry as "an art of imitation, for so Aristotle termeth it in his word Mimesis". For Sidney imitation by a poet leads eventually to glimpses of the ideal that lies behind the actual, which was an ingenious way to counter Plato's objections to poetry.

Shakespeare's sources, then, are wide, varied and deep and have provided scholars with swathes of research possibilities which they have taken up with great relish. One highly enjoyable and instructive way to study both artists, and expand your enjoyment in their work, is to look at their sources and what they do with them.

***

Shakespeare's sources have been so extensively researched, collected, referenced and written about, most strikingly in Geoffrey Bullough's monumental, eight volume, *Narrative and Dramatic Sources of Shakespeare*, that I will merely list some here as a quick guide to their all pervading prevalence. These sources not only come from a wide variety of places but are also handled in different ways at different points in his career. Both Dylan and Shakespeare grew more mature in their handling of source material as they gained experience in their respective fields. By the end of their careers, they meld together disparate borrowings from divergent sources and traditions, including, to significant effect, their own earlier work, to create complex new works.

Both artists utilise primary and secondary sources. Critics delight in referring to the former in Shakespeare's case, when they provide not just plot, character and themes but also direct lifts, as being, 'open upon Shakespeare's table as he wrote'. Shakespeare's primary sources across multiple plays include, among others, *Holinshed's Chronicles* and North's translation of Plutarch's *The Lives of the Noble Grecians and Romans*. We have previously looked at the influence of classical writers on Shakespeare and these all play their parts here, especially Ovid, Virgil, Seneca, Homer, and Plautus *et al.*

Holinshed's Chronicles is a history of Scotland, England and Ireland from their beginning up until its first publication in 1577. As well as being a direct source in, it has been estimated, at least a third of Shakespeare's plays, it was also a prime source for other writers who heavily influenced Shakespeare, especially Edmund Spenser and Christopher Marlowe. 'Holinshed' is the main source of Shakespeare's English History Plays, *Macbeth* and *King Lear*, amongst others. So closely does Shakespeare rely on the work that we can claim, with a relatively comforting certainty, that he used the second, revised edition of 1587.

As well as the goldmine of historical facts and background that it held,

Holinshed was particularly suitable for a dramatist's use due to the range of those who collaborated in its creation. This created a polyphonic account, ripe for characters to re-voice on stage. As 'the Holinshed Project' puts it:

"Among the authors and revisers were moderate Protestants (Raphael Holinshed, John Hooker), militant Protestants (William Harrison, Abraham Fleming), crypto-Catholics (John Stow), and Catholics (Richard Stanihurst, Edmund Campion). The upshot was a remarkably multi-vocal view of British history not only because of the contrasting choices of style and source material but also because the contributors responded very differently to the politics and religion of their own age. The importance of Holinshed's *Chronicles* for the understanding of Elizabethan literature, history, and politics cannot be overestimated."[4]

Plutarch's *The Lives of the Noble Grecians and Romans* also employed a fruitful approach for the dramatist's keen eye. The famous men chronicled in that work were placed side by side. It was a collection of 'Parallel Lives', chosen to highlight comparative strengths and failings, virtues and vices. *Julius Caesar, Antony and Cleopatra,*Coriolanus and *Timon of Athens* all rely, to varying degrees, on Thomas North's English translation of Jacques Amyot's lively French translation from a Latin rendering of Plutarch's Greek original.

Many of Shakespeare's plays also had direct, individual sources. These could be poetic or prose, and old stories or new tales from contemporary writers both English and Italian. They could be very well known or relatively obscure. The original inspirations for *Romeo and Juliet, Much Ado About Nothing, As You Like It, Othello, Pericles* and *The Winter's Tale* all fall into one or other of these categories. It also seems highly unlikely that Pierre de la Primaudaye's *The French Academy* was not at least part of the inspiration for *Love's Labour's Lost*. This was translated into English in 1586 and begins by telling the tale of four young gentlemen setting up an academic retreat in Anjou where they were to abjure sexual relations and withdraw from the society of their day.

Additionally, Shakespeare's plays were often new versions of previously performed works, *Richard III, King Lear* and the mysterious '*ur-Hamlet*' among others, or heavily influenced by successful plays by his contemporaries. Examples of these include Kyd's era-defining *The Spanish Tragedy* and *Hamlet*, and Marlowe's *The Jew of Malta* and *The Merchant of Venice*.

SOURCES

A new, and seemingly primary, Shakespearean source book has recently been discovered, namely, "*A Brief Discourse of Rebellion and Rebels*" by George North. As many as eleven of Shakespeare's plays are reputedly influenced in plot, theme and language by North's 1576 book which would make it potentially as large a source as anything outside Holinshed. It is therefore little wonder that Michael Witmore, director of the Folger Shakespeare Library, says: "If it proves to be what they say it is, it is a once-in-a-generation – or several generations – find."[5]

Then there were the secondary sources, again from a great range throughout the ages. Some of these re-occur often enough as to perhaps warrant the title of primary source. We find that the English history plays were also bolstered by Edward Hall's *The Union of the Two Noble and Illustre Families of Lancaster and York* as well as Samuel Daniel's *The Civil Wars between the Two Houses of Lancaster and York*. While Chaucer for example, (who is also repeatedly quoted in later Dylan lyrics), has a strong influence on *The Two Noble Kinsmen, Troilus and Cressida*, and *A Midsummer Night's Dream*.

The myriad of truly secondary sources is as expansive as you would expect from an extraordinarily bright mind, active in the exciting times of Elizabethan England with, perhaps personally enhanced, access to the book trade swirling around St Paul's. On those rare occasions when no primary source is available; *The Tempest*, for example, scholarship delves very deeply into what would be seen as more minor influences in other works.

What Shakespeare did with these sources provides a window into his unparalleled creative art and his dramatist's ability to develop plot and character. What he omits from his sources is everything that would prove a drag on the momentum of a performance. While sometimes he portrays characters much as they are in the sources, on other occasions he magnifies their roles or significantly minimises them. *Antony and Cleopatra* clings very closely to its main source, yet the character of Enobarbus is a major factor in the play while meriting only a mere mention in North's translation.

Sometimes Shakespeare simplifies the situations in his sources but mostly he complicates them, for example, by doubling the amount of identical twins in Plautus's *The Menaechmi* for his own *the Comedy of Errors*. He will happily swap people from different times and places into his timeframe and locations if it makes the play more dramatically effective. The old play *King Leir*, and all other variants of that tale had happy endings. It is hard to imagine the shock for the first Jacobean audience to witness Shakespeare's version with its terrible and terrifying conclusion.

The needs of Shakespeare's artistic aims are always served, and the sources used to facilitate that end. The pacing of the drama is of paramount importance; events, people and historical facts are all fashioned into contrasting scenes, arranged in movements like a piece of music, now loud, fast and bombastic, now quiet, soft and reflective, now brutal, vicious and without hope, then tender, forward-looking and forgiving. Comic and tragic, low humour and high sentiment are all drawn from a variety sources and re-arranged to exquisite dramatic effect.

A classical model existed for taking and transforming the work of those who had gone before. Ben Jonson, Shakespeare's friend and rival, wrote:

"The third requisite in our poet, or maker, is imitation, to be able to convert the substance or riches of another poet to his own use ... to draw forth out of the belt and choicest flowers, with the bee, and turn all into honey, work it into one refill and favour: make our imitation sweet; observe how the best writers have imitated, and follow them. How Virgil and Statius have imitated Homer; how Horace, Archilochus; how Alcaeus, and the other lyrics; and so of the rest."

Jonson was building on Horace and Seneca, who, like other ancient Romans, developed the idea from the Greeks. Thereby they were all enacting the very thing that they were describing.

The 'other lyrics' and 'the rest' form a river leading all the way to Bob Dylan who is another in the line of these imitator-transformers. Montaigne, a writer whom we know Shakespeare was familiar with and quoted, picked up on the same thread:

... The bees steal from this flower and that, but afterwards turn their pilferings into honey, which is their own; it is thyme and marjoram no longer. So the pupil will transform and fuse together the passages that he borrows from others, to make of them something entirely his own; that is to say, his own judgement. His education, his labour, and his study have no other aim but to form this."

This specific form of copying, known as *imitatio*, that is, the lengthy quotation with elaboration and modifications of a classical text, was actively encouraged and highly admired in Shakespeare's age. This technique plays a crucial role throughout Shakespeare's career. *Imitatio* is the way Shakespeare would have been taught to write. You learned by repeatedly imitating until you had mastered the rhetorical arts and then, perhaps, if gifted enough, added a little of your own into the well-drilled writing that reflected the work of classical genius.

The musically self-taught young Dylan put himself through something very similar. Again there was the seemingly endless repetition of the classic material, when he started out in New York by imitating Woody Guthrie, particularly, in every style and nuance until his own voice more and more became intertwined with that of the older songs. Then he began to write original words and performed them in styles and accents of his own.

Back in the Sixteenth Century, copying was the standard procedure; be it the admired *imitatio*, the pragmatic use of whatever was at hand or any step in-between. Shakespeare was, nonetheless, accused of plagiarism in the following passage from a 1592 pamphlet entitled: *Groats-worth of Witte, bought with a million of Repentance*:

"Yes trust them not: for there is an upstart Crow, beautified with our feathers, that with his Tygers hart wrapt in a Players hide, supposes he is as well able to bombast out a blank verse as the best of you: and being an absolute *Johannes fac totem*, is in his own conceit the only Shake-scene in a country. O that I might entreat your rare wits to be employed in more profitable courses: and let those Apes imitate your past excellence, and never more acquaint them with your admired inventions ... for it is pity men of such rare wits, should be subject to the pleasure of such rude groomes.'

'Shake-scene' clearly refers to Shakespeare, especially as it is followed by a play on a line from his *Henry VI Part Three*, Act I Scene iv: "O tiger's heart wrapped in a woman's hide".

These words are exceedingly important as an insight into Shakespeare's life and the jealousy which his early success had provoked. They have long been attributed to Robert Greene, but some scholars now contend that they were written by the dramatist Henry Chettle. Chettle himself denied that he had forged the document under the name of the dying Greene.

Whoever the author was, jealousy and snobbery were the motives behind the attack. The phrase, "upstart crow", is very deliberately chosen. We know crows to be highly intelligent, as did Aesop, despite the one that lost its cheese to the flattering fox, in his fable of 'the crow and the pitcher'. There was another Aesop fable where a vain jackdaw tried to impersonate more beautiful birds by putting on their discarded feathers. This is the image that became crystallised in the phrase 'borrowed plumes', and it is this fable to which Chettle or Greene is alluding.

'Putting on airs and graces' to quote another commonplace phrase, is what was being rallied against. The horror that a 'commoner' was using the words of his social 'betters' was behind the attack; that and the young man from Stratford's successful start to his career. Shakespeare's success was one element in a number of circumstances that had given rise to a fear of the new class of non-University writers, who were being educated at school, becoming successful in the theatre. This fear was realised when Middleton, Webster and Decker all followed in Shakespeare's wake.

The accusation obviously lacked any force in a time when copying was not seen as anything but the norm. Chettle soon issued an apology in which he turned the scorn shown towards Shakespeare's writing above into praise.

This incident provides an interesting illustration of the different attitudes towards *imitatio*, which was a wholly positive one and mere copying to which there was an indifference. That indifference would, in time, become the wholly negative view of plagiarism which we hold today. Janet Clare has analysed these reactions in her study of imitation in Renaissance theatre:

"Imitation invariably carries a positive charge and is associated with high culture, primarily in relation to classical models, whereas in some contexts the less lofty 'borrowing' veers towards a negative register. Popular theatre practice - as opposed to academic drama - was routinely dependent on borrowing rather than on imitation, although 'imitation' would appear to be the most appropriate term to describe the practice for taking over blank verse and dramatic patterns. Indeed, with playwrights appropriating materials, wholesale and local, the habit of re-cycling was so commonplace that it was rarely commented upon[6]."

SOURCES

Shakespeare had nothing to hide regarding his sources and often displayed them with pride. His beloved Ovid even appears on stage as a prop and in *Pericles* Shakespeare uses the dead English poet, John Gower, one of the sources for the play, as his chorus speaker. Gower was a link in a chain as he had told a tale that goes back to times of Greek antiquity. The play therefore commences with Gower saying: *"To sing a song that old was sung/From ashes ancient Gower is come"*. *Pericles*, in turn, quickly became one of the most referenced of all Shakespeare plays with more allusions to it in immediately succeeding drama than any of his other Jacobean plays.

***

That is a reminder, before matters become more complex regarding Dylan's use of sources, that Shakespeare, like Dylan after him, was a far greater influencer than influencee. So widespread and deep runs his influence that a list of even major works directly reflecting Shakespeare would appear so long as to seem endless. This began almost immediately, too, with references and tributes in numerous plays, Decker's allusions and, perhaps most significantly, Ford's magnificent 'commentary' on *Romeo and Juliet*, *'Tis Pity She's a Whore*. John Fletcher even wrote a sequel to *The Taming of the Shrew*, *The Tamer Tamed*, where, to all but the most unregenerate chauvinists' relief, Petruchio gets his comeuppance.

Bob Dylan's songs likewise have inspired answer-songs and parodies. As early as 1963 there was a song attacking Dylan and everything to do with him, to the tune of 'The Times They Are A-Changin'. Roberta Flack's re-positioning of 'Just Like A Woman' from a female perspective being a gender-change example to put alongside the many productions of Shakespeare where male and female roles are swapped. Dylan continues to be the master of re-interpreting or repositioning his own work. Although our evidence is painfully thin, we can assume the same of Shakespeare given that he worked in a field where constant editing and on-the-fly improvisation and re-interpretation were the order of the day. From what has survived, the Quarto and Folio versions of *King Lear*, and the various versions of *Hamlet* give credence to this view. With Dylan, we have on record a bounty of varied interpretations that is astonishing in depth, nuance and sheer quantity as he continues through the sixth decade of his career.

Adaptations of Shakespeare on screen and stage have continued unabated into modern times. *West Side Story* (*Romeo and Juliet*) *Kiss Me Kate* and *Ten Things I Hate About You* (both *The Taming of the Shrew*) being a few of the more famous. Tom Stoppard's *Rosencrantz and Guildenstern are Dead* is one of many plays based on Shakespeare. It is impossible to do justice, without writing a separate book on the matter, to the extent of his influence on the cultural landscape in the centuries after he wrote. *The Tempest* alone is directly responsible for Robert Browning's *Caliban Upon Setebos*, W.H. Auden's *The Mirror and the Sea*, and the science fiction film *Forbidden Planet* amongst others. This play's inspiration is legendary, incorporating T.S. Eliot's *The Waste Land*, giving the title to Aldous Huxley's *Brave New World* and an impressive slew of post-colonial writing.

One example of Shakespeare as influencer that I would like to mention here, as it is pertinent to a discussion near the end of this book on Dylan's Nobel Lecture, is that of Herman Melville's *Moby Dick*. Not only does that novel clearly reflect *Hamlet*, but it also echoes *Macbeth* and *King Lear* and rewrites Jaques' immortal, "*All the world's a stage*" speech from *As You Like It*, topped off with a Hamletesque flourish, in chapter 114:

"Would to God these blessed calms would last. But the mingled, mingling threads of life are woven by warp and woof: calms crossed by storms, a storm for every calm. There is no steady unretracing progress in this life; we do not advance through fixed gradations, and at the last one pause:—through infancy's unconscious spell, boyhood's thoughtless faith, adolescence' doubt (the common doom), then scepticism, then disbelief, resting at last in manhood's pondering repose of If. But once gone through, we trace the round again; and are infants, boys, and men, and Ifs eternally. Where lies the final harbor, whence we unmoor no more?"

Shakespeare's less direct influence is simply colossal, not only in poetry and drama which are forever under his influence, but all of Western Art and much of its philosophy and psychology would be immeasurably different without his fundamental, transcending and transforming influence.

In an understandably smaller, though still impressively large, universe, Dylan has had and continues to have a similarly immense impact. Not only have most forms of popular music in the last half-century been in large degrees shaped by his work, but his influence has spread through society impacting on politics, fashion, religion and ideologies. Musicians and songwriters constantly refer to him as their guiding light, as you might well imagine, but the wider artistic world continually does, too: authors, directors, actors and producers all regularly name-check Dylan as an influence in their lives and work. On receiving the Nobel Prize for literature the year after Dylan was given that accolade, interviewers pressed Kazuo Ishiguro to revive the controversy over the previous year's winner. Ishiguro was having none of this:

"Bob Dylan was my creative hero when I was growing up. When he won the Nobel, I was ecstatic. It's an added thrill that I follow directly in his footsteps."[7]

Many famous actors, including one of the leading Shakespearean thespians of our time, Mark Rylance, routinely acclaim Dylan as an inspiration. Some poets, perhaps understandably, if woefully mistakenly, have tried to snipe from what are far-away sidelines, but others have recognised Dylan's genius. Even the normally curmudgeonly Philip Larkin was won over, and through listening at the time rather than retrospectively, at that. This was Larkin in 1965:

"I'm afraid I poached Bob Dylan's *Highway 61 Revisited* out of curiosity and found myself well rewarded. Dylan's cawing, derisive voice is probably well suited to his material – I say probably, because much of it was unintelligible to me -and his guitar adapts itself to rock ('Highway 61') and ballad ('Queen Jane') admirably. There is a marathon 'Desolation Row', which has an enchanting tune and mysterious, possibly half-baked words."[8]

If that sounds qualified praise, we should recall their vastly different cultural milieus and how revolutionary and new Dylan was in 1965, as well as that unambiguous "well rewarded". We were later to find out that, once Larkin had had time to adjust to a poetic voice from a new source, or rather an old source renewed, Philip Larkin declared 'Mr Tambourine Man' to be the greatest song of all time.[9]

Aside from poets, actors, directors, producers who have proclaimed Dylan's direct influence are the legion of folk, blues, rock, country and pop performers who proudly display the same. When Dylan had seemed to "semi-retire", the Seventies' music scene responded with a blizzard of 'new Dylans'. The list of these included the following names: John Prine, Steve Forbert, Elliot Murphy, Loudon Wainwright III and Bruce Springsteen. Jimi Hendrix said that he would never have sung without having heard Dylan's voice first and Tom Waits's unique vocals were also given a boost by Dylan having been there before him. Countless musicians have covered Dylan's work in an attempt to latch on to the magic and to hope that some rubs off on them. Even rap and hip-hop artists have quoted and referred to Dylan songs in their lyrics. Joni Mitchell, later to turn into a harsh Dylan critic, credits his song, 'Positively 4th Street' with showing her that anything could be said in a song. Bruce Springsteen has often spoken about Dylan's influence in freeing his mind and showing him what could be done in rock music. Tom Petty said that: "He influenced my song-writing, of course. He influenced everybody's song-writing. There's no way around it. No one had ever really left the love song before, lyrically. So in that respect, I think he influenced everybody, because you suddenly realized you could write about other things.[10] Dylan's influence bestrode the Sixties and his direct influence on the Beatles, the Rolling Stones and the Byrds, all of whom have members with whom Dylan has collaborated, was inevitably passed on to their listeners and copiers.

One night, following a "Dylan is a plagiarist" media storm, Billy Bragg stopped his show to announce on stage that without Dylan as a leader to copy he, Bragg, would not even be there to play to the audience. He said the truth is that everyone else copies Dylan, and so the charges were ridiculous. *"The fiddler, he now steps to the road. He writes ev'rything's been returned which was owed"* as Dylan put it in 'Visions of Johanna', as early as the mid-Sixties.

Both of our bards have been copied endlessly and will continue to influence others forever more. Their words are repeatedly used in TV reports, especially as a lead-in or a summary point; newspaper headlines frequently quote them, as do sports commentators, advertisers and a whole range of communicators, some of whom will never have attended a Shakespeare play nor listened to Dylan. They may not even always be aware that they are quoting someone specifically at all, so embedded in our language have the artists' phrases become.

***

Perhaps this is also the time, before delving into the murky depths of copyright and plagiarism, to highlight both these magpie bards' supreme achievements in their powers of transmutation. And to remind ourselves that, in developing their own voice through imitation, they transformed all they touched into something transcendent, and something that speaks to, and influences, others in the ways that only bards can. The way they moulded their source materials, while honouring and enriching the traditions they took from; the manner in which they transformed, electrified and universalised the language that they used and imbued it all, somehow, with the unique imprint of "Shakespearean" or "Dylanesque" is, after all, the reason why they have become such huge influencers and repositories of source material themselves.

One of the most famous of Shakespeare's transmutations of his sources is the manner in which he transforms North's translation of Plutarch's *The Lives of the Noble Greeks and Romans* for the description of Antony first encountering Cleopatra. North's version reads as follows:

'She disdained to set forward otherwise but to take her barge in the river of Cydnus, the poop whereof was gold, the sails of purple, and the oars of silver, which kept stroke in rowing after the sound of the music of flutes, hautboys, citterns, viols, and such other instruments as they played upon in the barge. And now for the person of herself: she was laid under a pavilion of cloth of gold of tissue, apparelled and attired like the goddess Venus commonly drawn in picture, and hard by her, on either hand of her, pretty fair boys apparelled as painters do set forth god Cupid, with little fans in their hands with the which they fanned wind upon her.'

And this is Shakespeare, where the effect is best heard or, if that is not possible, read aloud

The barge she sat in, like a burnished throne
Burned on the water. The poop was beaten gold;
Purple the sails, and so perfumèd that
The winds were lovesick with them. The oars were silver,
Which to the tunes of flutes kept stroke, and made
The water which they beat to follow faster,
As amorous of their strokes. For her own person,

It beggared all description: she did lie
In her pavilion – cloth of gold, of tissue –
O'erpicturing that Venus where we see
The fancy outwork nature. On each side her
Stood pretty, dimpled boys, like smiling Cupids,
With divers-coloured fans, whose wind did seem
To glow the delicate cheeks which they did cool,
And what they undid did.

(*Antony and Cleopatra*, Act II, Scene ii)

This speech is by Enobarbus, a man we are encouraged to trust, and the nearest thing thus far in the play to an 'objective reporter'. His account of Cleopatra is a mesmerising one expressed in paradoxes, which is apt for a play that is so replete with those. Cleopatra is everywhere and nowhere in this description.

Where North enumerates, Shakespeare sensualises. The luxurious bounty of the verse is sumptuous and highly erotic. As copying goes this is in one way, that of repeated words and phrases, about as close as you can get, yet, in every way that matters, it is as far from copying as you can imagine.[11]

Dylan also repeatedly demonstrates the ability to take an existing piece of music, writing, or both together, and transform his source into something quite extraordinary and new. Dave Van Ronk, a leading figure in the early Sixties Greenwich Village folk scene, tells the story of the birth of Dylan's 'Chimes of Freedom' in his memoir, *The Mayor Of MacDougal Street*.

"Bob Dylan heard me fooling around with one of my grandmother's favorites, "The Chimes Of Trinity," a sentimental ballad about Trinity Church. He made me sing it for him a few times until he had the gist of it, then reworked it into the 'Chimes of Freedom'. Her version was better".

Dylan uses the chorus of this old song, credited to Michael J. Fitzpatrick (in 1895), for part of his own song. The original chorus went like this:

Tolling for the outcast, tolling for the gay,
Tolling for the millionaire and friends long pass'd away.
But my heart is light and gay

SOURCES

As I stroll down old Broadway
And I listen to the chimes of Trinity

Dylan rewrote this for his song's celebrated refrain. Singer Boxer John provides a faithful-to-the-original version on his *The Great Folk Heist*.[12] Comparing the two is instructive. Dylan here has taken one part of the song and built from it an enduring masterpiece. How Van Ronk could have thought 'her version was better' than Dylan's timeless, revelatory and visionary song is either sweetly loyal or deeply concerning.

As we listen to Dylan's song, we feel ourselves as one with the singer and his friends sheltering from the storm and watching the spectacular lightning. This grandeur scares us and lifts us as it illuminates the society huddled in the buildings below it. We, the listeners, are as transformed as the characters in the song, when the storm lifts and we return to normal life still holding the memories of the tempest's visions and awe-inspiring power. The alliteration and synaesthesia in phrases such as: *bells of bolts struck shadows in the sounds* takes over your mind and your senses as you listen.

Dylan's lyrics are reminiscent of Walt Whitman's 'A Song Of Myself' in their all-enveloping embrace. Both Whitman's 'Song' and Dylan's share many similar characters: outcasts, criminals, ill-judged prostitutes amongst others. In Whitman we have:

Embody all presences outlaw'd or suffering,
See myself in prison shaped like another man,
And feel the dull unintermitted pain.
...For me the keepers of convicts shoulder their carbines and keep watch, It is I let out in the morning and barr'd at night.
...Not a mutineer walks handcuff'd to jail but I am handcuff'd to him and walk by his side,
...Not a cholera patient lies at the last gasp but I also lie at the last gasp,

While in Dylan, in addition to his chorus, we have:
Tolling for the rebel, tolling for the rake
Tolling for the luckless, the abandoned an' forsaked
Tolling for the outcast, burnin' constantly at stake

Dylan's song swells to an overwhelming, all-embracing conclusion that extends empathy to everyone who is in need of it: *For the countless confused accused misused strung-out ones and worse/ And for every hung-up person in the whole wide universe.*

This has a feeling of largesse unfelt since Whitman, not only the Whitman of 'A Song of Myself' but also of 'The Sleepers' where he again becomes one with so many and shares their dreams. "I am the actor and the actress, the voter, the politician/ The emigrant and the exile, the criminal that stood in the box/He who has been famous, and he who shall be famous after today/The stammerer, the well-formed person, the wasted or feeble person."

Whitman identifies with and becomes a huge range of men and women, of all ages, colours and creeds, inside and outside the law. Dylan, from the starting point of an old romantic song, weds part of its refrain, now re-written, onto his own melody for the remainder of this poetic cry for freedom, reaches out to all of these, too, and more, in his cosmic, poetic embrace: 'every hung up person in the whole wide universe'.

In his early years, Dylan's copying and transforming route was often somewhat simpler than the one he used to create this haunting song. In those times, he normally just took an existing melody and wrote new words to it, in time honoured folk fashion. Source albums have been released detailing this and trying to incorporate the nearest of the many preceding variants to Dylan's songs that grew from them. There is an excellent reference work called *The Formative Dylan: Transmission and Stylistic Influences, 1961-1963* by Todd Harvey which not only lists Dylan's sources but often these sources' own sources, too, because songs are part of a chain that stretches way, way back. Dylan himself is well aware of this and sometimes will deliberately take inspiration from a very early ballad version, though on other occasions it can be any version that inspires him or catches his ear from then until his own time.

There has been controversy over plagiarism from the moment Dylan first tasted success, a success others, as with Shakespeare, resented. Biographer Robert Shelton noted that: "By the end of 1963, the folk scene was bitterly divided over whether Dylan was a song cribber or a composer working in the accepted tradition of building new songs on the skeletal remains of old folk songs."

SOURCES

Dylan has never hidden his method of song composition. As he wrote in "For Dave Glover", for the 1963 Newport Folk Festival program:

The folk songs showed me the way
They showed me that songs can say somethin human
Without "Barbara Allen" there'd be no "Girl From The North Country"
Without no "Lone Green Valley" there'd be no "Don't Think Twice"
Without no "Jesse James" there'd be no "Davy Moore"
Without no "Twenty one Years" there'd be no "Walls a Red Wing"[13]

Also, on the liner notes to his third album in 1964, Dylan wrote:

Yes, I am a thief of thoughts
not, I pray, a stealer of souls
I have built an' rebuilt
upon what is waitin'
for the sand on the beaches
carves many castles
on what has been opened
before my time[14]

He followed up this generously shared insight with another on his fifth album:

The Great books've been written. the Great sayings
have all been said/I am about t' sketch You
a picture of what goes on around here sometimes.[15]

Michael Gray's *Song and Dance Man III, The Art of Bob Dylan* details Dylan's many uses of the blues, including, as one example, Lightnin' Hopkins' 'Automobile Blues':

"The *Blonde on Blonde* song 'Leopard-Skin Pill-Box Hat' is neatly revealing about the way that even in his hippest, most radical and risky period, Dylan stood upon the bedrock of the blues. In one way, this song is utterly Dylanesque, and wholly redolent of that Warhol Factory New York City: so Sixties, so chic and fey, so knowing and druggy and poised, and engaging for its weird mix of energy and high comedy with its elaborate and ostentatious stance of ennui. Yet at the same time it is coach-built very closely upon the chassis of a Lightnin' Hopkins song from 1949, his 'Automobile (Blues)'.

"I saw you ridin' round, you was ridin' in your brand-new automobile. Yes, I saw you ridin' round, you was ridin' round in your brand-new automobile. Yes, you was sittin' there happy with your handsome driver at the wheel. In your brand-new automobeeeeel", and as Hopkins sings that extra last line, his voice takes that familiar downward curve, ending on that 'Dylanesque' long, sliding 'beeeel' that is a slippery mixture of a knowing sneer and some malicious envy. Dylan makes sly acknowledgement of his source in the last verse of his own song, with the in-joke admonition that 'you forgot to close the garage door'."[16]

It is not only musical forebears who impact on Dylan's writing, however. In Michael Gray's *Bob Dylan Encyclopaedia* entry on 'film dialogue in Dylan's lyrics', of which there are, incidentally, a large number that collectively form another treasure trove of allusions, he traces a line we looked at in chapter eight, on wordplay, to Don Siegel's 1958 movie, *The Lineup*. Dylan would have just turned seventeen when this film was released. It contains the line: "When you live outside the law, you have to eliminate dishonesty." Gray postulates this as the source for Dylan's pithier, harder hitting and unforgettable: *"to live outside the law you must be honest"*. This was the line, as discussed earlier, that Dylan had told Ginsberg was his 'most Shakespearean', at least up to that point in his career. It seems as though it was, aptly enough based, like so many of Shakespeare's lines, on something from the lips of an actor in a previous plot.

Most crucially, Dylan is an exceptionally well read person, and it is in the merging the artistic tributaries of music and performance with the literary that he achieves his unique status.

***

Dylan's English lessons seem to have stayed with him. His English teacher, B J Rolfzen proudly remembers how this pupil, known already for following his own path, was nonetheless always present and sat in the front row for his classes.[17] It would be interesting to know if W.H. Auden was one of the poets taught in those sessions. Auden provides an example of lighter, secondary literary sources and although he rarely features in books on Dylan, he has been mentioned in articles and fanzines. Also, Michael Gray, in his Dylan Encyclopaedia highlights Gavin Selerie[18] pointing out strong similarities between Auden's 'Victor' and Dylan's 'Lily, Rosemary and the Jack of Hearts'[19]

Auden echoes pop up often enough to make me feel that they are deliberate, or at least remembered. There is a very Auden-esque touch to some of the imagery in 'Farewell Angelina', especially in the world 'folding' in relation to the sky. Most of all there's Auden's 'Refugee Blues' which contains a number of lines that seem to echo Dylan's lyrics including: "Some are living in mansions, some are living in holes" which recalls *"You may be living in a mansion or you might live in a dome"* from 'Gotta Serve Somebody'. While "Saw a poodle in a jacket fastened with a pin, / Saw a door opened and a cat let in" always brings 'A Hard Rain's A-Gonna Fall' to my mind, as do other lines. "Stood on a great plain in the falling snow; / Ten thousand soldiers marched to and fro" reminds me of Dylan's '10,000 Men'. I hear flashes of Dylan elsewhere too, as I read Auden, in lines like: "Went down the harbour and stood upon the quay, / Saw the fish swimming as if they were free" and "Walked through a wood, saw the birds in the trees; / They had no politicians and sang at their ease." Another Dylan song and an Auden poem, both in ballad format, are compared by Adam Hammond in his thoughtful piece: "A Poetic High-Five Through the Ages: Bob Dylan's "As I Went Out One Morning" and Auden's "As I Walked Out One Evening.""[20] Hammond presents a good case for Dylan's song being an extended allusion to Auden's poem.

Such resonances should not be a surprise. Of all the poets from the 'high end', Auden is the one most steeped in music, and this was music of all kinds, including what was seen as low forms of popular music. He also shared Dylan and Shakespeare's fondness for nursery rhymes.

As he stepped into the twenty-first century, Dylan increasingly included lines from antiquity rather than the modern era. Professor of Classics at Harvard, Richard Thomas, sees this as one more step in Dylan's history of transfigurations, and as a very logical step:

"The voice of Odysseus may be heard on a number of the songs from *Tempest*, not least two of Dylan's favourites in performance, 'Early Roman

Kings' and 'Pay in Blood', songs he sings night after night. This method of composition is not to be thought of as mere quotation or citation. Rather, it is a creative act involving the transfiguring of song and of literature and of characters going back through Rome to Homer. It is one of the ways in which Dylan imagines and creates the worlds that he inhabits in his songs and in performance, especially since the early-Noughties. His song-writing has always come from, and drawn meaning from, other places, not least the worlds of the Greeks and Romans. In the process, Dylan has become part of a stream that flows from the beginning of Western literature to the present."[21] These and other literary references are discussed throughout this book, with Homer featuring strongly in the following chapter.

***

Dylan, as a modern writer, has the post-Romantic concept of artistic originality to contend with, with its disdain for plagiarism, and the legal minefields of copyright ownership. This last point, as witnessed in chapter four, was inextricably tied up with the opposition to his move from being a singer in the folk tradition in Greenwich Village to a Cuban-boot-heeled, global, popular culture icon in the mid-Sixties with copyrighted material in his name generating millions of dollars. It was a somewhat more complicated scenario than that of being booed for merely swapping an acoustic guitar for an electric one.

To add to this, there is the inescapable fact that Dylan is working with music as well as text and, with music, not standing on the shoulders of what has gone before is surely an impossibility. As Dylan wrote in an early prose poem, entitled "My Life in a Stolen Moment"[22]:

> I can't tell you the influences 'cause there's too many
> to mention an' I might leave one out
> An' that wouldn't be fair
> Woody Guthrie, sure
> Big Joe Williams, yeah
> It's easy to remember those names
> But what about the faces you can't find again

What about the curbs an' corners an' cut-offs
that drop out a sight an' fall behind
What about the records you hear but one time
What about the coyote's call an' the bulldog's bark
What about the tomcat's meow an' milk cow's moo
An' the train whistle's moan
Open up yer eyes an' ears an' yer influenced
an' there's nothing you can do about it

All writers, you imagine, read, but they do not fundamentally have to do so. Composers, on the other hand, have no choice at all. Before they write any music at all, they have, perforce, heard music. Even more than their literary brethren, composers do not create in a vacuum. If they did and created something that bore no resemblance to anything their predecessors had ever done, then we would not be able to take it in. We would be entering a philosophical area of speculation as to whether what we heard was music or noise of some unidentifiable kind. There are only so many keys on a piano and strings on a guitar, and while the combinations these can make in the structured realm of popular music are undoubtedly numerous, they are not infinite.

Popular music has always taken the form of new performers building on their predecessors, and in terms of the Sixties, one can think of the previous generations Rock and Rollers and Buddy Holly's, Elvis Presley's and Chuck Berry's influence on Dylan, the Beatles and the Stones. Or you can conjure up the influence of the Blues on Dylan and the Stones in particular of these three, but more broadly into a whole host of famous British and American performers. For a notorious example, it is hard to think of a Led Zeppelin song that is not taken from source, as the title to a *Rolling Stone* article highlights: "Led Zeppelin's 10 Boldest Rip-Offs."[23]

Dylan's borrowing, however, consists of a very complex mixture of approaches which, like Shakespeare's, can range from a striking phrase to an entire structure; be it thematic, metaphoric, or, in Dylan's case, musical. There is also the matter of Dylan's incomparable vocal gifts and the many voices he utilises even though each of the many is instantly identifiable as "Dylan".

Greil Marcus has spoken eloquently of Dylan's voice as a conduit of the voices of those who have gone before:

"It always has a particular howl, or a moan, in that voice. But that voice calls up many shadows, many ghosts, many forebears, and sometimes those people are very shadowy and sometimes they are absolutely distinct. It's in the way that he rewrites, reframes, re-sings old songs, with a knowledge of American music that may be beyond that of any archivist." [24]

Dylan lives at a time when individual authorial expression in artistic form is protected in law. Our current conception of an artistic creator, and especially a writer, is that they are sole owners of what they craft and that to copy that creation is to steal from them. At the same time, legal and cultural norms dictate that opprobrium is heaped upon those who imitate others and claim the work as their own.

Dylan's appropriations are, consequently, attacked in a way that Shakespeare's can never justly be. Such attacks inspire an immediate defence from Dylan's army of supporters. This defence is usually in the form of a double blast attributed to that arsenal of literary heavyweight T.S. Eliot, and claims: 'what Dylan does is okay because Eliot said that 'good poets borrow, great poets steal' and Eliot himself, especially in his masterpiece, *The Waste Land* does exactly what Dylan is being blamed for doing in his songs'.

The fundamental problem with this point of view is that neither of the claims it makes is true: Eliot did not say that, and nor did he 'do the same thing' in *The Waste Land*. What Eliot actually wrote was this:

"Immature poets imitate; mature poets steal; bad poets deface what they take, and good poets make it into something better, or at least something different. The good poet welds his theft into a whole of feeling which is unique, utterly different than that from which it is torn; the bad poet throws it into something which has no cohesion. A good poet will usually borrow from authors remote in time, or alien in language, or diverse in interest." [25]

So, as we can see, Eliot is arguing that good, mature poets indulge in the kind of inspirational transmutation of source material that we have looked at above. Rather than, as is so often claimed, by many people in many contexts, that Eliot advocates stealing others' work and passing it off as your own as something that is in any way justified or artistically admirable.

Nonetheless, it is obvious that the issue of taking from others is not one that concerned Eliot, rather it was what one did with these 'stolen goods' that determined if the act of appropriation was 'good' or 'bad'. There are certainly things that Dylan does of which Eliot's essay approves; the transforming of previous materials in to a new, artistic vision, the bolstering of a tradition of expression and introducing that to a new audience.

On the other hand, there are more contentious areas; but before progressing onto that thorny path, the second claim regarding Eliot has to be considered and dismissed. In *The Waste Land*, Eliot did indeed quote from a huge variety of sources in his impressive modernist collage and, as far as that goes, it can seem very like what Dylan does, especially on albums like *"Love and Theft"* and *Modern Times*. There is a crucial difference, though, in that Eliot painstakingly annotated his sources. He was very proud of them and therefore highlighted them. Dylan obviously cannot 'footnote' his songs. Yet there are sleeve notes and other ways of attributing credit to original sources. Dylan has, on occasion, availed himself of these. In the first of the album titles just quoted, *"Love and Theft"*, both the meaning and the quotation marks are an immediate tip-off as to what Dylan is up to on that delightful disc, as it alluded to Eric Lott's *Love and Theft: Blackface Minstrelsy and the American Working Class*. However, Dylan is also often criticised for not giving out any accreditation at all, and sometimes avoiding doing so to a significant degree. Ezra Pound would seem the closer parallel here, rather than T. S. Eliot.

Before looking at the particularly complicated case of musical copying, it is worth noting that there is an accepted state of 'unintentional copying' in all art, and it is one which has a long history in literature. Here, you could say that while immature artists constantly imitate, maturer ones suffer from cryptomnesia. Cryptomnesia is a condition that causes you to think that you have created something original, but, in reality, you have merely remembered something created by another artist via your subconscious. You have, in other words, plagiarised without realising that is what you have done. This, you might think, is a rather convenient theory to explain away plagiarism. However, there are many documented cases where artists have 'come clean' and confessed to having accidentally fallen into this state. Here are three prominent examples, though many more have admitted to falling into this category.

Umberto Eco describes coming across an old book in his collection that turned out to have inspired a passage in his celebrated novel, *The Name of the Rose*:

"I had bought that book in my youth, skimmed through it, realised that it was exceptionally soiled, and put it somewhere and forgot it. But by a sort of internal camera I had photographed those pages, and for decades the image of those poisonous leaves lay in the most remote part of my soul, as in a grave, until the moment it emerged again (I do not know for what reason) and I believed I had invented it."[26]

Professor Michael Mahr, studying cryptomnesia in literary works, replied to an interviewer: "In 1936 Robert Musil marks in his diaries that reading Jens Peter Jacobsen's 'Niels Lyhne' for the third time he remarked that he was influenced by it while composing a conversation between Agathe and Ulrich in the second volume of his Man Without Qualities . He adds: without knowing it, this scene was the Vorbild [the model]." [27]

Robert Louis Stevenson, from whom Dylan lifts phrases for his memoir, *Chronicles*, had a very similar incident to Eco when he re-read Washington Irvine's *Tales of a Traveller*. To his horror, Stevenson discovered that his renowned *Treasure Island* was a case where he could now see that "plagiarism was rarely carried farther".

Prior to that, Stevenson had noted cases of more straightforward copying which he had indulged in, also for *Treasure Island*. Those he justified in a dismissive manner, akin to what we hear from Dylan, later, but the 'cryptomnesia' examples shook him to the core.

If such unintentional borrowing can easily occur in the matter of plots, characters, themes and symbolism in prose writing, then it is unsurprising that it occurs so frequently in song-writing. The late Tom Petty, Dylan's one-time collaborator and touring partner, gave a clear insight into this realm of unintentional copying in the music business. Petty's song, 'I Won't Back Down' was judged to be the prototype for Sam Smith's hit 'Stay With Me'. Although the similarities were put down to 'pure coincidence' by a representative of Sam Smith, Smith nonetheless gave Tom Petty and Jeff Lynne a song-writing credit and a twelve and a half percent royalty stake. This was all settled amicably out of court. Petty's view was that: "All my years of song-writing have shown me these things can happen. Most times you catch it before it gets out the studio door but in this case it got by."[28]

Dylan arrived on the music scene at an earlier time and despite being excited by the rock'n'rollers in the mid-Fifties, he came to fame in the New York folk scene. There, as with plays in Shakespeare's times, a creative process existed whereby the artist used whatever came to hand and built upon what had gone before. The latter part of this was known as 'the folk process'. Charles Seeger, whose son Peter was the leading traditional light in that US folk scene, put it clearly: "The folk song is, by definition, and as far as we can tell, by reality, entirely a product of plagiarism."[29]

Dylan is quick to point that it often is the case that he is the only one blamed for copying when everyone else is doing the same thing, and, in this he has a strong case. As Paul McCartney put it in regards to the Beatles: "I'm always taking a little of this and a little of that. It's called being influenced. It's either called that or stealing. And what do they say? A good artist borrows; a great artist steals - or something like that. That makes us great artists then, because we stole a lot of stuff."[30] Clinton Heylin, in an introduction to his book, *It's One For The Money,* titled 'All Song Is Theft', notes that "*nothing* in Pop is original; everything comes from somewhere and (usually) someone identifiable. And often the only thing separating the rich from the poor is how well one of them has managed to disguise it."[31]

However, in a re-run of the jealous attacks caused by Shakespeare's early triumphs, Dylan's early success in New York in the Sixties brought envy and enmity upon his head. Dominic Behan, trying to stir up a lawsuit, has berated Dylan for stealing the tune of 'With God on Our Side' from Behan's 'The Patriot Game'. Conveniently for his hoped for pay-out, Behan neglected to mention that the melody is one that he took from an old folk song that had long ago passed into the public domain. There was a lot of publicity about this story, and it keeps re-surfacing and nearly always mentions Dylan as the only 'thief' in the story. The clemency expressed in Shakespeare's 'Sonnet 40', *I do forgive thy robbery, gentle thief* was never offered to Dylan.

This situation was heightened, and almost immeasurably complicated, by the burgeoning world of popular music, and the introduction of copyright into the scene where, as Charles Seeger observed, it simply did not fit, and the huge riches that Dylan and others began to make from their work.

Facing accusations of plagiarism, Dylan retorted:

What did I steal? Did I steal the word "the", the word "a", the word "so"? Everybody has to get their words from somewhere. Woody didn't write ten original melodies, but nobody ever called him a thief.[32]

The same debate has continued throughout the decades. In 2012 Dylan answered a question about not crediting his sources in the *Rolling Stone* interview by saying: *Oh, yeah, in folk and jazz, quotation is a rich and enriching tradition. That certainly is true. It's true for everybody, but me. I mean, everyone else can do it but not me. There are different rules for me.* [33]

In that same interview, Dylan erupted in a tirade which conflated those who complained of plagiarism with those who booed him for 'going electric'. As we have seen, that was a complex tale, with resentment at the concept of profiteering from what was seen as a communal art. Dylan was in no mood for examining complexities. Instead, he exploded:

"Wussies and pussies complain about that stuff. It's an old thing – it's part of the tradition. It goes way back. These are the same people that tried to pin the name Judas on me. Judas, the most hated name in human history! If you think you've been called a bad name, try to work your way out from under that. Yeah, and for what? For playing an electric guitar? As if that is in some kind of way equitable to betraying our Lord and delivering him up to be crucified. All those evil motherfuckers can rot in hell.

Rolling Stone: Seriously?

BD: *I'm working within my art form. It's that simple. I work within the rules and limitations of it. There are authoritarian figures that can explain that kind of art form better to you than I can. It's called song-writing. It has to do with melody and rhythm, and then after that, anything goes. You make everything yours. We all do it."*

The problem with the otherwise sound point of "we all do it" is that the sentence is unfinished. In a world of copyright protection, it should read something more like: "we all do it, but sometimes people are sued for it, and sometimes they aren't." Plus, crucially, sometimes the suing is done in Dylan's name.

Rod Stewart, fan of Dylan and coverer of then unreleased Dylan songs 'Only A Hobo', 'Tomorrow Is A Long Time' and 'Mama You've Been On My Mind' on his early albums, put out a song called 'Forever Young' that became a hit single. It shares not only its name with Dylan's famous song of the same title, but, to a significant degree, its general composition and thematic approach.

Rod Stewart's manager claimed that the name of Stewart's song came from the title of a film that Rod had seen, rather than from Dylan's song. Stewart's song was co-written with Jim Cregan and Kevin Savigar. Nonetheless, Stewart claims a very personal connection to it, telling *Mojo* magazine in a 1995 interview that, "I love 'Forever Young', because that was a real heartfelt song about my kids." The song has remained a favourite with the singer having gone on to officially release four different versions. With the similarities being unmistakable, Rod Stewart's management contacted Dylan's people and a 50-50 royalty split of the publishing rights was agreed.

Another hit, this one a monster, from which Dylan benefited financially was Hootie and the Blowfish's 'Only Want To Be With You'. Hootie's song is a touching tribute to Dylan's seminal album *Blood on The Tracks*. It quotes from 'You're A Big Girl, Now', 'Tangled Up In Blue' and, especially, 'Idiot Wind'.

These quotes are all introduced by the line, "Put on a little Dylan" giving the listener the impression that they are listening to the singer putting *Blood on The Tracks* on his turntable or CD-player as he talks to his girlfriend and then enjoying, as so many millions have, those magnificent songs. As the supreme relationship songs in popular music, they form the most apt of touchstones.

That did not stop a claim being made against the song on behalf of Dylan. We have no way of knowing if Dylan himself was aware of this. When you reach the stage, which Dylan did a very long time ago, of needing to have other people to take care of your business affairs, things are likely to happen without your knowledge. This is how Darius Rucker, Hootie's lead vocalist and rhythm guitarist, viewed it. In one of his many exuberant interviews on the Dan Patrick Show, Rucker put the decision and negotiations down to management people and commented that he doubted that Dylan 'knew anything about it'. It was reported that a very large out-of-court settlement was reached. Rucker also, however, stated that Dylan's management was aware of the use of Dylan's lyrics prior to the song becoming a big hit and only showed interest in it thereafter.

Dylan and Rucker ended up 'co-writing' another hit some years later. This was Rucker's first big solo success, 'Wagon Wheel'. This is another illuminating tale of musical ideas moving through the folk process. A wonderful couple of stabs at a song called 'Rock Me, Mama' featured on a bootleg album of Dylan out-takes from the soundtrack to the film, in which he appears as a character called 'Alias', *Pat Garrett and Billy the Kid*. This song, which I had long treasured, also impressed Old Crow Medicine Show's Critter Fuqua. He heard it on the bootleg, too, and his band released it in 2004 as co-written with Dylan and under the title 'Wagon Wheel'. Darius Rucker then recorded his version of this in 2013 and went on to have great success with it, winning the Grammy for Best Country Solo Performance.

Reflecting on what we have looked at, so far, regarding using others' material, copyright infringement, suing and being sued, it is worth remembering a few salient points. Firstly, it should not be forgotten in all this that Dylan has produced major musical and lyrical work that is totally original. I have never heard of any direct forbears for, say, 'Visions of Johanna' or 'Idiot Wind' to name just two, both of which are major songs in his canon.

Nor would Dylan be the first to ignore his own borrowings and sue others for lifting from him. It is claimed, in numerous reports, for one notorious example, that The Disney Corporation is built upon telling others' stories but woe betide anyone copying a single thing of theirs.[34]

In the same passage of the 2012 *Rolling Stone* interview quoted above, Dylan made two important points regarding his use of lines from Henry Timrod; firstly that he brings him wider exposure and sales, and secondly that it is not easy to weave such appropriations into a new song: *"And as far as Henry Timrod is concerned, have you even heard of him? Who's been reading him lately? And who's pushed him to the forefront? Who's been making you read him? And ask his descendants what they think of the hoopla. And if you think it's so easy to quote him and it can help your work, do it yourself and see how far you can get"*.

Dylan's last point there is an echo back down the centuries of the Roman poet Virgil defending himself from criticism over the use of lines from Homer the Greek's epics in his own epic poetry: "Why don't they try the same thefts?

They'll find out it's easier to snatch Hercules' club from him than a single line from Homer."[35] Furthermore, it is very far from being the case that 'Dylan' always sues. Rapper Chuck D, who has related on more than one occasion just how much he owes to "the Bobs" (Marley, Dylan and Womack) is well known for his Dylan allusions. Public Enemy's song "The Long and Whining Road" is a patchwork quilt of Dylan song titles, with four in the closing verse alone. Also, hip-hop singer, Sage Francis, as far as I am aware, faced no problems when he addressed Dylan in the song 'Hey Bobby', using variation on Bob's own words.

From the same musical background, we have the Beastie Boys, and we have the world of sampling which takes copying into a whole new area. *The Urban Dictionary* defines this technique as; "the process of taking brief segments of sound (from a song, movie or elsewhere) and using that sound to form another sound or musical piece". In our digital world, the potential uses are well nigh immeasurable, and the ease of trying things out makes many artists experiment widely. It has become a major part of the popular music scene. You are legally bound to ask for the copyright holders' permission to sample their work.

Rolling Stone traced the Bob Dylan and Beastie Boys connection and reported that:

"Quoth Mike D on Dylan: "He's one of the first b-boys, if not the first. What more to say?" The ultimate arbiters of New York boho cool, the snotty beat poets in the Beasties were naturally drawn to Dylan. Their landmark *Paul's Boutique* borrows a line from Dylan's protest-of-protests 'Maggie›s Farm' on their lovable bum tale 'Johnny Ryall.' And on '3-Minute Rule,' MCA even drops his own unique props: "I'm just chillin', like Bob Dylan.' Three years later, the boys would sample Dylan's 'Just Like Tom Thumb's Blues' for their 'Finger Lickin' Good' – a clearance that would ultimately cost them $700. Mike D told Boston Rock, "He asked for $2,000. I thought it was kind of fly that he asked for $2,000 and I bartered Bob Dylan down. That's my proudest sampling deal." Their upcoming *Hot Sauce Committee Pt. 2* is set to feature another sample of Dylan, a spoken word bit where he talked about the Boys on his satellite radio show."

A source of contention is that it is rare for Dylan, other than on his earliest releases, to directly credit his source on his record sleeves. It is true that he did name-check the notoriously litigious Willie Dixon on *Together Through Life* but this merely highlighted, more glaringly, the lack of other accreditation on the rest of the album and its immediate predecessors. On the other hand, Dylan is very open about his sources at other times and in other contexts. In 2004 he said:

"I wrote 'Blowin' in the Wind' in 10 minutes, just put words to an old spiritual, probably something I learned from Carter Family records. That's the folk music tradition. You use what's been handed down. 'The Times They Are A-Changin' is probably from an old Scottish folk song."[36]

Early in his career, Dylan explained that:

I don't even consider it writing songs. When I've written it I don't even consider that I wrote it when I got done...I just figure that I made it up or I got it some place. The song was there before I came along. I just sort of came and just sort of took it down with a pencil, but it was all there before I came around.[37]

Dylan provides similar accounts of his song-writing process down through the decades. There is, even for him, far less us, something magical and inexplicable about it all. In the 2004 interview just quoted, he also remarked that *"It's like a ghost is writing a song like that. It gives you the song and it goes away, it goes away. You don't know what it means. Except the ghost picked me to write the song."*

At other times he recalls the precise inspiration. He told Cameron Crowe, for the liner notes to *Biograph*, how he came to write that gloriously moving and celebratory song of nature, 'Lay Down Your Weary Tune': *"I wrote that on the west coast, at Joan Baez's house. She had a place outside Big Sur. I had heard a Scottish ballad on an old 78 rpm record that I was trying to really capture the feeling of, that was haunting me. I couldn't get it out of my head. There were no lyrics or anything, it was just a melody, had bagpipes and a lot of stuff in it. I wanted lyrics that would feel the same way. I don't remember what the original record was, but this was pretty similar to that, the melody anyway.*

And, again from the 2004 Hilburn interview:

Well, you have to understand that I'm not a melodist... My songs are either based on old Protestant hymns or Carter Family songs or variations of the blues form. What happens is, I'll take a song I know and simply start playing it in my head. That's the way I meditate ... I'll be playing Bob Nolan's 'Tumbling Tumbleweeds,' for instance, in my head constantly – while I'm driving a car or talking to a person or sitting around or whatever. People will think they are talking to me and I'm talking back, but I'm not. I'm listening to the song in my head. At a certain point, some of the words will change and I'll start writing a song.

This is reminiscent of Carole King describing how she plays "someone else's material that I really like, and that sometimes unblocks a channel." She went on to note, though, that "the danger in that is that you're gonna write that person's song for your next song."[38]

As for literary lifts, in some lyrics and prose Dylan does let you know when allusions are deliberate and, presumably, he wants these to be picked up by one or more listeners. Allusions can be mainly private, respectful acknowledgements of something that has moved the author in some way or another. I suspect that the use of the photograph from the cover of Larry Brown's book *Big Bad Love* being used as the cover to 2009's album, *Together Through Life* may fall into this category. However, that belief came about because I already knew that Dylan had mentioned being impressed by Brown's then latest book, *Father and Son*, which has parallels to *Big Bad Love*'s short stories, around about the time that *Time Out of Mind* came out. This is hardly common knowledge and so the allusion in the cover may just have been for Dylan's own amusement. Then again, perhaps not as it was so obvious, being a picture. At other times borrowed lines are celebrated lines from Shakespeare, Donne, Chaucer or classical writers and very often from such US heavyweights as Fitzgerald, Tennessee Williams, London, Hemingway, Twain and Poe. Sometimes the lines are harder to spot at first, but then turn out to be exact quotes which suggests that they are meant to be discovered.

There is, though, no definitive guide as to when allusions are deliberate and meant to be recognised, and it would be strange if there were, but there are some very helpful signs. Dylan's repeated use of the tropes of past times infusing or underlying later times, (Roman-Christian, US Civil and Independence wars, and the America of his own lifetime), constitute one clear category in which his references are deliberate, thought out and there to be noted. This is not to say that the songs concerned do not work well as songs without observing such facets, it is just that noticing them expands on the pleasurable experience of listening to them. It is like noting a similar thing in a Shakespeare play which, again, can be moving and fulfilling without the allusions being noticed. The added value they bring with them, in both cases, is a bonus.

Dylan's other 'nod and wink' to his listeners is when he 'doubles up' on his references. He alludes to a writer and then does so again to the same writer, and often the same piece, a few lines later. Examples of this appear later in Dylan's use of Virgil, Ovid and Homer in *"Love and Theft"*, *Modern Times* and *Tempest*. Dylan uses the same technique in his 2004 book, *Chronicles*.

Scott Warmuth has detailed a fine example of this: "... Dylan ends the sentence by calling "I Walk the Line," "a song that makes an attack on your most vulnerable spots, sharp words from a master." I present that the tail end of the sentence in question is clearly lifted from the work of Jack London's *White Fang*: 'White Fang was in a rage, wickedly making his attack on the most vulnerable spot. From the shoulder to wrist of the crossed arms, the coat sleeve, blue flannel shirt and undershirt were ripped in rags, while the arms themselves were terribly slashed and streaming blood.'

All this the two men saw in an instant. The next instant Weedon Scott had White Fang by the throat and was dragging him clear. White Fang struggled and snarled, but made no attempt to bite, while he quickly quieted down at a sharp word from the master.' "

In addition to the 'double confirmation', which Warmuth highlights, there is also a nudge as to what he is doing in the delicious pun of using the phrase 'sharp words from a master writer' with regard to a quote that includes the phrase 'a sharp word from the master'.

We have seen that, in both Shakespeare's time and in the folk process, appropriation is used as the basis for inventing new work. Stealing, lifting, copying, quoting, sampling, or whatever terms best fit, intentionally or otherwise, and then using what you have taken in whatever way you want, is both normal and praised. All of that has supposedly changed, as we live in a cultural climate that is supposed to abhor plagiarism and a legal one in which copyright acts have sharp, if uneven, teeth.

However, there is also a strong argument that such cultural perceptions, and their subsequent legal manifestations, mask the fact that there is, as the cliché has it, 'nothing new under the sun', and that all art is imitation and the only thing that is up for debate is the extent of the quality and recontextualisation of the 'new' work. At first this appears an extreme claim but given the evidence above and the following examples, post-Romantic times, up to and including or own day, seem not to differ radically to what went on before, perception and irregular copyright court cases aside. Many critics and artists tell us that this is the case.

Even the Romantics themselves struggled for originality, from the beginning to the end of their movement. Robert Burns, the bard we looked at earlier, and Dylan's 'inspiration', provided a bridge from the previous era into that of the Romantic Movement he played such a large part in creating. Burns' work was based as much on that of Robert Fergusson as the early Dylan's was on Woody Guthrie. Burns famously said that Fergusson was: "my elder brother in misfortune, by far my elder brother in the muse."

Samuel Taylor Coleridge, who along with Wordsworth launched the Romantic manifesto which prized individual originality as one of its guiding virtues, found the theory easier to promulgate than to practice. He once bemoaned how he could not write "without finding his poem, against his will and without his previous consciousness, a cento of lines that had pre-existed in other works".[39] While legend has it that Byron, a later Romantic, covered up the book he was copying from/being inspired by when someone entered the room while he was writing poetry.

Post Romantic thought has been torn between lauding originality and acknowledging a more prosaic truth. Mark Twain plainly noted that: "There is no such thing as a new idea. It is impossible. We simply take a lot of old ideas and put them into a sort of mental kaleidoscope. We give them a turn and they make new and curious combinations. We keep on turning and making new combinations indefinitely; but they are the same old pieces of colored glass that have been in use through all the ages".[40]

Back before it was even thought of as a problem, Shakespeare's character Timon expressed the idea of nothing being original best in this wonderful passage:

I'll example you with thievery.
The sun's a thief, and with his great attraction
Robs the vast sea. The moon's an arrant thief,

And her pale fire she snatches from the sun;
The sea's a thief, whose liquid surge resolves
The moon into salt tears. The earth's a thief,
That feeds and breeds by a composture stol'n
From gen'ral excrement; each thing's a thief.

(*Timon of Athens*, Act IV scene iii)

The moon, that symbol of lovers, dreamers and poets is figured as a mere reflection of an earlier, far brighter light. This is an extraordinary vision of the lack of originality in any art and it comes in a play indebted for its themes, language and observations to works by Plutarch and Lucian as well as an academic play entitled, unsurprisingly, *Timon*. This imagery of theft standing in for inspiration occurs in Dylan, too. He laments in the exquisite "Tears of Rage", "*why must I always be the thief*". In another context, Dylan sings "*If I was a master thief perhaps I'd rob them*" and in another, he implores the "*sad-eyed lady of the lowlands*" to "*stand with her thief*".[41]

Roland Barthes writes on the same theme of the absence of originality in his celebrated treatise, "The Death of the Author":

"We know that a text ... is a tissue of citations, resulting from the thousand sources of culture. ... the writer can only imitate a gesture forever anterior, never original; his only power is to combine the different kinds of writing ... the writer no longer contains within himself passions, humours, sentiments, impressions, but that enormous dictionary, from which he derives a writing which can know no end or halt: life can only imitate the book, and the book itself is only a tissue of signs, a lost, infinitely remote imitation."[42]

Musicians and novelists concur with this assessment. Late rock star Bowie answered the following question, posed by Cameron Crowe for *Playboy* in September 1976: "Since you put yourself first, do you consider yourself an original thinker?" by saying: "Not by any means. More like a tasteful thief. The only art I'll ever study is stuff that I can steal from. I do think that my plagiarism is effective. Why does an artist create, anyway? The way I see it, if you're an inventor, you invent something that you hope people can use. I want art to be just as practical. Art can be a political reference, a sexual force, any force that you want, but it should be usable. What the hell do artists want? Museum pieces? The more I get ripped off, the more flattered I get."

You feel that David Bowie, who like all his contemporary songwriters, had immersed himself in Dylan's albums, is channelling Dylan's 'Visions of Johanna' here as he makes his point. The novelist Thomas Mann called the process, in a very neat phrase, which perhaps leads us back to T.S. Eliot's 'mature poets', and is echoed in Bowie's 'tasteful thief', 'higher cribbing.' The outstanding Scottish poet Hugh MacDiarmid, whose later technique is the same as Dylan's, also shared Dylan's dismissal of those who object, declaring: "The greater the plagiarism the greater the work of art."

The folk process fits in with these viewpoints seamlessly. As Charles Seeger wrote while discussing the folk process: "Conscious and unconscious appropriation, borrowing, adapting, plagiarizing and plain stealing...always have been part and parcel of the process of artistic creation.[43]

Given that all art is seen to rest on the shoulders of what went before, there seems no reason for problems to arise, yet arise they do. This is due to lack of attribution and the slapping of a copyright on the individual result of appropriation of past material. This created early problems for Dylan, an example being 'Masters of War'. Dylan took the melody from the folk standard 'Nottamun Town' and wrote his own words to it. However, the particular arrangement he took was that sung by Jean Ritchie and belonged to her family. Jean Ritchie always acknowledged the self-evident fact that the song originally came from Britain, but the claim was that the specific arrangement Dylan used was her family's 'property'. As such Ritchie felt that she should have a song-writing credit. It has been reported that this claim was settled by a payment of $5,000[44].

A particularly strong example of controversy over Dylan and the "Trad. Arr" practice arose over his *Good As I Been to You* album. Dylan's versions of the songs he sings are so closely and clearly based on particular, individual recordings that his total lack of accreditation to his sources caused outrage. *The Folk Roots* review of the album was a release for their still pent-up rage at Dylan having 'betrayed' the folk scene three decades earlier. In an explosion not rivalled until Dylan's even angrier *Rolling Stone* 2012 interview, Ian Anderson wrote a scathing review highlighting the lack of accreditation below a photo of Dylan's face which was captioned: "thieving, clapped-out bastard." [45]

Later copies of the album did carry song accreditation but unfortunately compounded the original lack of any by being inaccurate, primarily in claiming two songs as being in the public domain when they were not and so further corrections had to be made. Dylan did not cease to use arrangements and not attribute them on later albums, so we can presume he was otherwise unmoved by such criticism. Perhaps he makes private communication with the artists concerned, perhaps he feels that they would feel proud to have him cover them, or perhaps he never thinks of these things at all until an interviewer annoys him by raising the matter.

In his music, then, Dylan follows unashamedly and repeatedly in the 'folk process'. Any quibbles that exist here fall into three categories: our (not his) cultural expectations; inconsistency in the area of claiming copyright while averring that 'anything goes, we all do it', and in the disputes arising from the fractious area of 'traditional arranged by'. Suing for breach of copyright may not have anything to do with Dylan himself and may or may not be guided by factors outwith our knowledge. In many cases, it has been documented that people have noticed Dylan copying from them but said nothing about it, except when asked in interview. Then they merely remark on how proud they are that he did so. It is also certainly true that for many people being covered by Dylan results in a boost in sales of their own work.

Dylan works in other artistic fields, too, and in his prose and painting he applies techniques of appropriation that have caused controversy and disquiet.

***

Similarly to 2001's album *"Love And Theft"*, Dylan's 2004 book, *Chronicles* is a patchwork quilt composed of lifts from elsewhere. In both cases the results were charming, moving and successful. Dylan had fulfilled Eliot's criteria that the artist must "make it into something better, or at least something different". The quotes from Jack London that we looked at earlier are only some that stem from his writing, and London is joined by Robert Louis Stevenson, Ernest Hemingway, Thomas Pynchon and others in having lines directly quoted. Most of the time you would never notice, and maybe he does not want you to, given how they have been so skilfully woven together; but as we have already observed, at other times he does and tips you off with two allusions, cheek by jowl. Dylan is also bound to know that such lifts will be discovered.

Many of the writers we have been discussing, including Shakespeare, deliberately put in quotations that they wanted to be discovered and so it should come as no surprise if Dylan does so, too. It was said of Shakespeare's favourite, Ovid, whom Dylan quotes extensively in the twenty-first century, that he wanted his lifts from Virgil to be noticed: "Ovid had liked it [a phrase from Virgil] very much and had done with it what he had done with many other verses of Virgil, not intending to filch it from him but rather to borrow it openly, precisely in order for his borrowing to be recognised."[46]

It is also far from laziness, on Dylan's part, in the case of the quotes from these authors and their peers. It would take a very long time to write all the pages using quotations as in the *White Fang* example above. Dylan has commented on how much effort the book took and to weave all his references from so many disparate sources would certainly be a laborious task. In many cases, writing a page of his own prose would surely be much easier and less time-consuming.

On the other hand, it is not just lines from literary masters that Dylan borrows. He also takes phrases from biographies, magazines and even a tour guide. This seems less arduous and more to do with saving himself time. A contemporary copy of *Time* is mined for early-Sixties New York atmosphere and a New Orleans Tour Guide for ambience for the chapter, set there, on the recording of *Oh Mercy*, in 1989.

This kind of thing has been done before by acclaimed literary craftsmen. Similar techniques, as we have already noted, were used by T.S. Eliot and the later Hugh MacDiarmid. We can add the illustrious name of James Joyce as a further example. Joyce gets mentioned in both *Chronicles* and the album, *Together Through Life*, whose title may be an added Joycean allusion[47]. Given that Dylan discussed Herman Melville in his Nobel lecture, one is tempted to think he may be pointing out that these revered figures wrote in ways similar to that for which he is criticised. Joyce was happy enough to be thought of by posterity as a 'scissors and paste man' because, as he readily admitted, that is what he basically was.

None of the above was raised in any of the hugely positive reviews which greeted *Chronicles*. Dylan was more than pleased with these. In 2006 he told *Rolling Stone*'s Jonathan Lethem: *"The reviews of this book, some of 'em almost made me cry – in a good way. I'd never felt that from a music critic, ever ... Most people who write about music, they have no idea what it feels like to play it. But with the book I wrote, I thought, 'The people who are writing reviews of this book, man, they know what the hell they're talking about.' It spoils you."*[48]

I have often wondered if he was making a joke because music critics are quick to spot his borrowings but with this book, critics did not seem to notice them at all. Perhaps Dylan was just enjoying getting a dig at music critics in the very pages of the leading music magazine, or perhaps was doing that and at the same time having fun with the idea that he had pulled the wool over the eyes of the book critics as far as his writing technique went. Or, most likely, he agrees with Joyce that to be a scissors and paste man is something of which to be proud. Proud, that is, as the creator of a new piece of art made out of the bits and pieces selected and woven together and agreeing with MacDiarmid that 'the greater the plagiarism the greater the art'.

In another field, his artwork, Dylan muddies rather than clears any areas of doubt about his method of conception. How one lets, or does not, that reflect back on his borrowing in *Chronicles* and his lyrics is probably an individual choice. What he does here does seem at times indefensible, although it has been predictably and stoutly defended. Perhaps though, to quote from his song 'Tight Connection To My Heart (Has Anyone Seen My Love?)', *"it was all a big joke/whatever it was about."*

For years now, Dylan has been producing a steady stream of artwork that hangs in galleries around the world and commands impressive prices. Many of the works have been traced to photographs or painting by both famous or seemingly random individuals. The resultant paintings replicate their source rather than interpret them. You come across comments on Social Media where people write: "Bob Dylan has copied/stolen my photograph, what should I do?" The people concerned are usually thrilled that Dylan has done so, I should add.

Matters reached a head with an exhibition of a set of paintings called *The Asia Series*, at the Gagosian Gallery in New York, which was originally touted in the official guide as being "a visual reflection on his travels in Japan, China, Vietnam, and Korea". Problems then arose when some of the paintings were discovered to be direct copies of others' photographs. The Dylan 'originals' sell for considerable sums, while 'signed prints' are also available and widely collected. These particular ones were stated to be a reflection of Dylan's own experiences. That was their 'Unique Selling Point' as the business community would call it.

The Gagosian Gallery was forced into releasing a very unconvincing defence: "While the composition of some of Bob Dylan's paintings is based on a variety of sources, including archival, historic images, the paintings' vibrancy and freshness come from the colors and textures found in everyday scenes he observed during his travels."

While it is true that Dylan is quoted in the brochure saying he *mostly* paints from real life and does use photographs amongst other items: "I paint mostly from real life. It has to start with that. Real people, real street scenes, behind the curtain scenes, live models, paintings, photographs, staged setups, architecture, grids, graphic design. Whatever it takes to make it work. What I'm trying to bring out in complex scenes, landscapes, or personality clashes, I do it in a lot of different ways. I have the cause and effect in mind from the beginning to the end. But it has to start with something tangible." Still, the tangible was not what he saw on his travels but instead others' photos replicated as paintings in a series that was purportedly a "visual reflection of his travels". Elsewhere the promotional material claimed: "He often draws and paints while on tour, and his motifs bear corresponding impressions of different environments and people. A keen observer, Dylan is inspired by everyday phenomena in such a way that they appear fresh, new, and mysterious."

No-one going to the exhibition could possibly have thought that the "everyday phenomena" were others' photographs rather than the trumpeted personal, Dylan experience when in Asia, which the phrase: "He often draws and paints while on tour" is clearly promoting.

A more robust defence was provided by Blake Gopnik in *The Daily Beast*[49]. "A headline in Artinfo.com asks if Dylan's painting are "ripped off." They aren't. They are mainstream contemporary art. Ever since the birth of photography, painters have used it as the basis for their works: Edgar Degas and Edouard

Vuillard and other favorite artists – even Edvard Munch – all took or used photos as sources for their art, sometimes barely altering them. Some of Matisse's greatest works riff on cheap postcards of North Africa...

... One year ago, one of the best shows in New York was the Metropolitan Museum's giant retrospective of John Baldessari, a veteran Los Angeles painter who not only bases many of his paintings on photos, but often pays other people to paint them. He calls Dylan's borrowings from photos a "no-brainer" that's not worth a moment's worry. "There are always going to be people who say art should be completely original. But what does that mean? Nobody comes out like the birth of Venus—all art comes out of art."

It would have been far more convincing had the Gagosian defended Dylan in these terms. The fact that they didn't makes me doubt the veracity of Gopnik's spirited article which went on to say:

"Given his subject matter, Dylan's "appropriations" may be especially cogent. By using old photos to explore the questionable notion of "Asian-ness," Dylan locks onto the clichés at its heart, in a way he couldn't have done by painting scenes from life ... The old photos let Dylan recycle standard Asian imagery in just the way our notions of Asian identity are based on recycled ideas. Dylan's series becomes a kind of compilation of our views of Asia, tied together into a tidy package by the old-fashioned medium of oil paint—a cliché used to talk about clichés."

To make matters even more intriguing, one of the contributors to the catalogue for this series was Richard Prince, in a piece that also appeared in *The New York Review of Books*.[50] Prince is another Gagosian artist who has faced complaints and controversies over paintings based on uncredited sources, including photographs. Richard Prince and Bob Dylan, according to some commentators, are involved in a wider, elaborate game of tweaking the noses of the establishment, critics and fans.

Controversy over plagiarism has followed each new Art Series, though this does not seem to be 'damaging the brand' in any significant manner. Also, similarly to literature and *Chronicles*, Dylan can look around him for others who create in a similar fashion to himself.

Andy Warhol, with whom Dylan had a chequered history, perhaps provided an example of taking from anywhere and everywhere, replicating whatever it was and claiming it as original art. As with Shakespeare in his plays and Dylan in his songs, whatever Warhol constructed out of his borrowed images was, always, ultimately and immediately identifiable as Warholian. It seems unlikely that Dylan would look to Warhol for anything more than a mere example, but perhaps Roy Lichtenstein could be an artist who gave some inspiration. The cover to Dylan's *Shot of Love* album certainly would suggest an influence. Lichtenstein's emphasis on parody and the appropriation of images from others may have played a part in forming Dylan's approach.

It is not just the paintings themselves that are composed through imitation. Dylan's foreword to another collection, *The Beaten Path*, at first seemed a refreshing insight into his approach to painting and an illuminating overview of his collection. In reality, though, Dylan was again playing games/plagiarising. His text is a tapestry of quotes lifted from the New Orleans Museum of Art, which had shown Dylan's *New Orleans Series*, website's "Glossary of Art Terms (with images.)" Scott Warmuth provides a comparison of the two documents, in his blog, which also details other source material, "Bob Dylan's The Beaten Path: Selling the Brooklyn Bridge"[51].

Still, it read impressively and even sounded Dylanesque at points but it is clear why people feel that Dylan often seems to be engaged in a complex series of ruses. The question is raised as to whether anyone should care about this. Perhaps Dylan is quite right to behave in this way if people are happy to go along with it. Sometimes it all makes me think of Salvador Dali doodling on and then signing napkins as a means of settling restaurant bills. 'Why not, if they accept it' being a popular view. Perhaps, though, it is all just 'a big joke'. The plagiarised introduction to *The Beaten Path* was published by *Vanity Fair* under the title "In His Own Words". Someone, somewhere, is surely having a laugh.

Lines in songs, prose, even seemingly casual asides in interviews, can at times be traced to specific sources where the linguistic similarities are far too close for it just to be coincidence. This forces you to ask yourself why he is doing it. Some of these references are very obscure, while others are more direct and, yet others, given his history and what he has already been found to lift from, are deliberately flaunted.

The further you pursue these allusions the more you realise that in everything Dylan writes and says, be it lyrics, prose or even interview comments, more and more connections to source material become apparent.

Then to top it all Dylan used his Nobel Literature Award Lecture to display his magpie tendency by using, of all things, student cheat guides, especially on *Moby Dick*, for some of his comments. Perhaps Dylan was making a number of points here. Melville himself was accused of plagiarising portions from one Amasa Delan for his story "Benito Cereno", and *Moby Dick*, as we have seen, is steeped in Shakespeare. Dylan may also be having fun at the Nobel Committee's expense. Using what is basically a cheat-your-way-out-of-reading-the-book on such an occasion would suit the impish spirit with which he is so often credited. On the other hand, that would all be guesswork and it may just have been lazy plagiarism. Dylan remains a master, both in and out of his art, at keeping everyone guessing.

***

Artwork is not what Dylan is going to go down in history for; it is his other work that will be enjoyed and studied by posterity. Such dubious behaviour in the other fields does, though, provide ammunition for detractors.

Outright condemnation is something Dylan has faced for close on six decades now, so it probably does not concern him. Fierce denunciations were not slow in coming from someone who seems to have spent many years wrapped in jealousy that she is not held in same esteem as Dylan. This songwriter told *The Los Angeles Times*: "Bob is not authentic at all," she said. "He's a plagiarist and his name and voice are fake. Everything about Bob is a deception. We are like night and day, he and I." So said Roberta Joan Anderson, whom you probably know by her 'fake name', Joni Mitchell. [52]

Dylan may face a steady stream of attacks, but he also has an army of ever-willing defenders. One of these, Robert Polito, commented insightfully in an article sub-titled: 'When Bob Dylan lifted lines from an obscure Civil War poet, he wasn't plagiarizing. He was sampling'. Polito points out the differences in styles of borrowing that Dylan uses: "We would scarcely realize we were inside a collage unless someone told us, or unless we abruptly registered a familiar locution. The wonder of the dozen or so snippets that

Dylan sifted from *Confessions of a Yakuza* for *"Love and Theft"* is how casual and personal they sound dropped into his songs - not one of those songs, of course, remotely about a *yakuza,* or a gangster of any persuasion. Some of Dylan's borrowings operate as allusions in the accustomed sense, urging us back into the wellspring texts. Timrod, I think, works as a citation we're ultimately intended to notice, though no song depends on that notice. Dylan manifestly is fixated on the American Civil War. [53]

The usual defence is more bluntly put as, 'it's just the folk process, so deal with it.' This does cover vast swathes of Dylan's prolific output; and if one fully accepts that process in all contexts, then no problem ever arises, and you accept it as the basis of all art. If you do, however, then you have to account for what seems a somewhat cavalier and inconsistent approach to the convention of copyright act enforcement and the subsequent claims made in this regard.

The worlds of creative art and copyright protection can never sit easily together. An illustration of that is the sobering realisation that dramatists in the modern world could never create and put on plays in a similar manner to how Shakespeare worked. If they tried to, they would very quickly find themselves facing litigation and their productions being banned. One wonders how much inspiring art has been lost because of this and how inhibiting a constraint it must represent to the development of artistic expression.

Dylan, overlooking his forays into the pop world, repeated his previous stance in 2012. In reply to the question, "When those lines make their way into a song, you're conscious of it happening?", in the *Rolling Stone* interview, Dylan said: *"Well, not really. But even if you are, you let it go. I'm not going to limit what I can say. I have to be true to the song. It's a particular art form that has its own rules. It's a different type of thing. All my stuff comes out of the folk tradition – it's not necessarily akin to the pop world."*

Better, by far, it is for us that Dylan has proceeded as he has, especially when you take into account that, despite some of the examples above, he often does pay tribute to those whose work he admires. If you follow Dylan's interviews and his Radio Show, and read *Chronicles,* then you will discover that he is very prepared to share his enthusiasms, inspirations and influences in those contexts. Without 'No More Auction Block' we would not have had 'Blowin' in the Wind', without old Scottish airs we would not have 'The Times They Are A-Changin' and 'Farewell Angelina', amongst others, without 'Nottamun Town' we would lack 'Masters of War' without 'La Bamba' we would not have 'Like A Rolling Stone', without 'Bottles of Wine' we would not have 'Buckets of Rain', that exquisitely perfect ending to Dylan's finest album, *Blood on the Tracks*. On and on that list could go, as could a similar one for Shakespeare, and so many gems would have been lost that it hardly bears contemplating.

Shakespeare and Dylan take source material, be it written, musical, performed or the language they hear on the streets and mould it instinctively into new visions that are stamped indelibly with their respective uniqueness. We instinctively feel this and we apprehend instantly that we are encountering something Shakespearean or Dylanesque, even though their work appears in so many disparate genres and styles and even though it is synthesised from sources that are traceable even as we hear them vocalised in fresh settings.

We follow their lead and investigate the work of those from whom they borrowed. Dylan's comment regarding Timrod is unquestionably true; a name seemingly forgotten was being talked about again and featured on the front pages of national newspapers. Dylan had lifted him from neglect, and in doing so proved the worth of Mark Twain's observation that "it is better to take what does not belong to you than to let it lie around neglected."[54] For many of his fans, Dylan has opened up the work of literary masters they would otherwise perhaps gone through life without encountering. As for music, Dylan has led so many people back to the wells from which he drinks himself, that it is hard to estimate how profound his influence on his listeners in this regard is. Suffice to say that generation after generation of listeners have discovered all manner of music, much of it hitherto obscure, because they discovered that this music had fed into the work of Bob Dylan.

Shakespeare, even more so, has led scholars, audiences and readers back to everyone who could conceivably have been thought to have influenced him. It is often claimed, with considerable justification, that our concentration on Shakespeare leads to a comparative neglect of work of genius by his contemporaries and near contemporaries. At the same time, however, it is our very fascination with Shakespeare's genius that ensures that his period in drama shall forever compel us. As a result, the stellar work of Marlowe, Jonson, Webster, Middleton and others of the time will continue to be extensively studied and performed.

From the convenience of using whatever is at hand to the transmutation of base metal into shining gold, both our bards create their art out of many strands of existing material. They fuse these into marvellous works which speak directly to us and continually inspire new generations of audiences and artists. By embedding the previous artistic streams at the centre of their art, they refresh the river that carries on after them to be added to by others who, like many in their audiences, have been inspired to delve backwards into the sources of these two artists, whose inspirational creations have moved them so deeply.

NOTES

1 Bate, Jonathan Jonathan Bate, *Soul of the Age: A Biography of the Mind of William Shakespeare* Random House Trade Paperbacks, 2010

2 Very directly when, as was Marlowe, describing Helen of Troy in *Troilus and Cressida*: "She is a pearl/ Whose price hath launched above a thousand ships." More diffusely in *Richard II*: "Was this face the face/That every day under his household roof/Did keep ten thousand men?"

3 John Jowet *Shakespeare And Text* Oxford University Press, U.S.A.Dec 7, 2007

4 http://www.cems.ox.ac.uk/holinshed/ – accessed February, 2018

5 Quoted by Michael Blanding in The New York Times, February 7, 2018

6 Janet Clare *Shakespeare's Stage Traffic: Imitation, Borrowing and Competition in Renaissance Theatre* Cambridge University Press, January, 2014

7 Quoted by Ron Charles in *The Washington Post*, "Books", October 5, 2017

8 Philip Larkin, in 'Jazz Review', Daily Telegraph, London, Nov 10, 1965

9 https://www.theguardian.com/books/2010/jun/27/philip-larkin-love-hate-women

10 An excerpt from *Conversations with Tom Petty [Omnibus]*by Paul Zollo. http://americansongwriter. com/2017/10/tom-petty-on-bob-dylan/ October 2017. This article was originally published on *americansongwriter.com in January 2012*

11 In passing, it can be noted that Shakespeare is, once again, telling a version of an already popular tale. There was a 1578 play in French which was translated into English in 1592, and there was Samuel Daniel's *The Tragedy of Cleopatra*, two years later, which proved popular enough to gain several reprints. Shakespeare's transformation of the story of the two lovers took it to an entirely new artistic level, or, rather, many other levels as its multilayered, opulent verse works on so many of them

12 "The Great Folk Heist is an album of folk songs that directly or indirectly influenced the earlier work of Bob Dylan. The songs have been traced back in time to some of their earliest incarnations

and have been lovingly arranged and given a new voice based on the emotional content of the lyrics and melodies." https://boxerjohn.com/the-great-folk-heist

13 "For Dave Glover" is not on Dylan's official site but appears in a number of unofficial collections of his writing. Including "Words Fill My Head" Bobcats International, 1990

14 Bob Dylan, https://www.bobdylan.com/albums/the-times-they-are-a-changin/ liner notes

15 Bob Dylan, https://www.bobdylan.com/albums/bringing-it-all-back-home/ liner notes

16 Michael Gray Song and Dance Man III, The Art of Bob Dylan Continuum International Publishing Group Ltd. 2002

17 BJ Rolfzen interviewed in Tales From A Golden Age DVD Chrome Dreams, Surrey UK 2004

18 Michael Gray quoting: Gavin Selerie 'Tricks and Training: Some Dylan Sources and Analogues', 'Telegraph no. 50'

19 Bob Dylan Lily, Rosemary And The Jack Of Hearts Copyright © 1974 by Ram's Horn Music; renewed 2002 by Ram's Horn Music

20 http://www.adamhammond.com/dylan-and-auden/ (accessed February 13, 2018)

21 Richard F Thomas Why Bob Dylan Matters Dey Street Book, US 2017

22 Bob Dylan Lyrics, 1962-1985 Paladin, Grafton books 1988

23 Gavin Edward, Led Zeppelin's 10 Boldest Rip-Offs" Rolling Stone June 22, 2016

24 James Mustich "Talkin' Bob Dylan" Barnes and Noble Review, October, 2010 https://www.barnesandnoble.com/review/talkin-bob-dylan accessed March 16, 2018

25 T.S.Eliot, "Philip Massinger," The Sacred Wood, New York: Bartleby.com, 2000

26 Umberto Eco Interpretation and Overinterpretation. Cambridge University Press, 1992

27 http://observer.com/2004/04/new-lolita-scandal-did-nabokov-suffer-from-cryptomnesia/ (accessed February 17, 2018)

28 https://www.rollingstone.com/music/news/sam-smith--tom-petty-settlement-20150126 Accessed February 20, 2018

29 Quoted in No Direction Home, Robert Shelton Beech Tree Books, 1986

30 Interview by Tom Mulhern Guitar Player July 1990 http://www.macca-central.com/macca-archives/guitarplayer.htm accessed July 13, 2018

Clinton Heylin Its One for the Money, Constable Robinson June 18, 2015

31 Ibid.

32 Bob Dylan 1963 quoted in No Direction Home Robert Shelton (Revised) Omnibus Press 2011

33 Bob Dylan, August 16th, 2012 issue of Rolling Stone. Interview by Mikal Gilmore

34 http://www.citypages.com/arts/5-times-disney-was-questionably-inspired-by-other-films/435693153

http://m.uk.ign.com/articles/2017/03/22/disney-accused-of-stealing-zootopia

https://archive.org/details/TheWaltDisneyCompanyAndShamelessPlagiarism

35 For more on this, see Richard F Thomas Why Bob Dylan Matters Dey Street Book, US 2017

36 Rock's Enigmatic Poet Opens a Long-Private Door, LA Times April, 2004. Robert Hilburn interviews Bob Dylan, April 2004. http://articles.latimes.com/2004/apr/04/entertainment/ca-dylan04/2

37 Anthony Scaduto, Bob Dylan W.H. Allen & Co. UK 1972

38 As quoted in Clinton Heylin Its One for the Money, Constable Robinson June 18, 2015

39 S.T. Coleridge Letter to Thomas Curnick, 1814, in Griggs 1959

40 Albert Bigelow Paine, Mark Twain, A Biography: The Personal and Literary Life of Samuel Langhorne Clemens, 1912. Available on Project Gutenberg: https://www.gutenberg.org/

SOURCES

files/2988/2988-h/2988-h.htm

41 Referencing Dylan's 'Positively 4th Street' and 'Sad-eyed Lady of the Lowlands' respectively

42 Roland Barthes, *The Death of the Author* http://www.tbook.constantvzw.org/wp-content/death_authorbarthes.pdf

43 Quoted in *No Direction Home*, Robert Shelton Beech Tree Books, 1986

44 Howard Sounes in *Down The Highway: The Life Of BobDylan*, Grove Press, 2001. There is also some extra background to the story, here: http://ryanhamiltonwalsh.tumblr.com/post/167560360886/masters-of-nottamun-town (accessed February 13, 2018)

45 Ian Anderson, *Folk Roots*, November 1992

46 Quoted in *The World of Ovid's Metamorphoses* By Joseph B. Solodow

47 Scott Warmuth: http://swarmuth.blogspot.com/2009/04/together-through-life-dispatch-6.html accessed March 2018

48 https://www.rollingstone.com/music/news/bob-dylan-signs-six-book-deal-20110118 accessed March 1, 2018

49 Blake Gopnik Love and theft: Bob Dylan accused of plagiarizing famous photos in his new art show https://www.thedailybeast.com/bob-dylan-accused-of-plagiarizing-famous-photos-in-his-new-art-show

50 http://www.nybooks.com/daily/2011/10/05/richard-prince-bob-dylan-fugitive-art/ accessed July 14, 2018

51 Scott Warmuth "Bob Dylan's The Beaten Path: Selling the Brooklyn Bridge" Dec 25, 2016.https://swarmuth.blogspot.co.uk/2016/?view=classic

52 Mitchell, incidentally, defends this seeming hypocrisy, according to Melinda Newman in the *USA Today*, by declaring that her name is simply a nickname derived from her given middle name, combined with her surname from when she took that of her then husband, Chuck Mitchell. It is an, erm, 'interesting' argument that a nickname from the middle name "Joan" is perfectly acceptable but first name "Bob" from first name "Robert" is seen as reprehensible

53 Robert Polito *Bob Dylan: Henry Timrod Revisited* https://www.poetryfoundation.org/articles/68697/bob-dylan-henry-timrod-revisited Accessed March 1, 2018

54 Merle Johnson, ed., More Maxims of Mark Privately Printed, New York (1927)

Chapter Ten

THE TEMPEST AND TEMPEST

We hear this fearful tempest sing

This chapter focuses on Shakespeare's play *The Tempest* and Dylan's album *Tempest*, and examines these individual works for aspects of their art that have been looked at in general in preceding chapters.

The situation is somewhat energised by the widely held, though eminently challengeable, assumption that *The Tempest* is Shakespeare's last solo-created work and, diving further into ever less supportable territory, is his farewell to the theatre and life in London. When it was put to Dylan that his album might be analogously his farewell to making albums and the sign of imminent retirement, he brusquely dismissed the idea. Dylan must have known that people would make the connection, despite there being no 'the' in his title, especially as he had been so frequently name-checking Shakespeare for years. That they homed in on the retirement link probably rankled with him, however.

Prior to looking into the intriguing parallels that exist between the two works, I will attend to this storm in a teacup. It should be stressed, from the outset, that the correspondences I then trace are analogies only and it is not a case of Dylan's album version of Shakespeare's play from just over 400 years before Dylan's 2012 release. Rather, it is the latest example of what this book has been exploring in the preceding chapters regarding parallels in their lives, works and cultural heritage.

***

The last play/last album connection has never gone away, as, following *Tempest*, Dylan has only put out new albums (two single discs and one triple set) that consist of him singing others' songs, most of which are strongly associated with Frank Sinatra. This chimes neatly enough with those who assert that *The Tempest* was the final solo-authored Shakespeare play before his final dramas, which are held to be collaborations with John Fletcher, his heir as the leading dramatist in the King's Men Company.

However, there are a number of factors which militate against this 'last play and therefore last album' claim; not least that there is no sound reason to be sure that *The Tempest* or *Tempest* are deliberately intended as the last solely written works of either man. Bob Dylan may well bring out a new album of originals[1]. Even if there is no further such album, there would still be no reason to assume with certainty that Dylan had planned *Tempest* as a farewell album when he was creating it. The same holds true of Shakespeare and *The Tempest*.

It is so often asserted, and so routinely accepted, that this play was Shakespeare's last non-collaborative work that you have to forcibly remind yourself that these assertions and this acceptance are built more on repetition than on solid fact.

It has even become common to see *The Tempest* referred to as Shakespeare's last play, even without the qualifier of 'solo authored'. This is demonstrably untrue. *The Tempest* was performed in 1611, as were *The Winter's Tale* and *Cymbeline*, more of which later. 1612 then saw both the lost play *Cardenio* and *The Two Noble Kinsmen*, while 1613 saw the final play in which Shakespeare was involved. This was titled *Henry VIII* in the First Folio, but *All is True* when performed in his lifetime. Critical orthodoxy views these to have been collaborations with John Fletcher, though there is a small minority of academics who have claimed *All Is True* to be all the bard's work and, therefore, his true final play.

The other claim, that *The Tempest* may not be his last play but is certainly the last one he wrote on his own, is certainly possible. Surprisingly, though, given the so oft-repeated assertions, there is no conclusive evidence one way or the other over which was written or produced last, *Cymbeline*, *The Winter's Tale* or *The Tempest*.

We do know that all three were performed in 1611, but we do not know the order they were written in, nor if the performance of *The Tempest* on November 1st was its debut. The people who state unequivocally that *The Tempest* is the final play do so because they see Prospero as being Shakespeare and the closing scene being a pre-planned farewell from Shakespeare to the theatre. This reductive interpretation has taken firm hold, even though Shakespeare was not saying goodbye to the theatre yet, and in spite of the fact that such an author-centric approach to art would not come into being until the Romantic era.

A self-perpetuating circular argument, as Dr Emma Smith has pointed out,[2] has grown up around this theory and it goes like this: '*The Tempest* must be Shakespeare's last "real" work as it has him saying "goodbye" via Prospero at the end. *The Tempest* has Shakespeare saying goodbye via Prospero at the end, and therefore *The Tempest* must be his last work.'

As it happens, the closing scenes of both *The Winter's Tale* and *Cymbeline* would be excellent farewells, too. The former is a reflective commentary on the magic of Shakespeare's art, and the latter has a self-undercutting, meta-theatrical, *tour-de-force* finale. Consequently, even in the dubious scenario of Shakespeare deciding in advance that a play was going to be his farewell, you could make an artistic case for any of the three of them.

Yet it is always *The Tempest* that is singled out because of the desperate need to force art into a biographical straitjacket which is forever presumptive, if not downright imaginary. This desire compels many to believe the play 'must be' Shakespeare talking directly to us.

Professor Marjorie Garber has described why this scenario has unfolded: "Fantasies attached to the notion of Shakespeare, including the fact that we can know something about him ... and the desire to actually have some kind of relationship ... this persistent, recurrent notion that this play is about Shakespeare's biography ... is again our cultural desire to have some intimate connection with Shakespeare."

This desire arises in many commentaries. Trevor Nunn's desire for this 'intimate connection', in the BBC series *Shakespeare Uncovered* leads him to make increasingly stronger claims as the documentary he narrates unfolds. From stating that his depressingly limiting starting point is that: "what still intrigues me about this play is what it tells us about Shakespeare himself" and describing it as "one of his most personal, almost autobiographical", Nunn then stretches his imagination to: "It is even possible that Shakespeare, who was also an actor, could have played the leading role himself. Then he adds:

"Shakespeare would have been 50 at the point of this play. Prospero is 50 – did he play Prospero? Why not? Was it not only his last play but his last performance?"

While we cannot completely rule out the possibility of this being what happened, we can certainly provide a list of answers to the question 'why not?' which shows how unlikely it is that it did. It is possible it was his last fully authored play, and indeed that has a reasonable chance of being true. It is possible, too, though less likely, that he saw himself as Prospero. It is also possible, but even less likely, that Shakespeare acted the part, and it is even more far-fetched to imagine that he anachronistically decided to write his own retirement speech, before not retiring.

Nunn ignores the overwhelming dubiety to which such a run of possibilities, piling up on top of each other, would lead. Instead, he claims each one as a distinct possibility, or probability, before culminating in presenting it as historical fact. He concludes the programme with the statement:

"For me, *The Tempest* will always be exceptional, not just because of its wisdom and humanity, because more than any of his other plays it leads us to the essence of the man who wrote them. My feeling is that it's in *The Tempest*, through the character Prospero, that we get closest to the workings of the mind of that genius William Shakespeare."

Immediately prior to that, Nunn had stacked the deck with statements that should have been challenged. His claim that Prospero is 50 in the play is an opinion, not a fact. His age is not firmly established in the text nor is there any reason why it should be. There are contradictory indications which have allowed him to appear anything from 25 to 70 onstage. If this first half of the claim is highly doubtful, then the second, that Shakespeare was 50 when he wrote the part, is simply untrue. The very oldest Shakespeare could have been was 47.

We are further (mis)informed that: "After writing *The Tempest* Shakespeare left London for good and returned to Stratford, just two years later he died. He was only 52." Three of the few facts we know for certain about Shakespeare at this juncture are as follows. Firstly, *The Tempest* was performed in 1611, so it could be written no later than that year. Secondly, Shakespeare died five not two, years later, in 1616. Thirdly, in-between these dates, in 1613, Shakespeare bought his first house in London, and it was strategically placed for someone who was working in the theatre.

Trevor Nunn is a very famous Shakespearean director and his love for Shakespeare's work in this documentary is very moving. As he builds up the case for the autobiographical reading, he gets carried away. This is natural, and even affecting, but someone, somewhere in the editing and production process should surely have tempered the rising certainty assigned to unknowable autobiographical claims and the deliberately misleading ending. Given the wide audience that TV reaches and the limitless opportunities for the recording being re-watched and re-broadcast, one can imagine how many viewers now erroneously believe that this is what happened at the end of Shakespeare's life.[3]

Marjorie Garber went on to provide a generous take on biographically intensive interpretations, after dismissing them as "fantasies":

"There is nothing wrong with these desires. There is nothing wrong even with this kind of reading. The fact that it's not historically accurate is not the end of the story, because the theatre is a magic place and we get out of there partly what we put into it. And so the very persistence of this fantasy, or wish, or reading or misreading is itself a kind of reading. It tells us a kind of story about the power of the play."

Nonetheless, Shakespeare was not retiring from London to Stratford. As Jonathan Bate wrote in *Soul of the Age*: "... at a London meeting in November 1614 with Greene, who had come to town in pursuit of Thomas Combe, the man proposing the enclosure. A firm sighting in London, just eighteen months before Shakespeare's death."[4]

That death was premature. Much is made of the average life expectancy in Shakespeare's time, but that average is heavily affected by the many deaths in childhood that were common then, and by the ravages of the plague(s). If you were fortunate enough to escape those, you could hope to complete the journey through Jaques' 'seven ages of man'. At the age of 53, in *Ode to Himself*, Shakespeare's contemporary, Ben Jonson, remarks that a recent stroke has turned his blood cold *before his years have made him old*, prior to promising that he is far from finished and will show everyone what he has still got to offer. This is the ode, with the magnificently grumpy opening verses in which, amongst other targets, Jonson dismisses Shakespeare's *Pericles* as a "moldy tale". Despite continuing to suffer from strokes, Jonson kept writing and lived to be 65.

Also, as mentioned earlier, there is the matter of Shakespeare buying property in London. Bate elaborates: "The only occasion on which Shakespeare bought as opposed to rented a property in London was in March 1613, when he purchased a substantial gatehouse close to the Blackfriars theatre. Even if this was primarily an investment property, the date of its purchase reveals Shakespeare's continuing commitment to London in his final years ... *All is True* was probably played at Whitehall for the court and Blackfriars for the gallants during the winter of 1613–14, before being staged at the new Globe the following summer. Shakespeare, then, is still at work in late 1613, maybe even some time into 1614. That he was still active at this time accords with the purchase of the Blackfriars gatehouse in 1613 and the meeting with Greene in London in the autumn of 1614. What kind of retreat to rural retirement is this?"[5]

On the other hand, not only was Shakespeare not retiring, but neither was Prospero. Instead, our fictive magus was going back to rule Milan. He was giving up his magic, the obsession with which had led him to lose Milan in the first place, but he was not retiring. In this way, you begin to feel that Prospero and Shakespeare are alike to an extent, but for the opposite of reasons than we are customarily led to believe.

In any case, Dylan seemed to go along with the widely-held assumption which holds that *The Tempest* is Shakespeare's final work when questioned on it. His mind doubtless was focussing elsewhere on the question's implications, as he dismissed the analogy between the works:

"Dylan's mention of Shakespeare raises a question. The playwright's final work was called *The Tempest*, and some have already asked: Is Dylan's *Tempest* intended as a last work by the now 71-year-old artist? Dylan is dismissive of the suggestion. "Shakespeare's last play was called *The Tempest*. It wasn't called just plain *Tempest*. The name of my record is just plain *Tempest*. It's two different titles."[6]

Dylan is perfectly correct in highlighting the dissimilarity in the titles. The definite article makes a vital distinction, as would an indefinite one. 'The Tempest', 'Tempest' and 'A Tempest' are all different. However, we have seen how regularly Dylan draws comparisons of himself to Shakespeare and, consequently, he would surely have been aware that his title would strike people this way, regardless of the obvious disparity. Not only does he name the title track '"Tempest"', even though it is about a ship hitting an iceberg with no tempest anywhere near the incident, but he had repeatedly mentioned Shakespeare in interviews for many years by this point. What seems to have irked him was that it was the 'retirement' implication that was taken up rather than anything more positive. This is more than understandable, especially given that nothing about the album suggests a swansong, *adios* or fond *adieu*.

Nevertheless, the longer that time passes without a follow-up to *Tempest*, the more it will be assumed that Dylan knew in advance that it would indeed be his farewell and the album will no doubt be reinterpreted in that light. The closing song, in particular, will come under scrutiny and, like the ending to *The Tempest*, often be made to carry an emotional weight of authorial intent that the existing evidence, when looked at objectively, simply does not support.

***

Regardless of their place in the exact chronological canons of the two artists, these two late works, *The Tempest* and *Tempest*, share many characteristics. Notwithstanding this, it would not be true to claim that Dylan's *Tempest* is akin to the works of so many other artists who recreate *The Tempest* in new works or use it as a direct foundation for their own visions. Instead, what we have are two individual works of art that we can view through the prisms of their shared sources; namely, the Classics, The Bible and Folk as well as in their characteristic wordplay and features relating to their position as writers creating texts as blueprints for live performances.

There are other positive parallels, too, which one can imagine Dylan would rather have been asked about than the question he did face. These range from basic similarities to analogous areas of interest that include: shipwrecks, reflecting back on own earlier works, the upsetting of social order, violence, and power. We will look at these areas before exploring the use of Classics, the Bible, Folk and the importance of performance.

There are a number of basic connections of significant import. Both album and play can be viewed as a series of visions and hallucinations. Both works feature shipwrecks; one conjured into existence in Shakespeare's play and an at times dream-like and fictitious rendition of a historical event in Dylan's song. Also, the tempest in Shakespeare's play was not natural but instead a magician's illusion and nor was there a real tempest when the Titanic sank. By naming his song 'Tempest' rather than "The Titanic", as it was in his source, Dylan presents his as a metaphorical tempest in which humanity finds itself storm-tossed and at the mercy of an inscrutable divine power.[7] The characters on his album struggle, search and attempt to persevere through life as though swimming through a turbulent sea that is ready to do them harm or finish them off at any moment. This is much the same case for most of the characters in *The Tempest,* and one assumes, that after he "abjures" his magic, it will be the same for Prospero, too. Prospero, though, does have the advantage that all his plans for dynastic succession, and their barring of Antonio's holding any power in the future, are in place, even if somewhat troublingly, for some, they have been secured through necromancy.

There is at least one straight Shakespeare reference on the album. This occurs in the song, "Pay in Blood" where we hear, in the final stanza: *"This is how I spend my days / I came to bury, not to praise"* which echoes Mark Antony's famous words, in *Julius Caesar*: *"I come to bury Caesar, not to praise him."* Additionally, some of the songs feature characters such as: The Rich man,

The Brothel Keeper, The Lady, The Boss, The Captain, The Bishop, Pity, Cupid, etc., that seem to come from early modern drama, or the Mystery Plays that preceded it, which reminds us again of Dylan's quote from his MusiCares' acceptance speech: *"These songs of mine, I think of as mystery plays, the kind that Shakespeare saw when he was growing up."* Like those plays and many of Shakespeare's, Dylan is still combining the sacred and the profane in the same manner we looked at in previous chapters. Not only in songs but even within the same verse, as here, from 'Narrow Way' where we move from sensual to sacred: *"I've got a heavy stacked woman, with a smile on her face/ And she has crowned, my soul with grace".*

That 'hard ground' shares with the Shakespeare play themes of violence, (attempted) murder, power, slavery, and a world social order that is in a state of upheaval. Dylan's album is filled with vividly detailed violence. Death and destruction are all around. 'Tin Angel' ends with all three protagonists dead, a woman, flanked by a dead husband and a dead lover, declaiming, theatrically: *"You died for me, now I'll die for you"* and then putting *"the blade to her heart and she ran it through"* sounds very Juliet-like. Even without being that specific, the closing bloodbath would not have been out of place on an Elizabethan or Jacobean stage. There's no Horatio here, forced to reluctantly stay alive 'in this harsh world' to tell the story. We have Dylan, though, in towering form to bear witness to the tale of the Boss, the Lady and Henry Lee.

Patrick Stewart recalled meeting director Rupert Goold for preliminary talks regarding Stewart taking on the role of Prospero for the 2008 Royal Shakespeare Company (RSC) production of *The Tempest*: "He talked about it being a violent play, and about the morality of the play being a strong issue, the wickedness that was always just under the surface, and danger too. And there was a political aspect. Not political in a colonial sense, but in the power struggles that exist between individuals – a kind of personal-political aspect". These words are equally applicable to *Tempest*.

Shakespeare and Dylan both look back to the civil wars of Roman times but often via the English and American Civil Wars respectively. Dylan's film *Masked and Anonymous* is built in very much the same spirit as his *Tempest* album and shares the same principles and approaches. Both *Masked and Anonymous* and *Tempest* maintain Dylan's favoured trope of merging the different periods of history. *The Tempest* and *Tempest* are equally concerned with how the past influences and is even replayed in the present. There is a telling moment in *Masked and Anonymous* where Dylan brings England into his theme of empires, past and present, dissolving and coalescing: The infuriating journalist, played by Jeff Bridges, is harassing Dylan's character, Jack Fate, and trying to goad him into responding: *"Have you been to England recently? It's not very English anymore. The Empire is finished. You got Big Ben and the Tower, but it's just a theme park. Sheesh, you got your start there, how does that make you feel, that the Empire is finished?"*

The doubling of "the empire is finished" ties in with both US and classical Rome, and the age old questions of Republic and Empire and who has the right to rule, in addition to bringing Shakespeare into the mix. These themes resound through both Shakespeare's play and Dylan's film and album, as do questions surrounding the make-up of the societies being ruled.

In shipwrecks, notions of nobility and class go out the same windows as everything else. In the opening storm in *The Tempest*, the boatswain puts the useless and vain lords in their place, in Act I Scene i:

ALONSO   *Good boatswain, have care. Where's the master? Play the men.*

BOATSWAIN   *I pray now, keep below.*

ANTONIO   *Where is the master, boatswain?*

BOATSWAIN   *Do you not hear him? You mar our labour - keep your*
              cabins. You do assist the storm.

GONZALO   *Nay, good, be patient.*

BOATSWAIN   *When the sea is. Hence! What cares these roarers for the name of*
              king? To cabin. Silence! Trouble us not.

Here, "roarers" cleverly puns the main meaning of 'waves' with the meaning of 'rioters', that is, the unruly mob overthrowing the social order.

This, in turn, doubly emphasises the boatswain's warning to Antonio not to "*assist the storm*". The ruler's interference is likely to lead to his doom in both the physical and social 'storms' that his actions are in danger of abetting.

While in Dylan's song, 'Tempest', as the great ship sinks, we hear of: "*All the lords and ladies / Heading for their eternal home*". It made no difference to the deadly waves if you came from any of "*The good, the bad, the rich, the poor*", because for sixteen hundred the finishing end was the same, regardless of social status. Nor, incidentally, does the Boss' social position save him from cuckoldry or death in 'Tin Angel'.

As befits later work, both play and album often hark back to previous dramas and records by their creators. Again they are following in Virgil's footsteps as he, too, movingly and effectively self-referenced his earlier poems in his later verses. This technique was something that Shakespeare had already mastered earlier as evidenced by *Twelfth Night* which affectionately references all his previous romantic comedies in a bravura farewell to that genre. Dylan has always been strong at setting up resonances with his earlier work but has been particularly so since his *Time Out Of Mind* album in 1997.

Delightful wordplay still abounds from the fertile pens of our bards. Shakespeare's language, as ever, is dazzling in a myriad of ways. There are set rhetorical flourishes; there is Caliban's alliterative style and sudden burst of sublime poetry, there are some startling modern sounding touches: "*who to advance and who/To trash for over-topping*". Our word-pairs are still present, too. A phrase originating, as previously mentioned, from *The Geneva Bible*, 'delicate and tender', appears in *Hamlet* but is here reversed to 'tender and delicate'. Others include the intriguing "backward and abysm". This phrase shows that Shakespeare is still experimenting with language as well as dramatic structure and effects. It occurs when Prospero is surprised at the very early memory of her infancy that Miranda provides. He asks:

But how is't
That this lives in thy mind? What seest thou else
In the dark backward and abysm of time?

(Act I Scene ii)

The use of backward as a noun signifying a period in the past was another first by Shakespeare. The combination of it with 'abysm' excited Dylan's friend, the poet Allen Ginsberg. Ginsberg, when teaching a class on *The Tempest* noted that: "....it's an interesting trick that he does by yoking two dissimilar or discordant words together; yoking together with an 'and' you get a little space – he does the same with "vast and middle" (in *Hamlet*) - backward *and* abysm."[8]

Dylan's wordplay also replays an old favourite, 'kill me dead" a tautology familiar from 'Cocaine Blues' and 'Shot of Love'. Hendiadys and associated word-pairing techniques are also well represented: 'Long And Wasted Years' – *cold and frosty*, 'Pay in Blood' – *steady and sure*, 'Early Roman Kings' – *sluggers and muggers* and "Tin Angel" – *cussed and cursed*. He even gives us an expanded version in 'Pay in Blood' – *life is short and it don't last long*. Dylan's verbal wit is continuously in evidence: *"hold your tongue and feed your eyes"*, he barks, and he still likes a paradox or two: *"The more I take the more I give/The more I die the more I live."*

Dylan has rarely sounded as Shakespearean as he does on this album[9] as Anne Margaret Daniel puts it: "The idioms and deliveries, phrasings and syntax of speech dating back to Shakespeare's day are alive and well in Dylan's *Tempest*"[10]. Additionally, the two works of art are very much concerned with the nature of language itself, again a theme we have noted through both artists' works. Caliban has a famous line about being taught Prospero and Miranda's language and the only benefit is being able to curse in it. The "gabble", as Miranda calls it, that he spoke before then is left ambiguously non-defined in the text. Caliban does, after all, know the name of his mother's deity, Setebos; he announces this in a manner that makes it seem that he did not learn it from Prospero or Miranda. If that is the case, and I am only proposing it hypothetically, Sycorax must have taught him how to say that at least.

Caliban's line, alluding to *Genesis*, which we consider later, about naming the sun and the moon returns us to the burning linguistic question of the time. The Biblical tale of Adam naming things is explored by Dylan in 'Man Gave Names To All The Animals', a song for children, and, therefore, aptly enough, one that would have been fitting for Miranda to have sung to Caliban.

The nature of language, and what he can do with it as an artist, was still on Dylan's mind, too, later in his career. *Tempest*, as we have seen, is closely aligned with Dylan's movie, *Masked and Anonymous* and we saw in the earlier chapter on wordplay that this involved deliberate linguistic experimentation.

Language is one of Shakespeare and Dylan's building blocks, as are music and the theatre. The two men remain innovatory towards all aspects of their art. Perhaps to take advantage of the indoor theatres affording space for musicians and suitable acoustics, Shakespeare made *The Tempest* one of his most musical plays. It is also the play where the songs are most fully integrated into the structure, theme and imagery of the drama. These songs had music composed for them by Robert Johnson[11], lutenist to the court of King James and composer of music for many plays of the era. The most famous song from the play, *Full Fathom Five*, is so highly regarded as to be often taken out of context and presented as a stand-alone text or song. It is important to remember, though, that in the play the song is telling a lie, and it is yet another illusion. Ferdinand's father is not under any water at all, far less five fathoms worth.

Shakespeare provides Caliban with what is a freedom-craving protest song, despite its internal contradiction:

CALIBAN   *No more dams I'll make for fish,*
           Nor fetch in firing
           At requiring,
           Nor scrape trencher, nor wash dish,
           Ban, ban, Ca-caliban
           Has a new master - get a new man.
           Freedom, high-day, high-day freedom, freedom high-day, freedom.

(Act II Scene ii)

That is not the only 'protest song' crying for freedom that we get in the play, as in Act II Scene ii we have Stephano and Trinculo singing:
Flout 'em, and scout 'em
And scout 'em, and flout 'em
Thought is free

As with the protest movements of the early Sixties, the music was here taken over by those in power. Ariel is again misleading characters with his music, this time by playing those symbols of communal, 'people's music', the tabor and the pipe. It is amusing to think for a moment of Prospero as 'The Man', using the rebellious under-classes' own music to dance to *his* tune.

As with music in theatre so we have theatre in music: after releasing *Tempest*, Dylan re-jigged his touring set list to include songs from the album at key junctures. He also inserted an interval into his performances and named the first and second parts, Act I and Act II. As discussed in chapter seven, playwright Conor McPherson has garnered significant success and acclaim for a play-musical based around Dylan songs, *Girl From The North Country*.[12]

The use of sources is another staple of the two bards' works that is repeated here. Two major examples are Shakespeare' use of Montaigne's essay, "Of The Cannibals" and Dylan's appropriation of the Carter Family's 'The Titanic'.

It is speculated that Shakespeare obtained copies of Montaigne from translator John Florio. Shakespeare had numerous potential connections with Florio, some of them so close that it seems improbable the men were not well acquainted. Indeed, many scholars see Florio as the source for the character of Holofernes in *Love's Labour's Lost*. If true, this would suggest that the acquaintance was not one that Shakespeare valued highly. The following passage from Florio's translation of Montaigne's 'Of the Cannibals', provides Shakespeare's character, Gonzalo, with an idealised vision of a nation:

". . . that hath no kind of traffike, no knowledge of Letters, no intelligence of numbers, no name of magistrate, nor of politike superioritie, no use of service, of riches or of poverty, no contracts, no successions, no partitions, no occupation but idle; no respect of kindred, but common, no apparell but natural, no manuring of lands, no use of wine, corne, or metal. The very words that import lying, falsehood, treason, dissimulations, covetousness, envie, detraction, and pardon, were never heard of amongst them."

Shakespeare imports this, verbatim at times, and places it in Gonzalo's mouth (rather than Caliban's, which would have more supported those persistent colonial readings of the play):

Gonzalo   *I'th'commonwealth I would by contraries*

> *Exècute all things. For no kind of traffic*
> *Would I admit; no name of magistrate;*
> *Letters should not be known; riches, poverty,*
> *And use of service, none; contract, succession,*
> *Bourn, bound of land, tilth, vineyard, none;*
> *No use of metal, corn, or wine, or oil;*
> *No occupation; all men idle, all;*
> *And women too, but innocent and pure;*
> *No sovereignty –*

(Act II Scene i)

Jonathan Bate sees this as Ovid's vision of the Golden Age refracted through Montaigne, and David Lindley writes: "The wording of Gonzalo's speech, however, is not taken straight from the first book of *Metamorphoses*, but from the version of its vision contained in Montaigne's Essay ' Of the Cannibals'. Montaigne is clearly Shakespeare's 'source' here, and yet it is extremely unlikely that he expected the audience to recognise the fact."[13].

It has been said, you suspect, firstly by an exhausted researcher, that there were 100,000 books written on Napoleon in the nineteenth century. A similar feeling and projected number would overcome you, were you to try and track down all the songs about the Titanic in the twentieth century. Dylan's melodic and lyrical model is, however, primarily that of the Carter Family's 'The Titanic'. To listen to the two songs one after another is to be struck by how closely Dylan adheres to this source, especially the opening stanzas, which directly supply whole lines:

The pale moon rose in its glory
She's drifting from golden west
She told a sad, sad story
Six hundred had gone to rest

The watchman was a-dreaming
Yes dreaming a sad, sad dream

He dreamed the Titanic was sinking
Out on the deep blue sea

There are some other lines that make their way into Dylan's song, but his soon spins out into its own orbit and Dylan's ending is very different to the sentimental close of the 'The Titanic'.

It is instructive to observe the use of sources more generally and in particular those from the shared cultural backgrounds of the two writers, especially in the areas of the Classics, the Bible and the folk tradition.

The Tempest and the Classics

The amount, depth and detail of the analyses that have traced the effects and implications of Virgil's *Aeneid* as a source text of *The Tempest* would astonish most modern audiences coming to the play for the first time.

As we have noted previously, Shakespeare and much of his contemporary and later audiences had an underlying knowledge of the classics. Consequently, Virgil can be seen to be hiding in plain view, everywhere, in *The Tempest*, despite being only specifically and unambiguously addressed on a few occasions. As D.A. Nuttall succinctly remarked when looking at this from the opposite perspective: "Shakespeare is seldom less Virgilian than when he is citing him"[14] John Pitcher has described Virgil's presence in *The Tempest* as 'spectral', Leah Whittington writes of it as "persistent but elusive", and Robert Wiltenburg sees *The Aeneid* as Shakespeare's primary source not in a direct sense but rather as "the story he is retelling"[15].

Certainly, the play is firmly set, despite all the writing and productions that relocate it to the 'New World', in the lands and sea of Aeneas' wanderings. Both works begin with shipwrecking storms. Aeneas was forced by a tempest to Carthage before leaving there for Italy. Additionally, a broad, structural comparison is evident. Both works start with a storm, which is later revealed to be supernaturally invoked, and the characters survive various trials, hallucinations and revelations to, hopefully, build a new and stable future.

The danger with pursuing 'spectral' presences is that one can be tempted to construct from them an all embracing structure that then struggles to contain what is, by its very nature, an open-ended and endlessly variable play-text. Therefore, I will turn first to what are seemingly the more fleshy manifestations of this Virgilian presence.

In Act III scene iii, just as Alonso, Sebastian, Antonio and the others are about to settle down to a banquet that has been laid before them by "Shapes", we get the stage direction: *Thunder and lightning. Enter ARIEL, like a harpy; claps his wings upon the table; and, with a quaint device, the banquet vanishes.* He then confronts the *"three men of sin"* with their crimes before: *"He vanishes in thunder; then, to soft music enter the Shapes again, and dance, with mocks and mows, and carrying out the table.*

This brings to mind the episode in Book III of *The Aeneid* where Virgil describes harpies attacking the banquet of another group of sailors who have been forced ashore by a storm:

...on the winding shore we build couches and banquet on the rich dainties. But suddenly, with fearful swoop from the mountains the Harpies are upon us, and with loud clanging shake their wings, plunder the feast; and with unclean touch mire every dish. Once more, in a deep recess under a hollowed rock, closely encircled by trees and quivering shade, we spread the tables and renew the fire on the altars; once more, from an opposite quarter o the sky and from a hidden lair, the noisy crowd with taloned feet hovers round the prey, tainting the dishes with their lips. [16]

An even clearer reference is that to the "widow Dido" and the "widower Aeneas" in a comical and revealing exchange, full of import, between the idealistic Gonzalo and the cynical Antonio and Sebastian:

GONZALO   *Methinks our garments are now as fresh as when we
put them on first in Afric, at the marriage of
the king's fair daughter Claribel to the King of Tunis*

SEBASTIAN   *'Twas a sweet marriage, and we prosper well in our return.*

ADRIAN   *Tunis was never graced before with such a paragon to
their queen.*

GONZALO   *Not since widow Dido's time.*

ANTONIO *Widow! A pox o'that! How came that widow in? Widow Dido!*

SEBASTIAN *What if he had said 'widower Aeneas' too?*

(Act II Scene i)

Gonzalo is talking of the pre-Virgil view of Dido. In this, the tragic queen founded Carthage and remained forever faithful to the memory of her dead husband, and committed suicide rather than undergo a forced re-marriage. Virgil's immortal version gave Dido her altogether different reputation. She is again glorious in that heart-breaking tale, where she again kills herself, but now because her lover Aeneas has left her to fulfil his destiny. This would, though, at least for those with hearts of stone and cynical eyes, deserve Antonio's scornful, and suggestive of sexual impropriety, dismissal: "Widow? A pox o'that'.

Prospero sees Miranda as being poised on the brink of one of these two paths of female behaviour and reputation and, by bringing in this classical backdrop, Shakespeare is encouraging the audience, as the play often does, to consider how the past interacts with the present. As we have seen, this is also a major theme for Dylan, especially in the twenty-first century. Claribel's politically arranged marriage to an African king illustrates further the concerns with which Prospero is struggling and juggling. Such problems did not only beset Prospero, and other rulers in *The Tempest*, but Shakespeare's King, too. James was, despite his avowed preference for Protestant mates for his children and his personal disapproval of arranged marriages, preparing to make politically expedient wedding matches for his son with powerful, Catholic royalty to ensure peace. History and fate had other ideas for his unfortunate offspring, however.

The third major and unmistakabe reference is when Ferdinand sees Miranda for the first time. He reacts to her in very much the same manner as Aeneas does when he first sees the Goddess Venus, who is his mother, though this is unbeknownst to him. She comes *"across his path, in the midst of the forest, with a maiden's face and mien ..."*: and Aeneas responds to her:

"... but by what name should I call you, maiden? for your face is not mortal

nor has your voice a human ring; O goddess surely! sister of Phoebus, or one of the race of Nymphs? Show grace to us, whoever you may be, and lighten this our burden. Inform us, pray, beneath what sky, on what coasts of the world, we are cast; knowing nothing of countries or peoples we wander driven hither by wind and huge billows. Many a victim shall fall for you at our hand before your altars."[17]

In *The Tempest*, Ferdinand, just like Aeneas, has landed in an unfamiliar land and he too meets a maiden and one so beautiful that he presumes her to be a goddess:

FERDINAND *Most sure, the goddess*
On whom these airs attend! Vouchsafe my prayer
May know if you remain upon this island;
And that you will some good instruction give
How I may bear me here: my prime request,
Which I do last pronounce, is - O you wonder! -
If you be maid or no?

MIRANDA *No wonder, sir; But certainly a maid.*

(Act I Scene ii)

Shakespeare may have been thinking of Virgil via Christopher Marlowe, who had already put this scene on the Elizabethan stage:

AENEAS But what may I, fair virgin, call your name,
Whose looks set forth no mortal form to view,
Nor speech bewrays ought human in thy birth?
Thou art a goddess that delud'st our eyes,
And shroud'st thy beauty in this borrowed shape.
But whether thou the sun's bright sister be,
Or one of chaste Diana's fellow nymphs,
Live happy in the height of all content
And lighten our extremes with this one boon,

> As to instruct us under what good heaven
> We breathe as now, and what this world is called
> On which, by tempests' fury, we are cast?
> Tell us, O tell us, that are ignorant;
> And this right hand shall make thy altars crack
> With mountain heaps of milkwhite sacrifice.

(Dido, Queen of Carthage[18] Act I Scene i)

Once these echoes put *The Aeneid* in your consciousness, other potential resonances are heard. Donna Hamilton is one of a number of critics who see Virgil clearly in Francisco's words when he suggests that Ferdinand may have survived in the lines beginning:" *Sir, he may live"* in Act II Scene i. As well as tracing an overarching, parallel arc in the two works, Hamilton compares the above with Virgil's: "and lo! from Tenedos, over the peaceful depths—I shudder as I tell the tale—a pair of serpents with endless coils are breasting the sea and side by side making for the shore. Their bosoms rise amid the surge, and their crests, blood-red, overtop the waves; the rest of them skims the main behind and their huge backs curve in many a fold." (2.203-8)

She comments that: "In constructing the passage that describes Ferdinand, Shakespeare appropriates for his own use several of the key verbs, nouns, and images that Virgil used for the snakes, and with a degree of exactness that leaves no doubt about their origin. Both Virgil and Shakespeare emphasize the power of the swimmers by describing them as high in the water. Virgil pictures the snakes as "breasting [incumbunt] the sea"; their "bosoms rise amid the surge [fluctus], and overtop [superant] the waves." Shakespeare follows Virgil when he writes that Ferdinand has been seen to *"beat the surges under him,"* has *"trod the water,"* and having *"breasted the surge"* has kept *"his bold head / 'Bove the . . . waves." "*[19]

Others trace Virgil's words both in the masque and in its abrupt conclusion and in the descriptions of drowned sailors. Over time, a skeleton of allusion has been uncovered throughout the play.

As we will see, Virgil is one of numerous classical authors referenced on Dylan's *Tempest*. Staying with Shakespeare for a time yet, however, it is striking that numerous and imposing critical edifices regarding *The Aeneid* and *The Tempest* have been built upon these bones. You can variously read Aeneas claimed as Ferdinand, Prospero and Caliban. As these analogies are not necessarily self-prohibitive, you can even read a mixture of them within the one critical view. The wide range of Virgilian takes that had been proposed for *The Tempest* became ever more expansive when the theme of imperial colonialism came to dominate critical theories and productions of the play. As *The Aeneid* is regarded as a key literary document detailing the founding of empires, this was, perhaps, inevitable. There is, however, no 'direct fit'. Instead, many critics, as Leah Whittington quotes of Craig Kallendorf, see Shakespeare as taking "not the precise substance of [Virgil's] colonial vision, but the process by which imperialism is questioned and qualified by 'further voices' that emerge in the drama".[20]

Popular, indeed dominant, though the colonial readings of *The Tempest* became, these relied on a blind eye being turned to basic points which spoke against them. Prospero is nothing like a colonist. He did not set out to conquer the island and plunder loot to be shipped back home. He was an outcast; shipwrecked, banished and left for dead. He arrives not with an army but with his infant daughter. Caliban is a one-off; he is not a subjugated race or culture. The action takes place in the Mediterranean and one mention of the Bermudas cannot alter that. Even the much quoted texts about voyages to the Americas that Shakespeare supposedly used as source material lie in the area of "likely assumption" rather than incontrovertible fact[21]. It is interesting to note, in passing, though, that two of these pamphlets refer to New World colonists as being like Dido and Aeneas. This also provides an illustration of how deeply embedded the classical myths were in the minds of Jacobeans.

Critical responses following *The Aeneid* trail deepened into complex readings regarding foundation myths of Britain, which were of prime importance at the time, given the unifying kingship of James the Sixth of Scotland and First of England. Much was being made of the legend of Aeneas' grandson, Brutus, with Trojan followers, founding Britain after killing the resident giants. James was depicted in text, picture and pageantry as the "second Brute". As is ever the case with *The Tempest*, the play allows itself to be moulded, to a large, but not total, degree, to fit the structure and imagery of this myth.

Professor Rowland Wymer, in a thoughtful piece, expands upon this tradition and focuses on the theme of how and why rulers are legitimised:"[22] What I wish to do is to read *The Tempest* in the light of myths about the origin of Britain, an approach which takes the play's questions about legitimate rulership beyond a narrowly conceived version of 'colonialism.'" Stepping away from narrow allegories, Wymer suggests that by interrogating the myths of Roman expansion and the creation of Britain, *The Tempest* encourages us to confront "the origins of all societies, the origins of all authority." Shakespeare's abiding questions over monarchical power and authority, according to Wymer, are answered in *The Tempest*:

"Neither Elizabeth nor James was an absolute ruler, nor could they hope to be. Their power was exercised as part of a complex network of overlapping jurisdictions. *The Tempest* also seems to recognise that, despite the manifest superiority of Prospero to Caliban, no ruler's power is ever truly absolute or beyond question. Some degree of co-operation and consent is always necessary from the governed, and in the play's Epilogue Shakespeare extends this insight so that it also applies to the artist's limited powers over his audience, forcing the actor playing Prospero to throw himself upon the mercy of the spectators, the mass of people who are the only final validation of whatever authority an artist or ruler claims."[23]

Others have reacted against such *Aeneid* readings by looking both backwards and forwards from it to two other classical literary giants; namely, Homer and Ovid. To take the latter firstly, Ovid is another 'spectral' presence throughout the play, according to Sir Jonathan Bate. Bate sees what he calls, with substantial justification, Shakespeare's 'favourite book', Ovid's *Metamorphoses*, reflected in *The Tempest*. The play's theme of transformation, as signified in that keystone song, 'Full Fathom's Five' certainly chimes with Ovid's masterpiece. It has also been claimed that the depiction of storms and wanderings allude to Ovid's poetry reflecting back on Homer and Virgil's poetry rather than coming in a straight line from the latter.

The one direct invocation of Ovid in *The Tempest* could hardly be more striking or important. The crucial speech where Prospero relinquishes his magical powers is, as has long been noted, taken almost straight from Arthur Golding's translation of *The Metamorphoses*. From Book Seven, there, we read:

Ye Ayres and windes: ye Elves of Hilles, of Brookes, of Woods alone,
Of standing Lakes, and of the Night approche ye everychone.
Through helpe of whom (the crooked bankes much wondring at the thing)
I have compelled streames to run clean e backward to their spring.
By charmes I make the calme Seas rough, and make y rough Seas plaine
And cover all the Skie with Cloudes, and chase them thence againe.
By charmes I rayse and lay the windes, and burst the Vipers jaw,
And from the bowels of the Earth both stones and trees doe drawe.
Whole woods and Forestes I remove: I make the Mountaines shake,
And even the Earth it selfe to grone and fearfully to quake.

While in The Tempest we have Prospero's lines, in Act V scene i, describing
his beloved magic which he realises that he must renounce:

Ye elves of hills, brooks, standing lakes, and groves,
And ye that on the sands with printless foot
Do chase the ebbing Neptune, and do fly him
When he comes back; you demi-puppets, that
By moon-shine do the green sour ringlets make,
Whereof the ewe not bites; and you, whose pastime
Is to make midnight mushrooms, that rejoice
To hear the solemn curfew; by whose aid -
Weak masters though ye be - I have bedimm'd
The noontide sun, call'd forth the mutinous winds,
And 'twixt the green sea and the azured vault
Set roaring war. To the dread rattling thunder
Have I given fire, and rifted Jove's stout oak
With his own bolt; the strong-based promontory
Have I made shake, and by the spurs pluck'd up
The pine and cedar: graves at my command
Have waked their sleepers, oped, and let 'em forth
By my so potent art.

Shakespeare's use of Medea's lines was not unique in his time. Thomas

Heywood's contemporaneous play on Classical myths, *The Brazen Age*, also features the lines: "The night grows on, and now to my black Arts, Goddess of witchcraft and darke ceremony/To whom the elves of hills, of brooks, of groves, of standing lake." Quoting Ovid's lines was clearly a means of providing extra meaning for many in the audience.

Shakespeare's care and intent are made doubly clear by Professor Jonathan Bate's observation that Shakespeare has supplemented Golding's translation with a phrase from the Latin original, *convulsaque robores* ('and rooted up oaks') for "rifted Jove's stout oak" as Golding never specified the species of tree.[24] According to Bate, recognition of the original and the parallels between Prospero and Medea are intended to bring the audience to the conclusion that Prospero's magic is, essentially, based on black magic, not white, and therefore must be abandoned. Additionally, Sycorax's connections to Medea further strengthen Prospero's analogies to Caliban's mother and, consequently, evil magic. These character parallels form one of the many instances of mirroring that make up *The Tempest*'s beguiling plot and cast.

Debates over white and black magic, plus Prospero's true character and intent, have rumbled on for centuries and will doubtless continue on for many more. Where one stands on this will determine one's interpretation of the entire play and for directors and cast it will be crucial in deciding how they stage their performance. The overwhelming importance of this Ovidian passage has led some commentators to attribute some, or all, of the references we looked at above in regard to The *Aeneid*, to Ovid's later re-workings of the same myths rather than from Virgil himself. They point out, for example, that the storm scene seems more redolent of *The Metamorphoses* than of The *Aeneid*.

There is another camp amongst the armies of interpreters of *The Tempest* who wish to move the focus away from Virgil, but instead of going forward to Ovid, they look back to Virgil's own source, Homer. *The Aeneid* was itself built upon those founts of Western Literature, Homer's *Iliad* and *Odyssey*. The latter tells of wanderings after a storm. Using Homer's epic style, Virgil expands upon the Grecian books and gives us another unforgettable epic, the tale of Aeneas, who established Rome after losing Troy. As well as similar key scenes in both, including storms, there are times when Virgil more or less directly translated from the Greek into Latin. The chain of influence always goes back to the epics we attribute to Homer, as they are the wellspring of all that was to follow. As Ralph Waldo Emerson wrote: "Read Tasso, and you think of Virgil; read Virgil, and you think of Homer". You could extend that list from Tasso onwards, writer by writer at your leisure. Thus, the argument follows, when you think of storms, think firstly not of Virgil or Ovid but of Homer, the progenitor.

Which brings us to Dylan's album and the Classics, remembering too that Dylan had dutifully, and extensively, name-checked Homer's *Odyssey* in his Nobel Prize for Literature lecture. As already noted, the Classics form a thread through Dylan's work. The schoolboy from the Latin Club in Hibbing even sang in Latin on 2009's *Chritmas in the Heart*. As we shall see, Greek influences have grown ever stronger in and continue up to his latest album release, of cover songs, Triplicate whose genesis he explained as: "*I was thinking in triads anyway, like Aeschylus, The Oresteia, the three linked Greek plays. I envisioned something like that.*"[25]

Tempest and the Classics

Tempest brought a partial change in Dylan's involvement with the classics when compared to his previous twenty-first century albums. The fascination with the 'past-in-the-present' was still very much to the fore. Modern day USA was still seen through a refraction of the American Civil War which itself was underpinned by the time when Rome moved from Republic to Empire after civil war, just before the time of Christ. However, Dylan was now turning from the Roman versions of old myths to their source in Homer. This backward investigation has parallels in Dylan's interest in Shakespeare sending him back to Spenser and Chaucer, both of whom he also brings into his songs, and the Mystery Plays. Similarly, from Virgil and Ovid he moves back to Homer. This is fitting when one recalls the musician and producer, T-Bone Burnett's remarks that: "There is no way to accurately or adequately laud Bob Dylan. He is the Homer of our time. The next Bob Dylan will not come around for another millennium or two, making it highly unlikely that it will happen at all."[26]

Ovidian lines which appeared in 'Workingman's Blues #2,' were to change in live performance. It was a change noted by all close Dylan followers, but its import was first spotted by Richard Thomas. The verse where Dylan takes the Ovid line "No one can claim that I ever took up arms against you" and sings it as *"No one can ever claim that I took up arms against you"* had gone. The following verse:

In you, my friend, I find no blame
Wanna look in my eyes, please do
No one can ever claim
That I took up arms against you

was now replaced by:

I'll be back home in a month or two
When the frost is on the vine
I'll punch my spear right straight through
Half-ways down your spine[27]

The 'Ovid' version still appears on *bobdylan.com*'s official lyrics as verse seven, though "Official Lyrics' also now have the "Homer" version in at least one of their many iterations. Professor Thomas explains the significance behind this alteration in the following perceptive observation:

"No sign of Ovid, except perhaps in the "fugitive's prayer." Instead, Dylan, perhaps led there by Ovid, had gone back to *The Odyssey*, with whose hero, "the man of twists and turns," he has long associated, specifically to Robert Fagles' 1996 Penguin translation of Homer's poem. Dylanologist Scott Warmuth gathered some of the Homeric intertexts, but what needs explaining is what these quotes are doing in Dylan's songs. Dylan transfigured is here quoting and channeling Odysseus, from Book 10 of *The Odyssey*, on the island of the witch and temptress Circe" – you too have shared a bed with the wrong woman," says Dylan in the Nobel lecture in June 2017 as he comes out and compares himself to Odysseus. The Greek hero is telling his host, King Alcinous, of going out to reconnoiter and killing a stag, dinner for his hungry crew, that some god sent his way:

Just bounding out of the timber when I hit him
Square in the backbone, halfway down the spine

And my bronze spear went punching clean through—
He dropped in the dust, groaning, gasping out his breathe[28] "

This move to Homer, and specifically *The Odyssey*, was continued in *Tempest* whose songs are replete with lifts straight from Fagles' translation.

At first glance, you would not think there is any particular reason to connect *The Odyssey*'s "despite so many blows" with *"How I've survived so many blows"* in "Pay in Blood". By the time you get to that line in *The Odyssey*, however, you have read, soon before it, this passage:

You, you're a reckless fool—I see that. So,
the gods don't hand out all their gifts at once,
not build and brains and flowing speech to all.
One man may fail to impress us with his looks
but a god can crown his words with beauty, charm,
and men look on with delight when he speaks out.
Never faltering, filled with winning self-control,
he shines forth at assembly grounds and people gaze
at him like a god when he walks through the streets.
Another man may look like a deathless one on high
but there's not a bit of grace to crown his words.
Just like you, my fine, handsome friend. Not even
a god could improve those lovely looks of yours
but the mind inside is worthless.

Here you can find the source for the 'Pay in Blood's' *"Just like you, my handsome friend"*[29] as well as, from 'Tin Angel': *"You're a reckless fool, I can see it in your eyes"* and *"with a worthless mind"* plus *"She has crowned my soul with grace"* from 'Narrow Way'. From Fagles' readily available translation of *The Odyssey*, we can discover further quotations that turn up on Tempest. For example, "I'll lead you there myself at the break of day", appears, in identical form, on 'Duquesne Whistle'. Live performances of 'Long and Wasted Years', (a wistful song which otherwise exemplifies Orsino's 'strain' with 'a dying fall') soon boasted the following verse:

My enemy slammed into the Earth
I don't know what he was worth
But he lost it all, everything and more
What a blithering fool he took me for'

This alludes directly to Homer's account of Odysseus glorying in the success of his 'nobody' trick and the Cyclop's defeat: *To think how my great cunning stroke had duped them one and all ... such a blithering fool he took me for."*

Furthermore, a number of lifts are evident in 'Roll on John': *"Rags on your back just like any other slave"* and *"They tied your hands and they clamped your mouth"* echo "throwing filthy rags on his back like any slave" and "clamped his great hands on the man's mouth" from the same translation of Homer's epic. Others from the same song include *"Your bones are weary, you're about to breathe your last"* (*Odyssey*: "I'm bone-weary, about to breathe my last" plus two that lie cheek by jowl in the epic (*"They'll trap you in an ambush"* and, the word for word, *"You been cooped up on an island far too long"*) :

'Which god, Menelaus, conspired with you
to trap me in ambush? seize me against my will?
What on earth do you want?'
'You know, old man,'
I countered now. 'Why put me off with questions?
Here I am, cooped up on an island far too long,

Possibly the most important one, however, comes in this couplet from 'Pay in Blood': *"How I made it back home nobody knows / Or how I survived so many blows.* Dylan refers to this again in his Nobel Lecture when discussing Odysseus' journey home. After mentioning how he 'survived so many blows', Dylan continued: *"He's one against a hundred, but they'll all fall, even the strongest. He was nobody. And when it's all said and done, when he's home at last, he sits with his wife, and he tells her the stories"*. In both cases we are being encouraged to remember how Odysseus tricks the Cyclops when asked for his name:

I will tell you. But you must give me a guest-gift
as you've promised. Nobody—that's my name. Nobody—
so my mother and father call me, all my friends."

In addition, the Cyclops whom Odysseus is addressing has just drunk 'drugged wine', which is something else specifically addressed both in "Pay in Blood" *"Someone must have slipped a drug in your wine"* and in Dylan's Nobel Lecture: *"Drugs have been dropped into his wine"*.

Thomas further sees the 'Odysseus as Nobody' theme in the lines from "Early Roman Kings" that follow on immediately from ' ... house of death':
"One day you will ask for me/
There'll be no-one else that you'll want to see" Thomas makes a detailed case for this being intentional, whether he convinces you there or not, there is no ambiguity over the song's following segment:

I can strip you of life
Strip you of breath
Ship you down
To the house of death

This unquestionably comes from the same Fagles' translation, where we find: "Would to god I could strip you of life and breath / and ship you down to the House of Death".

The ancient past in the present, or in the recent past and in Dylan's lifetime, is once again the theme, here in 'Early Roman Kings'. The title refers simultaneously to the ancient Romans distributing corn to the people and a New York gang of the late Sixties and early Seventies.

Shakespeare's *Coriolanus*, set in early Roman history, opens with scenes of public disorder over the lack of such corn distribution. This was also a cause issue of riots contemporaneously in Shakespeare's hometown, where privation through lack of food was not helped by the Bard storing grain to inflate its price.

For obvious reasons the gang is commonly assumed to have been an Italian one, though this has been disputed by some. As far as this song is concerned, the Italian assumption fits in with the other Italian references and I presume Dylan takes the gang as having been so. The song also plays on past and present in other ways, this time the mafia, interleaved with a line from Juvenal. We will stick with Homer for now, however, and return to Richard Thomas and his contention that: "What I think hasn't been noticed is the song's continuing after the direct Homeric quote with creative allusion that can't be caught by the computer programs that some people out there are feeding Dylan's lyrics into. After the verbatim quotes, the singer continues "One day / You will ask for me / There'll be no one else / That you'll wanna see." "No one" is of course the Homeric speaker, and the Homeric addressee will not be seeing anyone."[30]

Thomas thinks it likely Dylan was led into "becoming Odysseus" by Ovid's identification of the same thing happening to him in *Tristia*, the very poetry of exile that Dylan mined so effectively on *Modern Times*:

"Like Dylan, Ovid was a trickster, and he was also attracted to Odysseus ("Ulysses" for the Romans), the ultimate trickster and lyre-playing teller of tales true and tall: "Sing to me, Muse, of a man full of many twists and turns," as The Odyssey begins, a fine description of Odysseus, Ovid, and Bob Dylan." As the good professor points out, Ovid, in his exile, wrote a long, wry comparison of himself with the wandering Odysseus and reckoned throughout it that his own fate was far worse than his fictional Greek forerunner's. This comparison concluded with the lines:

He had his loyal companions
His faithful crew: my comrades deserted me
at the time of my banishment. He was making for his homeland,
A cheerful victor: I was driven from mine—
fugitive, exile, victim. My home was not some Greek island,
Ithaca, Samos— to leave them is no great loss—
but the City that from its seven hills scans the world's orbit,
Rome, centre of empire, seat of the gods.[31]

Professor Thomas observes that, by "the end of the fourth book of these poems, Ovid takes the comparison even further and has more or less become Odysseus, as he relives the journey" and sees the same development in Dylan: "Ovid 'transfigured' himself into Odysseus, as Dylan would say, and Dylan, who had taken on the voice of Ovid on *Modern Times*, then followed suit and on *Tempest* got himself back to where it all began—with an intertextual brilliance that shows exactly how he sees his art and how to conjure up the longdead souls of the poets he has been reading."[32] Dylan thus, on the *Tempest* album, finishes the journey he started when, in live performances, he replaced Ovid lines with Homer's in 'Workingman's Blues #2'.

Further support for his theory comes from the album cover, which features a river-goddess from the base of the Pallas-Athene Fountain statue outside the Parliament building in Vienna. Athene, known in *The Odyssey* as Athena, Pallas Athena or Pallas, is the protective Goddess of Odysseus.[33] More grist to the mill is added because, while performing songs from *Tempest*, Dylan has had, as Thomas explains: "a classical statue next to him onstage. It is a river goddess, a likeness of a statue group of Pallas Athena ... The same river goddess is on the cover of Tempest. Why? I would say because Dylan transfigured into Odysseus, the wandering survivor of so many blows, quite naturally has with him a statue associated with the goddess, has taken her on as his divine patron."[34]

Odysseus was still on Dylan's mind in the year following his Nobel lecture. In that lecture, referring to *The Odyssey*, he had said: *"You too have shared a bed with the wrong woman. You too have been spellbound by magical voices, sweet voices with strange melodies."* In interviews, he kept up the same connecting train of thought. In March 2017, Dylan used the subject of Joan Baez to return to Odysseus. On Dylan's official website, there was a "Q&A" with Bill Flanagan, which included a question so preposterously out of the blue and inappropriate that one has no doubt that the same person that answers it, in effect, posed it:

BF   What do you think of Joan Baez?

BD   *She was something else, almost too much to take. Her voice was like that of a siren from off some Greek island. Just the sound of it could put you into a spell. She was an enchantress. You'd have to get yourself strapped to the mast like Odysseus and plug up your ears so you wouldn't hear her. She'd make you forget who you were.*[35]

Thomas rightly shows how Dylan identifies himself with Odysseus in his Nobel Lecture, because you inevitably think of Dylan when you read, or hear Dylan, describing someone *"on that long journey home", "He's a travelin' man, but he's making a lot of stops"*, and *"rambled this country all around"*.

I would like to add that the focus on "winds" in the speech's depiction of Odysseus is also very Dylanesque. "He's trying to get back home, but he's tossed and turned by the winds. Restless winds, chilly winds, unfriendly winds. He travels far, and then he gets blown back."[36] Winds have always been very key to Dylan's career, and pivotal, career-changing, art-defining classics have 'wind' in the title. 'Blowin' in the Wind', 'Idiot Wind' and 'Caribbean Wind'. Many famous lines involve the wind, such as: *"You don't need a weather man/To know which way the wind blows"*. One of the many "in" jokes on the *"Love And Theft"* album is to hear Dylan sing, *"Sometimes it's just plain stupid/To get into any kind of wind"* in 'Floater (Too Much To Ask)'. While, in 'Make You Feel My Love' Dylan sings a verse not unlike his description of Odysseus in the Nobel Lecture, twenty years later:

The storms are raging on the rolling sea
And on the highway of regret
The winds of change are blowing wild and free
You ain't seen nothing like me yet

It is noteworthy, that with his lines from *The Odyssey* in 'Roll on John', Dylan could be seen as bringing to John Lennon a similar identification with Odysseus. If this were the case, it would, added to the other accolades for Lennon's work, interleaved as they are with lines from the revolutionary, genius English artist-poet William Blake, turn this tribute into something of extraordinary stature. I am not fully convinced that is what is going on here. This is because so much is happening in this deceptively simple song that its overall intent seems less clear than it would first appear. On closer listening, the song becomes either more diffuse or more complex depending on the level of one's appreciation of the track. A line such as *"down in the quarry with the quarrymen"* suggests that there must be more to it than first meets the ear. Dylan is clearly drawing our attention to a second use of 'quarry' over and above its role in the name of an early Beatles incarnation, the name of which was taken from the local school anthem and provided a nice pun on 'rock'. A sad note, in passing, that quarry is much used in Fagles' translation of *The Odyssey* as the word for that which is hunted. Poor John Lennon was a 'quarry man' in more ways than one.

310

A quick reminder of the phrases straight from Homer: *"Rags on your back just like any other slave/ They tied your hands and they clamped your mouth"*, *"Your bones are weary, you're about to breathe your last"* *"You been cooped up on an island far too long"*. The first two lines here occur in a verse that seems far removed from the ongoing story of Lennon's life:

Sailin' through the trade winds bound for the south
Rags on your back just like any other slave
They tied your hands and they clamped your mouth
Wasn't no way out of that deep dark cave

Not only are the middle two lines from *The Odyssey* but the last one probably, given all the other references, is at least on one level, a nod to the Cyclops' cave. By bringing his identification with Odysseus into a tribute to Lennon, Dylan is, inadvertently I would presume to suggest, opening up the possibility, if this proves to be his last non-covers album, of a future filled with wild theories of Dylan (as Odysseus/Lennon) bidding farewell to his art in a way that would match those of Shakespeare bidding farewell to his art in *The Tempest*.

Ovid has not disappeared entirely. Scott Warmuth traces the lines *"Nothing is more wretched than what I must endure"* and *"They strip your useless hopes away"*, from "Pay in Blood" back to Ovid. Additionally that song, in particular, though also the album in general, certainly portrays a level of savage violence similar to that which the artistic director of the RSC, Gregory Doran, posits as Ovid's attraction for Shakespeare.[37] Although violence is hardly restricted to Ovid alone, there are times when his victims and perpetrators come to mind. As well as a large number of violent deaths, the album features some eye-opening phrases. 'Pay in Blood', delivered with a magnificently, menacing swagger, includes the unforgettable: *"I got something in my pocket make your eyeballs swim/I got dogs that could tear you limb from limb."* These are visceral enough on the album but were taken to an even more gut-wrenching level as Dylan toured in the years following the album's release with his set list revolving around *Tempest* tracks, which were carefully placed at pivotal points in the set.

Another classicist who made his way onto the songs on *Tempest* is someone we've noted in Dylan's work before: Juvenal. Scott Warmuth posited a possible connection between Dylan's *"Gonna put you on trial in a Sicilian court,"* to Juvenal, *Satire 6*, "Her household's governed with all the savagery/ Of a Sicilian court". While this may seem far-fetched at first, Susanna Morton Braund's translation Warmuth is quoting from here has provided the source for Dylan lines previously, and there are others on this album. Also from *Satire 6*, we have, "the pimp was already dismissing his girls" which brings a line from 'Tempest' to mind: *"Davey the brothel keeper / Came out, dismissed his girls"*.[38] As monolithic a presence as the Classic writers appear, and yet more references pepper *Masked and Anonymous* and recent Dylan interviews, perhaps an even greater impact on the two bards' work has come from the Bible. Needless to say, it also holds great sway in 'the two tempests'. We will look at these in turn, beginning with Dylan's album.

Tempest and *The Bible*

In his 2012 *Rolling Stone* interview Dylan commented, regarding *Tempest*, that: "It's not the album I wanted to make, though. I had another one in mind. I wanted to make something more religious." Perhaps because I am so accustomed to him playing games in his interviews, I took this as Dylan cutely drawing attention to the strong religious imagery and themes that run throughout *Tempest*. Sometimes it is quite subtle and almost subliminal, yet at other points it is very much to the fore. Biblical imagery occurs throughout the album, unsurprisingly from someone who still refers to Jesus as "our Lord" in that same interview, but is most highly concentrated in selected songs. 'Narrow Way' is a prime example. This song uses as its base a biblical passage that has appeared in previous Dylan songs, most hauntingly in 1979's impassioned 'When He Returns': *"Truth is an arrow and the gate is narrow that is passes through"* The Biblical text is:

13 Enter ye in at the strait gate: for wide is the gate, and broad is the way, that leadeth to destruction, and many there be which go in thereat:

14 because strait is the gate, and narrow is the way, which leadeth unto life, and few there be that find it.

(Matthew 7:13-14)

It is a passage that is also alluded to in a Hank Williams' song, 'I Saw the Light', which ends:

I was a fool to wander and astray
Straight is the gate and narrow the way
Now I have traded the wrong for the right
Praise the lord I saw the light.

Dylan said to Jon Pareles in 1997: "I believe in Hank Williams singing 'I Saw the Light.' I've seen the light, too."[39]

'Narrow Way' also includes a direct reference to the Eucharist, *"For a drink of wine and a crust of bread"* as well as references to grace, to Jesus, possibly to the Resurrection or at least the fear of non-Resurrection as a doubt-filled Christ struggles with his thoughts in the desert. Moreover, the narrator is heard to be dragging a plough and, that old Dylan favourite, *"drinking from an empty cup"* (there are those doubts again), among many other biblical echoes. *"Look down angel, from the skies, help my weary soul to rise,"* sings Dylan, in a sentiment he has expressed at other times. Dylan's song ends with a renunciation of violence and a move toward reconciliation that mirrors Prospero at the end of *The Tempest*.

'Pay in Blood' is another one of the most biblically inflected, as well as one of the most Homeric, tracks on the album. It packs a mighty double punch, fittingly enough for a song that functions as the engine-room of the album and was central to so many live shows in the years that followed its release.

The phrase 'pay in blood' itself, over and above any other connotations it evokes, has to put one in mind of Jesus paying for the sins of humankind with His blood. It is inconceivable that the connotation would not occur to Dylan even if he also means something else by it. The song overall addresses the violence of the image, rather than anything obviously sacred, but the but the connection is unavoidably there. The image of Christ's blood purifying the sins of others recurs throughout the Bible but I would take particular note of *Revelation* 1:5, as *The Book of Revelation*, it seems to me, is the key biblical text on this album: "and washed us from our sins in his own blood" . In his interview with *Rolling Stone* when the album was released, Dylan named a number of books that were important for his imagery but he elected to place

The Book of Revelation in pole position and in isolation before going on to add the others:

RS: Clearly, the language of the Bible still provides imagery in your songs.

BD: *Of course, what else could there be? I believe in the Book of Revelation. I believe in disclosure, you know? There's truth in all books. In some kind of way. Confucius, Sun Tzu, Marcus Aurelius, the Koran, the Torah, the New Testament, the Buddhist sutras, the Bhagavad-Gita, the Egyptian Book of the Dead, and many thousands more. You can't go through life without reading some kind of book.*

A number of interpretations have drawn differing conclusions; most convincingly Richard Thomas' Odysseus attribution. It is not only perfectly possible, but characteristically the case, that Dylan, like Shakespeare, can be making both a classical and biblical allusion with the same phrase and hence, by utilising this technique, be dealing with ancient history, the time of the American Civil war and today, simultaneously.

As with all the plays and albums in both Shakespeare and Dylan's later careers, one can hear echoes of their earlier work. *"I could stone you to death for the wrongs that you done"* brings 'Rainy Day Women #12 and 35' to mind with its associated biblical backdrop (see chapter 4). While the phrase *"Man can't live by bread alone"* from 'Narrow Way' recalls a couplet from "Something's Burning Baby": *"You can't live by bread alone, you won't be satisfied/You can't roll away the stone if your hands are tied"*; both drawing on that Biblical commonplace.

"I'm sworn to uphold the laws of God", is growled defiantly in another line and we hear two of Dylan's most street-wise re-phrasings of biblical matters since the opening verse of 1965's 'Highway 61 Revisited'. Firstly we have a 'prove that you are the Son of God' challenge : *"You've got the same eyes that your mother does/If only you could prove who your father was"* and then the downright blunt: *"I saw you buried and I saw you dug up"*.

The biblical allusions are particularly strong in the album's final two songs or, as I tend to hear them, 'the final song and the epilogue'. The title track 'Tempest' is studded with lines and images of the Bible. Dylan delivers a rich, nuanced vocal that sounds all-knowing and all-encompassing as he delivers lyrics which contrastingly display, on the surface at least, a surprising naivety.

There is no solace for the victims of the appalling tragedy, however, or at least not in the sense of understanding the Divine Plan behind it. As ever in such situations, we are left with: *"But there is no understanding / For the judgement of God's hand."* It is sung majestically and beautifully, but for all that such aphorisms appear to be the flimsiest of flimsy cop-outs to the non-faithful. Nonetheless, that is still less distressing than the widely held, and much sung, theory that the sinking was divine punishment for man's hubris in believing he had built an unsinkable ship.

The theme of the Apocalypse, which had been prominent in Dylan songs for over half a century by this point, is still strong on 'Tempest'. *"The promised hour was near"* and *"'The veil was torn asunder'"* Dylan solemnly intones, and most crucially of all, when singing of the Captain: *"He read the Book of Revelation / And he filled his cup with tears."*

The beginning of Christ's life is signified by the lines, *"He saw the starlight shining / Streaming from the east"* and the couplet, *"The veil was torn asunder / Between the hours of twelve and one"* links the sinking of the Titanic to the moment of His death. The *King James Version* records, in Mathew 27, that: "And Jesus cried out again with a loud voice, and yielded up His spirit. Then, behold, the veil of the temple was torn in two from top to bottom; and the earth quaked, and the rocks were split...".

The inclusion of the song 'Roll on John', after what seems the natural album closing track, 'Tempest', raises a number of questions. For a considerable number of people, those questions can only be answered by positing another John, or other Johns, to join the ex-Beatle, John Lennon, in the verses, primarily St John the Apostle.

For a variety of reasons, the homage to John Lennon does seem a rather odd choice for Dylan to have made as the closing track of *Tempest*. Firstly, there's the time element, as it was released over twenty-two years after the former Beatle was slain. This topic was broached in the 2012 *Rolling Stone* interview in which Dylan suggested that it had been written some time previously:

RS You also have a song about John Lennon, "Roll on John," on this album. What moved you to record this now?

BD *I can't remember – I just felt like doing it, and now would be as good a time as any. I wasn't even sure that song fit on this record. I just took a chance and stuck it on there. I think I might've finished it to include it. It's not like it was just written yesterday. I started practicing it late last year on some stages.*

Dylan and Lennon's relationship was a mixture of admiration, commonality and a huge dose of rivalry. Dylan's admiration for the Beatles' early work is well known and documented, as is the fact that the Beatles all looked up to him. It is a mutual admiration that still continues with the surviving Beatles. Dylan remarked, in 2007, that: "*... to this day, it's hard to find a singer better than Lennon was, or than McCartney was and still is. I'm in awe of McCartney. He's about the only one that I'm in awe of. He can do it all. And he's never let up. He's got the gift for melody, he's got the gift for rhythm, he can play any instrument. He can scream and shout as good as anyone, and he can sing a ballad as good as anyone. And his melodies are effortless, that's what you have to be in awe of.... he's just so damn effortless. I just wish he'd quit (laughs). Everything that comes out of his mouth is just framed in melody.*" On hearing this Paul McCartney was particularly pleased because, as he put it: "we all thought Bob was the coolest".

They certainly did. Back in the Sixties, Lennon talked about *The Freewheelin' Bob Dylan:* "For three weeks in Paris, we didn't stop playing it, we all went potty about Dylan." Starr and McCartney admired Dylan greatly, while George Harrison simply adored him. Harrison once told Tom Petty that Dylan "is so great he makes Shakespeare look like Billy Joel". This was said in jest, no doubt, but you sometimes wonder to what degree, given Harrison's attitude toward Dylan. As for Lennon, if anything he took things even further because he clearly wanted to *be* Dylan. Dylan's influence on Lennon's song-writing was immediate, profound and long-lasting. Lennon produced the Dylanesque song of sexual intrigue "Norwegian Wood" and Dylan responded to that with his superb song, of considerably more complex sexual intrigue, 'Fourth Time Around' on *Blonde on Blonde.* At first, this went down very badly with Lennon, though his opinion changed later:

"I was very paranoid about Dylan's version of it. I remember he played it to me when he was in London. He said, 'What do you think?' I said, 'I don't like it.' I didn't like it. I was very paranoid. I just didn't like what I was feeling.

I thought it was an out and out skit, you know, but it wasn't. It was great. I mean, he wasn't playing any tricks on me. I was just going through the bit."[40]

Lennon always seemed to be "going through the bit" with Dylan. In the mid-Sixties, their lives, the kind of music they were playing, their fame and their status came together briefly, but this did not last. Their paths became very different, and Lennon always seemed aggrieved, in the nineteen seventies, that Dylan was on a different one to him. A resentment doubtless whetted by the obvious sway that Dylan's writing had on his own, while there was nary a sign of a counter lyrical influence.

Lennon continued, for the rest of his cruelly short life, to veer from resentment to admiration in precisely the manner of that quote from his 1968 interview with *Rolling Stone*. For every comment praising Dylan, there were put downs, jibes and parodies studded with mocking mimicry. You are reminded of Ben Jonson's comments on Shakespeare as they see-sawed between taunts and praise. The more this went on, the more it was clear that Lennon must still be in Dylan's thrall, which would inevitably lead to another bout of bad-feeling from Lennon.

Lennon's last parodies of Dylan, some versions of which circulated amongst collectors before being released on official posthumous collections, were of Dylan's 'Gotta Serve Somebody'. In public, Lennon had spoken out in defence of Dylan's right to become a Christian, singing songs of his faith. Lennon was puzzled by it, but said that Dylan should be allowed to do his own thing. However, either from the album, *Slow Train Coming* and/or Dylan's Saturday Night Live appearance playing 'Gotta Serve Somebody', Lennon got the inspiration for a mean-spirited parody, called 'Serve yourself' of which he went to the trouble of making no fewer that twelve versions, over the next year. Yoko Ono, rather unconvincingly, tried to explain it away as a joke, but Lennon's view was clear from the considerably more succinct diary entry for September the fifth, 1979: 'Gotta Serve Somebody'... guess he wants to be a waiter now."

Dylan, you would think, would have been hurt, but perhaps he was long used to barbs and parodies by then and, anyway, he would have expected that there would be the compensatory praise to come as Lennon's cycle of admiration and resentment spun round again. This time, however, that spinning cycle was stopped by a bullet.[41]

It is illuminating to compare 'Roll on John' with 'Lenny Bruce', another tribute song to a dead icon that came out long after the time of death. Bruce died on August 3, 1966, and the song was released on 1981's *Shot of Love*. Those of us lucky enough to have seen the European leg of the 1981 World Tour were treated to pre-release live versions. Many devoted Dylan fans heartily dislike the song. I have always had a soft spot for it, but I have found myself in a small minority in this regard. The reasons given for disliking it are that it is clichéd, sentimental and simple to the point of being simple-minded. Yet that is not how I hear it. Dylan sings it powerfully and movingly. The lines *"they stamped him and labelled him"* surely sum up exactly what both Bob Dylan and Lenny Bruce hated and was what Dylan was so fiercely fighting against at the time of Bruce's passing. The lines: *"he sure was funny, and he sure told the truth, / and he knew what he was talking about"* are a marvellous tribute and exactly the kind of thing one would aspire to have on one's gravestone. One is a fine tribute on its own, but both combined produce something exceptional for which to be remembered and it is this that the song duly celebrates. Incidentally, that combination of veracity and humour is also a perfect summary of the role of a Shakespearean Fool.

The Lennon/Beatles history that Dylan recounts in this song is extremely 'clichéd', perhaps to evoke the TV coverage of Lennon's death through the repetitive short clips rolling around on 24-hour news. Or perhaps it is meant to reflect the way modern history comes pre-packaged now, in TV 'sight-bites'. We know by heart the stock footage that depicts the early 1960s: civil rights marches/ police with Alsatian dogs attacking blacks who were protesting in the South/Martin Luther King's speech in Washington, an event at which Dylan and Baez sang his songs together. Perhaps with 'Blowin' in the Wind' playing in the background as the newsreel clips run. Then there are the later Sixties: Vietnam war being summed up in about three minutes showing: the dropping of Agent Orange/Napalm strikes/ the naked girl running from the burning village/ the anti-war protesters/ napalm strikes with Jimi Hendrix singing Dylan's "All Along the Watchtower" in the background / Americans and their allies scrambling to escape from the US Embassy building/ Fade to black. This has become the way that complex, multi-year history is portrayed. It is the tele-visual equivalent of fast food.

There are a number of references in the song, however, that do not fit, either easily or at all, with any history of Lennon, potted or otherwise: 'island', 'cave', 'slave', 'voyage,' that curious double-use-in-one-line of "quarry" and the entire penultimate verse.[42]

Neither Manhattan nor Britain make sense regarding the way 'island' is used, explanations for the relevance of 'cave' and 'slave' to Lennon's life have not been convincing, and while Lennon did make a vital voyage, you do not feel that is what is being alluded to here. Though, intriguingly enough for this chapter, it was a life-changing voyage to Bermuda, as this account explains.[43]

These non-Lennon references are the signal for the emergence of biblical readings of the song. Leading on from the Watchman on the preceding track, 'Tempest', reading the *Book Of Revelation*, it has been posited that 'John' sometimes refers to John Lennon and sometime to the accredited author of that book, St John the Apostle. I believe that it was long-term Dylan commentator, John Stokes who first proposed this to me, in a private e-mail, and others were to follow, with Kees de Graaf, in particular, writing extensively on this interpretation. In this view, the island is Patmos, the quarry is where the Apostle, now in his nineties, was subjected to forced labour, and the voyage is the one that brought him from Ephesus to Patmos. He was indeed 'a slave', 'in rags' and so, at this point, there does seem to be a great deal going for the theory. The explanation of the cave is not persuasive, however:

"However, when it says: 'Wasn't no way out of that deep dark cave' this also means that there is at the same time something positive and uplifting in this phrase. John was now ready to receive this vision and could not leave that cave until he had written down on a scroll all that 'he saw and heard'. John's sworn testimony about how he received the messages is written down in the first chapter of the Book of Revelation."

The cave seems far more likely to fit another set of references, which de Graff acknowledges, that of the Cyclops in *The Odyssey*. Homer's lines, as mentioned previously, are peppered throughout this song and cover 'the island', 'the slave in rags', 'the ambush', 'weary bones' and 'breathing last'. The effect is of Dylan being Odysseus-like. This song's mythic presentation of Lennon has been viewed in the same way as many heard 'Lenny Bruce', that is, as being about its author as well as the dead comedian.

Speaking of the cave, this takes us back not just to *The Odyssey* and Cyclops, but also to *The Aeneid* and to *The Tempest*'s theme of Ferdinand and Miranda as an opposite mirroring of Aeneas and Dido. The latter pair consummated their love with sex, outside marriage, in a cave and it is this that Ferdinand refers to when he rejects the temptations of fornication: "*the murkiest den ... shall never melt/Mine honour into lust*". The only 'cheating' that goes on in their cave is when he plays Miranda falsely at chess. Add this to the 'voyage to Bermuda', and you begin to again ponder the relationship between the island of this song and that of Shakespeare's play.

Whether you incline towards John the Apostle, Homer or a mixture of both to accommodate the non-Lennon lines, you are still left with a verse that does not chime with any combination of Beat, Biblical or Homeric interpretation. I am referring to the penultimate stanza with its opening three lines:

"*Roll on, John, roll through the rain and snow*
Take the right-hand road and go where the buffalo roam
They'll trap you in an ambush before you know"

While it is true that Lennon was 'ambushed', there was no "they" involved, instead the murder was committed by a loner, and, in any case, 'the buffalo roam' and 'right hand road', between them, unmoor us from all previous referents. Kees de Graaf quotes one theory covering this and thus brings to three the number of "Johns" in his interpretation:

"I want to give special thanks to Dave Richards who pointed out to me that the 'John' referred to this verse may refer to John Smith, (1580-1631) who was an Admiral of New England, a soldier, explorer, and author. Smith is said to have played an important role in the establishment of the first permanent English settlement in North America. Apart from the Indian tribes, the local weather is said to have been the biggest threat for these early Jamestown settlers. That is why it says '*roll on John through the rain and snow*'; Dave Richardson pointed out to me that 'Pocahontas, daughter of the chief of the Powhatan Indian tribe, warned Smith about her tribe's plot to ambush and kill John Smith in 1608, when this Powhatan tribe invited them to their land on supposedly friendly terms'; This may be the reason why it says: '*they trap you in an ambush before you know*'.

'John' Lennon and 'John' Smith and 'John' the Apostle may have in common that their lifetime work was done far away from their home land, across the sea and both Smith and Lennon led a sort of British invasion. The invasion that John the Apostle led was of much greater importance, it hugely set up the invasion of the gospel throughout the entire world."[44]

This may be an ingenious theory, but neither it, nor the combination of the elements of the song I have discussed, sit easily with me. As with many of the detailed interpretations claiming that the epilogue in *The Tempest* shows Prospero/Shakespeare as a Catholic sympathiser or Prospero as the Antichrist incarnate in the figure of the Pope, I feel I am being taken very far away from the experience of encountering the song or the play. In trying to analyse why this is so, I end up, as always do by returning to performances.

Shakespeare and Dylan raise questions, and they do not often answer them, or at least not textually. The raising is enough, and it is often the whole point. To come to terms with these questions, you have to trust the performance you are currently witnessing or considering. We do not have the luxury of any Shakespeare performance directed by him, or with him acting in it, but his play-texts act as a guide to directors and actors on how they can perform certain parts of the play. They are not bound to follow his embedded guidance, but it is often there and always invaluable.[45] We will be looking at one of these when discussing the moment Prospero asserts that he forgives his brother, only to immediately undercut what he has just uttered. We do, on the other hand, have Dylan singing "Roll on John" and in more than one version.

The album version opens quite beautifully with thoughtful, melancholic falling chords. Dylan's knowing, sad vocal is immensely expressive, especially of the title phrase. Also, just to hear Dylan intone the famous Beatle line: "I heard the news today, oh boy..." is irresistibly moving for those of us of a certain age and background, and the expressiveness of his finishing phrase is spine tingling. It is only when you pay closer attention to the words that seemingly non-fitting references in some of the lines strike you. In particular, the verse with the mention of roaming buffalo, and its sudden switch from sea to road travel.

Dylan first played 'Roll On, John' live at Blackpool, forty-five miles north of Liverpool, on the same coast facing out to America across the ocean, on

November 24, 2013. Unusually, after years of varying his set-list from night to night, Dylan had settled on a standard set in which the closing songs were 'All Along the Watchtower' and 'Blowin' in the Wind'. As the former ended, and the crowd prepared for the latter, Dylan slipped, instead, into a song from an album half a century later. This was a soft, intimate rendition of 'Roll on John' and Dylan dropped the penultimate stanza entirely. With that absent, it felt much more of a straightforward tribute to Lennon, despite the other lyrics that seem to come from, and refer to, other stories still being present.

There was a cheer of recognition as the music began. Debuts are always acclaimed in Dylan concerts and are usually a surprise, but this particular one was hoped for, almost expected even, in this location. An even louder cheer greeted the first mention of the title phrase (and it was acclaimed on repetition, thereafter). The applause intensified after the *"From the Liverpool docks to the red-light Hamburg streets"* line, and it was quite clear those cheering had no critical words such as 'cliché' or 'sentimental' in their minds. Two nights later, in London, the version was different again, as, blessedly, is the case when following Dylan tours. If anything, this one was even more wistfully intimate and Dylan's diction became far clearer as the song progressed. Once more, there was no doubt that the majority of the audience was taking it as a straight Dylan tribute to a dead Beatle. Again the "buffalo" verse was dropped. A minority may also have been thinking of St John the Apostle, and an even smaller minority may have thought of the Homer intertextuality, but you somehow doubt it was more than a very few, if any. At the next show, the final song reverted to 'Blowin' in the Wind'. 'Roll on John' has not been played live since that night.

The epilogue to Shakespeare's *The Tempest*, like this epilogue to Dylan's album, *Tempest*, provokes heated debate over potential religious readings. Interestingly, epilogues were not always part of the performance in Shakespeare's day. Indeed, they may have only appeared on set occasions or in certain locales. Similarly, many Dylan fans I know either never play or do not regularly play 'Roll on John'. Just like Dylan, they are *'not sure if that song fits on this record'*. Instead, they stop the album after the end of the title track; though others I know are appalled by this behaviour. Both play and album are significantly altered by the inclusion, or exclusion, of their respective 'epilogues'.

The Tempest and The Bible

When discussing *The Tempest*, Doctor Charles Moseley of Cambridge University remarked: "This is absolutely unquestionable: the twin pillars on which Western culture is built, which Shakespeare can take for granted, are the Bible and the Classics. It is sheer folly to ignore that fact. It is not my business to tell you what to believe, but it is my business to tell you what you should know." Biblical phrases and themes appear throughout, from a passing point to the all-embracing movement of the entire play. Caliban remembers how Prospero taught him *'to name the bigger light, and how the less, that burn by day and night'.* Shakespeare's original audience would pick up on the reference to *Genesis 1:16: 'God then made two great lights: the greater light to rule the day, and the lesser light to rule the night'.* It probably now goes unnoticed by many, perhaps most, in the UK and other Western European nations. For centuries, The Bible was a source that did not even need to be thought about, it was just there. This is a situation that has changed for many, though certainly not for Dylan nor, perhaps, a significant portion of his audience, in America at least. Larger story arcs, however, are still recognisable to all, and the late romances in Shakespeare all share a similar movement that is suffused with biblical import.

Shakespeare's play is a profound exploration of the key concepts of mercy and forgiveness. The play on one level is a deep meditation on the nature of these and their qualities of transcendence. Given his time and society, it is obvious that Shakespeare would view these concepts primarily in a Christian light. All the major characters in the play have someone to forgive and/or mercy to entreat. There is a movement from disruptive crime or sin to reconciliation, forgiveness and re-unification by way of a period of suffering, loss and searching. This is both the model for classical epics and for *The Bible*. The spiritual pattern is clear: innocence, sin, exile, suffering, repentance, penance, mercy, forgiveness and ultimate joy and reconciliation. The late romances are often viewed as a multi-play meditation on these transcendent qualities of mercy and forgiveness.

In *The Tempest*, this move to forgiveness and reconciliation is inspired by the spirit, Ariel. Ariel, unlike fallen humankind, can hear the heavenly music of the spheres. Ariel it is who steers the revenge-driven Prospero onto a path of virtue and mercy. Having trapped and tormented Prospero's enemies, as instructed, Ariel pities them and tells Prospero: *"if you beheld them now, your affections / Would become tender."* Prospero seems taken aback by the suggestion: *"Does thou think so spirit?"* Ariel convinces him with a devastatingly simple phrase that carries profound insight: *"Mine would, sir, were I human."* Stung into clarity by this, Prospero pivots away from tragic revenge toward mercy and the play can thus now move on to a resolution akin to the comic tradition:

> *And mine shall.*
> *Hast thou, which art but air, a touch, a feeling*
> *Of their afflictions, and shall not myself,*
> *One of their kind, that relish all as sharply*
> *Passion as they, be kindlier moved than thou art?*
> *Though with their high wrongs I am struck to th' quick,*
> *Yet with my nobler reason, 'gainst my fury*
> *Do I take part. The rarer action is*
> *In virtue than in vengeance.*

(Act V Scene i)

Forgiveness is to replace vengeance and all are to be reconciled. That at least is the aim, and that is how the play is often summarised. Shakespeare being Shakespeare, to our eternal gratitude, does not portray life's great questions as susceptible to such easy answers. As ever in *The Tempest,* you can make a very good case for this, but it is not the whole story. It certainly is the major movement of the play, and the crucial moral arc, but it is not unquestioned nor is it achieved with full success. Alonso sees the error of his ways, repents and is forgiven; so far, so good. Prospero says he forgives all, but it is almost impossible to perform the following exchange without the old rancour immediately pulling the rug from under the feet of his "Welcome all", given words such as, "infect" and "rankest":

PROSPERO *Welcome, my friends all!*

[Aside to SEBASTIAN and ANTONIO]
>   *But you, my brace of lords,*
>   *were I so minded,*
>   *I here could pluck his highness' frown upon you*
>   *And justify you traitors: at this time*
>   *I will tell no tales.*

SEBASTIAN   *The devil speaks in him!*

PROSPERO   *No.*
>   *For you, most wicked sir, whom to call brother*
>   *Would even infect my mouth, I do forgive*
>   *Thy rankest fault - all of them - and require*
>   *My dukedom of thee, which perforce I know*
>   *Thou must restore.*

(Act V Scene i)

Antonio and Sebastian may have signalled some manner of repentance on stage in the original production, but we will never know if that were the case. There is no indication of it in the text we have. Antonio has his crown and dukedom taken from him by Prospero; but he neither asks for forgiveness nor proactively returns what he usurped. You wonder what this means for the future. More than any other play, *The Tempest* leaves you wondering about the future.

What happens to Caliban, for example, is a question that exercises the mind. Does he stay behind and re-inherit the island and there "seek grace" or does Prospero's acknowledgement that this "thing of darkness" is "mine" mean that Caliban will be with Prospero? It should be noted, too, that Prospero's reaction to Caliban's admission of folly and determination to "seek grace" is a curt "Go to, away", as he orders Caliban and the drunken plotters off to 'handsomely trim' his cell as a precondition to pardoning them.

How will Ferdinand and Miranda's idealistic marriage, brought about by magic trickery, after all, to fulfil Prospero's dynastic scheming, sustain itself in the real world? Ferdinand attempted to dupe Miranda at chess. Clearly, a deliberate point was being made here as there is no plot reason that necessitates it. Are we to take it as an omen that Ferdinand will not be faithful or just that a life of politics awaits them with its inherent deceit and falsehood? Many questions throng in our heads as we leave the theatre, but the most nagging ones of all surround the figure of the unapologetic Antonio.

Prospero's forgiveness had initially been conditional on the penitence of all who had committed crimes against him, but neither Sebastian nor Antonio proffer any. Prospero goes ahead and forgives them anyway, but his anger is still palpable in the lines above. This can, and has, been interpreted as Prospero overcoming his innate anger and desire for vengeance, and reaching the full Christian ideal of forgiveness. He shows mercy even to those who have done him wrong and who refuse to repent. Yet it takes quite some dramatising to turn the ending into a scene of complete reconciliation with Antonio standing, unrepentant, on stage. Mercy and forgiveness are undoubtedly in triumphant ascendancy; however, they are not quite wholly victorious as the action ends.

The action ending is not the end of the play, however, or at least not as it is always now staged. As mentioned previously, there is an epilogue that has been the cause of much commentary and controversy. The epilogue is a source of concentrated biblical allusion that further emphasises the theme of mercy and forgiveness through the pardoning of sins and, once again, it is an area of *The Tempest* that has encouraged different, and opposing, interpretations.

The epilogue ends with a religiously infused plea that takes the customary request for applause to an entirely higher plane and merges it with the play's grand movement toward mercy and forgiveness:

And my ending is despair,
Unless I be relieved by prayer
Which pierces so, that it assaults
Mercy itself, and frees all faults.
As you from crimes would pardon'd be,
Let your indulgence set me free.

If we had previously been experiencing the epilogue as spoken by the actor playing Prospero, we are now faced with the thought that it may be Prospero speaking in character. The epilogue can be played in a variety of ways: Prospero as Prospero the character, the actor who has played Prospero speaking as himself on behalf of the cast, or Prospero speaking as Shakespeare. Further to that, for those with the biographical obsession which leads eventually to Trevor Nunn's wishful imagining, the interpretation can be: 'Prospero as the actor, and that actor being Shakespeare himself'.

There are a lot of "ifs" to be granted before getting to that last scenario, but, were we to grant them all, it certainly would give a special meaning to any performance in which that happened. This hypothetical scenario would have likely only occurred in a performance where the author got a portion of the takings, possibly the opening night in Shakespeare's time. In other words, even if the somewhat far-fetched idea of Shakespeare personally imploring the audience via the epilogue ever took place, then it is extremely unlikely to have happened at every performance. The difference in effect from when it did and did not happen would have been profound. Such an overload of biographical and meta-theatrical import, I suggest, also would leave no room for thoughts of the Bible and the intricacies of the word "indulgences" with which we are about to concern ourselves.

Punning to the last line, Shakespeare plays on the double meaning of 'indulgence'. On the one hand, he is asking the audience to indulge him with applause which will bring the entertainment to a close and free him and the rest of the cast from their duties at the playhouse. On the other hand, following on from the earlier line, *"Clap for me so I can know that I succeeded / This will pardon me for my sins"* he is making a very specific religious reference. In the Catholic confession of Christianity, 'indulgence' is also the technical term for being released from punishment for your sins. It is this remission from sin that Hamlet's father craves, because he was sent to death with an uncleansed soul. The selling of indulgences by the Catholic Church, that is, sinners buying exemption or remission from punishment, is thought to be the single biggest driver behind the Protestant Reformation. It is difficult to imagine a more loaded term on which to end the epilogue.

This usage has been taken in a wide variety of ways, from Shakespeare merely availing himself of a term well known in a country that had, after all, been Catholic for many years and whose population still were immersed in its metaphors and symbols. The master playwright and wordsmith using the perfect word that was at hand, in other words. Others though see it as very pointed and as an affirmation of Shakespeare's 'secret Catholicism' while yet others see it as linking Prospero back to dark magic and see him as a representative of the Pope as Anti-Christ. In this reading:

"Prospero has already renounced his most superstitious practices that connote the Antichristian aspect of his characterization and concomitantly the usurping power of the papacy: the storms, inversion of trees and resurrections, and he is leaving the island. He nevertheless appears obstinately Catholic in his need for the prayers of others when he begs the audience in his Epilogue: '... release me from my bands / With the help of your good hands.' He then tells them '... my ending is despair / Unless I be relieved by prayer.' (Epilogue 9–10; 15–16) These comments suggest continuing adherence to the old religion with its belief in the power of other people's prayers to aid the soul of the deceased through the pains of Purgatory. They, therefore, engage with the 1606 Oath of Allegiance that was 'intended to separate Roman Catholics who adhered to the doctrine that a pope could depose a temporal ruler from Roman Catholics who did not hold this view and could be therefore considered loyal subjects'. This implication of unreformed Roman Catholicism sets Prospero apart from Caliban, who, like a good Protestant, will seek for grace personally." [46]

This quote comes from an article by Lynn Forest-Hill, that builds on the work of Rowland Wymer and others on what Hill calls 'the Albina myth'. Although references to those works seem absent, we are assured that it "engages with a growing body of criticism that analyses early modern drama from the perspective of insular literary tradition". This foundation myth of Britain is promoted alongside the Antichrist theme as being central to *The Tempest's* meaning. However, Forest-Hill does, to her credit, acknowledge that "There are admittedly problems with using the Albina myth as an interpretive tool for *The Tempest*." I would add that the theory is not alone in that regard. In fact, there are problems with all the theories that attempt or claim to fully 'explain' the play.

Forest-Hill's article is full of historical facts, and those are fascinating in their own way, yet the conclusions it comes to are far from any feeling I have had when watching the play. Perhaps that is because I am 'a man out of time'. Forest-Hill contends that: "That audience would also have been familiar with the religious and political conflict attributed to the Antichrist in sixteenth and seventeenth-century England when this character was constantly used as a metaphor for the abuse of power by the papacy." This view is also held by others. Bernard Capp writing about the vogue for reading the *Book of Revelation* as a commentary on what was then the present, remarks that: "During the first half of Elizabeth's reign there developed a general consensus that the Pope was the Antichrist and that the end of the world was at hand".[47]

Every shade of meaning in-between embracing and denouncing Catholicism has also been fully explored and added to the large library of non-denominational Christian readings that have been published. With *The Tempest*, theories abound, and the play invites these in the same way that it inspires so many artists to use it as a basis for their own creations, whether as a source, a jumping off point, or a philosophical and poetic counterpoint. As Anne Barton wrote, in a quote that is so pithy and accurate that David Lindley begins his introduction to the *New Cambridge Shakespeare* with it: "*The Tempest* is an extraordinarily obliging work of art. It will lend itself to almost any interpretation, any set of meanings imposed upon it: it will even make them shine." She also counsels caution with her prefatory remark to those sentences: "What is remarkable, however, is the degree of plausibility which even the wildest theories seem to possess."[48]

We can add a further word of caution regarding the epilogue, and that is whether or not it was often performed. A double ruled line precedes it in the First Folio, unlike the others in that precious volume[49]. The play works beautifully without it, magnificent though it is as a closing speech. Different scholars have different ideas about when such an epilogue would have been performed. Some contend it would only have been added on for court appearances, others that it was designed for the indoor Blackfriars Theatre. Another theory, as alluded to earlier, suggests it was only played when the author was deriving a portion of the gate money. It is intriguing to think that this passage, which has been so pored over as the basis for interpretations of the play as a whole, and central to the design of so many productions in their lead-up to it, may have been originally viewed as a mere add-on for special occasions. It seems unlikely that we will ever know whether that was the case or not, with any degree of certainty, but we do know how ever-present and often performance defining it has become in our own time. Unlike Dylan's epilogue to his *Tempest*, this one is always now played.

The other major religious theme of the play is that of the Apocalypse, 'the promised end' as it was described in *King Lear*. As with Dylan, eschatological concerns are often present in Shakespeare's work, and *The Tempest* returns, just as Dylan's *Tempest* does, to those old favourites *Isaiah* and the *Book of Revelations*. The Apocalypse is one of the key strands of imagery in Shakespeare's play, though I would, however, urge some caution over the danger of taking this too far. It is one thing to deepen one's pleasure by discovering metaphors, themes and resonances that are shared with other works, myths and sacred texts but quite another to make those discoveries the entire story. The dreariest expositions on *The Tempest*, and *Tempest* alike, are those that force radically unstable texts into a straitjacket. Both Shakespeare and Dylan have always created works that raise questions and open thoughts up rather than close them down. These misreadings are exponentially increased when people propose that the works are direct biblical rewrites. That compels both texts, by nature open-ended, to be read rather than experienced in performance. Nonetheless, you can confidently state, regarding both album and play, that the *Book of Revelations* has been read and cups have been filled with tears.

The first parallel between *The Tempest* and the Apocalypse of John is that they both have the same composition. Stephen Marx summarises the four parts of this:" A) an introduction of setting and participants and movement to another world B) a pageant displaying a series of battles in which good triumphs and evil is defeated, followed by depictions of resurrection, judgement and the dissolution of the world C) a new pageant combining re-creation with marriage D) the closing of the vision and a return to the setting of this world."[50]

Secondly, there is the masque: "our revels now have ended" Prospero says, when he has to interrupt it. 'Revels' is derived from 'revelations', a connotation it has here as well as its technical usage related to the concluding, harmonious dance at court masques for noble families. [51]

The intertwining of masques and the Apocalypse goes back to the 'early Roman kings', to borrow Dylan's song title. Both reveal a message of divine import. In the case of pageantry, this was to bolster the divine right of kings. Shakespeare refers to such processions of divine royalty into London in his play *Richard II* and almost certainly took part in one himself in 1604. This was when King James could, finally, enter London in triumph as the plague threat had at last receded. The Chamberlain's Men, now to be called The King's Men, took their place in the grand procession. The words that acclaimed James upon his entry into the city were straight out of *Revelation:* "If then it was joyous with hats, hands, and hearts, lift up to heaven to crie King James, what is it now to see King James come, therefore, O worthiest of Kings as a glorious bridegroome through your Royall chamber"[52]. This was a reflection of the final advent of the highest king of all into the city of New Jerusalem with Satan, along with Gog and Magog, having been finally defeated. Christ, the bridegroom of his Church, is triumphant: *Let us be glad and rejoice, and give glory to him, for the marriage of the Lamb is come, and his wife hath made herself ready* (Revelations 19).

It is also noteworthy that Jerusalem is known as Ariel, as in *Isaiah 29*, "Ariel, the city where David dwelt" (1) ... "And the multitude of all the nations that fight against Ariel, even all that fight against her and her munition, and that distress her, shall be as a dream of a night vision" (7).

The masque is another transformation, one leading to a moment of revelation as does the Apocalypse. Edgar Alan Poe picked up on this meaning for his *The Masque of the Red Death*, with its lead character tellingly named Prince Prospero. Dr Christopher Rollason has written perceptively of this in relation to Dylan's album and Shakespeare's play:

"Haunting the album's intertextual aisles is the ghost of Edgar Allan Poe, whom I have discovered there no less than three times! The opening track, 'Duquesne Whistle', (co-written by Dylan with Robert Hunter), has the phrase "at my chamber door", which, like the title track's "nameless here for evermore", comes directly from Poe's celebrated poem 'The Raven' (as earlier referenced by Dylan in 1965's 'Love Minus Zero / No Limit'). It is worth noting that Poe's poem itself includes the word "tempest" twice, and the song 'Tempest' mourns the Titanic's dead in a lament – "Sixteen hundred had gone to rest / The good, the bad, the rich, the poor / The loveliest and the best" – that recalls another poem by Poe, 'The City in the Sea' ("Where the good and the bad and the worst and the best / Have gone to their eternal rest").[53] "

It is always good to be reminded that apparent sources need not necessarily be direct. Shakespeare can come to Dylan through Poe, or Eliot and Auden, both of whom wrote poetry inspired by *The Tempest,* and a host of others. The same is true for Blake via Ginsberg, and the Bible through Shakespeare and so forth. Rollason touches inadvertently on another secondary source when he remarks in the same piece:

"The singer-songwriter's latest opus lives and thrives under the sign of intertextuality, literary and musical – as of course does all his work, and even more so his more recent production. Such is announced by the title "Tempest" itself, which, whatever Dylan's own disclaimers, inevitably recalls Shakespeare's late-period masterpiece "The Tempest" (which Dylan had earlier cited, in the phrase "the stuff dreams are made of" from his unreleased early-Eighties song 'City of Gold")[54]."

That is not a direct quote from *The Tempest* but instead comes from the film *Casablanca's* misquote, deliberately or intentionally, of Shakespeare's phrase. Dylan has a number of lines from Humphrey Bogart films sprinkled throughout his songs, and this is another. Shakespeare's phrase is: "*We are such stuff/As dreams are made on*"[55]. The 'on' is a perfect fit for the play with its insistent meta-theatrical message. Dreams are *built upon* what the audience is viewing, that is both the real audience and the audience of the masque in the play. What we see as reality is built upon illusion. For the film *Casablanca* the 'of' ending suits the message, that is, the idea that the characters' love-story *consists of* a Hollywood fantasy and has to be abandoned for reality. This 'consists of' is also the meaning in Dylan's song.[56]

In *The Tempest* too, dreams and visions must end:

Our revels now are ended; these our actors,
As I foretold you, were all spirits, and
Are melted into air, into thin air;

And, like the baseless fabric of this vision,
The cloud-capped towers, the gorgeous palaces,
The solemn temples, the great globe itself,
Yea, all which it inherit, shall dissolve
And like this insubstantial pageant faded,
Leave not a rack behind.

(Act IV Scene i)

Steven Marx and others see the conclusion of *The Tempest* to reflect that of *Revelation*, the final book of the Bible. (I can almost feel the call of the "last album and last play" argument, intensifying here as I type this.) We are back to St John and the island of Patmos. Marx writes: "the "opening outward" from Patmos and Prospero's island dissolves barriers between seer and reader, performer and audience, vision time and "real" time. Once the New Jerusalem is reached by John, it immediately fades, and he never returns to the heavenly court." Judith E. Tonning takes this to its logical conclusion in her article: *Like this Insubstantial Pageant, Faded': Eschatology and Theatricality in The Tempest*[57], the abstract for which reads:

"This article sets the theatrical self-reflexivity of The Tempest in relation to its concern with eschatology, arguing that in Prospero's staged apocalypse (culminating in an aborted masque) the play imitates the literalist, royal interpretations of the Book of Revelation underlying the Jacobean court masque in order to expose the insufficiency of such interpretations. In their stead, the ending of the play introduces a self-conscious form of drama which, like the sacramental liturgy, seeks not to arrest and hypostatise presence, but to stir desire for eschatological encounter in and through an acceptance of the temporality and limitation of the ordinary."

For Lynn Forest-Hill, with her combination of the foundation myth of Britain and Prospero as the Papal Anti-Christ, this all adds to her theory that: "The train of revelation that emerges in *The Tempest* may be seen as mimetic ... the process by which the nation moved from the earliest form of 'primitive' Christianity, to willing servitude under Roman Catholic hegemony, through awakening resentment, to a more rational selfhood grounded in the

Protestant doctrine of grace. By looking back to literary traditions, Caliban's prior claim to the Island is established in mythical terms and Prospero takes on the characteristics of an Antichrist figure as well as a usurper: a perversion of the evangelical Constance."

***

I note, therein, the term 'literary tradition' and while I do not wish to demean that, literary tradition is one thing, but for a dramatist, it is the creation of live performances that matters. The director and cast have to decide how they will present the main characters, the pivotal lines and the ending. It is over forty years now since I first saw a performance of *The Tempest* and the many and varied productions I have since witnessed were all different in tone and import, even when seeing the same version at different times. The text in performance is infinitely variable.

Even one line can change the whole ambience and meaning of the experience. *"This thing of darkness, I acknowledge mine"*, for example. Certain productions heavily emphasised a psychoanalytical reading and the line was Prospero's acceptance of the bestial part of his human nature. In one of the Prospero-as-nasty-colonist versions, the line was, chillingly, about an enslaved Afro-American. It is difficult for 'literary tradition' to manage such malleable text. This is particularly so when there are no words at all, but only action. A noteable example of this was in the RSC production where Simon Russell Beale's Ariel spat in Prospero's face upon being granted his freedom. Those who witnessed this were shocked into a new interpretation.

The last few productions I have attended of the play have all been strikingly different in tone and effect. The first of the two 2016 productions that I saw was at The Wanamaker Theatre at the Globe. Designed to replicate the experience of visiting the Blackfriars theatre in Shakespeare's day, this magnificent indoor, wooden, candlelit arena is such a thing of beauty that you are transported even before the stage magic begins. This was Dominic Dromgoole's farewell as artistic director at the Globe and was a brave choice given that 2013's *The Tempest* there, with the wonderful Roger Allam as Prospero, had been so wildly and widely acclaimed. He knew what he was doing, though, and it was a subtle interpretation with Pippa Nixon's marvellously nuanced Ariel bringing out many of the themes and concerns of the play to a powerful emotional effect. Trinculo and Stephano engaged in the kind of audience interaction that can make their minor roles so crucial to the overall impact and this was carried forward, to a far greater degree, in the next production I saw that year.

This was at the Cambridge Shakespeare Festival, an annual event that sees forty-odd professional actors perform eight plays in two batches of four, running simultaneously, through July and August in the wonderful outdoor setting of the gardens of Cambridge Colleges.

Such prop-light locations release the directors from any obligation to provide naturalistic staging and this is intensely liberating, as the absence of any cluttering distractions results in complete focus on the action and words as brought to life by actors' bodies and tongues. The next benefit of such intimate settings is that these very actors spend much of the evening interacting with us, the audience, and thus draw us into the performance as willing participants.

Watching a play with the actors very close to the audience and in natural daylight highlights how much can be portrayed through gesture and facial movement. An intimate bond is created between audience and actors and this is fully exploited when the actors freely interact with their audience which is not separated by the infamous "fourth wall".

In Cambridge that summer, Jemima Watling was entrancing throughout as Ariel and played her with such shimmering grace that you ached for her to be given her longed-for freedom. The farewell scene with Ian Recordon's Prospero was performed with a beautiful balance of understatement that nonetheless held emotional depth and significance. There was no spitting in the eye here, though I will admit to my own being decidedly watery. Meanwhile at the other extreme of light and dark, of air and earth, we were shown an unforgettable Caliban by her brother, Lawrence Watling, who entered the play by crawling forward towards the audience with madly staring eyes and his tongue protruding. On he came, and on, and right up to the woman in the front of the picnicking area as though he were a dog about to lick her face. She bravely kept her composure as he pushed his visage so very close to touching hers with his tongue. Having shown her mettle, that particular woman was to be middle of so much interaction that she must have felt she was one of the cast by the evening's end.

The star 'interacter' of all, though, was Ella Sawyers as Trinculo in a part that is ready-made for such improvised fun. Sawyers exploited this to the full, and she remained very much in character as she ate and drank her fill from her enthusiastic pilfering of the audience's picnic rations. Such spontaneous interaction gives rise to feelings of camaraderie and shared laughter. This helps to demystify Shakespeare and return him to his original position, that of a crowd-pleasing producer of entertainment.

Then in 2017, I saw a production that could hardly have been more different. The possibility of moving plays indoors to the Blackfriars Theatre in winter created the possibility for new 'special effects' in Shakespeare's late plays. Honouring that innovative tradition, the Royal Shakespeare Company put on a spectacular, cutting-edge production featuring, amongst other digital splendours, an Ariel avatar trapped in a huge tree. Ariel was projected as a hovering, malignant harpy whose movements were controlled by an actor, in a special suit, via sensors all over his body and head. The banquet scene was another projection, one of a whole series of digital special effects throughout.

As with Dylan, the words on the page are one thing and the performative experiences are something else; something that is infinitely variable and, when live and unrecorded, both ephemeral in nature and individually unique to each audience member.

Sir Ian McKellen, interviewed by David Lindley, and quoted in the introduction to the *New Cambridge Shakespeare* edition, 2002, remarked: "I've never felt so strongly in a play that the meaning does not belong to the actor's perception of what the play is ... The audience's imagination is much, much less controlled by the actors ... than in almost any other." This reminds us of Barthes' conclusion in his famous treatise *The Death of the Author* which held that meaning ultimately resides with each recipient of a work of art: "... *the whole being of writing: a text consists of multiple writings, issuing from several cultures and entering into dialogue with each other, into parody, into contestation; but there is one place where this multiplicity is collected, united, and this place is not the author, as we have hitherto said it was, but the reader: the reader is the very space in which are inscribed, without any being lost, all the citations a writing consists of; the unity of a text is not in its origin, it is in its destination"*[58]. For a reader, yes, and this is at least as true for an audience member at a play or a concert.

Dylan does not play whole albums live, but *Tempest* songs were quickly integrated into his set-lists and came to dominate them throughout 2013. 'Pay in Blood' was a highlight on most nights, and after an uncertain start it quickly came to outstrip the album version in a downright scary live incarnation. In addition to 'Duquesne Whistle' and 'Early Roman Kings' also appearing earlier in the set, three of *Tempest's* finest songs provided an ending triplet to the main set. Each night they formed a ladder of increasing achievement. A fine 'Scarlet Town' was followed by an exquisite 'Soon After Midnight', adding subtly altered nuances to the studio version, but most transformed and transfixing was 'Long And Wasted Years' which was played as a visual and audio climax to the night (pre-encores). The song had become a dynamic delight bursting out of the short, slight and yet seemingly immense frame of Dylan standing stage centre and projecting out into infinity.

In that and following years, the songs from *Tempest* played off and around the other songs in Dylan's set-list, their new setting producing divergent resonances to those we experience when listening to them on the album release. The balance between them also altered on different nights and different legs. 'Pay in Blood' and 'Long and Wasted Years' were always central to the sets but their respective dominance of the night could vary as could how they interacted with other dramatic highlights from outwith the album, such as 'Forgetful Heart'. As with *The Tempest*, as stressed throughout this book, the words are endlessly flexible in performance.

***

To return to those words, now, and to repeat an earlier observation: the same line in a Shakespeare play or a Dylan song can reference both classical and scriptural texts simultaneously. Given that the Bible is suffused with classical thought and writing, this can occur both intentionally and unintentionally. However, it is also a deliberate effect with which Shakespeare was always adept and one that shows up increasingly in Dylan's later work.

In *The Tempest,* this effect is noticeable in everything from the grand scale to the small detail. The arc of moving from revenge to forgiveness and reconciliation is that of classical epics as well as the teaching of *The Bible.* Aeneas was supposed to follow this, although at the very end he could not bring himself to follow his father's instructions and 'spare the defeated', as it is written in the Virgil line which Dylan incorporated into 'Lonesome Day Blues'.

Shakespeare deftly entwines the classical and the scriptural when he has Ariel interrupt the lords' banquet. The reference to *The Aeneid* is combined with Ariel accusing Alonso, Antonio, and Sebastian of being "three men of sin". While even the most classically rich of scenes, the masque, has, via the symbol of the rainbow a simultaneous allusion to the divine providence of the ancient gods and the Christian one.

When I first heard Dylan sing, in 'Scarlet Town': "I touched the garment but the hem was torn", I immediately thought of the woman who was miraculously cured after touching the hem of Christ's cloak as he passed by. Wrapped up in the folk and biblical elements, I missed the classical allusions of the verse as a whole. Richard Thomas did not:

"One verse of the song, the sixth, points in its entirety to Rome and adds a new ingredient, that of Christians under Rome or in Rome:

On marble slabs and in fields of stone

You make your humble wishes known

I touched the garment but the hem was torn.

In Scarlet Town where I was born

"Marble slabs and in fields of stone" has an ancient world feel to it, perhaps the Roman Forum, while the next lines point toward biblical lands and to the woman in the Gospel of Luke 8.43–48 who makes her humble wishes known by touching the hem of Jesus's garment as Jesus passes by, and is immediately cured of her chronic bleeding. Dylan may even be channeling Sam Cooke's or some other version of the gospel song "Touch the Hem of His Garment." But the biblical and the Roman have always been side by side, ever since he saw The Robe, or stood on the stage at Hibbing High acting the role of that Roman soldier."[59]

This reminds us of Dylan's threefold vision that superimposes the present, as well as the American War of independence and Civil War, plus the period encompassing the move from Roman Republic to Empire and the coming of Christ on top of one another. For Ovid and Timrod we now have Homer and the Quaker, John Greenleaf Whittier. Whittier was a poet, pamphleteer, editor and political activist, amongst other achievements and roles, who lived for most of the nineteenth century and he was, like Dylan, influenced by Robert Burns. Whittier was, until being quoted by Dylan at least, most famous for his work on, and his writing which promoted, the abolition of slavery. Slavery is very much on Dylan's mind as that Homer line in "Roll on John" and even the briefest listen to 'Pay in Blood' will inform you. The slavery and Civil War references on *Tempest* slide, in the fashion of previous albums, from ancient history to US history and back again. In the misty past of linguistic derivation, the root word for tempest was *tempus*, which means 'time'. The word 'tempest' perhaps originally signified a storm so severe that it appeared to disrupt time, bringing chaos and flux in its wake. The theme of the past in the present keeps recurring in both *The Tempest* and *Tempest*. In the interview to coincide with the album's release, Dylan spoke passionately about slavery, the American Civil War and the continuing effect of this past on the present day:

RS Do you see any parallels between the 1860s and present-day America?

BD *The United States burned and destroyed itself for the sake of slavery. The USA wouldn't give it up. It had to be grinded out. The whole system had to be ripped out with force. A lot of killing. What, like, 500,000 people? A lot of destruction to end slavery. And that's what it really was all about. This country is just too fucked up about color. It's a distraction. People at each other's throats just because they are of a different color. It's the height of insanity, and it will hold any nation back – or any neighborhood back. Or any anything back. … It's doubtful that America's ever going to get rid of that stigmatization. It's a country founded on the backs of slaves. … It's the root cause. If slavery had been given up in a more peaceful way, America would be far ahead today. Whoever invented the idea 'lost cause'? There's nothing heroic about any lost cause. No such thing, though there are people who still believe it.*

Civil War erupts on the Titanic, in a verse of 'Tempest', in phrases taken from the Bible and that again simultaneously link the present, Civil Wars and Biblical times:

Brother rose up against brother
In every circumstance
They fought and slaughtered each other
In a deadly dance

As well as collecting numerous John Greenleaf Whittier poetic sources for lines on *The Tempest*[60], Scott Warmuth also notes that: "The sixth verse of 'Narrow Way' begins with, "This is hard country to stay alive in." I think that Dylan is referencing a key line from the 1953 film *Escape From Fort Bravo*. The film is about a Union prison fort that holds Confederate soldiers." Additionally, there are some more explicit references to the US Civil War and the War of Independence, the most obvious being in 'Narrow Way': "Ever since the British burned the White House down".[61]

The after-effects of the US Civil War were given an extra intertextual touch at the end of the second stanza of 'Tempest'. Dylan sings: "*Sailing into tomorrow/To a gilded age foretold*"[62] despite the official lyrics having "a golden age" as the lyric. *The Gilded Age: A Tale of Today* was a novel that recurring Dylan touchstone, Mark Twain, co-wrote about political corruption in the wake of the war. Noteworthily for my book, that title itself is an allusion to a passage from Shakespeare's *King John*, whose theme informs the novel:

SALISBURY

Therefore, to be possess'd with double pomp,
To guard a title that was rich before,
To gild refined gold, to paint the lily,
To throw a perfume on the violet,
To smooth the ice, or add another hue
Unto the rainbow, or with taper-light
To seek the beauteous eye of heaven to garnish,
Is wasteful and ridiculous excess.

(Act IV, scene ii)

The third major pillar of shared cultural background is that of the folk tradition in its widest sense, embracing music, fairy tales, legends and nursery rhymes

The folk tradition

Shakespeare's late romances are built from a core of Western culture's folklore, myth and fairy stories. Such romances go back to time immemorial with their tales of sorcery, children in danger, wicked stepmothers and magic islands away from everyday reality, where common perception is subverted. All of these are in *The Tempest*, alone, as are the fairytale elements of a father trying to protect his daughter, upon her reaching sexual maturity, from the wickedness in the wider world. A handsome prince even comes to marry her. We also have the biblically resonant tale of brother usurping brother, as well as a stolen crown and other themes as old as all these. The play has all the strangeness and wonder that fairy tales evoke.

Dylan's album, too, is filled with the fantastic, the supernatural, the grotesque and the mythic. He most obviously explores his folk roots in 'Tin Angel' and 'Scarlet Town', but they appear throughout the album, and all the way to the last track's title and its closing words. The title of that song is but a comma away from being identical to the folk song 'Roll On, John', which Dylan sang on the Cynthia Gooding Show in 1962 in a voice as old as he was young. John Peter Morris pointed out to me that the closing lines echo those of the old Scottish song, *I Once Loved a Lass*. That song's melody was appropriated by Dylan, along with some of its metaphorical bent, for his 'Ballad in Plain D' on 1964's *Another Side of Bob Dylan*, which makes this less likely to just be coincidence. '*I Once Loved a* Lass', ends:

The men o' yon forest they askit o' me
How many strawberries grow in the saut sea?
I answered them back wi' a tear in my e'e
'How many ships sail in the forest'?
O dig me a grave and dig it sae deep
And cover it owre wi' flooers sae sweet
And I will lie doon there and tak' a lang sleep.

And maybe in time I'll forget her.

Dylan's closing verse line is: "Cover him over and let him sleep"[63]. The rest of the stanza consists of further intertextuality with two William Blake lines sandwiching one from a bedtime prayer.

'Tin Angel' is an extraordinarily dark and foreboding song, straight from the territory of the Child Ballads. Its pounding, ominous beat makes the doomed cast of characters it holds seem as predestined to death as the passengers on the Titanic on the succeeding track, 'Tempest'. It is a tale of sexual cheating, murder and suicide that harks back for centuries and has forerunners in Dylan's recording history. These include, 'Blackjack Davy" and 'Love Henry' from 1993's *Good As I Been To You* and 1994's *World Gone Wrong*.

It is, as Dylan sings on 'Tempest', *"a sad, sad story"* and it is also an old, old story going all the way back to an ancient Scottish ballad that is known in many variants there and throughout the world. I think I first heard it, as a child, as 'Johnny Faa'. Johnny can become Davy and with a dash of the Gypsy line – 'The Raggle Taggle Gyspsies-O', 'The Egyptian Laddie', 'Gypsy Laddie' – drop the Faa and become known as Gypsy Davy and hence onto Blackjack Davy. Child Ballad number 200 first appeared in print in the early Eighteenth Century.

Dylan mixes in a reference to Henry Lee, he of 'Love Henry', a song that can be traced back to Child Ballad 68, 'Young Hunting' and appeared on Dylan's album *World Gone Wrong*. Dylan perhaps also sprinkles in a touch of the border ballad, 'Matty Groves' as he conjures up his fierce 2012 contribution to a genre he has already invested in so heavily and tellingly.

'Scarlet Town' opens with the same line as Barbara Allen, another song with a Dylan past: "In Scarlet town where I was born". Incidentally, 'Tin Angel' also alluded to 'Barbara Allen' when its line *""You died for me, now I'll die for you"* "echoed Barbara Allen's emotional peak of "Sweet William died for me today/I'll die for him tomorrow."

'Barbara Allen' was a hard, tough song but Dylan ups the ante considerably on that front, with some brutal lines in the Fallen World of Scarlet Town. In the earlier, 'Soon After Midnight' we had been told that *"Charlotte's a harlot, dresses in scarlet"* and harlotry is very much in evidence here, too, as you would expect from the title, including *"my flat-chested junky whore"* in a town where it is pointedly, *"all right there for ya"*. There's a lot more to the song than this, though, with nursery rhyme, perhaps classical, and biblical allusions amidst the violence and squalor. *"I'm staying up late and I'm making amends/While the smile of heaven descends"* the narrator sings in a couplet that is as surprising on first listen as it is welcome. Just as the lines "Sweet William died for me today/I'll die for him tomorrow" did in 'Barbara Allen', so this couplet brings a sudden shaft of light into a dark song. Dylan sang Barbara Allen in his early Village Folk days and it was a highlight of the first year in what became known as the 'Never Ending Tour', in 1988.

It is worth noting, too, that Gillian Welch, known for her Dylan covers among other successes, opens her 2011 album *The Harrow & The Harvest* with a song called, 'Scarlet Town', co-written with David Rawlings. This dark re-working of folk tropes, both lyrical and musical, appears on an album that has been seen as engaging with Dylan's song 'Standing In The Doorway'.[64]

***

Turning now to the reception given to intertextuality on *Tempest*, we find that there is an assumption that if a poet puts together a string of quotations from various sources that it is artistic intertextuality and highly admirable but that if a songwriter does the same then it is lazy, insincere and lacking in value. Perhaps this explains, to a degree at least, why some people have said that Dylan is just throwing a bunch of quotations from any old place into the songs and stitching them together without any thought for overall meaning. They use some of Dylan's own words to back up this view, though on closer inspection Dylan is not saying exactly the same thing. What Dylan does say, raises interesting questions over intent and control, conscious and instinctive creation.

When talking of *Moby Dick* in his Nobel acceptance speech, Dylan remarked that everything is mixed in. *"All the myths: the Judeo Christian bible, Hindu myths, British legends, Saint George, Perseus, Hercules – they're all whalers. Greek mythology, the gory business of cutting up a whale. Lots of facts in this book, geographical knowledge, whale oil – good for coronation of royalty – noble families in the whaling industry. Whale oil is used to anoint the kings. History of the whale, phrenology, classical philosophy, pseudo-scientific theories, justification for discrimination – everything thrown in and none of it hardly rational. Highbrow, lowbrow, chasing illusion, chasing death, the great white whale, white as polar bear, white as a white man, the emperor, the nemesis, the embodiment of evil. The demented captain who actually lost his leg years ago trying to attack Moby with a knife."*

Dylan here provides quite an apt summary of how his own *Tempest* feels on first listens: *everything thrown in and none of it hardly rational. Highbrow, lowbrow, chasing illusion, chasing death.* The more you listen, though, the more things cohere, questions arise and overall shapes and feelings emerge to dominate how you hear and appreciate it as a whole. Even putting aside for a moment the dubiety in trusting anything Dylan says about his own work, were he really to have just *'thrown everything in and hope it stuck'*, he did so from sources he knows intimately. Like any artist, he creates on conscious and subconscious levels with the balance of craft and inspiration always a fluid one, even though the balance is markedly different at various points in his long and storied career. He has talked of songs coming to him from above and using him as conduit. This traditional Romantic vision of inspiration from the Muses, using the human artist as a means to expressing something over which the artist has no control, is an extreme example of the author being divorced from the meaning of his work. It points up, however, the complete non-necessity of the creator understanding what their creation 'means' to use that reductive phrase. Dylan knows that it is what art provokes, invokes and inspires that is most important. It is part of a critic's job to concern themselves with meaning, not the artist's.

Dylan continued his Nobel Lecture from above by asking: *"So what does it all mean?"* He also provided the answer: *"Myself and a lot of other songwriters have been influenced by these very same themes. And they can mean a lot of different things. If a song moves you, that's all that's important. I don't have to know what a song means. I've written all kinds of things into my songs. And I'm not going to worry about it – what it all means. When Melville put all his old testament, biblical references, scientific theories, Protestant doctrines, and all that knowledge of the sea and sailing ships and whales into one story, I don't think he would have worried about it either – what it all means."*

As with all art, it is the creation, in this case the song, that matters and not any potential authorial intent. In that sense it is true that you do not "have to know what a song means". However, what Dylan is saying here is not the same as saying 'throw absolutely anything at the wall and hope it sticks'. On *Tempest*, the quotes from Homer are very aptly chosen. Many of the quotes originate from a speech where the old champion shows how far ahead of the young pretenders he still is, which is exactly how Dylan sounds like he views himself as his swaggering vocals and dynamic music roar from your speakers. At the same time, the Bible and Folk are in his DNA and so Dylan does not need to search for relevance, as it is at his fingertips. Even if we are to believe the image of Dylan carelessly 'tossing them in', then he would still instinctively and unerringly 'toss them in' at just the right time; and he would still be, consciously or sub-consciously, selecting these particular lines and phrases from the vast store available.

Also, as we have seen, Dylan himself gave a very different view of the process to that of merely throwing quotes together. In a 2012 reply to a question about quoting/lifting from Confederate poet Timrod on *Modern Times*: " ... *if you think it's so easy to quote him and it can help your work, do it yourself and see how far you can get".*

In *Rolling Stone* in 2012 Dylan gave an account of the album's creation which gets to the centre of the matter: "Tempest *was like all the rest of them: The songs just fall together. It's not the album I wanted to make, though. I had another one in mind. I wanted to make something more religious. That takes a lot more concentration – to pull that off 10 times with the same thread – than it does with a record like I ended up with, where anything goes and you just gotta believe it will make sense."*

This sounds like a man trusting the instincts that have served him so well previously: *"like the rest of them...fall together... anything goes and you just gotta believe it will make sense."*

To reiterate, the focus on authorial intent or interpretation is, in any case, a red herring. As Michael Stipe, of the band REM, once remarked: "I really don't want to reveal anything about a character, I maintain that my take, my interpretation of what my songs are about, is, in the whole world, the least important take. I wrote them but that does not give me some divine insight into their meaning".[65]

What counts are the works of art created, not the authors' purpose. We know very little about Shakespeare's intent anywhere in his plays, nor how much is collaboration, and we do not even know who or how many people wrote *The Odyssey*, and this has no effect whatsoever on the power of the works or our appreciation of them. Consciously or subconsciously, Dylan has used classical, scriptural and folk elements to create the songs on *Tempest*. These are his ubiquitous sources, as are the wider literary and cultural elements that he adds to the mix. In the case of 'Ain't Talkin' from earlier in the century, he presents us with a version without any Ovid quotes at all on *Tell-Tale Signs* and a different take, on *Modern Times*, with more than ten lines from Ovid's exile poems added to create a seamless new whole.

Dylan continued his Nobel speech with the following words: "*John Donne as well, the poet-priest who lived in the time of Shakespeare, wrote these words, 'The Sestos and Abydos of her breasts. Not of two lovers, but two loves, the nests.' I don't know what it means, either. But it sounds good. And you want your songs to sound good.*" Dylan is once again having some fun here. Donne knew exactly what he meant, and Dylan knows that Donne did so. The sexually explicit elegy, commonly referred to as "To his Mistress Going to Bed", is not at all obscure. The lines Dylan quotes only seem so when taken out of context from the extended and intricate conceit encouraging the mistress to uncover her body for the lustful lover. Donne's use of the ocean voyage as a metaphor for each part of his lovers' body is a technique Dylan himself has used too, through house fixtures in 'Temporarily Like Achilles' on *Blonde On Blonde* for one, outstanding, example. Donne names the cities on either side of the Hellespont, which are famed in lovers' literature due to the myth of Hero and Leander.

Made famous in Shakespeare's day by Marlowe, and referenced more than once by Shakespeare himself, the famous tale of Leander swimming nightly to his love was also a favourite of Lord Byron who went so far as to replicate the dangerous swim. Dylan has named Byron as a poet he particularly admires and gave his early Sixties girlfriend, Suze Rotolo, a book of Byron's poems, signed from "Bob Byron Dylan. Dylan's son Jesse's middle name is

Byron.[66] Given the phrases, prominence in Greek myth, its obvious use as a sexual metaphor, as well as its connections to Shakespeare, Donne and Byron, I think we can safely say that Dylan does know what it means.

This Donne quote, with its bawdy humour, its examination of empire, power politics, the nature of the Christian divine and its interest in Classical mythology and symbolism, delightfully brings together many of the themes of this book and both *The Tempest* and *Tempest*. Again, as with the Homer quotes in this speech and many of the remarks in the *Rolling Stone* 2012 and various Bill Flanagan interviews, Dylan is giving us only slightly oblique hints as to what he is up to in his own work. It is noteworthy that *Moby Dick* is itself constructed, to a significant degree, out of Shakespeare's writing.

Dylan's hopeful '*you gotta believe it will all make sense*' is a hope fulfilled in such beautiful songs as 'Soon After Midnight' and 'Long and Wasted Years' and powerful ones like 'Pay in Blood' and 'Tin Angel'. Of course, as this book is meant to testify, you do not find the meaning in the text alone. With a song, the music and, with Dylan especially, the vocal carries you along and gives you a deeper meaning than mere words alone can, however well-chosen those words are.

***

The Tempest and *Tempest* are fine works within the stellar canons of their creators. They are not the very best either has to offer, but that is hardly a crime given, to name but a few, the likes of *King Lear*, *Hamlet*, *Macbeth* and *Blood on the Tracks*, *Blonde on Blonde*, *Highway 61 Revisited*. They are dynamic, inventive, and mesmeric. Each exemplifies many of the themes of this book. Both, too, are particularly strong on the idea of the influence of the past on the present. Dylan had further illuminating words on this in his 2012 *Rolling Stone* interview:

The thing about it is that there is the old and the new, and you have to connect with them both. The old goes out and the new comes in, but there is no sharp borderline. The old is still happening while the new enters the scene, sometimes unnoticed. The new is overlapping at the same time the old is weakening its hold. It goes on and on like that. Forever through the centuries. Sooner or later, before you know it, everything is new, and what happened to the old? It's like a magician trick, but you have to keep connecting with it.[67]

"*A magician's trick*", is most apt for our context in this chapter. More importantly, our two bards keep 'connecting with it' and creating things anew through performance art. Directors and cast have to make decisions on how they will put on their next production of *The Tempest*. No matter what key choices are made, the best will still leave it as open as possible and allow you to leave the theatre with thoughts, questions and wonder ringing in your head.

Dylan's *Tempest* album is fixed for now, though there could be a later release in *The Bootleg Series* with alternate versions, but is pregnant with much that is only revealed after multiple listens. However, the songs in performance can become anything he wishes; harder, softer, faster, slower, more rock, less rock, angrier, more wistful *et cetera*. The possibilities in performance are as endless as the musical settings and vocal inflections that Dylan may choose to give them. Were his so-called 'never-ending tour" to revert, from its current to its earlier habits, songs could change from night to night, appearing and disappearing from the set lists and changing from rock to folk to blues to reggae and back to rock again.

Also, there are always new productions and new performances. Spring 2018 saw Dylan return on tour to Europe. At the same time Robert Carsen's French language version of *The Tempest* was on stage at the legendary *Comédie-Française* in Paris. The translation for Carsen's production was by Jean-Claude Carrière, who is most famous for his collaborations with Luis Buñuel. Dylan told John Landau in 1978 that Buñuel was his favourite director.[68] Remembering that Dylan said that if he cannot see a Shakespeare play in English, then the next best thing is to see Shakespeare performed in another language, it is to be hoped that he may have found a way of catching a performance amidst his own busy and *Tempest* touched run of shows.

NOTES

1 His previous albums of solo-authored songs came out in 1997, 2001, 2006 and 2012 and, so, if the sequence continues, perhaps we can look forward to a new album of original songs in 2019

2 Dr Emma Smith, https://podcasts.ox.ac.uk/series/approaching-shakespeare accessed November 7, 2017

3 There was an even lower point in the series when it gave a platform to the ludicrous conspiracy

theories about Shakespeare not being Shakespeare but being a noble instead. This kind of group flourishes in the age of social media and is, lamentably, also supported by some of the greatest Shakespearean actors that we have in current times, as it was here in the *Richard II* episode. For some reason, these people can accept that Mozart wrote and played symphonies at six but not that someone from Stratford could write plays as a grown man. As with similarly outlandish theories, enormous claims are made from the flimsiest of starting points while ignoring the breathtaking scale of the deception they are proposing and the almost religious leap of faith you would need to make to think it was achievable. One example, among the myriad that come to mind: it is claimed that Shakespeare could not possibly have known about the Court and therefore it was a nobleman that wrote them (not that class prejudice has anything to do with this, you understand, they hastily add). There's no consideration that De Vere (the current favourite after Bacon and Marlowe's proponents have dwindled in time, though there are still some around) would have been highly unlikely to know anything about felt-making or Warwickshire accents and local flower names from the region. Over and above all this, it is surely the plays that matter, not the author. Certainly, that is what everyone in Shakespeare's age would have thought, unlike our own, celebrity infatuated days

4 Jonathan Bate, *Soul of the Age: A Biography of the Mind of William Shakespeare Random House Trade Paperbacks, 2010*

5 *Ibid.*

6 Bob Dylan, August 16, 2012 issue of *Rolling Stone*. Interview by Mikal Gilmore.

7 That metaphorical tempest did have a physical aspect to it in Dylan's initial thoughts. There is no mention of an iceberg in the song but in very early draft papers seen by Richard Thomas at The Dylan Institute in Tulsa, the intriguing entries in very sketchy lyric beginnings include: "Tempest blew ~~the hull apart~~ hole;" "Tempest tore a[ugly]gash." (This discovery is to appear in the afterword to the paperback edition of Richard F Thomas *Why Bob Dylan Matters*, the original hardback was by Dey Street Book, US 2017)

8 Allen Ginsberg, Teaching class, http://www.openculture.com/2014/03/hear-allen-ginsbergs-short-free-course-on-shakespeares-play-the-tempest-1980.html accessed November 11,[th] 2017

9 I wrote an article on "The Two Bards" to accompany the website for my book *Shakespeare in Cambridge*, Amberley Press, UK

10 Anne Margaret Daniel *Tempest*, Bob Dylan and the Bardic Arts, in *Tearing the World Apart: Bob Dylan and the Twenty-First Century* , Eds. Nina Goss, Eric Hoffman. University Press of Mississippi 2017

11 A name with coincidental reverberations for Dylan aficionados, being the same as that of the legendary delta blues guitarist who has had such a profound influence on Dylan's work

12 One of the stars of that show, Sheila Atim, won an Olivier Award for Best Supporting Actress In A Musical and enormous acclaim for her rendition of Dylan's "Tight Connection To My Heart". She is currently playing, and singing, as Emilia in *Othello* at the Globe

13 Press, 2002

14 D.A. Nuttall "Virgil and Shakespeare" in Ed. Charles Martindale, *Virgil and his Influence*: Bimillennial Studies, Bristol Classical publications, 1984

15 Robert Wiltenburg, 'The *Aeneid* in *The Tempest*,' in *Shakespeare Survey* 39 (1987), pp. 159-68; Pitcher, John . " A Theater of the Future: *The Aeneid* and The Tempest ." *Essays in Criticism 34* (1984); Nuttall, A. D. "Virgil and Shakespeare." Ed. Martindale, *Shakespeare's Virgil: empathy and The Tempest* Leah Whittington (Chapter 4 in *Shakespeare and Renaissance Ethics* edited by Patrick Gray, John D. Cox. Cambridge University Press, 2014)

16 *The Aeneid* Translation by H.R. Fairclough

17 *Ibid.*

18 Christopher Marlowe, *The Complete Plays*, Everyman, J.M. Dent, London 1999

19 Virgil and The Tempest *The Politics Of Imitation* Donna B. Hamilton Ohio State University Press Columbus, 1990

20 Leah Whitington Shakespeare's Virgil : empathy and The Tempest quoting Craig Kallendorf The Other Virgil: "Pessimistic" Readings of *The Aeneid* in Early Modern Culture . Oxford : Oxford UP , 2007

21 After considering the various pamphlets, David Lindley concludes, in his introduction to the New Cambridge Shakespeare edition, that "it is difficult to demonstrate that any of these individual texts were direct sources for the play".

22 Rowland Wymer. *"The Tempest and the Origins of Britain." Critical Survey Volume 11, issue 1, March 1999*

23 Wymer, Rowland *Ibid.*

24 Bate, Jonathan *Shakespeare and Ovid*, 1993

25 Q&A with Bill Flanagan March 22, 2017 https://www.bobdylan.com/news/qa-with-bill-flanagan/ accessed January 12, 2019

26 T-Bone Burnett in the foreword to 2004's reprint of Sam Shephard's *Rolling Thunder Logbook* De Capo, 2004

27 Bob Dylan. *The Lyrics: 1961-2012* Simon & Schuster UK; UK edition (November 8, 2016)

28 Richard F Thomas *Why Bob Dylan Matters* Dey Street Book, US 2017

29 Nb. Unfortunately, some verses are not on the official lyrics site

30 Richard F Thomas *op. cit.*

31 Ovid: *The Poems of Exile: Tristia and the Black Sea Letters* translated by Peter Green, University of California Press, 2005

32 Richard F Thomas *op. cit.*

33 In Roman mythology the Goddess is called Minerva and Odysseus is named Ulysses

34 Richard F Thomas *op. cit.*

35 https://bobdylan.com/news/qa-with-bill-flanagan/ accessed October 20, 2017

36 Bob Dylan, Nobel Lecture https://www.nobelprize.org/nobel_prizes/literature/laureates/2016/dylan-lecture.html
Accessed October 17, 2017

37 *Ovid from the RSC: The World's Greatest Storyteller* BBC TV November 2017

38 Scott Warmuth, https://www.pinterest.com/scottwarmuth/a-tempest-commonplace/

39 Bob Dylan, quoted by Jon Pareles 1997 N.Y. Times News Service

40 *Rolling Stone* interview, November 23, 1968

41 It is noteworthy that Dylan included the phrase: 'Shine your light' on 'Roll on John' as it was a key one on 'Precious Angel' from the *Slow Train Coming* album

42 The line is filled with puns. The pre-Beatles were named after the Quarry Bank school song, pulling from it a neat pun on quarry as rock:

Quarry men old before our birth

straining each muscle and sinew

toiling together Mother earth

conquered the rock that was in you

In the same way that the name Beatles incorporates "beat" and aurally puns on beetles, intentionally aligning them with the Buddy Holly's Crickets.

43 https://beatle.wordpress.com/2007/01/11/john-lennon-the-sailor-whatever-gets-you-through-the-storm/ accessed December 27, 2017

44 De Graff, Kees: Bob Dylan's 'Roll on John' – *lyric analysis* http://www.keesdegraaf.com/media/Misc/1882p17psou9fm1e1d41g5m9gfs11p81.pdf

45 John Barton's *Playing Shakespeare* dramatises many examples of this. It is available as a book but to get the proper effect, it is essential to watch the DVD showing Barton working with actors including Peggy Ashcroft, Judi Dench, Ben Kingsley, Ian McKellen and Patrick Stewart

46 Lynn Forest-Hill, Giants and Enemies of God: the relationship of Caliban and Prospero from the perspective of insular literary tradition. Shakespeare Survey 59. Pp 239-253, 2006.

47 Capp, Bernard. "The Political Dimension of Apocalyptic Thought." *The Apocalypse in English Renaissance Thought and Literature*. Eds. C.A Patrides & Joseph Wittreich. Ithaca, NY: Cornell University Press, 1984

48 Anne Barton, Editor, *The Tempest, New Penguin Shakespeare*,1968.

49 *Henry IV Part One*, also has a special arrangement for its epilogue, though it is completely different with an ornate, special, layout

50 Steven Marx, *A Masque of Revelation:*The Tempest*as Apocalypse* Cal Poly University San Luis Obispo 93407 undated

51 From which we have the current meaning of festivities, especially family-centred ones, such as 'Christmas revels'

52 Quoted in John Nichols, The Progresses, Processions, and Magnificent Festivities of King James the First. London, 1828

53 Dr Christopher Rollason: *Bob Dylan, "Tempest": Intertextuality, Shakespeare And Edgar Allan Poe* https://rollason.wordpress.com/2012/09/09/bob-dylans-tempest-intertextuality-shakespeare-and-edgar-allan-poe

54 The song has now been released on The Bootleg Series Vol. 13: Trouble No More 1979–1981 (November 2017)

55 A phrase, incidentally, which perfectly encapsulates the message of Dylan's song, 'Series of Dreams' and the accompanying video

56 *There is a city of love/Way from this world, stuff dreams are made of/Fear of no darkness, stars high above/There is a city of love*

57 Judith E. Tonning, Like this Insubstantial Pageant, Faded': Eschatology and Theatricality in The Tempest. Literature and Theology, Volume 18, Issue 4, 1 December 2004, Pages 371–382

58 Roland Barthes, *The Death of the Author* http://www.tbook.constantvzw.org/wp-content/death_authorbarthes.pdf

59 Richard F Thomas *op. cit.*

60 Warmuth, Scott https://www.pinterest.com/scottwarmuth/a-tempest-commonplace/

61 The lyrics on the official Bob Dylan website have 'white house', but I have no doubt that the phrase calls for initial capitals

62 Perhaps "gilden" is the closest to what Dylan actually sings, I concede, but it certainly begins "gild" not "gold". The 'gilded age' phrase also cropped up in an April 2012 article in *The New Yorker*. Daniel Mendelsohn. *Unsinkable: Why we can't let go of the Titanic*: "But overshadowing everything is the problem of money and class. The Titanic's story irresistibly reads as a parable about a gilded age in which death was anything but democratic..."

63 It sounds like "cover 'em" on the album, and is often printed as this, but it sounded like "him" at the Blackpool concert and this is how it appears on the official website lyrics page, though we have to bear in mind that this is often an unreliable source

64 J.L. Wall "The Harrow and the Harvest": Dylan in the Doorway Cryin https://ordinary-times.com/2011/07/19/the-harrow-and-the-harvest-dylan-in-the-doorway-cryin/ accessed August 23, 2018

65 Quoted by Sean O'Hagan in *The Laughing Cavalier, "Guardian Lifestyle"* April 14,2001. Available online at: *https://www.theguardian.com/lifeandstyle/2001/apr/14/weekend.seanohagan* accessed December 3, 2017

66 http://nodepression.com/article/bob-dylan%E2%80%99s-nobel-lecture-heard-melodies-are-sweet accessed 21, August 2018

67 Bob Dylan *Rolling Stone* interview 2012

68 Bob Dylan *Rolling Stone* interview, January 26, 1978

Chapter Eleven

CONCLUSION

The chapter on 'the two tempests' to a large degree already provides this study with its conclusion. It recaps and illuminates, by example, most of the main points in preceding chapters. Included in those are Shakespeare and Dylan's use of biblical, classical and folk sources, their exhilarating wordplay, and the wide variety of ways they use source material. Also illustrated is the sacred symbolism that infuses their work and how religious debate swirls around them. The difficulties encountered by solely literary-bound interpretations of performing art are also highlighted. Their qualities as bards arise, to an extent, and there is even an example of a Shakespeare line appearing in a Dylan song. However, the emphasis on these last three is stronger in the book as a whole and there were two chapters of the book which could not be represented in the discussion of 'the two tempests'. Firstly, the opposition to their art and secondly any example of Dylan appearing in a Shakespeare production, as neither category was applicable.

Once added, these complete the summary of this book. The two late works also exemplified the way that both writers continually raise questions which leave us inspired and enlightened through their art. They have always done so. 'Blowin' in the Wind's' questions are answered by the way Dylan asks them. And Dylan's first major anthem is as alive and vital as ever, though one cannot help but wish that it did not still need to be heard. Dylan has continued to ask pertinent questions throughout his career, as Shakespeare did before him.

The centre of this comparative study has been the magical way their work inspires audiences, this is why it brought us to a fitting conclusion. Dylan asserted in his semi-fictive memoir *Chronicles* that for him:

"Folk music was a reality of a more brilliant dimension. It exceeded all human understanding, and if it called out to you, you could disappear and be sucked into it. I felt right at home in this mythical realm made up not with individuals so much as archetypes, vividly drawn archetypes of humanity, metaphysical in shape, each rugged soul filled with natural knowing and inner wisdom. Each demanding a degree of respect. I could believe in the full spectrum of it and sing about it. It was so real, so more true to life than life itself. It was life magnified.[1]

This precisely describes my own feelings on first encountering both Dylan and Shakespeare.

Dylan, in 2011, also declared that:

"...what you gotta understand is that I do something because I feel like doing it. If people can relate to it, that's great; if they can't, that's fine, too. But I don't think I'm gonna be really understood until maybe 100 years from now. Because what I've done and what I'm doing, nobody else does or has done ... And when I'm dead and gone people will realise that, and then they'll try to figure it out. There's all these interpreters around, but they're not interpreting anything except their own ideas. Nobody's come close."[2]

This book contends that we can reduce that hundred years' wait by counter-intuitively looking backwards for over four times that span. We can 'come closer' than the interpreters Dylan dismisses in this comment by tracing the parallels in the creative work of these two giants of performing and literary arts and the opposition they had to overcome. This is especially the case when we take into account the way they use language which illuminates our daily speech and has made us take them to our hearts as bedrocks of our culture.

Or at least we can if we always keep in mind those words that make our hearts and soul tremble in anticipation of life-changing artistic experiences: "Ladies and Gentlemen, please take your seats as tonight's performance is about to commence...".

NOTES

1 Bob Dylan, *Chronicles* Volume One, Simon and Schuster, 2005

2 Mick Brown: Bob Dylan: *The way he sang made everything seem like a message* https://www.telegraph.co.uk/culture/music/bob-dylan/8480252/Bob-Dylan-The-way-he-sang-made-everything-seem-like-a-message.html accessed August 11, 2018

Interviews

1965   Man, poetry is just bullshit, you know? I don't know about other countries, but in this one it's a total massacre. It's not poetry at all. People don't read
poetry in this country – if they do, it offends them; they don't dig it. You go to
school, man, and what kind of poetry do you read? You read Robert Frost's "The
Two Roads", you read T. S. Eliot – you read all that bullshit and that's just bad, man,
It's not good. It's not anything hard, it's just soft-boiled egg shit. And then, on top of
it, they throw Shakespeare at some kid who can't read Shakespeare in high school,
right? Who digs reading, *Hamlet*, man? All they give you is *Ivanhoe, Silas Marner,
Tale of Two Cities* – and they keep you away from things which you should do. You
shouldn't even be there in school. You should find out from people. Dig! (Paul J
Robbins Interview, Santa Monica, California 26 March 1965)

1966   "Rimbaud? I can't read him now. Rather read what I want these days.
'Kaddish' is the best thing yet. Everything else is a shuck. I never dug Pound or El-
iot. I dig Shakespeare. A raving queen and a cosmic amphetamine brain." To Robert
Shelton, Lincoln, Nebraska, March 12, 1966. Quotes in Shelton, *No Direction Home*
(*Author's note, it may be worth mentioning at this point that Dylan later wrote in* Chronicles
that he never read Pound, he mentions Pound's Nazism, but that he read and liked Eliot.)

1978   That's because the songs are intense. There's a wide range of emotions
there. To me it's like a Shakespeare play, you know, even after all these years, you
know, you can still go and see a group doing Shakespeare. It might not be the way
it was, you know, when, you know, it was happening but it's a pretty fair account
of it, and this is the same way, the songs all run together in a way that if you was
going to sit down and break 'em all down you'd have some kind of story there. You
really would. It's that... it's more... it's a play. And I'm singing all the songs. Maybe
all the elements are out there. You know, a lot of these songs I could see better,
you know, with more, I could see them definitely being more romantic and using
different elements of theatre but I can't do everything, you know. (Marc Rowland
interview 23rd September 1978, (collected in John Baldwin's privately published
Fiddler Now Upspoke Volume 3.)

1978   (Ginsberg: "Pound's Cantos are constructed in this way — image to
image.") Dylan: Every great work of art is when you think about it. Shakespeare.

The point to get is that the film is connected by an untouchable connective link. (Ginsberg and Dylan discussion to promote *Renaldo and Clara*)

1985   It's like people studying literature. Who do they read? They read Shakespeare. Literature must have been at a high level when Shakespeare was writing his plays. You can't say that today if you go and see a play. It's going to be very far down the line from Shakespeare. The same way with rock n' roll, rhythm and blues, and all that. We're living in a time where you can still feel it. It might be remote, but you can still feel it, whereas fifty or sixty years from now, it's only going to be a dream. How many radio stations play Howlin' Wolf or Jimmy Reed or Muddy Waters? Most young black guys don't even know who those people are.
And
At certain times I read a lot of poetry. My favorite poets are Shelley and Keats. Rimbaud is so identifiable. Lord Byron. I don't know. Lately if I read poems, it's like I can always hear the guitar. Even with Shakespeare's sonnets I can hear a melody because its all broken up into timed phrases so I hear it. I always keep thinking, 'What kind of song would this be?' (Interview with Denise Worrell, "'It's All Right in Front': Dylan on Life and Rock" in Time Magazine 25 November 1985)

1988   ... of course nobody writes like Shakespeare either, but you know, it doesn't matter those things can still be performed. They don't have to be written – just like folksongs.
And
Have you ever seen a Shakespeare play? I mean, it's like the English language at its peak where one line will come out like a stick of dynamite, and you'll be so what-was-that! But then the other stuff is rolling on so fast you can't even think, and then you have to struggle to catch up to where you are in the present. And folk songs are pretty much like the same way. Of course, nobody writes like Shakespeare either, but, it don't matter. Those things can still be performed. They don't have to be written, just like folk songs. Quoted in the *Miami Times* by Kathryn Baker, interview entitled "Love Me or Leave Me" September 1988. A syndicated piece, throughout September in various newspapers; the interview took place in the first week of August.)

1991   The world don't need any more poems, it's got Shakespeare.
And
(Paul Zollo, Song Talk: People have a hard time believing that Shakespeare really

wrote all of his work because there is so much of it. Do you have a hard time accepting that?) Dylan: People have a hard time accepting anything that overwhelms them. (*Song Talk* Interview, Beverly Hills, California 4 April 1991)

1997   But I'm not the songs, it's like somebody expecting Shakespeare to be Hamlet, or Goethe to be Faust. If you're not prepared for fame, there's really no way you can imagine what a crippling thing it can be. (David Gates Interview, Santa Monica, California September 1997)

2001   I've had a God-given sense of destiny. This is what I was put on earth to do. Just like Shakespeare was gonna write his plays, the Wright Brothers were gonna invent an airplane. (Christopher John Farley Interview for *Time* Magazine 17 September 2001)

2005   It was just more rural back then. That's what people did. You could see guys in blackface. George Washington in blackface or Napoleon wearing blackface. Like, weird Shakespearean things. Stuff that didn't really make any sense at the time. And people had other jobs in the carny team. I saw somebody putting make-up on getting back from running the Ferris wheel once. And I thought that was pretty interesting. (Jeff Rosen interviews for *No Direction Home* Source: Official DVD release 2005)

2011   One song is always using a line from another song to brace it. But then goes off on another tangent. Minstrels did it all the time. Weird takes on Shakespeare plays, stuff like that. It's just done automatically. (John Elderfield interview, Spring 2011)

2015   I like to see Shakespeare plays, so I'll go – I mean, even if it's in a different language. I don't care, I just like Shakespeare, you know. I've seen *Othello* and *Hamlet* and *Merchant of Venice* over the years, and some versions are better than others. Way better. It's like hearing a bad version of a song. But then somewhere else, somebody has a great version.
And
I need all kinds of songs – fast ones, slow ones, minor key, ballads, rumbas – and they all get juggled around during a live show. I've been trying for years to come up with songs that have the feeling of a Shakespearean drama, so I'm always starting with that. (Robert Love interview Saturday February 7, 2015)

Speeches

2015 Musicares

I'm glad for my songs to be honored like this. But you know, they didn't get here by themselves. It's been a long road and it's taken a lot of doing. These songs of mine, they're like mystery stories, the kind that Shakespeare saw when he was growing up. I think you could trace what I do back that far. They were on the fringes then, and I think they're on the fringes now. (Musicares Acceptance Speech Feb 6, 2015.)

2016 Nobel Banquet

I was out on the road when I received this surprising news, and it took me more than a few minutes to properly process it. I began to think about William Shakespeare, the great literary figure. I would reckon he thought of himself as a dramatist. The thought that he was writing literature couldn't have entered his head. His words were written for the stage. Meant to be spoken not read.

When he was writing Hamlet, I'm sure he was thinking about a lot of different things: "Who're the right actors for these roles?" "How should this be staged?" "Do I really want to set this in Denmark?"

His creative vision and ambitions were no doubt at the forefront of his mind, but there were also more mundane matters to consider and deal with. "Is the financing in place?" "Are there enough good seats for my patrons?" "Where am I going to get a human skull?" I would bet that the farthest thing from Shakespeare's mind was the question "Is this literature?"

But, like Shakespeare, I too am often occupied with the pursuit of my creative endeavors and dealing with all aspects of life's mundane matters. "Who are the best musicians for these songs?" "Am I recording in the right studio?" "Is this song in the right key?" Some things never change, even in 400 years. (Speech by Bob Dylan given by Azita Raji, US Ambassador to Sweden, at the Nobel Banquet on 10 December 2016.)

2017 Nobel Lecture

That's what songs are too. Our songs are alive in the land of the living. But songs are unlike literature. They're meant to be sung, not read. The words in Shakespeare's plays were meant to be acted on the stage. Just as lyrics in songs are meant to be sung, not read on a page. And I hope some of you get the chance to listen to these lyrics the way they were intended to be heard: in concert or on record or however people are listening to songs these days. (Lecture for The Nobel Prize in Literature 2016, dated 5 June 2017)

It is over forty years since I read my first critical book on Shakespeare. As the decades have passed I have read many books, journals and blogs. Added to that there are the radio and TV documentaries, audio Shakespeare courses and podcasts that I have absorbed over the years, as well as numerous discussions with directors, actors, scholars and enthusiasts. Consequently, it is impossible to remember the exact influence each of these has had upon this book but they are all thanked for their undoubted contributions.

The same holds true with Dylan, and is enhanced by my close connection with nearly all of the major figures in Dylan studies. I have had the fortune of long standing friendships with Michael Gray, Clinton Heylin, Stephen Scobie and the late Paul Williams, and as well as publishing and reviewing their writing, I have conducted in-depth interviews with each author. Their influence, and that of their various publications, is therefore pervasive, as is that of many other Dylan scholars and aficionados over the years, especially those who contributed to my magazines dedicated to his work. Additionally, I have reviewed a substantial number of publications on Dylan, as they have come out, since 1991 and I am sure they have all left a mark on my own thinking.

The selective bibliography that follows is, therefore, solely of the books that I returned to specifically while writing this book.

Shakespeare Editions:
The Shakespeare edition used throughout, unless embedded in quotes from another critic, is *The New Cambridge Shakespeare* series of individually edited plays. General Editor 1984-1990 Philip Brockman and; from 1990-1994 Brian Gibbons.

Additional The Tempest editions:
Ed: Kermode, Frank Arden II, Bloomsbury 1988
Ed: Vaughan Virginia Mason and Vaughan Alden T., Arden III, 2003
Ed: Orgel, Stephen Oxford University Press, 2008

Dylan Lyrics:
Bob Dylan's lyrics do not have a definitive edition. Due to this, I refer wherever possible to those on the official website, www.bobdylan.com, though this is necessarily supported by: Dylan, Bob *The Lyrics: 1961-2012* Simon & Schuster UK; UK edition (8 Nov. 2016) and Dylan, Bob *Lyrics 1962 - 1985* Paladin, Grafton books 1988

Discrepancies exist between these three and between them and the other alternate official Lyric editions. Additionally, and most crucially, between all of these and what Dylan actually sings on record, far less when performing live. Performance art once again is found to be misrepresented by the printed word. I have endeavoured to navigate the resultant complexities clearly in the text, aided by endnotes.

(*Anon.* privately published): *The Fiddler Now Upspoke* A Collection of Bob Dylan's Interviews

Desolation Row Promotions, UK 1995

Bate, Jonathan *Soul of the Age: A Biography of the Mind of William Shakespeare* Random House Trade Paperbacks, 2010

Barton, John *Playing Shakespeare* Methuen, 1984

Davies, Oliver Ford *Performing Shakespeare* Nick Hern Books, London, 2007

Dylan, Bob *Tarantula* MacGibbon & Kee Ltd., London, 1971

Dylan, Bob *Chronicles* Simon and Schuster, 2004

Gray, Michael *The Bob Dylan Encyclopedia,* Continuum International, 2006

Greenblatt, Stephen *Will in the World: How Shakespeare Became Shakespeare*. Jonathon Cape, 2004

Gurr, Andrew, *The Shakespearean Stage 1574-1642 4th Edition* Cambridge University Press, 2009

Hansen, Adam *Shakespeare and Popular Music Paperback* Continuum, 2010

Frank Kermode *Shakespeare's Language* Farrar, Straus and Giroux, 2001

Martin, Linda and Segrave, Kerry *Anti-Rock: The Opposition To Rock 'n' Roll* Da Capo Press.1993

Pauline Kiernan *Filthy Shakespeare: Shakespeare's Most Outrageous Sexual Puns* Quercus, 2006

Palfrey, Simon, *Doing Shakespeare* London: The Arden Shakespeare, 2005

Richmond, Hugh Macrae *Shakespeare's Tragedies Reviewed,* Peter lang Publishing 2015

Ricks, Christopher *Visions of Sin*. Published by Ecco, HarperCollins, 2004

Sanders, Julie *Shakespeare and Music: Afterlives and Borrowings* Polity,2013

Thomas, Richard F *Why Bob Dylan Matters* Dey Street Book, US 2017

Wells, Stanley, *Shakespeare, Sex, and Love* Oxford University Press, 2012

Wissolik, Richard David and McGrath, Scott *Bob Dylan's Words* Eadmer Press, USA, 1994

Eds: Braunmuller and Hattaway, A. R. And Michael *The Cambridge Companion to English Renaissance Drama* (Cambridge: Cambridge University Press, 1999)

Ed: Bulman, James *shakespeare, theory and performance* Routledge 1996

Eds: Carson and Karim-Cooper, Dr Christie and Farah, *Shakespeare's Globe: A Theatrical Experiment* (Cambridge: Cambridge University Press, 2008)

Eds: Dollimore, Jonathan, Sinfield, Alan *Political Shakespeare: Essays in Cultural Materialism,* Manchester University Press, 1994

Eds: Hansome-Reeves and Escolme, Stuart and Bridget, *Shakespeare & The Making of Theatre* Basingstoke, Palgrave Macmillan, 2012

Eds: Maguire and Smith Laurie and Emma *30 Great Myths about Shakespeare* Chichester: Wiley-Blackwell, 2012

Ed: Shaughnessy, Robert *Shakespeare in Performance* (New Casebooks) MacMillan Press Ltd., 2000

Eds: Wells and Stanton, Stanley and Sarah, *The Cambridge Companion to Shakespeare on Stage* (Cambridge: Cambridge University Press, 2002)

As I was completing this book at the end of 2018, Santa presented me with *Tearing the World Apart: Bob Dylan and the Twenty-First Century* edited by Nina Goss and Eric Hoffman. This contains an article by Anne Margaret Daniel entitled: *"Tempest,* Bob Dylan and the Bardic Arts". I have added three references to this. Guessing by the publication date Ms Daniel was thinking along similar lines to me in 2015-2016 when I first brought the two bards together for an article that gave birth to this volume.

Acknowledgements:

Shakespeare and Dylan have been central to my adult life. To properly acknowledge everyone would consequently entail listing most of the people I have known, starting with my father, the late James Muir, who introduced me to literature in the first place. To obviate such a long list of names, I restrict myself here only to those who have directly influenced this publication. Enormous thanks are due to the readers of my original draft chapters: Chris Green, Pia Parviainen, Rowland Wymer, Tara Zuk and Graham Hall. Although they all already know how grateful I am, it is good to be able to acknowledge this publicly and to urge the last two named to bring into print their original and stimulating ideas for their own books. I look forward to the day when I can return the favour they did me here. As well as corrections, a host of interesting other ideas were brought up and talked over as the drafts were discussed and the book took shape. Had we but world enough, and time, a plethora of new paths are there, waiting, to be explored.

Special thanks are due to Jeff Rosen and David Beal as the book would not be the same without the use of Dylan's lyrics, reproduced here by their kind permission. Similar accolades to 'go-between extraordinaire', Derek Barker, formatting whiz-kid Tracy Barker, and Mark Neeter at Red Planet for all their help and work.

My gratitude also goes to James Adams, Mick Gold and to *Bob Dylan ISIS* magazine where my first thoughts and predictions on Dylan and academia appeared some years ago, well before he won the Nobel Prize for Literature, and all of which have come to pass in the intervening time. They also reprinted the article that was the genesis of this book, and which was sent to Dylan's office not long before that award was bestowed, having originally appeared on a website supporting my book *Shakespeare in Cambridge*.

Another worthy recipient of thanks is Professor Richard Thomas who, through no fault of his own, was at first a first cause of aggravating delay and enforced rewriting. Once met, though, a kindred spirit was immediately detected, and he has since become a source of support, encouragement and friendship.

BOB DYLAN ON
RED PLANET

www.redplanetmusicbooks.com

Index